What Can She Know?

What Can She Know?

Feminist Theory and the
Construction of Knowledge

Lorraine Code

Cornell University Press

Ithaca and London

First published 1991 by Cornell University Press.

International Standard Book Number 0-8014-2476-3 (cloth)
International Standard Book Number 0-8014-9720-5 (paper)
Library of Congress Catalog Card Number 90-55755
Printed in the United States of America
Librarians: Library of Congress cataloging information
appears on the last page of the book.

⊗ The paper in this book meets the minimum requirements
of the American National Standard for Information Sciences
Permanence of Paper for Printed Library Materials, ANSI Z39.48-1984.

For Jacqueline, David, and Jonathan Code
for what I have learned from them

All the interests of my reason, speculative as well as practical, combine in the three following questions:

1. What can I know?
2. What ought I to do?
3. What may I hope?

The first question is merely speculative. We have, as I flatter myself, exhausted all the possible answers to it, and at last have found the answer with which reason must perforce content itself, and with which, so long as it takes no account of the practical, it has also good cause to be satisfied.

—Immanuel Kant, *Critique of Pure Reason*

Contents

Preface

Throughout the reconstructions and refinements in feminist theory since the 1970s, one focal point, one rallying claim, has demanded and continues to demand ritual incantation. Simone de Beauvoir states the claim as early (in English) as 1952: "Representation of the world, like the world itself, is the work of men; they describe it from their own point of view, which they confuse with absolute truth."[1] Aida Hurtado reiterates it in 1989, in terms that attest to the categorial refinements effected in feminist theory during the intervening years: "Each oppressed group in the United States is positioned in a particular and distinct relationship to white men, and each form of subordination is shaped by this relational position."[2] In this book I engage critically with the *epistemology* made by professional philosophers of the mainstream, one of the more arcane and esoteric artifacts of men. It is an artifact, in the main, of white men, articulated, as it turns out, from their point of view, yet upheld as a source of 'absolute truth' about how the world should be known and represented.

It may seem that epistemology, from its location within professional philosophy, could have minimal bearing on feminist projects. My claim, however, is that institutionalized disciplines that produce knowledge about women, and position women in societies according

[1]Simone de Beauvoir, *The Second Sex*, trans. H. M. Parshley (New York: Vintage, 1972), p. 161.
[2]Aida Hurtado, "Relating to Privilege: Seduction and Rejection in the Subordination of White Women and Women of Color," *Signs: Journal of Women in Culture and Society* 14 (Summer 1989): 833.

to the knowledge they produce, are informed by versions of and variations on the methods and objectives that received epistemologies authorize. These disciplines, among which I include biology and most of the social sciences, have found women inferior in countless ways, have been unable to accord them a place as historical agents, and have presumed to interpret women's experiences for them, in versions often unrecognizable to the women themselves. In the folklore of most western societies women are represented—partly in consequence of a spill-over of that disciplinary knowledge—as incapable of having knowledge of the best and most rational kind. Hence places in the social structure are reserved for them which assume their epistemic inferiority and block their access to authoritative intellectual and social-political status.

According to its self-presentation, the central assumptions of epistemology are neutral and universally applicable. The criteria of objectivity and neutrality that govern its search for truth—together with 'truth' itself—are criteria and goals that 'most people' would unthinkingly endorse. Hence epistemology looks as if it should be immune to feminist critique, should count as explicitly gender-neutral and indeed as a model of disengaged neutrality. Yet I contend that mainstream epistemology, in its very neutrality, masks the facts of its derivation from and embeddedness in a specific set of interests: the interests of a privileged group of white men.

One focus of my critique, then, is the 'particular and distinct' kinds of subordination that mainstream epistemology produces—often invisibly—for *women's* knowledge and women's positions on the philosophical-epistemological terrain. In the early chapters, where my analysis centers on epistemology itself, I often aggregate men, for professional philosophers comprise a markedly homogeneous group: middle class, university educated, and predominantly white. The women whose positions I contrast with theirs—the oppressed, 'Other' group—are the women whose projects are often marginalized in the very neutrality and dislocatedness of 'the epistemological project'. My analysis of epistemology, and of mainstream philosophy, in the first four chapters is an institutional-political analysis, in which the 'institution' under scrutiny comprises the range of practices—research, conference presentations, articles in learned journals, books, other scholarly-professional activities in the academy and its correlates—that constitute professional philosophy. Yet its impact is not restricted to the institution, for philosophers commonly claim to speak not just for philosophers, but for 'all men'. Hence my analysis focuses also upon the limited purview of that claim, with its pretensions to 'embrace women' and to speak for the interests and projects of women and men who are not members of the select group of knowledge and epistemology makers.

In the first four chapters, then, I engage in a critical dialogue with the dominant epistemology of the Anglo-American mainstream to unmask its claims to occupy a neutral, transcendent place outside the epistemic struggles and responsibilities central to people's lives, however various their histories and locations. I examine its claims to stand aloof from the hierarchies of power and oppression that produce and inform those struggles and from the accountability they require. Philosophical beliefs about knowledge and authority inform and are informed by social conceptions of what it is—ideally—to be a good knower and about how knowledge confers expertise. Although it cannot be true that epistemologists speak to—or for—'all men', the effects of embedded epistemological assumptions in legitimating and/or suppressing knowledge, authorizing knowers, and establishing expertise extend far beyond the academy, with widespread social-political implications.

My project is to interrogate mainstream Anglo-American epistemology from within and without. The internal critique that I develop from my position as a white, middle-class, privileged member of the profession—albeit differently privileged from many epistemology makers—engages with such pivotal ideals and regulative principles as objectivity (with its suppression of subjectivity), value-neutrality, and rational autonomy. It works at once with these principles and against them, to reveal their contribution to the inclusions and exclusions that the epistemological project underwrites. The external critique examines the cognitive practices that the epistemology of the mainstream legitimates and denigrates, to reveal their implications for the efforts of women and other 'eccentric' groups to claim cognitive authority.

Particularly in the internal analysis, the women I discuss—often, it may seem, generically—are the privileged, educated white women who have been simultaneously attracted to philosophy and uneasily positioned within it. Issues of race, ethnicity, and other sites of marginalization are less prominent in this part of the analysis, again because of the relative homogeneity of this group. I do not ignore the fact that many women are advantaged and empowered by the resources philosophy offers. Nor do I argue that all women are disadvantaged equally and alike by its presuppositions and the practices it informs. But I maintain that the epistemology of the mainstream works from engrained assumptions about *who* can be a knower.

Hence I concentrate, in Chapters 3 and 4, on an analysis of the construction and position of 'the autonomous reasoner'—first in his appearances as the representative moral agent; and then in his activities as a paradigmatic cognitive agent. I elaborate a conviction that subjectivity—moral and cognitive agency—is produced in developmental processes, and that developmental theories contribute to understanding subjectivity. Yet developmental analyses have to be materially located, for all practices, including parenting and child development, are grounded in social-economic relations. People raise children differently, and subjectivity is differently constructed, within these groundings.

In Chapters 5, 6, and 7 the analysis is primarily external. I engage with the politics of knowledge that mainstream epistemology informs, even at a considerable distance from the ivory towers of the academies where the rhetoric of objectivity and scientific neutrality is born and nurtured. There I look at the place of knowledge in shaping social structures that are unevenly responsive to human interests. I analyze the content of knowledge about women, a set of specific asymmetries in the relative positioning of women and privileged white men on the epistemic terrain, and the distribution of cognitive resources in societies of unequal power and privilege.

The project, despite this initial presentation, is as much constructive as critical. Yet it has no blueprint, no set of plans that dictates the shape of its product. Feminists are sometimes hesitant to locate themselves critically, wary of representing feminism as negative, reactive, bereft of positive proposals. I have tried in this book to engage in critiques that are at once resourceful and resistant: showing where intransigent practices have to be challenged and undone, yet making plain in the challenge that the point is not to wipe the slate clean, to stop trying to know, to desist from evaluating and debating knowledge. Constructive proposals are often frankly experimental, taking the form of asking how it would be if things were done differently, suggesting what some of those differences might be, revealing their transformative potential. Knowledge is crucial to every aspect of human lives; its possession is empowering, its deprivation enervating and disabling. Women have to be in positions where they can know, if they are effectively to challenge the oppressions that have shaped their lives. Epistemologies have to be constructed that can produce these emancipatory effects.

This book has been a long time in the making. I would not have been able to complete it without advice and help. It will be clear from the text that my greatest debt is to the feminist theorists and activists on whose work I have drawn—not always in ways that they would have wanted me to—for the development of my argument.

Parts of Chapters 1 and 2 are based on material reworked from my "Is the Sex of the Knower Epistemologically Significant?" published in *Metaphilosophy* 12 (July/October 1981). Chapter 3 and part of Chapter 4 are based on material from my "Second Persons," in Marsha Hanen and Kai Nielson, eds., *Science, Morality, and Feminist Theory* (Calgary, Alberta: University of Calgary Press, 1987; copyright © *Canadian Journal of Philosophy*), and from "Autonomy Reconsidered," published in *Atlantis* 13 (Spring 1988). Sections of Chapter 5 are based on my article "The Tyranny of Stereotypes," in Kathleen Storrie, ed., *Women: Isolation and Bonding; The Ecology of Gender* (Toronto: Methuen, 1987; copyright © Canadian Research Institute for the Advancement of Women). Chapter 6 reworks material from my "Credibility: A Double Standard," in Lorraine Code, Sheila Mullett, and Christine Overall, eds., *Feminist Perspectives: Philosophical Essays on Minds and Morals* (Toronto: University of Toronto Press, 1988). This material is used here with permission.

I am grateful to the Social Sciences and Humanities Research Council of Canada for a Strategic Grant, which I held from 1984 to 1987, during which time I conceived the project and wrote drafts of the early chapters; and to the Department of Philosophy at the University of Waterloo, and Brian Hendley, its chair, for making space available to me for that work. The Social Sciences and Humanities Research Council of Canada provided further support, from 1987 to 1990, in the form of a Canada Research Fellowship, which enabled me to complete the manuscript. I am grateful to the Women's Studies Research Group at York University and its chair, Joan Gibson, for sponsoring me to hold the fellowship at York; and to the Department of Philosophy for providing me with a teaching home. A Visiting Research Fellowship at the Queen Elizabeth House Centre for Cross-Cultural Research on Women, at Oxford University, in the summer of 1985, provided added stimulation for the project. From May to September 1986, as a Visiting Fellow at the Humanities Research Centre of the Australian National University in Canberra, I revised Chapters 3 and 4. A Mellon Fellowship at Brown University, during the first six months of 1989, where I taught in the Philosophy Department and participated in the weekly research seminar at the Pembroke Center for Feminist Research, provided helpful insights for the final work on the manuscript.

Colleagues and friends have provided valuable criticisms and support. I especially thank Joan Gibson for extensive comments on the manuscript, Alison Wylie for helping me to sort out the first four chapters, and Hilary Kornblith for his encouragement and careful comments at various stages of the publication process. Genevieve Lloyd, Jane Martin, Richard Schmitt, and Carole Stewart read and commented on parts of the project. Several anonymous readers and discussants at conferences and meetings where I have presented parts of the book in progress made constructive suggestions. My greatest debt is to Murray Code, who has lived with this project from its inception, read and reread drafts of every chapter, and offered untiring criticism, advice, and support—as well as technical assistance without which the book would never have emerged onto paper.

LORRAINE CODE

Toronto, Ontario

What Can She Know?

CHAPTER ONE

Is the Sex of the Knower
Epistemologically Significant?

The Question

A question that focuses on the knower, as the title of this chapter does, claims that there are good reasons for asking who that knower is.[1] Uncontroversial as such a suggestion would be in ordinary conversations about knowledge, academic philosophers commonly treat 'the knower' as a featureless abstraction. Sometimes, indeed, she or he is merely a place holder in the proposition 'S knows that p'. Epistemological analyses of the proposition tend to focus on the 'knowing that', to determine conditions under which a knowledge claim can legitimately be made. Once discerned, it is believed, such conditions will hold across all possible utterances of the proposition. Indeed, throughout the history of modern philosophy the central 'problem of knowledge' has been to determine necessary and sufficient conditions for the possibility and justification of knowledge claims. Philosophers have sought ways of establishing a relation of correspondence between knowledge and 'reality' and/or ways of establishing the coherence of particular knowledge claims within systems of already-established truths. They have proposed methodologies for arriving at truth, and criteria for determining the validity of claims to the effect that 'S knows that p'. Such endeavors

[1]This question is the title of my paper published in *Metaphilosophy* 12 (July–October 1981): 267–276. In this early essay I endorse an essentialism with respect to masculinity and femininity, and convey the impression that 'positive thinking' can bring an end to gender imbalances. I would no longer make these claims.

are guided by the putatively self-evident principle that truth once discerned, knowledge once established, claim their status *as* truth and knowledge by virtue of a grounding in or coherence within a permanent, objective, ahistorical, and circumstantially neutral framework or set of standards.

The question 'Who is S?' is regarded neither as legitimate nor as relevant in these endeavors. As inquirers into the nature and conditions of human knowledge, epistemologists commonly work from the assumption that they need concern themselves only with knowledge claims that meet certain standards of *purity*. Questions about the circumstances of knowledge acquisition serve merely to clutter and confuse the issue with contingencies and other impurities. The question 'Who is S?' is undoubtedly such a question. If it matters who S is, then it must follow that something peculiar to S's character or nature could bear on the validity of the knowledge she or he claims: that S's *identity* might count among the conditions that make that knowledge claim possible. For many philosophers, such a suggestion would undermine the cherished assumption that knowledge can—and should—be evaluated on its own merits. More seriously still, a proposal that it matters who the knower is looks suspiciously like a move in the direction of epistemological relativism. For many philosophers, an endorsement of relativism signals the end of knowledge and of epistemology.

Broadly described, epistemological relativists hold that knowledge, truth, or even 'reality' can be understood only in relation to particular sets of cultural or social circumstances, to a theoretical framework, a specifiable range of perspectives, a conceptual scheme, or a form of life. Conditions of justification, criteria of truth and falsity, and standards of rationality are likewise relative: there is no universal, unchanging framework or scheme for rational adjudication among competing knowledge claims.

Critics of relativism often argue that relativism entails incommensurability: that a relativist cannot evaluate knowledge claims comparatively. This argument is based on the contention that epistemological relativism entails conceptual relativism: that it contextualizes language just as it contextualizes knowledge, so that there remains no 'common' or neutral linguistic framework for discussion, agreement, *or* disagreement. Other critics maintain that the very concept 'knowledge' is rendered meaningless by relativism: that the only honest— and logical—move a relativist can make is once and for all to declare her or his skepticism. Where there are no universal standards, the argument goes, there can be no knowledge worthy of the name. Opponents often contend that relativism is simply incoherent because of its inescapable self-referentiality. Relativism, they argue, is subject to the same constraints as every other claim to knowledge and truth. Any claim for the truth of relativism must itself be relative to the circumstances of the claimant; hence relativism itself has no claim to objective or universal truth. In short, relativism is often perceived as a denial of the very possibility of epistemology.[2]

Now posing the question 'Who is S?'—that is, 'Who is the knowing subject?'—does indeed count as a move in the direction of relativism, and my intention in posing it is to suggest that the answer has epistemological import. But I shall invoke certain caveats to demonstrate that such a move is not the epistemological disaster that many theorists of knowledge believe it to be.

It is true that, on its starkest construal, relativism may threaten to slide into subjectivism, into a position for which knowledge claims are indistinguishable from expressions of personal opinion, taste, or bias. But relativism need not be construed so starkly, nor do its *limitations* warrant exclusive emphasis. There are advantages to endorsing a measure of epistemological relativism that make of it an enabling rather than a constraining position. By no means the least of these advantages is the fact that relativism is one of the more obvious means of avoiding reductive explanations, in terms of drastically simplified paradigms of knowledge, monolithic explanatory modes, or privileged, decontextualized positions. For a relativist, who contends that there can be many valid ways of knowing any phenomenon, there is the possibility of taking several constructions, many perspectives into account. Hence relativism keeps open a range of interpretive possibilities. At the same time, because of the epistemic choices it affirms, it creates stringent accountability requirements of which knowers have to be cognizant. Thus it introduces a moral-political component into the heart of epistemological enquiry.[3]

There probably is no absolute authority, no practice of all practices or scheme of all schemes. Yet it does not follow that conceptual schemes, practices, and paradigms are radically idiosyncratic or purely subjective. Schemes, practices, and paradigms evolve out of communal projects of inquiry. To sustain viability and authority, they must demonstrate their adequacy in enabling people to negotiate the

---

[2]I consider some of these objections to relativism at greater length in "The Importance of Historicism for a Theory of Knowledge," *International Philosophical Quarterly* 22 (June 1982): 157–174.

[3]I discuss some of these accountability requirements, and the normative realism from which they derive, in my *Epistemic Responsibility* (Hanover, N.H.: University Press of New England, 1987).

everyday world and to cope with the decisions, problems, and puzzles they encounter daily. From the claim that no single scheme has absolute explanatory power, it does not follow that all schemes are equally valid. Knowledge is qualitatively variable: some knowledge is *better* than other knowledge. Relativists are in a good position to take such qualitative variations into account and to analyze their implications.

Even if these points are granted, though, it would be a mistake to believe that posing the 'Who is S?' question indicates that the circumstances of the knower are *all* that counts in knowledge evaluation. The point is, rather, that understanding the circumstances of the knower makes possible a more *discerning* evaluation. The claim that certain of those circumstances are epistemologically significant—the sex of the knower, in this instance—by no means implies that they are definitive, capable of bearing the entire burden of justification and evaluation. This point requires special emphasis. Claiming epistemological significance for the sex of the knower might seem tantamount to a dismissal, to a contention that S made such a claim only because of his or her sex. Dismissals of this sort, both of women's knowledge *and* of their claims to be knowers in any sense of the word, are only too common throughout the history of western thought. But claiming that the circumstances of the knower are not epistemologically definitive is quite different from claiming that they are of no epistemological consequence. The position I take in this book is that the sex of the knower is one of a cluster of *subjective* factors (i.e., factors that pertain to the circumstances of cognitive agents) constitutive of received conceptions of knowledge and of what it means to be a knower. I maintain that subjectivity and the specificities of cognitive agency can and must be accorded central epistemological significance, yet that so doing does not commit an inquirer to outright subjectivism. Specificities count, and they require a place in epistemological evaluation, but they cannot tell the whole story.

Knowers and the Known

The only thing that is clear about S from the standard proposition 'S knows that p' is that S is a (would-be) knower. Although the question 'Who is S?' rarely arises, certain assumptions about S as knower permeate epistemological inquiry. Of special importance for my argument is the assumption that knowers are self-sufficient and solitary individuals, at least in their knowledge-seeking activities. This belief derives from a long and venerable heritage, with its roots in Descartes's quest for a basis of perfect certainty on which to establish his knowledge. The central aim of Descartes's endeavors is captured in this claim: "I shall have the right to conceive high hopes if I am happy enough to discover one thing only which is certain and indubitable."[4] That "one thing," Descartes believed, would stand as the fixed, pivotal, Archimedean point on which all the rest of his knowledge would turn. Because of its systematic relation to that point, his knowledge would be certain and indubitable.

Most significant for this discussion is Descartes's conviction that his quest will be conducted in a private, introspective examination of the contents of his own mind. It is true that, in the last section of the *Discourse on the Method*, Descartes acknowledges the benefit "others may receive from the communication of [his] reflection," and he states his belief that combining "the lives and labours of many"[5] is essential to progress in scientific knowledge. It is also true that this individualistically described act of knowing exercises the aspect of the soul that is common to and alike in all knowers: namely, the faculty of reason. Yet his claim that knowledge seeking is an introspective activity of an individual mind accords no relevance either to a knower's embodiment or to his (or her) intersubjective relations. For each knower, the Cartesian route to knowledge is through private, abstract thought, through the efforts of reason unaided either by the senses or by consultation with other knowers. It is this individualistic, self-reliant, private aspect of Descartes's philosophy that has been influential in shaping subsequent epistemological ideals.

Reason is conceived as autonomous in the Cartesian project in two ways, then. Not only is the quest for certain knowledge an independent one, undertaken separately by each rational being, but it is a journey of reason alone, unassisted by the senses. For Descartes believed that sensory experiences had the effect of distracting reason from its proper course.

The custom of formulating knowledge claims in the 'S knows that p' formula is not itself of Cartesian origin. The point of claiming Cartesian inspiration for an assumption implicit in the formulation is that the knower who is commonly presumed to be the subject of that

---

[4]René Descartes, *Meditations*, in *The Philosophical Works of Descartes*, trans. Elizabeth S. Haldane and G. R. T. Ross (Cambridge: Cambridge University Press, 1969), 1:149.
[5]René Descartes, *Discourse on the Method of Rightly Conducting the Reason and Seeking for Truth in the Sciences*, in ibid., pp. 124, 120.

proposition is modeled, in significant respects, on the Cartesian pure inquirer. For epistemological purposes, all knowers are believed to be alike with respect both to their cognitive capacities and to their methods of achieving knowledge. In the empiricist tradition this assumption is apparent in the belief that simple, basic observational data can provide the foundation of knowledge just because perception is invariant from observer to observer, in standard observation conditions. In fact, a common way of filling the places in the 'S knows that p' proposition is with substitutions such as "Peter knows that the door is open" or "John knows that the book is red." It does not matter who John or Peter is.

Such knowledge claims carry implicit beliefs not only about would-be knowers but also about the knowledge that is amenable to philosophical analysis. Although (Cartesian) rationalists and empiricists differ with respect to what kinds of claim count as foundational, they endorse similar assumptions about the relation of foundational claims to the rest of a body of knowledge. With 'S knows that p' propositions, the belief is that such propositions stand as paradigms for knowledge in general. Epistemologists assume that knowledge is analyzable into propositional 'simples' whose truth can be demonstrated by establishing relations of correspondence to reality, or coherence within a system of known truths. These relatively simple knowledge claims (i.e., John knows that the book is red) could indeed be made by most 'normal' people who know the language and are familiar with the objects named. Knowers would seem to be quite self-sufficient in acquiring such knowledge. Moreover, no one would claim to know "a little" that the book is red or to be in the process of acquiring knowledge about the openness of the door. Nor would anyone be likely to maintain that S knows better than W does that the door is open or that the book is red. Granting such examples paradigmatic status creates the mistaken assumption that all knowledge worthy of the name will be like this.

In some recent epistemological discussion, emphasis has shifted away from simple perceptual claims toward processes of evaluating the 'warranted assertability' of more complex knowledge claims. In such contexts it does make sense to analyze the degree or extent of the knowledge claimed. Yet claims of the simple, perceptual sort are still most commonly cited as exemplary. They are assumed to have an all-or-nothing character; hence they seem not to admit of qualitative assessment. Granting them exemplary status implies that, for knowledge in general, it is appropriate to ask about neither the circumstances of the knowing process nor who the knower is. There would be no point to the suggestion that her or his identity might bear on the *quality* of the knowledge under discussion.

Proposing that the sex of the knower is significant casts doubt both on the autonomy of reason and on the (residual) exemplary status of simple observational knowledge claims. The suggestion that reason might function differently according to whose it is and in what circumstances its capacities are exercised implies that the manner of its functioning is dependent, in some way, on those circumstances, not independent from them. Simple perceptual examples are rendered contestable for their tendency to give a misleading impression of how knowledge is constructed and established and to suppress diversities in knowledge acquisition that derive from the varied circumstances— for example, the sex—of different knowers.

Just what am I asking, then, with this question about the epistemological *significance* of the sex of the knower? First, I do not expect that the question will elicit the answer that the sex of the knower is pertinent among conditions for the existence of knowledge, in the sense that taking it into account will make it possible to avoid skepticism. Again, it is unlikely that information about the sex of the knower could count among criteria of evidence or means of justifying knowledge claims. Nor is it prima facie obvious that the sex of the knower will have a legitimate bearing on the qualitative judgments that could be made about certain claims to know. Comparative judgments of the following kind are not what I expect to elicit: that if the knower is female, her knowledge is likely to be better grounded; if the knower is male, his knowledge will likely be more coherent.

In proposing that the sex of the knower is epistemologically significant, I am claiming that the scope of epistemological inquiry has been too narrowly defined. My point is not to denigrate projects of establishing the best foundations possible or of developing workable criteria of coherence. I am proposing that even if it is not possible (or not *yet* possible) to establish an unassailable foundationalist or coherentist position, there are numerous questions to be asked about knowledge whose answers matter to people who are concerned to know well. Among them are questions that bear not just on criteria of evidence, justification, and warrantability, but on the 'nature' of cognitive agents: questions about their character; their material, historical, cultural circumstances; their interests in the inquiry at issue. These are questions about how credibility is established, about connections between knowledge and power, about the place of knowledge in ethical and aesthetic judgments, and about political agendas and the responsibilities of knowers. I am claiming that all of these questions are epistemologically significant.

The Sex of the Knower

What, then, of the sex of the knower? In the rest of this chapter—and this book—I examine some attempts to give content to the claim that the sex of the knower *is* epistemologically significant.[6] Many of these endeavors have been less than satisfactory. Nonetheless, I argue that the claim itself is accurate.

Although it has rarely been spelled out prior to the development of feminist critiques, it has long been tacitly assumed that S is male. Nor could S be just any man, the apparently infinite substitutability of the 'S' term notwithstanding. The S who could count as a model, paradigmatic knower has most commonly—if always tacitly—been an adult (but not *old*), white, reasonably affluent (latterly middle-class) educated man of status, property, and publicly acceptable accomplishments. In theory of knowledge he has been allowed to stand for all men.[7] This assumption does not merely derive from habit or coincidence, but is a manifestation of engrained philosophical convictions. Not only has it been taken for granted that knowers properly so-called are male, but when male philosophers have paused to note this fact, as some indeed have done, they have argued that things are as they should be. Reason may be alike in all men, but it would be a mistake to believe that 'man', in this respect, 'embraces woman'. Women have been judged incapable, for many reasons, of achieving

[6]In this chapter I discuss the *sex* of the knower in a way that may seem to conflate biological sex differences with their cultural elaborations and manifestations as *gender* differences. I retain the older term—albeit inconsistently—for two reasons. The first, personally historical, reason connects this text with my first thoughts on these matters, published in my *Metaphilosophy* paper (see note 1, above). The second, philosophically historical, reason reflects the relatively recent appearance of 'gender' as a theoretical term of art. In the history of 'the epistemological project', which I discuss in these early chapters, 'sex' would have been the term used, had these questions been raised.

[7]To cite just one example: in *The Theory of Epistemic Rationality* (Cambridge: Harvard University Press, 1987), Richard Foley appeals repeatedly to the epistemic judgments of people who are "like the rest of us" (p. 108). He contrasts their beliefs with beliefs that seem "crazy or bizarre or outlandish . . . beliefs to most of the rest of us" (p. 114), and argues that an account of rational belief is plausible only if it can be presented from "some nonweird perspective" (p. 140). Foley contends that "an individual has to be at least minimally like us in order for charges of irrationality even to make sense" (p. 240). Nowhere does he address the question of who 'we' are. (I take this point up again in Chapter 7.)

knowledge worthy of the name. It is no exaggeration to say that anyone who wanted to *count* as a knower has commonly had to be male.

In the *Politics*, Aristotle observes: "The freeman rules over the slave after another manner from that in which the male rules over the female, or the man over the child; although the parts of the soul are present in all of them, they are present in different degrees. For the slave has no deliberative faculty at all; the woman has, but it is without authority, and the child has, but it is immature."[8] Aristotle's assumption that a woman will naturally be ruled by a man connects directly with his contention that a woman's deliberative faculty is "without authority." Even if a woman could, in her sequestered, domestic position, acquire deliberative skills, she would remain reliant on her husband for her sources of knowledge and information. She must be ruled by a man because, in the social structure of the *polis*, she enjoys neither the autonomy nor the freedom to put into visible practice the results of the deliberations she may engage in, in private. If she can claim no authority for her rational, deliberative endeavors, then her chances of gaining recognition as a knowledgeable citizen are seriously limited, whatever she may do.[9]

Aristotle is just one of a long line of western thinkers to declare the limitations of women's cognitive capacities.[10] Rousseau maintains that young men and women should be educated quite differently because of women's inferiority in reason and their propensity to be dragged down by their sensual natures. For Kierkegaard, women are merely aesthetic beings: men alone can attain the (higher) ethical and religious levels of existence. And for Nietzsche, the Apollonian (intellectual) domain is the male preserve, whereas women are Dionysian (sensuous) creatures. Nineteenth-century philosopher and linguist Wilhelm von Humboldt, who writes at length about women's knowledge, sums up the central features of this line of thought as follows:

[8]Aristotle, *Politics*, trans. Benjamin Jowett, in *The Basic Works of Aristotle*, ed. Richard McKeon (New York: Random House, 1941), 1260b.

[9]I discuss the implications of this lack of authority more fully in Chapters 5 and 6. See Elizabeth V. Spelman, *Inessential Woman: Problems of Exclusion in Feminist Thought* (Boston: Beacon, 1988), for an interesting discussion of some more complex exclusions effected by Aristotle's analysis.

[10]It would be inaccurate, however, to argue that this line is unbroken. Londa Schiebinger demonstrates that in the history of science—and, by implication, the history of the achievement of epistemic authority—there were many periods when women's intellectual achievements were not only recognized but respected. The "long line" I refer to is the dominant, historically most visible one. Schiebinger, *The Mind Has No Sex? Women in the Origins of Modern Science* (Cambridge: Harvard University Press, 1989).

"A sense of truth exists in [women] quite literally as a sense: . . . their nature also contains a lack or a failing of analytic capacity which draws a strict line of demarcation between ego and world; therefore, they will not come as close to the ultimate investigation of truth as man."[11] The implication is that women's knowledge, if ever the products of their projects deserve that label, is inherently and inevitably *subjective*—in the most idiosyncratic sense—by contrast with the best of men's knowledge.

Objectivity, quite precisely construed, is commonly regarded as a defining feature of knowledge per se.[12] So if women's knowledge is declared to be *naturally* subjective, then a clear answer emerges to my question. The answer is that if the would-be knower is female, then her sex is indeed epistemologically significant, for it disqualifies her as a knower in the fullest sense of that term. Such disqualifications will operate differently for women of different classes, races, ages, and allegiances, but in every circumstance they will operate asymmetrically for women and for men. Just what is to be made of these points—how their epistemological significance is to be construed—is the subject of this book.

The presuppositions I have just cited claim more than the rather simple fact that many kinds of knowledge and skill have, historically, been inaccessible to women on a purely practical level. It is true, historically speaking, that even women who were the racial and social 'equals' of standard male knowers were only rarely able to become learned. The thinkers I have cited (and others like them) claim to find a rationale for this state of affairs through appeals to dubious 'facts' about women's natural incapacity for rational thought. Yet deeper questions still need to be asked: Is there knowledge that is, quite simply, inaccessible to members of the female, or the male, sex? Are there kinds of knowledge that only men, or only women, can acquire? Is the sex of the knower crucially determining in this respect, across all other specificities? The answers to these questions should not address only the *practical* possibilities that have existed for members of either sex. Such practical possibilities are the constructs of complex social arrangements that are themselves constructed out of historically specific choices, and are, as such, open to challenge and change.

Knowledge, as it achieves credence and authoritative status at any

---

[11]*Humanist without Portfolio: An Anthology of the Writings of Wilhelm von Humboldt*, trans. with intro. by Marianne Cowan (Detroit: Wayne State University Press, 1963), p. 349.

[12]I analyze this precise construal of objectivity in Chapter 2.

point in the history of the male-dominated mainstream, is commonly held to be a product of the individual efforts of human knowers. References to Pythagoras's theorem, Copernicus's revolution, and Newtonian and Einsteinian physics signal an epistemic community's attribution of pathbreaking contributions to certain of its individual members. The implication is that *that* person, singlehandedly, has effected a leap of progress in a particular field of inquiry. In less publicly spectacular ways, other cognitive agents are represented as contributors to the growth and stability of public knowledge.

Now any contention that such contributions are the results of independent endeavor is highly contestable. As I argue elsewhere,[13] a complex of historical and other sociocultural factors produces the conditions that make 'individual' achievement possible, and 'individuals' themselves are socially constituted.[14] The claim that individual *men* are the creators of the authoritative (often Kuhn-paradigm-establishing) landmarks of western intellectual life is particularly interesting for the fact that the contributions—both practical and substantive—of their lovers, wives, children, servants, neighbors, friends, and colleagues rarely figure in analyses of their work.[15]

The historical attribution of such achievements to specific cognitive agents does, nonetheless, accord a significance to individual efforts which raises questions pertinent to my project. It poses the problem, in another guise, of whether aspects of human specificity could, in fact, constitute conditions for the existence of knowledge or determine the kinds of knowledge that a knower can achieve. It would seem that such incidental physical attributes as height, weight, or hair color would not count among factors that would determine a person's capacities to know (though the arguments that skin color *does* count are too familiar). It is not necessary to consider how much Archimedes weighed when he made his famous discovery, nor is there any doubt that a thinner or a fatter person could have reached the same conclusion. But in cultures in which sex differences figure prominently in virtually every mode of human interaction,[16] being female

[13]See chap. 7, "Epistemic Community," of my *Epistemic Responsibility*.

[14]I discuss the implications of these points for analyses of subjectivity in Chapter 3.

[15]I owe this point—and the list—to Polly Young-Eisendrath, "The Female Person and How We Talk about Her," in Mary M. Gergen, ed., *Feminist Thought and the Structure of Knowledge* (New York: New York University Press, 1988).

[16]Marilyn Frye points out: "Sex-identification intrudes into every moment of our lives and discourse, no matter what the supposedly primary focus or topic of the moment is. Elaborate, systematic, ubiquitous and redundant marking of a distinction between two sexes of humans and most animals is customary and obligatory. One *never* can ignore it." Frye, *The Politics of Reality: Essays in Feminist Theory* (Trumansburg, N.Y.: Crossing Press, 1983), p. 19.

or male is far more fundamental to the construction of subjectivity than are such attributes as size or hair color. So the question is whether femaleness or maleness are the kinds of subjective factor (i.e., factors about the circumstances of a knowing subject) that are constitutive of the form and content of knowledge. Attempts to answer this question are complicated by the fact that sex/gender does not function uniformly and universally, even in western societies. Its implications vary across class, race, age, ability, and numerous other interwoven specificities. A separated analysis of sex/gender, then, always risks abstraction and is limited in its scope by the abstracting process. Further, the question seems to imply that sex and gender are themselves constants, thus obscuring the processes of *their* sociocultural construction. Hence the formulation of adequately nuanced answers is problematic and necessarily partial.

Even if it should emerge that gender-related factors play a crucial role in the construction of knowledge, then, the inquiry into the epistemological significance of the sex of the knower would not be complete. The task would remain of considering whether a distinction between 'natural' and socialized capacity can retain any validity. The equally pressing question as to how the hitherto devalued products of *women's* cognitive projects can gain acknowledgment as 'knowledge' would need to be addressed so as to uproot entrenched prejudices about knowledge, epistemology, and women. 'The epistemological project' will look quite different once its tacit underpinnings are revealed.

Reclaiming 'the feminine'

Whether this project could or should emerge in a *feminist epistemology* is quite another question. Investigations that start from the conviction that the sex of the knower *is* epistemologically significant will surely question received conceptions of the nature of knowledge and challenge the hegemony of mainstream epistemologies. Some feminist theorists have maintained that there are distinctively female—or feminine—ways of knowing: neglected ways, from which the label 'knowledge', traditionally, is withheld. Many claim that a recognition of these 'ways of knowing' should prompt the development of new, rival, or even separate epistemologies. Others have adopted Mary O'Brien's brilliant characterization of mainstream epistemology as "malestream,"[17] claiming that one of the principal manifestations of

[17]See Mary O'Brien, *The Politics of Reproduction* (London: Routledge & Kegan Paul, 1980).

its hegemony is its suppression of female—or 'feminine' knowledge. In this section I sketch some classic and more recent arguments in favor of feminine 'ways of knowing' and offer a preliminary analysis of their strengths and shortcomings.

Claims that there are specifically female or feminine ways of knowing often find support in the contention that women's significantly different experiences (different, that is, from men's experiences) lead them to know 'the world' differently (i.e., from the ways men do). A putatively different female consciousness, in turn, generates different theories of knowledge, politics, metaphysics, morality, and aesthetics. Features of women's experiences commonly cited are a concern with the concrete, everyday world; a connection with objects of experience rather than an objective distance from them; a marked affective tone; a respect for the environment; and a readiness to listen perceptively and responsibly to a variety of 'voices' in the environment, both animate and inanimate, manifested in a tolerance of diversity.

Many of these features are continuous with the attributes with which the dominant discourse of affluent western societies characterizes a good mother. Indeed, one of the best-known advocates of a caring, maternal approach both to knowledge and to a morality based on that knowledge is Sara Ruddick, in her now-classic article "Maternal Thinking." Maternal thinking, Ruddick believes, grows out of the *practice* of caring for and establishing an intimate connection with another being—a growing child. That practice is marked by a "unity of reflection, judgment and emotion . . . [which is] . . . no more relative to its particular reality (the growing child) than the thinking that arises from scientific, religious, or other practice"[18] is relevant to scientific or religious matters alone. Just as scientific or religious thought can structure a knower's characteristic approach to experiences and knowledge in general, Ruddick believes that attitudes and skills developed in the attentive and painstaking practices of caring for infants and small children are generalizable across cognitive domains.

Ruddick's celebration of values traditionally associated with mothering and femininity is not the first such in the history of feminist thought. Among nineteenth-century American feminists, both Margaret Fuller and Matilda Gage praised women's intuition as a peculiarly insightful capacity. Fuller, for example, believed that women have an intuitive perception that enables them to "seize and delineate with unerring discrimination" the connections and links among the

---

[18]Sara Ruddick, "Maternal Thinking," *Feminist Studies* 6 (1980): 348. I develop a critical analysis of Ruddick's position in Chapter 3. It should be noted that in Ruddick's 1989 book, *Maternal Thinking: Toward a Politics of Peace* (Boston: Beacon, 1989), she addresses some of the issues I raise about the essentialism of this earlier article.

various life forms that surround them.[19] In this respect, she maintains, women are superior to men. And Gage believed that women have unique intellectual capacities, manifested especially in an intuitive faculty that does not "need a long process of ratiocination" for its operations.[20] Both Fuller and Gage, albeit in quite different contexts, advocate legitimizing this suppressed and undervalued faculty whose deliverances, they believe, are attuned to and hence better able to reveal the secrets of nature and (for Gage) of spirituality, than masculine ratiocinative practices.

This nineteenth-century belief in the powers of female intuition is echoed in the work of two of the best-known twentieth-century radical feminists, Shulamith Firestone and Mary Daly. For Firestone, there are two sharply contrasting modes or styles of response to experience: an "aesthetic response," which she links to femaleness and characterizes as "subjective, intuitive, introverted, wishful, dreamy or fantastic, concerned with the subconscious (the *id*), emotional, even temperamental (hysterical)"; and a technological response, which she describes as masculine: "objective, logical, extroverted, realistic, concerned with the conscious mind (the ego), rational, mechanical, pragmatic and down-to-earth, stable."[21] Firestone's claim is not that the aesthetic (= the feminine) should dominate, but that there should be a fusion between the two modes. To overcome patriarchal domination, she believes, it is vital for the aesthetic principle to manifest itself in all cultural and cognitive activity and for technology to cease operating to exclude affectivity.

Daly's concern with spirituality and with the celebration of witchcraft places her closer to Gage than to Fuller. Daly invokes the metaphor of spinning to describe the creation of knowledge and to connect the process with women's traditional creative activities. She claims that "Gyn/Ecology Spins around, past, and through the established fields, opening the coffers/coffins in which 'knowledge' has been stored, re-stored, re-covered . . . [where] its meaning will be hidden from the Grave Keepers of tradition." These "Grave Keepers" are the arbiters of knowledge in patriarchal culture: the men who determine the legitimacy of knowledge claims. In consequence of their forced adherence to masculine epistemic norms, Daly contends, "women

[19]Margaret Fuller, *Woman in the Nineteenth Century* (1845; New York: Norton, 1971), p. 103.
[20]Matilda Jocelyn Gage, *Women, Church, and State* (1893; Watertown, Mass.: Persephone, 1980), p. 238.
[21]Shulamith Firestone, *The Dialectic of Sex: The Case for Feminine Revolution* (New York: Bantam 1971), p. 175.

are encouraged, that is, dis-couraged, to adapt to a maintenance level of cognition and behavior by all the myth-masters and enforcers." Gyn/Ecology is a process of breaking the "spell of patriarchal myth"—by which Daly means all 'received' knowledge in patriarchal cultures—"bounding into freedom"; weaving "the tapestries of [one's] own creation."[22] Once freed from patriarchal myth, women will acquire the knowledge they need to validate their pleasures and powers as marks of their own authority and to unmask patriarchy. Daly's is a vision of female empowerment.

Some theorists maintain that research into the lateralization of brain function reveals 'natural' female-male cognitive differences. The findings of this research are frequently interpreted to indicate that in men, "left-brain" functions predominate, whereas "right-brain" functioning is better developed in women. Evidence that women have better verbal skills and fine motor coordination, whereas men are more adept at spatial skills, mathematics, and abstract thinking, is cited as proof of the existence of female and male cognitive differences. Depending on the political orientation of the inquirer, such findings are read either as confirmations of male supremacy and female inferiority or as indications of a need to revalue 'the feminine'. Among the celebratory interpretations are Gina Covina's claim that women, whom she describes as more "rightbrained" than men, deal with experience "in a diffuse non-sequential way, assimilating many different phenomena simultaneously, finding connections between separate bits of information." By contrast, men, whom she labels "leftbrained," engage typically in thinking that is "focused narrowly enough to squeeze out human or emotional considerations . . . [and to enable] . . . men to kill (people, animals, plants, natural processes) with free consciousnesses."[23] For Covina, there are 'natural' female-male differences. They are marked not just descriptively but evaluatively.

If brain-lateralization studies, or theories like Daly's and Firestone's, can be read as demonstrations of women's and men's *necessarily* different cognitive capacities, then my title question requires an affirmative answer. But it is not clear that such conclusions follow unequivocally. Consider the fact that allegedly sex-specific differences are not observable in examinations of the structure of the brain itself, and that in small children "both hemispheres appear to be equally

[22]Mary Daly, *Gyn/Ecology: The Metaethics of Radical Feminism* (Boston: Beacon, 1978), pp. xiii, 53, 57, 320.
[23]Gina Covina, "Rosy Rightbrain's Exorcism/Invocation," in G. Covina and Laurel Galana, eds., *The Lesbian Reader* (Oakland, Calif.: Amazon, 1975), p. 96.

proficient."[24] At most, then, it would seem, the brain may come to control certain processes in sexually differentiated ways. Evidence suggests that the brain *develops* its powers through training and practice.[25] Brains of creatures presented with a wide variety of tasks and stimuli develop strikingly greater performance capacities than brains of creatures kept in impoverished environments. As Ruth Bleier points out, "the biology of the brain itself is shaped by the individual's environment and experiences."[26]

Bleier notes the difficulty of assessing the implications of lateralization research. She observes that there are just as many studies that find no sex differences as there are studies that do, and that variability within each sex is greater than variability between them.[27] Janet Sayers suggests that it is as plausible to argue that sex differences in the results of tests to measure spatial ability are the results of sex-specific strategies that subjects adopt to deal with the tests themselves as it is to attribute them to differences in brain organization. She points out that there is no conclusive demonstration that differences in brain organization actually *"cause* sex differences in spatial ability."[28] It is not easy to see, then, how these studies can plausibly support arguments about general differences in male and female cognitive abilities or about women's incapacity to enter such specific domains as engineering and architecture, where spatial abilities figure largely.

These are just some of the considerations that recommend caution in interpreting brain-lateralization studies. Differences in female and male brain functioning are just as plausibly attributable to socio-cultural factors such as the sex-stereotyping of children's activities or

[24]See Gordon Rattray Taylor, *The Natural History of the Mind* (London: Granada, 1979), p. 127. In an earlier article Taylor points out that "if the eyelids of an animal are sewn up at birth, and freed at maturity, it cannot see and will never learn to do so. The brain has failed to develop the necessary connections at the period when it was able to do so." Taylor, "A New View of the Brain," *Encounter* 36, 2 (1971): 30.

[25]In this connection Oliver Sacks recounts an illuminating story of a fifty-nine-year-old, congenitally blind woman with cerebral palsy, whose manual sensory capacities, he determined, were intact and quite normal. But when he met her, she had no use of her hands, referring to them as "useless lumps of dough." It became apparent that her hands were functionless because she had never used them: "being 'protected', 'looked after', 'babied' since birth [had] prevented her from the normal exploratory use of the hands which all infants learn in the first months of life." This woman first learned to use her hands in her sixtieth year. Oliver Sacks, "Hands," in *The Man Who Mistook His Wife for a Hat and Other Clinical Tales* (New York: Summit, 1985), p. 57.

[26]Ruth Bleier, "Lab Coat: Robe of Innocence or Klansman's Sheet?" in Teresa de Lauretis, ed., *Feminist Studies / Critical Studies* (Bloomington: Indiana University Press, 1986), p. 65.

[27]Ibid., pp. 58–59.

[28]Janet Sayers, *Biological Politics* (London: Tavistock, 1982), p. 103.

to differing parental attitudes to children of different sexes, even from earliest infancy. It would be a mistake to rely on the research in developing a position about the epistemological significance of the sex of the knower, especially as its results are often elaborated and interpreted to serve political ends.[29]

Now Fuller, Gage, Ruddick, Firestone, Daly, and Covina evidently believe—albeit variously—in the effectiveness of *evaluative reversals* of alleged differences as a fundamental revolutionary move. Philosophers should acknowledge the superiority of feminine ideals in knowledge acquisition as much as in social life and institutions, and masculine ways of thought should give way, more generally, to feminine ways. These recommendations apply to theoretical content and to methodology, to rules for the conduct of inquiry, and to principles of justification and legitimation.

The general thesis that inspires these recommendations is that women have an edge in the development and exercise of just those attributes that merit celebration as feminine: in care, sensitivity, responsiveness and responsibility, intuition and trust. There is no doubt that these traits are commonly represented as constitutive of femininity. Nor is there much doubt that a society that valued them might be a better society than one that denigrates and discourages them. But these very traits are as problematic, both theoretically and practically, as they are attractive. It is not easy to separate their appeal from the fact that women—at least women of prosperous classes and privileged races—have been encouraged to cultivate them throughout so long a history of oppression and exploitation that they have become marks of acquiescence in powerlessness. Hence there is a persistent tension in feminist thought between a laudable wish to celebrate 'feminine' values as tools for the creation of a better social order and a fear of endorsing those same values as instruments of women's continued oppression.

My recurring critique, throughout this book, of theoretical appeals to an *essential* femininity is one I engage in from a position sensitive to the pull of both sides in this tension. By 'essentialism' I mean a belief in an essence, an inherent, natural, eternal female nature that manifests itself in such characteristics as gentleness, goodness, nurturance, and sensitivity. These are some of women's more positive

[29]Sayers notes: "So germane do . . . findings about sex differences in brain organization appear to the current political debate about the justice of continuing sexual inequalities in professional life that they are now regularly singled out for coverage in newspaper reports of scientific meetings." Ibid., p. 101. See Lynda Birke's elaboration of this point in her *Women, Feminism, and Biology* (Brighton: Harvester, 1986), p. 29.

attributes. Women are also represented, in essentialist thought, as naturally less intelligent, more dependent, less objective, more irrational, less competent, more scatterbrained than men: indeed, essential femaleness is commonly defined against a masculine standard of putatively *human* essence.

Essentialist attributions work both normatively and descriptively. Not only do they purport to describe how women essentially *are*, they are commonly enlisted in the perpetuation of women's (usually inferior) social status. Yet essentialist claims are highly contestable. Their diverse manifestations across class, race, and ethnicity attest to their having a sociocultural rather than a 'natural' source. Their deployment as instruments for keeping women in their place means that caution is always required in appealing to them—even though they often appear to designate women's *strengths*. Claims about masculine essence need also to be treated with caution, though it is worth noting that they are less commonly used to oppress men. Essential masculine aggressiveness, sexual needs, and ego-enhancing requirements are often added, rather, to reasons why women should remain subservient. Perhaps there are some essential female or male characteristics, but claims that there are always need to be evaluated and analyzed. The burden of proof falls on theorists who appeal to essences, rather than on those who resist them.

As I have noted, some of the thinkers I have cited advocate an evaluative reversal, in a tacit acceptance of stereotypical, essentialist conceptions of masculinity and femininity. To understand the import of the tension in feminist thought, these stereotypes need careful analysis. The issues of power and theoretical hegemony that are inextricably implicated in their maintenance need likewise to be analyzed. As an initial step toward embarking on this task I offer, in the remainder of this section, a critical analysis of three landmark articles that engage with malestream epistemology with the intention of revealing grounds for feminist opposition to its traditional structures.

(i) In her early piece, "Methodocracy, Misogyny and Bad Faith: Sexism in the Philosophic Establishment," Sheila Ruth characterizes mainstream philosophy in its content, methodology, and practice as male, masculine, and masculinist. Noting, correctly, that most philosophers—even more in the late 1970s than in the 1990s—are men, Ruth maintains that the content of their philosophy reflects masculine interests and that their standard methodologies reflect imperialist masculine values, values whose normative status derives from their association with maleness. Ruth writes that "philosophical sexism, metasexism . . . is epistemological, permeating philosophy to its roots—the structure of its methods and the logic of its criticism." She argues that "what should not be is the raising of . . . male [intellectual] constructs to the status of universals—the identification of male constructs with allowable constructs so that women cannot 'legitimately' think, perceive, select, argue, etc. from their unique stance."[30] For Ruth, the sex of the knower *is* epistemologically significant at a fundamental level, with all-pervasive implications.

This essay attests to the surprise and anger occasioned by early 'second wave' feminist realizations that theories that had posed, for centuries, as universal, neutral, and impartial were, in fact, deeply invested in furthering the self-interest of a small segment of the human population. Such realizations brought with them a profound shock, which often resulted in an insistence on affirming contrary, feminine interests and values. These early contributions often appear flawed from the present stage of feminist theoretical development, and I shall draw attention to some of those flaws as reasons why I would not, today, wholeheartedly endorse Ruth's claims.[31] They are worthy of rearticulation, though, for this article is one of the classics of feminist philosophy which created space for the development of subsequent critiques.

There is much that is right about Ruth's contentions, but two interconnected problems make it impossible to agree completely with her: the assumptions that "male constructs" exercise a unified, univocal hegemony and that women occupy a single "unique stance." I have argued in the first section of this chapter that epistemological relativism is a strong position because it creates the possibility of raising questions about the *identity* of knowers. It opens the way for analyses of the historical, racial, social, and cultural specificity of knowers and of knowledge. Now its value would be minimal were it possible to demonstrate that cognitive activity and knowledge have been conceived in exactly the same way by all knowers since the dawn of philosophy. Precisely because it allows the interplay of common threads *and* of specific variations, relativism has a significant explanatory capacity. This capacity is tacitly denied in an account such as Ruth's, based, as it apparently is, on implicit claims about essential, eternal conceptions of femininity and masculinity, mirrored in constant interpretations of knowing and knowledge. In the face of histor-

---

[30]Sheila Ruth, "Methodocracy, Misogyny, and Bad Faith: Sexism in the Philosophic Establishment," *Metaphilosophy* 10, 1 (1979): 50, 56.

[31]My *Metaphilosophy* article is another pertinent example. Allan Soble criticizes the essentialism of my argument in "Feminist Epistemology and Women Scientists," *Metaphilosophy* 14 (1983): 291–307.

ical, ethnographic, political and class-based evidence to the contrary, the onus would fall on Ruth, should she still wish to defend these claims, to demonstrate the constancy of the concepts.

Their assumed rigidity presents a still more serious problem. The content Ruth gives to masculinity and femininity plays directly into their essentialist, stereotypical construal in late-twentieth-century western societies. Yet there is no better reason to believe that feminine and masculine characteristics are constant across a complex society at any one time than there is to believe in their historical or cross-cultural constancy. Norms of masculinity and femininity vary across race, class, age, and ethnicity (to name only a few of the axes) within any society at any time. An acceptance of the stereotypes results in a rigidity of thinking that limits possibilities of developing nuanced analyses. In this article it creates for Ruth the troubling necessity of defining her project both *against* and *with reference to* a taken-for-granted masculine norm. No single such norm is discernible in western thought, yet when Ruth's positive recommendations in favor of different philosophical styles are sketched out by contrast with that assumed norm, their explanatory power is diminished. Ruth is right to assert that women have had "no part in defining the content of philosophical speculation, but they have had even less influence over the categories of concern and the modes of articulation."[32] The predominance of feminine and masculine stereotypes in her argument points to an unhappy implication of such early arguments for evaluative reversal: namely, that had women had such influence, their contribution would have been as monolithic as the 'masculine' one.

The broadest of Ruth's claims remains her strongest: philosophy has oppressed women in ways that feminists are still learning to understand. My point is that analyses of this oppression need to be wary lest they replicate the very structures they deplore. Much depends, in the development of feminist projects, on how women's oppression is analyzed. It is important to prevent the reactive aspects of critical response from overwhelming its creative possibilities. Ruth's analysis leans rather too heavily toward the reactive mode.

(ii) In another early, landmark article, "The Social Function of the Empiricist Conception of Mind," Sandra Harding confronts stereotypes of femininity from a different direction. Her thesis is that "the empiricist model of mind supports social hierarchy by implicitly sanctioning 'underclass' stereotypes." Emphasizing the passivity of know-

---

[32]Ruth, "Methodocracy, Misogyny, and Bad Faith," p. 54. In my thinking about Ruth's article I am indebted to Jean Grimshaw's discussion in her *Philosophy and Feminist Thinking* (Minneapolis: University of Minnesota Press, 1986), pp. 53–55, 81–82.

ers in Humean empiricism, Harding contends, first, that classical empiricism can allow no place for creativity, for historical self-consciousness, or for the adoption of a critical stance. Second, she discerns a striking similarity between 'the Humean mind' and stereotypical conceptions of women's minds: "formless, passive, and peculiarly receptive to direction from outside."[33] Her intention is to show that an espousal of empiricist theory, combined with an uncritical acceptance of feminine stereotypes, legitimates manipulative and controlling treatment of women in the social world. There are striking echoes, as Harding herself notes, with the Aristotelian view of woman's lack of rational authority: a lack that, for Aristotle, likewise justifies women's inferior social position.

Present-day empiricists would no doubt contend that Harding's equation of empiricism with a 'passive' epistemology and theory of mind has little validity, given the varieties of contemporary empiricism in its transformations under the influence of philosophers such as Quine.[34] Yet even if Harding has drawn only a caricature of 'the Humean mind', her account has a heuristic value in highlighting certain tendencies of orthodox, classical empiricism. Empiricism, and its latter-day positivist offspring, could indeed serve, either as a philosophy of mind or as a theory of knowledge, to legitimate under the guise of objectivity and impartial neutrality just the kinds of social practice feminists are concerned to eradicate. The impartiality of empiricist analysis, the interchangeability of its subjects of study, work to provide rationalizations for treating people as 'cases' or 'types', rather than as active, creative cognitive agents.[35] Such rationalizations are common in positivistic social science.

More intriguing is a 'double standard' Harding discerns in classical empiricist thought. The *explicit* picture of the Humean inquirer, she maintains, is of a person who is primarily passive, receptive, and hence manipulable. Yet the very existence of Hume's own philosophy counts as evidence that he himself escapes that characterization. His intellectual activity is marked by "a critical attitude, firm purposes and a willingness to struggle to achieve them, elaborate principles of inquiry and hypotheses to be investigated, clarity of vision, precision, and facility at rational argument."[36] This description of the *implicit*

[33]Sandra Harding, "The Social Function of the Empiricist Conception of Mind," *Metaphilosophy* 10 (January 1979): 39, 42.
[34]See especially Lynn Hankinson Nelson, *Who Knows: From Quine to a Feminist Empiricism* (Philadelphia: Temple University Press, 1990). Because Nelson's book was published after my manuscript was completed, I have not discussed it in this book.
[35]I discuss this consequence of empiricist thinking more fully in Chapter 2.
[36]Harding, "Social Function of the Empiricist Conception of Mind," pp. 43, 44.

Humean inquirer, Harding notes, feeds into standard gender stereotypes, in which men come across as "effective historical agents" while
women are incapable of historical agency.

Harding accuses the promulgators of the classical empiricist conception of mind of false consciousness. Their own theoretical activity
exempts *their* minds from the very model for which they claim universal validity: the contention that no one is a self-directed agent, everyone is a blank tablet, cannot apply to the authors themselves. Hence
the empiricists presuppose a we/they structure in which 'they' indeed are as the theory describes them, but 'we', by virtue of our
theoretical creativity, escape the description. In consequence, "the
empiricist model of mind . . . functions as a self-fulfilling *prescription*
beneficial to those already in power: treat people as if they are passive
and need direction from others, and they will become or remain able
to be manipulated and controlled."[37] Harding maintains that the implicit distinction between active empiricist theorist and passive ordinary inquirer maps onto the stereotypical active male/passive female
distinction and acts to legitimate the social and political consequences
of that stereotype in androcentered power structures.

Now it is not easy to show that Harding is right either to find an
implicit 'double standard' in Humean thought or to suggest that de-
marcations of the two 'kinds' of knower are appropriately drawn
along sexual lines. Hume himself may have meant merely to distinguish a philosopher at his most sophisticated from an ordinary 'vulgar' thinker. His elitism may have been intellect- or class-related,
rather than sex-related. If Harding is right, however, the Humean
'double standard' would suggest that the sex of the knower is epistemologically significant, in that it designates men alone as capable of
active, creative, critical knowing—and of constructing epistemological theories. By contrast, women are capable only of receiving and
shuffling information. Even if she is mistaken in her Humean attributions, then, the parallels Harding draws between the intellectual elitism that empiricism can create and sexual elitism find ample confirmation in the social world. The common relegation of women to low-
status forms of employment, which differ from high-status employment partly in the kinds of knowledge, expertise, and cognitive authority they require, is just one confirming practice.[38]

What ensures Harding's paper a place in the history of feminist
critiques of philosophy is less the detail of its Hume interpretation

[37]Ibid., p. 46.
[38]An example of the hierarchy of cognitive relations created by such assumptions is
the theme of Chapter 6.

than its articulation of the political implications of metaphysical theses. In the face of challenges such as these, which have been more subtly posed both in Harding's later work and elsewhere as feminist thought has increased in sophistication, the neutrality of such theses can never be taken for granted. Should it be declared, the onus is on its declarers to demonstrate the validity of their claims. So despite the flaws in Harding's analysis, her article supports my contention that the sex of the knower is epistemologically significant. If metaphysical theories are marked by the maleness of their creators, then theories of knowledge informed by them cannot escape the marking. Whether the case can be made that both theoretical levels are thus marked, without playing into sexual stereotypes, is a difficult question, but the evidence points compellingly toward the conclusion that the sex of a philosopher informs his theory-building.

(iii) The influence of stereotypically sex-specific traits on conceptions of the proper way to do philosophy is instructively detailed in Janice Moulton's analysis of "The Adversary Method," as she perceptively names it. Moulton shows that a subtle conceptual "conflation of aggression and competence"[39] has produced a paradigm for philosophical inquiry that is modeled on adversarial confrontation between opponents. This conflation depends, above all, on an association of aggression with such positive qualities as energy, power, and ambition: qualities that count as prerequisites for success in the white, middle-class, male professional world. Moulton questions the validity of this association in its conferral of normative status on styles of behavior stereotypically described as male. Yet what is most seriously wrong with the paradigm, she argues, is not so much its maleness as its constitutive role in the production of truncated philosophical problems, inquiries, and solutions.

The adversarial method is most effective, Moulton claims, in structuring isolated disagreements about specific theses and arguments. Hence it depends for its success on the artificial isolation of such claims and arguments from the contexts that occasion their articulation. Adversarial argument aims to show that an opponent is wrong, often by attacking conclusions implicit in, or potentially consequent on, his basic or alleged premises.[40] Under the adversarial paradigm,

---

[39]Janice Moulton, "A Paradigm of Philosophy: The Adversary Method," in Sandra Harding and Merrill B. Hintikka, eds., *Discovering Reality* (Dordrecht: Reidel, 1983), p. 151.

[40]I am agreeing with Moulton's association of the paradigm with maleness in using the masculine pronoun to refer to its practitioners—even though many women have learned to play the game well.

the point is to confront the most extreme opposing position, with the object of showing that one's own position is defensible even against such stark opposition. Exploration, explanation, and understanding are lesser goals. The irony, Moulton claims, is that the adversarial paradigm produces bad reasoning, because it leads philosophers to adopt the mode of reasoning best suited to defeat an opponent—she uses "counterexample reasoning" to illustrate her point[41]—as the paradigmatic model for reasoning as such. Diverse modes of reasoning which might be more appropriate to different circumstances, tend to be occluded, as does the possibility that a single problem might be amenable to more than one approach.

Moulton's analysis lends support to the contention that the sex of the knower is significant at the 'metaepistemological' level where the legitimacy of epistemological problems is established. The connection between aggressive cognitive styles and stereotypes of masculine behavior is now a commonplace of feminist thought. Moulton's demonstration that such behavior constitutes the dominant mode—the paradigm—in philosophy, which has so long claimed to stand outside 'the commonplace', is compelling. She shows that mainstream philosophy bears the marks of its androcentric derivation out of a stereotypically constructed masculinity, whatever the limitations of that construction are.

Like all paradigms, the adversarial method has a specific location in intellectual history. While it demarcates the kinds of puzzle a philosopher can legitimately consider, a recognition of its historical specificity shows that this is not how philosophy has always been done nor how it must, of necessity, be done. In according the method (interim) paradigm status, Moulton points to the historical contingency of its current hegemony. The fact that many feminist philosophers report a sense of dissonance between the supposed gender neutrality of the method and their own feminine gender[42] puts the paradigm under serious strains. Such strains create the space and the possibilities for developing alternative methodological approaches. Whether the sex of the knower will be methodologically and/or epistemologically significant in such approaches must, for now, remain an open question.

---

[41]Moulton, "Paradigm of Philosophy," p. 159.

[42]See, for example, Genevieve Lloyd's observation that "the exercise of writing feminist philosophy came out of [her] experience of dissonance between the supposed gender neutrality of philosophy and [her] gender." Lloyd, "Feminist Philosophy and the Idea of the Feminine" (manuscript, 1986), p. 22.

Knowledge, Methodology, and Power

The adversarial method is but one manifestation of a complex inter-weaving of power and knowledge which sustains the hegemony of mainstream epistemology. Like the empiricist theory of the mind, it presents a public demeanor of neutral inquiry, engaged in the disinterested pursuit of truth. Despite its evident interest in triumphing over opponents, it would be unreasonable to condemn this disinterest as merely a pose. There is no reason to believe that practitioners whose work is informed by these methodological assumptions have ruthlessly or tyrannically adopted a theoretical stance for the express purpose of engaging in projects that thwart the intellectual pursuits of women or of other marginalized philosophers. Could such a purpose be discerned, the task of revealing the epistemological significance of the sex of the knower would be easy. Critics could simply offer such practitioners a clear demonstration of the errors of their ways and hope that, with a presumption of goodwill on their part, they would abandon the path of error for that of truth and fairness.

Taking these practitioners at their word, acknowledging the sincerity of their convictions about their neutral, objective, impartial engagement in the pursuit of truth, reveals the intricacy of this task. Certain sets of problems, by virtue of their complexity or their intrinsic appeal, often become so engrossing for researchers that they override and occlude other contenders for attention. Reasons for this suppression are often subtle and not always specifically articulable. Nor is it clear that the exclusionary process is wholly conscious. A network of sociopolitical relationships and intellectual assumptions creates an invisible system of acceptance and rejection, discourse and silence, ascendency and subjugation within and around disciplines. Implicit cultural presuppositions work with the personal idiosyncracies of intellectual authorities to keep certain issues from placing high on research agendas. Critics have to learn how to notice their absence.

In "The Discourse on Language," Michel Foucault makes the astute observation that "within its own limits, every discipline recognizes true and false propositions, but it repulses a whole teratology of learning."[43] The observation captures some of the subtleties involved in attempting to understand the often imperceptible workings of

---

[43]Michel Foucault, "The Discourse on Language," in *The Archaeology of Knowledge*, trans. Alan Sheridan (New York: Pantheon, 1972), p. 223.

hegemonic, usually masculine power in mainstream philosophy. A discipline defines itself both by what it excludes (repulses) and by what it includes. But the self-definition process removes what is excluded (repulsed) from view so that it is not straightforwardly available for assessment, criticism, and analysis. Even in accepting mainstream avowals of neutral objectivity, critics have to learn to see what is repulsed by the disciplinarily imposed limits on methodology and areas of inquiry. The task is not easy. It is much easier to seek the flaws in existing structures and practices and to work at eradicating them than it is to learn to perceive what is not there to be perceived.

Feminist philosophy simply did not exist until philosophers learned to perceive the near-total absence of women in philosophical writings from the very beginning of western philosophy, to stop assuming that 'man' could be read as a generic term. Explicit denigrations of women, which became the focus of philosophical writing in the early years of the contemporary women's movement, were more readily perceptible. The authors of derogatory views about women in classical texts clearly needed power to be able to utter their pronouncements with impunity: a power they claimed from a 'received' discourse that represented women's nature in such a way that women undoubtedly merited the negative judgments that Aristotle or Nietzsche made about them. Women are now in a position to recognize and refuse these overt manifestations of contempt.

The covert manifestations are more intransigent. Philosophers, when they have addressed the issue at all, have tended to group philosophy with science as the most gender-neutral of disciplines. But feminist critiques reveal that this alleged neutrality masks a bias in favor of institutionalizing stereotypical masculine values into the fabric of the discipline—its methods, norms, and contents. In so doing, it suppresses values, styles, problems, and concerns stereotypically associated with femininity. Thus, whether by chance or by design, it creates a hegemonic philosophical practice in which the sex of the knower is, indeed, epistemologically significant.

CHAPTER TWO

Knowledge and Subjectivity

Objective/Subjective—and Other Dichotomies

The assertion that knowledge is, inextricably, subjective *and* objective will seem outrageous to theorists of knowledge who believe that 'knowledge' is demarcated in virtue of its *objective* validity from such inferior cognitive products as opinion and belief. Mainstream epistemologists commonly contrast objectivity with the subjective ephemerality of speculation, fantasy, and hearsay. In this chapter, however, I contest the validity of the subjective/objective contrast in its starkest interpretations. My claim in Chapter 1 that the sex of the knower is epistemologically significant introduces a *subjective* factor— a factor that pertains to the specific, subjective 'nature' and circumstances of knowers—into the conditions that bear on the nature, possibility, and/or justification of knowledge. Hence it amounts to a claim that knowledge is indeed both subjective and objective. If this claim is taken seriously, the term 'knowledge' itself needs to be recast so that it can retain its referential and descriptive scope while relinquishing some of its presumption to objectivity.

The recasting will amount to a dissolution—a deconstruction—of the traditional objective/subjective dichotomy. Yet admitting subjective factors into the conditions that make knowledge possible does not yield a thoroughgoing subjectivism that would deny sense to the term 'knowledge'. Indeed, 'pure objectivity' is excessively venerated, I suspect, because philosophers fear that the subjectivism commonly identified with relativism in *its* starkest construal is the only alternative. Such a conviction suggests that 'objectivity' and 'subjectivity' must be construed as dichotomous, polarized terms. Were they not held in dichotomous opposition, an interplay between subjective and objective factors might be revealed in the creation of all knowledge worthy of the label. The implications of this possibility are the subject of this chapter.

The objective/subjective dichotomy is but one of several dichotomies that have structured mainstream Anglo-American epistemology and have become a central focus of feminist analysis. My point in challenging their validity is not to dispute the value of distinctions—even sharp distinctions—for clarification and analysis. But constructing distinctions as polar opposites, conceiving their boundaries as fixed and rigid, and confining inquiry within the limits those boundaries impose are unduly restrictive of philosophical insight. When theorists use such dichotomies to mark distinctions that are both hierarchical and polar, they establish a set of exclusionary, oppressive constraints and imbalances. By contrast, the approach to knowledge I shall sketch highlights possibilities of reciprocal interaction between and among such constructs.

In mainstream theory of knowledge, a persistent set of dichotomies sustains a (possibly unconscious, often implicit) institutionalization of 'masculine' modes and a concomitant denigration of 'feminine' modes in philosophical styles, problems, and methods. Feminist theorists have argued, persuasively, that dichotomous thinking is peculiarly characteristic of malestream thought. Understanding the connections between the 'maleness' of the thought and its dichotomous structure does risk invoking the very stereotypes I am concerned to reject. So examinations of the problem must be mindful of this danger. But the idea that there are connections between these dichotomies and male intellectual hegemony is prima facie plausible just because of the fact that so many deeply entrenched dichotomies run parallel to a taken-for-granted male/female dichotomy, not just descriptively but evaluatively. The dichotomies thus afford conceptual support for social and ideological structures that preserve the privileged places occupied by an elite group of men in the social order and designate the disadvantaged places reserved for women and other less privileged people.

The relation of the objective/subjective dichotomy to the male/female dichotomy is apparent from the fact that, in the philosophical tradition, women are often (albeit perhaps unthinkingly) consigned to an insignificant place in a community of knowers on the basis of claims that *their* 'knowledge' is hopelessly subjective. Such claims are commonly based on women's purported incapacity to rise above the practical, sensuous, and emotional preoccupations of everyday life. Hence women are judged unfit for the abstract life of pure reason in which true knowers must engage. So a set of dichotomies continuous with the subjective/objective dichotomy is invoked: theory/practice, reason/emotion, universal/particular, mind/body, abstract/concrete. They demarcate a set of categories—the lefthand one of each pair—by which knowledge is distinguished from aspects of experience deemed too trivial, too particular, for epistemological notice. The alignment of the righthand terms of these pairs with (stereotypical) femininity is well established. Hence there are good reasons for feminists to engage critically with the dichotomies and to take issue with the political assumptions they sustain about women's lack of cognitive authority.

Dichotomies are especially problematic in that they posit exclusionary constructs, not complementary or interdependent ones that could shade into one another or function as 'mixed modes' rather than absolutes. In dichotomous thinking the opposed terms are like Aristotelian contradictories, which must conform to the principle of the excluded middle. Everything has to be *either* A *or* Not-A, for A and Not-A exhaust all possibilities. Continuity between the terms is a logical impossibility. Not-A is the privation or absence of A; everything must be either one or the other, for the rigid either/or distinctions marked by the dichotomies cover the entire universe of discourse. Yet as Nancy Jay aptly cautions, the use of such dichotomies distorts most people's cognitive experiences, "for there are no negatives there." Jay contrasts Durkheimian starkly dichotomous thinking with Weber's more fluid approach, which construes distinctions as contraries rather than contradictories. She argues that no appeal to 'the laws of thought' could demonstrate either the 'naturalness' or the necessity of A/Not-A construals. By contrast, Aristotelian contraries, symbolized as A/B distinctions, admit of a continuity between the terms and find a positive reality in both. According to Jay, A/Not-A forms of thinking are suited primarily to a "purely formal logic without reference to the existential world."[1] Applied directly to the world, they become instruments of oppression and social control.[2]

Dichotomous thinking is implausibly simplistic, then, in the obli-

---

[1]Nancy Jay, "Gender and Dichotomy," *Feminist Studies* 1 (1981): 48, 51.
[2]Referring to Jay's article, Nancy Hartsock notes that "the not-A side is . . . associated with disorder, irrationality, chance, error, impurity. . . . Radical dichotomy functions to maintain order." Hartsock, "Foucault on Power: A Theory for Women?" in Linda Nicholson, ed., *Feminism/Postmodernism* (New York: Routledge, 1990), p. 162.

gations it imposes on cognitive agents to opt for one or the other 'side' of the pair. A knower must either value objectivity absolutely or succumb to the vagaries of subjectivity run wild: there is no middle ground. Subjectivity becomes everything chaotic and unstable that exhibits none of the defining features of objectivity. Hence it has no epistemic value. Yet things in the world, however variously people experience them, are rarely so clearly distinguished. If the overriding aim is to acquire an understanding of the experiential world, then it is not easy to see how a mode of thinking that is formal rather than experientially based can contribute to that end.

Now the dissolution of a dichotomy does not render its terms meaningless. Rather, it denies both terms the absolute force that the oppositional structure of the dichotomy confers. With that thought in mind, I want to raise two kinds of objection against the objective/subjective dichotomy, with its implication that 'purely objective' knowledge is alone worthy of epistemological attention. I want to challenge the beliefs, first, that some knowledge is entirely objective, some entirely subjective; and second, that knowledge properly so-called is all objective or all subjective. With respect to the first belief, I claim that knowledge is, necessarily and inescapably, the product of an intermingling of subjective and objective elements. The second belief implies either that any intrusion of subjectivity would vitiate a body of knowledge, a thesis, or a theory qua knowledge, or—if knowledge can be declared all subjective—that extreme relativism, even solipsism, is the only possible consequence. I maintain that it is a mistake to read 'subjective' as a pejorative term, yet that it is equally mistaken to underrate the epistemic value of objectivity. Rather, specific instances of knowledge fall along a continuum, where some are more purely objective; others manifest a greater interplay of subjectivity and objectivity; others again are more purely subjective. A viable theory of knowledge that is in touch with the diversity of cognitive experiences has no place for the standard objective/subjective dichotomy, nor for any other dichotomy according to which knowledge is *better* to the extent that it is purely rational, theoretical, abstract, or universal. The construction of the nature and status of knowledge I propose does not extol pure objectivity; hence it accords the opposed terms of traditional dichotomies a textured reading that can reveal their place in the situated experiences of cognitive agents.

In the third section of this chapter, I consider the role of subjectivity in the construction of knowledge. First, though, it is important to examine a commonly maintained connection between the objective/subjective dichotomy and a fact/value dichotomy, according to which knowers worthy of the title are perfectly neutral in their knowing. At the intersection of these dichotomies, an assertion that specific interests motivate inquiry and shape results amounts to a heresy against the true faith. For serious knowledge seekers, objectivity and value-neutrality are virtually synonymous. These assumptions are often defended (where they are not regarded as self-evident) with the contention that value-directed inquiries are indistinguishable from inquiries based on whim. The products of whimsy could not be called objective, because there can be no criterion for choosing between them, and each one is, therefore, as good as any other. By contrast, objective knowledge is declared value-neutral and presented as a collection of impartial and wholly disinterested facts or truths.

Some feminist theorists have argued that declarations of value-neutrality serve only to mask androcentric bias. As Sandra Harding puts it: "From the perspective of feminist theory and research, it is *traditional* thought that is subjective in its distortion by androcentrism—a claim feminists are willing to defend on traditional objectivist grounds."[3] Her suggestion is as apt as it is provocative, although it would be preferable, I think, to appeal to *quasi*-traditional grounds. Few feminists would want to defend their claims according to objectivist grounds dichotomously (i.e., traditionally) construed. Moreover, few feminists would claim value-neutrality for their own inquiries, which have avowedly political motivations in their feminist commitments. The point is to demonstrate the possibility of accommodating political (= subjective) considerations while maintaining as strict an objectivity as is possible—and reasonable—within them: to show that, often, objectivity requires taking subjectivity into account.

Objectivity

The assumption of value-neutrality at the heart of the received view of objectivity owes much to the pride of place accorded to scientific knowledge, with *its* alleged value-neutrality, among human intellectual achievements. Epistemologists commonly evaluate knowledge per se according to its success in approximating the methodological and epistemological criteria of the physical sciences. Implicit in the veneration of objectivity central to *scientific* practice is the conviction that objects of knowledge are separate from knowers and investiga-

[3]Sandra Harding, *The Science Question in Feminism* (Ithaca: Cornell University Press, 1986), p. 138.

tors and that they remain separate and unchanged throughout investigative, information-gathering, and knowledge-construction processes. According to standard scientific orthodoxy, universal and general laws can be formulated on the basis of empirical observations; and such laws enable a researcher to predict—in a purely disinterested manner—how objects will be affected by, or behave in, certain controlled circumstances. In fact, even if no practicing scientist would articulate so pure and simple a conception of objectivity as a regulative ideal, such perfect objectivity is tacitly upheld as the feature that distinguishes knowledge from belief, opinion, and fantasy. Even if no practicing scientist believes it is possible to achieve such perfect objectivity, mainstream epistemologists commonly assume that knowledge properly so-called must be modeled on scientific criteria, construed in these stringent objectivist terms.

Harding notes that defenders of value-neutrality, purity, and objectivity in science defend 'scientific method' with the contention that "science's logic and methodology, and the empirical core of scientific facts these produce, are totally immune from social influences; that logic and scientific method will in the long run winnow out the factual from the social in the results of scientific research."[4] Yet descriptions of 'science' which enforce a belief in this kind of objectivity are generally derived from a rarefied conception of *physics*, which is seen as the purest of all sciences, distinguished by a methodology that is immune to social influence. In other words, the 'scientific method' that is accorded paradigm status is the method of only one highly specialized—and in many ways atypical—species of scientific practice. The subject matter of physics is much less complex than the subject matters of biology or the social sciences, Harding notes. Nor is there any reason to assume that the alleged methodological purity of physics is characteristic of the methodology of most other sciences. Hence physics is a poor choice of paradigm for scientists and, derivatively, for theorists of knowledge.

If this commonly endorsed ideal of objectivity is only of narrowly

[4]Ibid., p. 40. In her "Introduction: Is There a Feminist Method?" to her edited collection *Feminism and Methodology* (Bloomington: Indiana University Press, 1988), Harding distinguishes *methods* of data collection from *methodologies* of examining, analyzing, and conducting experiments with data, and from *epistemologies*, which specify justification procedures. In the present discussion I do not hold the terms apart so neatly. Even for positivists and their objectivist descendants, epistemology depends on methods and methodology. For feminists, as for other critics of positivism, it is not possible to detach the context of discovery (= the methods and methodology) from the context of justification (= the epistemology): methodological practices are matters of direct epistemological concern. Harding's distinctions would be compatible with a discovery/justification division that is inimical to the position I am arguing here.

local relevance (i.e., strictly speaking, only within the confines of physics), the epistemological implications are noteworthy. Yet they require careful elaboration to avoid advancing a view that I do not endorse: namely, that scientific knowledge is indeed the paradigm of knowledge per se. Theorists who accord scientific knowledge paradigm status maintain that other kinds of knowledge, in other domains, are—and should be—modeled on scientific knowledge in their sources, their methodology, the subject-object relation they assume, and their criteria of truth, evidence, and verification. It is doubtful that scientific knowledge has ever deserved that status; yet in historical periods when it is thus venerated, other kinds of knowledge are denigrated in consequence. One striking example is the period marked by the ascendancy of positivism, with its project of developing a unified science in which the social sciences would be modeled on the assumptions and methodology of physics. The effects of this project are still visible, particularly in the hegemony enjoyed by behaviorism in psychology. Feminist dismay over the decontextualized, ahistorical, circumstantially blind treatment of human subjects that behaviorism legitimates is but one—albeit a crucial one—of the reasons for disputing the paradigmatic position of (physical) science.

These points notwithstanding, conceptions of scientific methodology are constitutive of mainstream constructions of the nature and possibilities of human knowledge. My claim that the ideal of objectivity central to that methodology does not live up to its pretensions has epistemological implications despite my unwillingness to accord paradigmatic status to scientific inquiry. Scientists, particularly physicists, claim to work from the purest (and starkest) conception of objectivity, from which all other construals of this ideal derive. If the ideal in its purest form is not workable even as physicists construe it, then it follows by *analogy* (if not from granting it paradigm status) that ideals of objectivity upheld elsewhere will be equally, or even more, contestable.

Challenging the paradigmatic status of physics opens the way for arguments against the purity of objectivity from other directions. The fact that perfect, positivistic objectivity is not easy to achieve in other areas, except by distorting the subject of study, raises questions about whether the alleged supremacy—and immunity—of physics is justifiable. Rather than arguing that other disciplines (such as biology, anthropology, or psychology) are underachievers with respect to objectivity because they fall short of the ideal standards of physics, it becomes imperative to ask why physics has been so established a paradigm of objectivity. Harding attributes the "success" of physics, in part, to the fact that it looks "either at simple systems or simple aspects of complex systems." She claims that the ability of models of these systems to make reliable predictions derives from the fact that "they are conceptualized as self-contained and deterministic."[5] To the extent that it confines its investigations to these systems, physics is remarkably successful and apparently objective in the purest sense. But it can no more be commended for this aspect of its methodology than other cognitive enterprises can be condemned for proceeding differently. No methodology is self-justifying.

The physics-derived conception of objectivity depends on a peculiar construal of the relations between knowing subjects and their objects of knowledge. According to Elizabeth Fee: "It is not the subjectivity of the scientist that is seen as producing knowledge so much as the objectivity of the scientific method: subjectivity, indeed, is regarded with suspicion, as a possible contaminant of the process of knowledge production, and one which must be governed by stringent controls."[6] The scientist, and likewise the knower, is like the subject of the 'S knows that p' proposition: a place holder in the research project, whose *identity*—his genius, inspiration, eccentricities, predilections, blindnesses; his privileges of class, race, ethnicity, and gender—is irrelevant to his research practice. Perfect neutrality marks his detached and distanced observation of the object in conditions carefully controlled to maximize objectivity.

When this methodology is translated into social scientific contexts, in which human beings are the objects of study, a further suppression of subjectivity occurs. Theories and research methodologies in the social sciences 'objectify' the human subjects they study. Experiments are designed to predict human behavior and to analyze it quantitatively, for only behavior amenable to statistical analysis is judged worthy of scientific study. The methodology produces explanations of personality and of social structures that take into account neither the consciousness of the subjects studied nor the meanings and interpretations of their experiences for these subjects. Human behavior, then, is conflated with other observational data. The possibility that a subject might not remain separate and unchanged throughout an experiment or inquiry, that she or he could intentionally defy the behavior-governing rules that a researcher 'discovers', is rarely entertained.

[5]Harding, *Science Question*, p. 44.
[6]Elizabeth Fee, "Women's Nature and Scientific Objectivity," in Marian Lowe and Ruth Hubbard, eds., *Woman's Nature: Rationalizations of Inequality* (New York: Pergamon, Athene Series, 1983), p. 11.

When such a possibility is considered, efforts are made to control it out of significance.

Now feminist critiques often center on the contention that objectivity is an inherently male construct. Fee notes that the objectivity believed to characterize scientific knowledge production "is specifically identified as a male way of relating to the world. Science is cold, hard, impersonal, 'objective'; women, by contrast, are warm, soft, emotional, 'subjective'."[7] Knowledge produced in seemingly objective ways carries an authority that mirrors, reinforces, and probably also derives from masculine authority. Its alleged derivation from detached, pure thought permits it to claim superiority over modes of thought infected with emotional involvement and feeling. Out of this conception of the autonomy of scientific knowledge the conviction emerges that 'real' knowledge must be autonomous, detached from the subjective idiosyncrasies and circumstances of both 'observer' and 'observed'; abstract, independent, and depersonalized. The separation between subject and object implicit in the ideal leads many feminists to see the veneration of objectivity as an explanation for men's alienation from nature (and from women), which reaches a pinnacle in the abstract theories and truths that scientists produce.

Science and knowledge production are often represented as pure in yet another way: as unsullied by thoughts about the uses to which knowledge might perchance be put. The separation that objectivists assume between facts and values supports the conclusion that facts are 'just facts' and worth pursuing for their own sake. Questions about the social and/or moral consequences of discovery can, consequently, be designated as separate matters with which scientists—or knowledge seekers—need not, qua scientists, concern themselves. Scientists can absolve themselves from moral-political responsibility by invoking the overriding value of objectivity. Presenting their findings in an impersonally objective manner ("the facts show"), speaking with the authority of their institutional position, masks the identity— indeed, the existence—of the cognitive agents whose values, in effect, shape and guide the inquiry. The facts, allegedly, speak for themselves; the values on which they are based are suppressed. Such is the mythology of science and, by extension, of the knowledge purportedly modeled on, or judged according to, scientific standards.

Now the picture of objectivity in knowledge—and scientific knowledge—I have sketched may seem to caricature a set of practices that only approximate some of these features some of the time. Yet

7Ibid., p. 13.

this ideal of objectivity claims a remarkable degree of respect in epistemological, scientific, social scientific, and other circles. Practitioners who do not conform to it often think that they do or believe that ideal objectivity is their ultimate goal. It is odd that so seemingly unattainable a goal should have such a persistent regulative force. One plausible explanation connects with a fairly common belief about the overwhelming and uncontrollable nature of feeling and emotion. Objectivity appeals so strongly because of its construction as distinct and separate from the vagaries of emotional life. Hence it can offer a refuge of clarity and certainty, free from the apparent irrationality of emotions. Some feminists argue (albeit on essentialist grounds) that a distrust of feeling characterizes masculine ways of thinking and hence provides another reason why the goal of objectivity has, in practice, been peculiarly attractive to men.

A specifically epistemological explanation for the nature of standard constructions of objectivity relates to the specimens of knowledge, inherited from the empiricist tradition, that are commonly cited as paradigmatic. I am referring now not to the paradigmatic status of scientific knowledge with respect to knowledge per se, but to the simple observational claims that scientific knowledge, along with most 'ordinary' knowledge, holds as paradigmatic *within* a body of knowledge. Privileging these sorts of knowledge claim—"The book is red," "The door is open"—is part of the positivist inheritance. The practice derives from the early empiricist and later positivistic conviction that all knowledge, scientific and 'ordinary', can be broken down into observational 'simples' that are foundational in providing a basis of certainty for systems of knowledge constructed on them. Sense-data theorists, and some more recent empiricists, share this view of the role of simple observational statements in a body of knowledge.

There is, at first glance, something persuasive about the belief that such knowledge claims are both fundamental and paradigmatic. Developmentally, simple observational truths do seem to be the first bits of knowledge that an infant acquires as she or he learns to recognize and manipulate everyday, medium-sized objects in the immediate environment. It seems, too, that an infant or child is properly objective in these early cognitive experiences: that she or he *comes across* objects and learns to identify and deal with them without preconceptions and without altering their properties in so doing. Objects ordinarily remain independent of a child's knowing; and those same sorts of objects in adult life—cups, spoons, chairs, trees, and flowers—seem to be the simplest and surest of the things one knows.

They are *there* to be observed and known, they are reasonably constant even through change, and they seem, on the whole, to exist independently of a person's cognitive efforts—hence to be objectively knowable and known. In the search for a simple example of what standard knowers know "for sure," knowledge claims of this sort are obvious candidates. So it is scarcely surprising that they should count as paradigmatic, should be constitutive of received definitions of knowledge *and* objectivity.

Yet when one considers how basic and crucial the necessity of knowing other people is, paradigms, knowledge claims, and objectivity take on quite a different aspect. In fact, knowing other people is at least as worthy a contender for paradigmatic status as knowledge of medium-sized, everyday objects. Developmentally, recognizing other people, learning what can be expected of them, is both one of the first and one of the most essential kinds of knowledge a child acquires. An infant learns to respond *cognitively* to its caregivers *long before* it can recognize the simplest of physical objects. Evidence about the effects of sensory deprivation on the development of cognitive agency shows that a child's capacity to make sense of its physical environment is intricately linked with its caregivers' construction of that environment. I am not suggesting that knowing other people should become *the* new epistemological paradigm, but I am asserting that it is has equally strong claims to paradigm status, despite worries that purists might have about allowing for more than one kind of paradigm.

Knowledge of other people develops, operates, and is open to interpretation at different levels; it admits of degree in ways that knowing that the book is red does not. Hence it is qualitatively different from the simple observational knowledge commonly constitutive of epistemological paradigms. It is not easy to subsume it under the analyses appropriate for empirical paradigms. 'Knowing how' and 'knowing that' are implicated in the process, but they do not begin to tell the whole story. These considerations may create the impression that this kind of knowledge is philosophically unmanageable. Yet the contrast between its multidimensional, multiperspectival character and the stark simplicity of standard paradigms raises questions, rather, about the practice of granting exemplary status to the standard paradigms.

The contention that people are *knowable* may sit uneasily with psychoanalytic claims about the unconscious, and postmodern critiques of theories that presuppose a unified self. I want at once to acknowledge this tension and to maintain it.[8] Feminists do, in practice, often find that they know people well enough to know who can be counted on and who cannot, who makes a good ally and who does not. Yet knowing other people, precisely because of the fluctuations and contradictions of subjectivity, is an ongoing, communicative, interpretive process. It can never be fixed or complete: any fixity that one might claim for 'the self' is at best a fixity in flux; but something must be fixed to 'contain' the flux even enough to permit references to and ongoing relationships with 'this person'. Assumptions that one knows another person have to be made within the terms of this tension.

Generalizing an interpretive approach of this sort to other kinds of knowledge can afford a safeguard against dogmatism and rigidity. Knowledge of other people is possible only in a persistent interplay between opacity and transparency, between attitudes and postures that elude a knower's grasp, and traits that seem to be clear and relatively constant. Hence knowers are kept on their cognitive toes: the 'more-or-lessness' of this knowledge constantly affirms the need to reserve and revise judgment. Yet ongoing personal and political commitments cannot be left undecided: they require affirmation that people know one another well enough to be able to go on. In the requirement that it accommodate change and growth, this knowledge contrasts further with traditional paradigms that deal, on the whole, with objects of knowledge that manifest a high degree of permanence. In knowing other people, a knower's subjectivity is implicated, from its earliest developmental stages; in such knowledge her subjectivity develops and changes. Analogous reconstructions and changes often occur in the subjectivity of the person(s) she knows. Nor are the knower/known positions fixed. Hence such knowledge works from a conception of subject-object relations different from that implicit in appeals to simple empirical paradigms. Claims to know a person are open to negotiation between knower and 'known', where the 'subject' and 'object' positions are always, in principle, exchangeable. In the process, it is vital to watch for discrepancies between a person's sense of her own subjectivity and a would-be knower's conception of what it is like to be her; yet neither the self-conception nor the knower-conception can claim absolute, ultimate authority, for the limits of self-consciousness constrain the process just as closely as the interiority of mental processes and experiential constructs and their unavailability to observation.

[8]I discuss the nature and implications of the tension in greater detail in Chapter 3.

The fact that perfect, objective knowledge of other people is not possible gives no support to a contention *either* that 'other minds' are radically unknowable *or* that such knowledge as people may claim of one another never merits the label 'knowledge'. Traditional philosophical assumptions to the effect that people are opaque to one another surely count as one reason why this knowledge has had minimal philosophical attention. Knowledge, as the tradition defines it, is *of* objects. Only when people can be assimilated to objects is it possible to know them. This long-standing assumption is challenged by my claim that knowing other people is a paradigmatic knowing.

The process of knowing other people requires constant learning: how to be with them, respond to them, act toward them. In this respect, too, it complements the more common sense-perceptual paradigms. In fact, if those paradigms were also taken from situations in which people had to *learn* to know, rather than from the operation of taken-for-granted adult expectations, the complexity of knowing even the simplest of things would not so readily be masked, and the fact that knowledge can be qualitatively evaluated would be more clearly apparent. Consider the strangeness a traveler experiences in a country and culture where she has to suspend judgments about the identity and nature of all manner of things from simple artifacts, to flora and fauna, to customs and cultural phenomena. These experiences show that acquiring the ability to make informed observations, judgments, and requests is a slow and tentative process. Participation in such situations opens a different perspective on fundamental assumptions that people are accustomed, unthinkingly, to make.

The fact that an agent's subjectivity is differently implicated in knowing other people from knowing everyday objects may create the impression that this knowledge is, indeed, largely subjective. Such a conclusion would be hasty and unwarranted. There *are* objective facts that one has to respect if the knowing is to be good of its kind: facts that (together with numerous subjective ones) constitute "the person one is" at any historical moment.[9] Only certain stories can accurately be told about a person; others simply cannot. 'External' facts are the most obvious constraints: facts about age, sex, race, place and date of birth, height, weight, and hair color: the information that appears on a passport. That information is objective on any ordinary understanding of objectivity. A good deal of other information is reasonably objective in much the same way: facts about major life events such as

[9]The phrase is Elizabeth V. Spelman's, in her paper "On Treating Persons as Persons," *Ethics* 88 (1978): 151.

marriage or divorce, childbirth, siblings, education, employment, abode, and travel; facts about skills such as knowing how to play a musical instrument, ride a bicycle, build furniture, cook, operate a computer, speak Russian.

The crucial and intriguing fact about knowing people—and the reason why it affords insights into problems of knowledge—is that even if one could know all the facts about someone, one would not know her as the person she is. No more can knowing all the facts about oneself, past and present, guarantee self-knowledge. Yet none of these problems raises doubts that there is such a creature as the person I am, or the person she or he is, now. Nor do they point to the impossibility of knowing other people.

Persistent problems in finding criteria that would determine *when* one knows another person explain philosophical reluctance to count knowing people as knowledge that bears epistemological investigation. Yet my suggestion that such knowledge is indeed a model—a paradigm—for a wide range of knowledge, and not merely inchoate and unmanageable, recommends itself the more strongly on consideration of the extent to which cognitive practice is grounded on such knowledge. Here I refer not just to everyday interactions with other people, but to the specialized branches of knowledge that claim institutional authority. Educational theory and practice, psychology, sociology, anthropology, law, some aspects of medicine and philosophy, politics, history, and economics, to mention only the obvious examples, all depend for their epistemic credibility and validity on implicit appeals to knowing people. This fact makes it all the more curious that observation-based knowledge of material objects, and the methodology of the physical sciences, should hold sway as the paradigm—and paragon—of intellectual achievement. But the results of according observational paradigms continued veneration are evident in the reductive approaches of behaviorist psychology. They are apparent in parochial impositions of meaning on the practices of other cultures still characteristic of some areas of anthropology,[10] and in the simple translation of present-day descriptions into past cultural contexts which characterizes some historical and archaeological practice. But feminist, hermeneutic, and postmodern critiques are slowly succeeding in requiring objectivist social scientists to reexamine their presuppositions and practices.

I am proposing that, if epistemologists require a *scientific* model,

[10]Bleier observes, however, that feminist cultural anthropologists are on the way to "taking over the field" ("Lab Coat," p. 62), just as feminist field primatologists have done, and transformed it.

then a reconstructed social science can offer a better paradigm than natural science—or physics—for knowledge as such. Harding contends that "a critical and self-reflective social science should be the model for all science, and . . . if there are any special requirements for adequate explanations in physics, they are just that—special."[11] My proposal is that social scientific practice based on a commitment to knowing people as well as possible is a worthy epistemological paradigm tout court.

Social science would not displace physics in order to make way for repudiating claims to objectivity in the model discipline, as though physics and its derivative disciplines alone could safeguard objectivity. Social scientific inquiry is objectively constrained by the same factual-informational details that constrain all attempts to know people: physical, historical, biographical, environmental, climatological, social structural, and other *facts* constitute its 'objects' of study. These facts are available for objective analysis, though there is no doubt that they are open to varying and sometimes careless degrees of interpretation and to political construction. Social scientific investigations focus also on purposeful and learned behavior, on preferences, intentions, and meanings, often with the aim, Harding notes, of explaining "the origins, forms, and prevalence of apparently irrational but culturewide patterns of human belief and action." Such phenomena cannot be measured and quantified to provide results comparable to those obtainable in a controlled physics experiment. Yet this fact neither destroys social scientific objectivity nor reestablishes the methodology of physics as better, either in itself or in the results it produces. Harding rightly maintains that "the totally reasonable exclusion of intentional and learned behaviors from the subject matter of physics is a good reason to regard inquiry in physics as atypical of scientific knowledge-seeking."[12] I am arguing that it is equally atypical of knowledge-seeking as such. Intentional and learned behaviors are indeed subjective attributes, but there is no good reason to believe that taking subjectivity into account *entails* abandoning objectivity. Rather, once theorists acknowledge the oddity, and peculiar insularity, of the physics-derived conception, with its suppression of subjectivity, it becomes increasingly urgent to contest the ideal in areas of inquiry where *subjectivities* are the 'objects' of study. (The incongruity of this formulation mirrors the incongruity of the practice it addresses.)

[11]Harding, *Science Question*, p. 44.
[12]Ibid., pp. 47, 46.

There is no conflict, then, between my insistence on the limitations of the traditional conception of objectivity and contentions that the construction of knowledge is *objectively* constrained by the (changing, open-ended, but roughly specifiable) possibilities of 'human nature' and by the (also changing, but specifiable) nature of 'the world'. It is no more possible to obliterate a revolution, a war, a famine, a political regime, or a form of oppression by thinking them away than it is to will a mountain or a chair to vanish. Facts about wars and political events and attitudes may be open to more varied interpretations than mountains and chairs, and records can be falsified, but there *are* facts to be documented, interpreted, and falsified. Activists constantly encounter them in their efforts to effect social and political change. It is also true that human biology exercises constraints on cognitive agency. The facts of having a certain kind of sensory apparatus, and bodies that fall within certain ranges of size and agility, structure possibilities of experience, shaping and limiting possible ways of knowing.

Claims about natural cognitive constraints of this sort are difficult to substantiate definitively. Biological fluctuations are effected by the activities an organism engages in and by ecological, environmental, and/or evolutionary conditions; and ideological beliefs infect standard, 'malestream' interpretations of the significance of biology. The brain-lateralization studies I discuss in Chapter 1 are a case in point. Research designed to demonstrate basic 'natural' differences between female and male brain capacity is enlisted to explain women's inferior positions in society in general and in cognitive achievement in particular. Such studies commonly take inadequate account of the role of social-environmental structures in the construction both of differences in abilities and skills and—more significantly—of differences in brain organization itself.[13] Nonetheless, human sensory-motor equipment dictates possibilities of experience within a significant range and hence creates and limits possibilities of knowledge acquisition. Human hands can play pianos and use computer keyboards, but human eyes cannot see ultraviolet, and human beings cannot fly unaided. These constraints shape experiential possibilities objectively.

Feminists have been rightly concerned to contest the alleged 'naturalness' of many capacities and characteristics. There is no doubt that appeals to 'human nature' which claim it as a constraint on knowledge construction derive as much from political interests as from straightforward observation and description. Received theories of hu-

---

[13]Cynthia Eagle Russett examines some historical manifestations of this 'role' in *Sexual Science: The Victorian Construction of Womanhood* (Cambridge: Harvard University Press, 1989).

man nature are commonly the constructs of a privileged intellectual elite and consistently derived from its own experiences. Nor is 'the physical world' timeless and eternal. Like the world of which they are part, human beings evolve and change. They are amply capable of effecting transformations both in their own being and in the world itself. Yet the minimal constraints that derive from the 'reality' of the world and of cognitive agency constitute a residual set of objective limits on adequate, responsible inquiry. All the terms of the discussion may be problematic, contestable, and in need of subtle analysis, but none is rendered meaningless or useless. Nor is it reasonable to conclude that knowledge modeled on knowing people would be recast as a purely social product, unconstrained by objectivity.

This last point requires special emphasis. Philosophers tend to argue that if knowledge is less than purely objective, then it must follow that reality itself is socially constructed: there are *no* facts of the matter and hence there is no point in trying to discover how things 'really' are. This argument reveals the tenacity of philosophical adherence to a strict fact/value distinction. Philosophers fear that a claim that neither science nor knowledge per se can be value-neutral entails the further claim that knowledge and human interests are inextricably bound together *and* that radical subjectivism is the only option.

Just such a consequence is assumed and endorsed in the work of feminist theorists Liz Stanley and Sue Wise, who equate value-neutrality with positivism and condemn both together. Contending that positivism assimilates "social reality, social 'objects' and events" to physical reality, Stanley and Wise criticize positivistic acceptances of "the existence of an 'objective' social reality."[14] They argue that there is, in fact, *no* such objective reality: there is only my reality, or yours, or ours, continually negotiated and managed by us, either separately or collectively. The conception of 'reality' to which positivist social scientists improperly assimilate social reality is the same rarefied and highly specialized reality that physical science claims for its objects of study. Stanley and Wise maintain that there is a radical disjunction between the 'reality' of the objects of physics and 'social reality'. In consequence, they endorse a radical subjectivism for which, indeed, there are no objective social truths. There is only my truth or yours, ours or theirs.

Now it is easy to understand Stanley and Wise's motivations in making these assertions. The dominant influence of positivistic en-

---

[14]Liz Stanley and Sue Wise, *Breaking Out: Feminist Consciousness and Feminist Research* (London: Routledge & Kegan Paul, 1983), p. 108.

deavors to develop a unified science, with all sciences modeled on physics, tempts critics to conclude that there simply is no reality of the sort that behavioristic psychologists, for example, claim to know. Confrontations with the governing assumptions of quantitative sociological and historical analysis, and of parochial anthropological research, reinforce this conclusion. Such social scientific projects can only 'succeed' by ignoring the fact that their objects of study are *conscious* beings whose consciousness often influences, and even determines, the outcome of the most carefully controlled experiments.[15] Masculine analyses of women's experiences often simply *get it wrong* from the point of view of the women themselves.

The very idea that they 'get it wrong' indicates that there is something to be 'got right'. Stanley and Wise believe that the owner or author of an experience is uniquely and solely in a position to manage and negotiate *that* 'reality': only she can get it right. This conclusion is part of the subjectivism they espouse. Again, it is easy to understand their reasons. The problem is that their view of social reality is as much of a caricature as the rarefied view of physical reality that philosophers of science draw on to demonstrate the pure objectivity of physics. Just as the received view of physical reality regards material objects as permanent and independent of any observer, so this view of social reality regards that 'reality' as transient and dependent on the experiencer. The malleability of social reality is read according to its most extreme interpretation just as, in positivistic constructions of physics, the separateness of the known from knowers is given *its* most extreme interpretation.

Now Stanley and Wise would surely reject any suggestion that sexism, class and racial injustices, women's oppressions, or women's biological experiences are "all in their minds." Hence they evidently believe in social realities that are less individually constructed, managed, and negotiated than they imply. Were there no facts about women's circumstances, there would be nothing to investigate, criticize, and know.

It is crucial to recognize, as Stanley and Wise in fact do, that it is impossible to understand experiences and behaviors without taking into account both the social context and the meaning—the signifi-

[15]Rhoda Unger comments that behaviorist psychology "has limited itself to the study of behaviors that are devoid of much meaning for the human subject—of either sex—and has had to examine these subjects in a context that eliminates any opportunity for the selection of alternative behaviors." Unger, "Psychological, Feminist, and Personal Epistemology: Transcending Contradictions," in M. Gergen, ed., *Feminist Thought and the Structure of Knowledge*, p. 125.

cance—of the event for its experiencer/author. But a contention that there are *no* objective social realities would obliterate the purpose of feminist political projects. The findings of feminist research and analysis could be dismissed as one idiosyncratic way of seeing the world, no better than any other way. They could even be dismissed as manifestations of ideological paranoia. There is no doubt about the need for persistent and responsible self-criticism in feminist research and for acknowledging the self-referentiality of every inquirer's position. Her position is as revisable, as negotiable, as the 'negotiated' reality she studies. She can, at most, construct a temporally, culturally, and geographically located analysis, according to the best evidence available. But such an acknowledgment does not deny that there are right and wrong descriptions of social realities or that evidence needs to be counted, objectively, as evidence.

For evidence to count, there must be some objective truths about women's circumstances. The same truths may not hold in just the same way for all women, and it may be impossible to argue that no one's *interests* are served by the circumstances under analysis—that is, the facts of the matter will probably not be interest- (= value-) free. Analyses of women's exploitation, as Jean Grimshaw notes, "cannot always be worked out by the explication of everyday experience alone. The activities of things such as multinational corporations are usually extremely remote from everyday experience, yet they have profound effects on women's lives. And these effects do not depend for their existence on the recognition accorded to them."[16] Women's lives and experiences are constructed in ideology-saturated cultural locations, and there are facts, open to analysis, about how ideological effects operate—even though there may be no ideology-free space from which to conduct such analyses. Ideologies themselves are open to interpretation, misreading, and distortion. Yet 'interpretations' often come in the form of concrete institutions and practices. The existence of multinational corporations attests to the social embeddedness of capitalist ideology, and there are facts about how that ideology affects people's lives. So there emerges a picture of objective facts, open to multiple interpretations, analyzable from various perspectives. Facts may change and evolve in processes of interpretation and critique; hence 'reality' is indeed open to social structuring. Social practices, attitudes, institutions are far from constant, yet neither are they mere ephemera of a researcher's imagination. They are *there*, present for analysis. Facts may mean different things to different

[16]Grimshaw, *Philosophy and Feminist Thinking*, p. 102.

people, affect some people profoundly and others not at all: hence they are both subjective and objective.

Subjectivity

Breaking the spell of timelessness, detachment, universality, and absoluteness reveals that knowledge is subjective and objective in several fairly uncontroversial ways. Some aspects of subjectivity that play a constitutive role in the construction of knowledge are a subject's (i) historical location; (ii) location within specific social and linguistic contexts, which include racial, ethnic, political, class, age, religious, and other identifications; (iii) creativity in the construction of knowledge, with the freedoms and responsibilities it entails; and (iv) affectivity, commitments, enthusiasms, desires, and interests, in which affectivity contrasts with intellect, or reason in the standard sense.[17] These constituents are subjective in the sense that they derive from the circumstances and practices of subject-knowers. They are interwoven, in that they work together and are mutually efficacious. I separate them only for purposes of analysis.

Positivistic and postpositivistic theories of knowledge declare the existence—and necessity—of a radical split between reason or intellect and emotion. This split connects with the fact/value distinction, deriving its force, in part, from a belief that value judgments are purely emotive, hence neither verifiable nor falsifiable. They must therefore be prevented from contributing to the construction of knowledge properly so-called. Positivists and postpositivists contend that sense perceptions, which are replicable by all normal observers in normal circumstances, feed directly into the intellect, where knowledge is produced—rationally, objectively, and dispassionately. Emotion, by contrast, is the aspect of subjectivity that makes it most suspect. Emotions should be controlled, and the possibility that they could be integral to the construction of knowledge is hardly to be conceived. Any attempt to claim a legitimate (and, indeed, vital) place for emotion in the creation, growth, and/or justification of knowledge amounts, on this view, to a surrender to a subjectivism of the most solipsistic and idiosyncratic variety.

The conception of emotion on which such a condemnation turns is

[17]Because it is *reasonable* to feel certain emotions in certain circumstances, a contrast between emotion and *intellect* is more plausible than one between reason and emotion. I continue sometimes to draw a reason/emotion contrast for the sake of locating the discussion within standard terminology.

a curious one. It is at least as extreme, and as distortedly so, as the conceptions of rationality and objectivity with which it contrasts. The assumption is that emotional response is ineluctably whimsical and unstable, erratic, idiosyncratic, and irrational: that uncontrolled hysteria is the paradigmatic emotion. (The femaleness of hysteria is no mere accident.) The idea that it is *reasonable* to feel emotions in certain circumstances, and that when someone does *not* feel concern, joy, sorrow, or pleasure under some conditions, then her or his close associates may be puzzled or worried, bears no weight. Yet emotions such as curiosity, interest, amazement—all of which make sense in certain circumstances—are necessary to the construction of knowledge: without them, many inquiries would never have been undertaken or sustained. Indeed, investigations are often prompted by rage, frustration, political necessity, enthusiasm, or despair. Outraged users need to know the facts about the Dalkon Shield; political urgency requires the accumulation of facts about environmental pollution. Even if such an inquiry is sustained throughout by such affective motivation, its results can stand up to viable criteria of objectivity. Emotion and intellect are mutually constitutive and sustaining, rather than oppositional forces in the construction of knowledge.[18]

The systematic denigration of emotion connects closely, in the privileged domains of western societies, with an association of emotionality with femaleness. Recall the descriptive and evaluative parallels marked by the dichotomies I discuss in the first section of this chapter. A recognition of the parallel structures of the objective/ subjective, reason/emotion, and male/female dichotomies suffices to show how intricate a task it is for feminists to reclaim emotion as a contributor to the construction of knowledge. A reclamation appears at once to reaffirm the femaleness of the undervalued righthand terms in the dichotomies and to accept female essentialism. Hence a project of establishing the cognitive role of emotion risks engaging in a politically suspect glorification of unreason *against* the ascendancy of reason. Feminists are rightly wary of identifying themselves with the forces of irrationality and hence of vindicating the condemnations that allegedly uncontrollable femininity has invited—and gained— throughout the centuries. What, then, should be done?

The most promising answer is that theorists of knowledge need to engage in critical analyses of the suppression of subjectivity against

[18]See in this connection Alison Jaggar's "Love and Knowledge: Emotion in Feminist Epistemology," in Alison M. Jaggar and Susan R. Bordo, eds., *Gender/ Body/Knowledge: Feminist Reconstructions of Being and Knowing* (New Brunswick, N.J.: Rutgers University Press, 1989).

which the standard ideal of objectivity defines itself. The ideal, which evolved out of Baconian science, Cartesianism, empiricism, and positivism, is a historically and locally specific intellectual value whose emergence is marked by a variety of motivations, anxieties, and aspirations. Empiricists' beliefs in the passivity of the observer, together with their mechanistic conceptions of a nature that functions without the intervention and/or cooperation of the detached observer, is one apparent source of present-day conceptions of objectivity. According to the ideal, observers stand—and *should* stand—dispassionately (i.e., *un*emotionally) at a distance from the objects of their observation. Neither the subjectivity of the observer nor, where applicable, of the observed is relevant to the information-gathering process.

The control that a mechanistic approach to nature promises is one of its strongest points of appeal. The controlling, exploitative—and allegedly dispassionate—dominant science in western culture bears the marks of the hierarchical view of the cosmos that (Baconian) empiricist philosophers endorsed. That view, which derives from the idea of a Great Chain of Being, places man hierarchically above woman (closer to the angels and to God), and human beings above animals, plants, and inanimate nature. It appears to have gained ascendancy, in part, because of the justification it provides for human exploitation of nature: because of its efficacy in serving the *interests* of the powerful. Hence for all its self-proclaimed objectivity, there is evidence that its hegemony is sustained by *subjective* forces: by interests and self-interest. It is difficult to evade the conclusion that the very ideal of objectivity that urges the suppression of subjectivity (emotionality) is itself as much a product of emotional circumstances (*subjective* enthusiasms and interests) as it is the product of a 'natural' flowering of intellect detachedly knowing the world.

It is not surprising that epistemological ideals should derive out of human interests. Indeed, it would be more implausible, more counterintuitive, to believe that they do not: human cognitive agents, after all, have made them. Why would they not bear the marks of their makers? A recognition that human interests are indeed implicated in these ideals does not, prima facie, invite censure. It does enjoin a sustained moral-political alertness to the need for analysis and critique, in every instance, of the sources out of which claims to objectivity and neutrality are made. More pointedly, the recognition forces the conclusion that if the ideal of objectivity is not established in accordance with its own demands, then it has no right to the theoretical hegemony to which it has laid claim.

Now Lynda Birke argues that, historically, the mechanistic scheme coexisted from the Middle Ages through the Renaissance and into the seventeenth century, with organic, holistic—and somewhat romantic—philosophies whose cosmic vision revolved around a belief in the harmony of the whole and of the place of human beings within it.[19] She documents her thesis persuasively. Her consequent proposal that the ascendancy of mechanistic explanations of nature and of empiricist philosophy in the seventeenth and eighteenth centuries should be read as a shift away from an organic view, toward the development of a culture/nature opposition, is plausible, if still controversial. Even if the organic view Birke discerns did not have hegemonic status, the case she makes for there being alternative cosmic ideals in circulation allows theorists to understand the rise of mechanistic thinking and of ideal objectivity as contingent moments in the growth of western culture. These are no purely natural, necessary developments. Hence the reign of objective reason is open to a challenge that casts in question its claims to universality and eternality. Even today, Birke maintains, there are societies that see their culture as "embedded in, and a significant part of, nature." Hence, she argues, "the nature-culture opposition as we now know it is not only culture-specific: it is also historically specific."[20] Evidence for the historical and cultural specificity of the suppression of emotions and affectivity argues that the issue is indeed one of interests and forces that are still alive, ready to be tapped and regenerated. Despite the traditional alignment of subjectivity with femininity, and its consequent denigration, female philosophers are by no means the only defenders of alternative modes. The sources Birke cites are primarily male.

Birke's analysis does not show that there is anything inherently *wrong* with mechanism and the ideals it endorses. Instead, she demonstrates the *contestability* of its hegemonic status, revealing it as a selected alternative rather than as a necessary moment in a unilinear history. There is a Foucauldian point to be made about the purpose of historical studies such as Birke's: a point common to Foucault's early, 'archaeological' works and his later, 'genealogical' ones. Studies of this kind do not, in fact, reveal a rational necessity in the development of world views and the evolution of theories. Rather, they show that such processes are less rational, more random, than the putatively monolithic western tradition pretends. Hence there are gaps, spaces for other possibilities. Hegemony is always contingent,

[19]Birke, *Women, Feminism, and Biology*, p. 113. For an extended argument about the 'death of nature' at the birth of the new science, see Carolyn Merchant, *The Death of Nature: Women, Ecology, and the Scientific Revolution* (New York: Harper & Row, 1980).
[20]Birke, *Women, Feminism, and Biology*, pp. 108, 109.

derivative from happenstance, dependent on and constitutive of prevailing power structures, achieved through the elision of other projects. It is always unstable.

Recent psychohistorical studies by Susan Bordo and Naomi Scheman have analogous implications for feminist deconstructions of ideal
objectivity. Both (albeit variously) trace the ascendancy of the ideal
back to *emotional* rather than purely rational or intellectual origins,
representing it as an attempt to establish a refuge against overwhelming emotional discomfort occasioned by the impact of Cartesian skepticism. In "The Cartesian Masculinization of Thought,"[21] Bordo
focuses on the images of anxiety, confusion, and separation which
permeate Descartes's *Meditations*, prompting him to develop strategies to preserve himself from vertigo. In "Othello's Doubt/ Desdemona's Death: The Engendering of Scepticism," Scheman describes Othello's doubt as an "unease at the heart of the experiences
of immersion in the world and connectedness to others." Othello's
adoption of Iago's objectivist view of the world is motivated by the
same impulse, she maintains, as that which "informs Descartes' *Meditations* and the subsequent course of Western science and epistemology."[22] Bordo attributes the origins of skeptical discomfort to a separation from the organic female universe of the Middle Ages; Scheman
sees its source in a disintegration of "an apparently stabler (mis)re-
membered earlier world."[23]

Dispassionate observation and scientific objectivity promise control over unruly emotions. They confer the power that is needed to
obliterate frightening perspectival distortions and to establish clarity,
certainty, and stability. No such security is available in the seductiveness of experienced nature, in the kaleidoscopic and dazzling realm
of sensory (bodily) experiences, or in the fragility of human relationships. The detached observer, who can control his emotions with his
reason, and nature with his knowledge, can escape the vagaries and
uncertainties of the evanescent sensory world to dwell in a realm of
objective truth. The achievement of this security requires detachment
not only from the observed world but, in Cartesian thought, from his
own body, which is amenable to the same mechanistic descriptions as
the rest of the sensory world.[24]

[21]Susan Bordo, "The Cartesian Masculinization of Thought," *Signs: Journal of Women
in Culture and Society* 11 (Spring 1986): 439–456.

[22]Naomi Scheman, "Othello's Doubt/Desdemona's Death: On the Engendering of
Scepticism," in Judith Genova, ed., *Power, Gender, Value* (Edmonton: Academic Printing
and Publishing, 1987), pp. 113, 114.

[23]Ibid., p. 117.

[24]Richard Bernstein's account of the 'Cartesian Anxiety' that makes objectivism so
tempting and relativism so terrifying complements these analyses. See his *Beyond*

Rationalists and empiricists, for all their differences, are united in endorsing this conception of ideal objectivity. Both identify knowledge with power (power over the 'self' in Cartesian terms, over nature in Baconian ones), and both applaud an impartial, disinterested stance for knowers, who must suppress temptations to enthusiasm for, or other engagement with, their objects of knowledge. Both empiricists and rationalists argue against epistemic dependence either on an inquirer's emotional responses or on other persons as sources of knowledge. Bordo notes: "empathetic, associational, or emotional response obscures objectivity, feeling for nature muddies the clear lake of the mind."[25] Similarly, knowledge seekers should rely on their own independent efforts, for dependence on other people slides readily into a powerless position of reliance on opinion and hearsay. Knowledge worthy of that name, then, is possible only for inquirers who can purge their minds of distorting and disruptive emotional and personal influences.

For Bordo, Cartesian objectivism is of a piece with, and indeed consequent on, a seventeenth-century "flight from the feminine." Rationalists and empiricists were of one mind, she maintains, in their conviction that the essential epistemic task (both practical—in empirical science—and theoretical) was to tame "the female universe." Ideal objectivity is the *masculine* epistemological stance that a knower must adopt if this project is to be carried out successfully. This stance is, above all, *detached* "from the particularities of time and place, from personal quirks, prejudices, and interests, and most centrally, from the object itself."[26] To develop this detachment, a knower had to neutralize all traces of emotional unruliness and of the 'female' mystery that such unruliness implies.

The subject-object relation that the objectivist model assumes is peculiarly unthreatening. It is marked, as Scheman notes, by an absence of the reciprocity that is an integral part of knowing a friend. A nonsymmetrical power relation over the object of knowledge precludes any possibility of reciprocal interaction. In the fortress of certainty erected to alleviate Cartesian anxiety, knowing other people could have no place—not to mention a paradigmatic place. The ambiguity and approximation of knowing other people could offer no promises of certainty to dispel anxiety. Knowing other people, even peripherally, cannot be unresponsive, emotionless, and neutral. Only

---

Objectivism and Relativism (Philadelphia: University of Pennsylvania Press, 1983), esp. chap. 1.
[25]Bordo, "Cartesian Masculinization of Thought," p. 453.
[26]Ibid., pp. 453, 454, 451.

in behaviorist and statistical analyses can it pretend adherence to ideal objectivity. Such knowledge may indeed promise control and a high degree of certainty. Its pretensions to *know* its subject matter in any responsible sense are highly contestable.

The metaphysics of the person that underpins the objectivist model (and *excludes* knowing persons from its purview) depicts human subjects as essentially solitary, separate, self-subsistent beings, fundamentally opaque to one another. For Descartes, as for Othello, connection with such beings is dangerous, threatening. The possibility of developing intersubjective knowledge of other people, of benefiting from commonality and mutual concern, simply does not enter the picture. Knowledge, Bordo claims, is achieved through "measurement rather than sympathy."[27] It is knowledge of a strangely unpeopled world that this model legitimates, and the consequences for its practical and professional applications are striking. Fee, for example, observes that physicians are so trained that "if [a] . . . patient's subjective experience does not fit readily into [their] trained perception of objective reality, then the experience must be discounted."[28] There is no place—no claim to epistemological status—for knowledge that takes account of the specificities of subjectivity, agency, and experience.

For both Scheman and Bordo, these moves to ensure certainty in knowledge evince a need to guard against the anxiety consequent on a radical separation from the world. For both, that anxiety is characteristic of (stereotypically conceived) male experience. Scheman claims that the ambivalence that permeates *Othello* and the *Meditations* is inevitable in a world where men are expected to dominate women. The need to ward off ambivalence prompts an anxiety that urgently seeks refuge in objectivism. Drawing on psychoanalytic literature, Scheman contends that this ambivalence has its source in a conflict between an infantile dependency on, and an equally strong desire to be independent from, the mother. Woman is experienced, at once, as a source of nurturance and life and as a threat to infantile omnipotence and the assertion of independent selfhood. The structures of the conflict are different for female children, who are not expected, in dominant privileged western cultures, to separate from their mothers as male children are but are encouraged to maintain connection, identification, and a level of dependence. There is no doubt that dependence is a frequent source of ambivalence for women, too, in their later lives, but it is the structures

[27]Ibid., p. 450.
[28]Fee, "Women's Nature and Scientific Objectivity," p. 23.

of masculine ambivalence that are at issue for Scheman. Her point is that a sense of powerlessness and alienation fluctuates, in male consciousness, with an urge to dominate and control. To maintain the ascendancy of the latter, a man must establish complex ideological and intellectual (= antiemotional) structures. Connection with other people is neither an unequivocal option *nor* a basis for epistemic assurance.

Out of an existential anguish, then, arises the need to develop a position of cognitive autonomy and epistemic control, "a relationship with nature in which [one's] own identity and status are not at risk."[29] This need accounts for the *engendering* of skepticism. Experiential engagement either with the material world or with other intelligent beings would only undermine the basis of epistemic certainty.

In Bordo's work and—to a lesser extent—in Scheman's, there is a troubling romanticism: a nostalgic appeal to an earlier closeness to nature, a claim for the existence of a connectedness that would be difficult to document. I am assuming that it is legitimate to read references to a 'misremembered world' either as a projection of alternative possibilities or as interpretative history. Hence I am putting worries about historical accuracy aside, for the sake of elaborating Bordo's and Scheman's plausible claims about the emotional appeal of objectivity. Like Birke's analyses, their claims about the specifiable, localizable, and exclusionary history of ideal objectivity create space for deconstructing the ideal by reconstructing the processes of its formation. A critical redirection of the goals and methodologies of inquiry has the emancipatory potential to grant a hearing to voices suppressed by the dominant discourse.

Identifications of empiricism, rationalism, and objectivity with masculinity are both problematic and illuminating. They invoke essentialist claims that are the inverse of essential femininity. There is no doubt that ideals of objectivity and stereotypical masculinity mirror one another quite closely. Nor is there any doubt that the rhetoric of 'natural' male supremacy sustains the power structures that ensure male privilege and oppress women. But attributions of essential maleness efface differences among men and claim a natural necessity for characteristics that are in fact typical only of an elite group of white men in specific situations of power, property, and political privilege. However widespread male dominance may be, its practices are differently engaged in by men of different classes and races within patriarchal societies, and differently, too, in different societies and cultures. Like essential femaleness and ideal objectivity, ideal or

---

[29]Scheman, "Othello's Doubt/Desdemona's Death," p. 121.

essential masculinity is a specific cultural-social construct, not a manifestation of natural essence.

Nonetheless, as many insightful feminist studies reveal, philosophical practices that extol ideal objectivity and ascribe to a scientific
model of knowledge manifest persistent associations with the characteristics of ideal masculinity. Even the ideal of reason is defined by
excluding characteristics commonly associated with 'the feminine'.[30]
Hence feminists need to understand these associations and to develop strategies for constructing epistemological positions and regulative ideals that are not so clearly aligned with androcentric values and
their inevitable constructions of femaleness and femininity as 'less
than' maleness and masculinity. The problem is to devise alternatives
that neither presuppose an 'essential' femaleness nor appeal to 'feminine' values that are just as unrealistically pure and unequivocal as
ideal objectivity and masculinity.

Addressing one aspect of this problem, Bordo notes a crucial difference between present-day analyses of gender and 'gender-inflected'
styles as social constructs, and a nineteenth-century doctrine of female
moral superiority.[31] The nineteenth-century doctrine illustrates the
pitfalls of a female essentialism that accords high value to stereotypically female traits in order to entrust women with the moral guardianship of society and to establish separate spheres of male and female
influence. This ideology underpins the doctrine of complementarity,
of women's relegation and confinement to a 'private' realm and of
their potential and often actual exploitation as caregivers and nur-
turers. If present-day analyses can displace complementarity with a
critical revaluation of dominant 'masculine' modes and suppressed
'feminine' ones, to make possible a politics of difference that works
across a range of positions and attributes, then a disruption of malestream hegemonic epistemological presuppositions may be possible.
A more playful interplay of differences could divert appeals to essentialism that seem to require distinctively feminine and distinctively
masculine epistemological positions, incommensurable and immune
to reciprocal critique and influence.

Projects directed toward blurring the lines of essentialism need to
take critical note of the studies of child-raising practices in middle-
class affluent white American nuclear families, produced by such
researchers as Dorothy Dinnerstein, Nancy Chodorow, and Carol
Gilligan.[32] Child raising in these families is commonly represented as

[30]See Genevieve Lloyd, *The Man of Reason* (London: Methuen, 1984).
[31]Bordo, "Cartesian Masculinization of Thought," p. 455.
[32]See Dorothy Dinnerstein, *The Mermaid and the Minotaur: Sexual Arrangements and
Human Malaise* (New York: Harper Colophon Books, 1976); Nancy Chodorow, *The*

the social norm of gender construction. These studies show that male children in such families are consistently nurtured into adults for whom objectivist, masculine ways are right and 'natural', while female children are nurtured to become adults for whom connectedness, closeness, and empathy are 'natural'. In short, the gendered associations of these qualities derive from a statistically small segment of the population, whose way of life has a disproportionally large normative role in establishing social standards. Written at a stage in the development of 'second wave' feminism when difference was receiving less attention than commonality, these analyses take scant account of the partiality of their own conclusions. Yet they reveal some of the dangers of conceiving reconstructive feminist projects as efforts simply to revalue 'the feminine' or to incorporate it into 'the masculine'. It is not easy to claim unequivocal value for connectedness over detachment or to identify feminine values straightforwardly with warmth and goodness. Associations of 'female' connectedness with cooperation are just as oversimplified as associations of 'male' separation with competition. Evelyn Fox Keller and Helen Moglin, in fact, argue that cooperation is sometimes *facilitated* by differentiation and autonomy. Drawing attention to "the many kinds of conflict that emerge from too strong an identification between mothers and daughters,"[33] they offer one cogent reason why a feminist rewriting of epistemology cannot simply reclaim devalued feminine values. These values, too, are riddled with ambiguity and contradiction. Ideal objectivity may institutionalize stereotypical male subjectivity; but displacing it with an analogous female subjectivity in just the same role is assuredly not the best solution.

Creativity, Culture, and Language

The position I have been developing in this critique of objectivism is predicated on a belief that knowledge is a construct that bears the marks of its constructors. In the previous section I have shown that its claims to objectivity are derivative of culturally constituted male experiences. They derive out of the subjective, affective preoccupations of privileged, paradigmatic knowers. In this section I argue that other

Reproduction of Mothering: Psychoanalysis and the Sociology of Gender (Berkeley: University of California Press, 1978); and Carol Gilligan, *In a Different Voice: Psychological Theory and Women's Development* (Cambridge: Harvard University Press, 1982).

[33]Evelyn Fox Keller and Helen Moglin, "Competition and Feminism: Conflicts for Academic Women," *Signs: Journal of Women in Culture and Society* 1 (Spring 1987): 500.

dimensions of subjectivity, such as the creativity, and the historical, cultural, and linguistic locations of the constructors, are likewise visible in the construct.

Creativity and Cultural Location

The importance of creativity in the production of knowledge finds its best-known philosophical articulation in the philosophy of Immanuel Kant. Knowledge, for Kant, is the product of a creative synthesis of the imagination. The imagination mediates between understanding and sensibility (= sense perception), categorizing experience and constructing knowledge out of it. In this process, knowers are active, selecting and discriminating aspects of experience on which they impose a structure and unity. An interplay between subjective and objective elements is taken for granted in Kantian epistemology. There is no contradiction in claiming that knowledge is indeed formed or produced through the creative cooperation of perception and thought, while asserting that knowledge is objective. The material world is knowable only to the extent that it is accessible to creative synthesizing, however elastic the limitations of that activity and however extendable it is by technological or other means. Cognitive projects constantly have to deal with surprises: they come up against aspects of experience that cannot be altered at will: aspects that affirm the objective independence of 'reality' from cognitive structuring. 'Reality' dictates the nature of the synthesis, within broad limitations, as does the cognitive equipment of the organism.[34]

Cognitive possibilities themselves, however, are shaped by such subjective factors as the historical, cultural, and linguistic 'locatedness' of every inquirer. Any critical analysis of abstract, universalist models of knowledge which takes subjective cognitive circumstances into account will reveal that a knower's location in history is constitutive of her or his possibilities of knowing.[35] It was no more possible for a mathematician of Plato's day to know non-Euclidean geometry than it was for him to know Marxist theory or to know how to use a telephone. The impossibility derives not from the 'truth' or 'untruth' of non-Euclidean geometry at that time, but from the fact that it constituted an order of novelty that could not be accommodated within 'state of the art' geometrical knowledge. 'State of the art' knowledge

[34]The nature of the realism implicit in these claims is discussed at greater length in chap. 5 of my *Epistemic Responsibility*.
[35]I examine the implications of historical location more fully in "The Importance of Historicism for a Theory of Knowledge."

exerts a strong determining influence in knowledge construction: at certain historical periods, certain ways of structuring experience are unavailable tout court. A complex structure of conceptual, political, and 'knowledge accumulation' factors produces the conditions that make knowledge possible.

Such factors work in interconnected ways to shape the cognitive possibilities even of the privileged women who are the alleged peers and equals of hegemonic male knowers. It would be an exaggeration to claim that the closed doors of institutions of academic learning, at certain periods of history, actually produced female stupidity. But it is not at all fanciful to see those closed doors as evidence of a perception of women's place in the intellectual world which, in turn, shaped their academic and intellectual choices. Evidence about the adaptability of human brains, and about the need to acquire skills at early developmental stages, suggests that if women are actively *or* passively excluded from early training, 'higher' levels of knowledge will be inaccessible, even in imagination, to most of them. Exceptions can always be cited, but their rarity merely supports the larger point. Christine Peirce's 1975 observation remains apt: "certain abilities of persons can be manifested only in circumstances of cooperativeness. One cannot, for instance, manifest intelligence in an interpersonal situation with someone priorly convinced of one's stupidity."[36] Social expectations ensure that even the most privileged women, in eras of masculine ascendancy, have difficulty gaining access to authoritative learning. Despite its class and racial variations, epistemic discrimination of this general sort has no counterpart as a form of discrimination against men. At issue here are what Jill Matthews calls "patterns of probability"; she remarks, "The value of such patterns is that they establish the boundaries of probability. Everything is possible; only some events are probable in any particular society."[37] Analogously, and for structural reasons, only some cognitive achievements are probable for women at any particular time in history, in any society. These probabilities also vary across class, race, and other specificities, but gender lines establish a distinct and irreducible set of variations.

[36]Christine Peirce, "Philosophy," in *Signs: Journal of Women in Culture and Society* 1 (Winter 1975): 493. Londa Schiebinger notes that "without proper training and access to libraries, instruments and networks of communication, it is difficult for anyone—man or woman—to make significant contributions to knowledge" (*Mind Has No Sex?* p. 12). Yet she reminds her readers that women's exclusion from institutions of learning has not been uniform throughout history and that official institutions were not the only sites of the production of knowledge.

[37]Jill Julius Matthews, *Good and Mad Women: The Historical Construction of Femininity in Twentieth-Century Australia* (Sydney: Allen & Unwin, 1984), p. 30.

Language

Knowledge is discursively, linguistically constructed. Its construction varies across natural languages and within the discursive practices and disciplinary structures of linguistic communities. Languages
and discourses reflect, structure, and are structured by embedded
metaphysical assumptions about the nature of 'reality'. They show
what objects, events, and experiences a linguistic community considers worth naming and how that community constructs the relations of objects and events to one another. There are notable differences from one language to another about the appropriateness and
legitimacy of divisions and classifications. (The fact that Eskimos have
thirty-six words for 'snow' is often cited to illustrate this point.)
Whether such differences recommend a radical linguistic relativism,
which would entail incommensurability from language to language,
remains an open question.[38] At a time when theorists are familiar
with the influence of Wittgenstein's philosophy and with Foucault
and postmodernism, it would be unacceptable to characterize language as a neutral or transparent medium through which experiences
pass untouched on their way to becoming knowledge. Problems of
interpretation, understanding, and evaluation attend all speech acts
and linguistic exchanges: most acts of communication are—more or
less successfully—acts of translation. Feminists have contended that
women in patriarchal societies have to perform these acts of translation twice over: to translate both from idiolect to idiolect and from an
androcentered language into a language that can achieve some connection with their experiences.[39] More recent feminist analyses of
difference and diversity point to a still more complex process. Translation has to take place not just across gender lines, but across lines
constituted by race, ethnicity, class, sexual preference, and age. These
lines crisscross to form meanings that construct difference variously,
according to the variables pertinent to specific situations and negotiations. It is rarely legitimate, prior to conversation and interpretation,
to assume the existence of 'a common language'.[40]

[38]I argue this point at greater length in my "Language and Knowledge," *Word:
Journal of the International Linguistics Association* 31 (December 1980): 245–258.

[39]In the early years of the 'second wave', such suggestions came most notably from
Dale Spender, in *Man Made Language* (London: Routledge & Kegan Paul, 1980); Robin
Lakoff, in *Language and Woman's Place* (New York: Harper & Row, 1975); and Mary Daly,
in *Gyn/Ecology*. Andrea Nye, in chap. 8 of her *Feminist Theory and the Philosophies of Man*
(London: Croom Helm, 1988), offers an extensive analysis of feminist preoccupations
with issues of language, drawing on French feminism and postmodernism as well as
upon Anglo-American writings.

[40]The allusion is to the title of Adrienne Rich's collection of poetry *The Dream of a
Common Language: Poems 1974–1977* (New York: Norton, 1978).

The relativistic implications of these claims mirror the relativistic implications of affirming the epistemological significance of the specificity of cognitive agents and of the consequent perspectival differences. Translation and communication succeed often enough in practice to suggest that extreme relativism is implausible. Yet the rarity of perfect translation and the translinguistic elusiveness of many concepts and ideas recommend respect for a significant measure of relativism. Perhaps it is logically possible for all linguistic utterances to be translated into any other language without remainder.[41] But in practical terms, conceptual barriers are often difficult to assail. The power of discourse to shape experiences, to reconstruct them so that their 'owners' can scarcely recognize them, or to exclude them from view is a palpable fact that arguments about logical possibilities cannot gainsay.

In her early, path-breaking critique of the standard English lexicon, Dale Spender argues that there is gender-bias in the construction of meanings and in the apportioning of 'linguistic space'.[42] Women are excluded from processes of naming and of meaning-construction, and women's interests and experiences occupy but a small part of both everyday and institutional vocabularies. Linguistically, it is a man's world, where woman's place is defined and maintained by 'man made language' in innumerable subtle ways. Hence women must learn to speak a language that does not, in effect, speak of 'their own' experiences.

The most interesting examples are not just the now popularly recognized uses of the generic 'man' and 'he', which undoubtedly reflect and maintain women's invisibility. That example is part of a larger picture of language as an enforcer of women's powerlessness which feminists began to assemble with Spender's work and other studies of the 1970s and early 1980s. Sociological evidence about male control and dominance in 'private' conversations and about the contestedness of women's right to speak in 'public'—together with the difficulties they face in claiming this right—reveal a stark power differential constituted along gender lines.[43] Evidence shows that women's careful, tentative, often reticent speech patterns strengthen commonplace beliefs about their lack of authority. Lexical evidence that female in-

---

[41]Certainly this is Donald Davidson's conviction in his now-classic refutation of linguistic relativism, "On the Very Idea of a Conceptual Scheme," *Proceedings and Addresses of the American Philosophical Association* 47 (1974): 5–20.

[42]Spender, *Man Made Language*.

[43]A classic collection of studies that reveal this power differential is Barrie Thorne and Nancy Henley, eds., *Language and Sex: Difference and Dominance* (Rowley, Mass.: Newbury House, 1975). The collection contains an excellent annotated bibliography.

feriority is linguistically encoded—in diminutives (poetess), in valuational asymmetries ('spinster' is less positive than 'bachelor'), in varied adjectival assignments (soft, fragile versus hard, tough), and in the tendency even of politically claimed titles (Ms.) to acquire a pejorative connotation—demonstrates how the semantic dimension of a language can mirror a social sex/gender system.

It is true that these early studies assume a unified dominant male voice and an equally unified, marginalized and repressed female voice. To claim adequacy to the present historical moment they would need to diversify and specify those voices much more subtly, to allow for a broader range of speaking positions. Subsequent emphasis on differences has made it necessary for feminists to engage in more finegrained analyses of the interweavings of knowledge, gender, race, and class, to mention only some of the differences that often count. But for these more discriminating analyses to begin, patterns of the reciprocal constitution of knowledge, gender, and language had to be drawn with broad, bold strokes. Hence the significance of these early studies in bringing these matters to feminist awareness should not be occluded by uneasiness over the inadequacies consequent on their essentialism. They open an area of discussion that is particularly valuable to feminist epistemological inquiry. Feminists need to understand the androcentricity of malestream epistemology: its near-exclusive concentration on men's experiences, masquerading as 'human' experiences, and counted as the sources of knowledge. If the language is tailor-made to express those experiences, and if women's experiences simply fall through the spaces in that same language, the androcentricity of the theory is scarcely a surprise. The difficulty is to find a solution, particularly in the face of an apparent tendency of surface reforms to slide into asymmetrical valuations. To mount a successful critique of sexist language, according to Andrea Nye, theorists cannot "take words as simple stand-ins for objects that can be rearranged at will, or assume that there is a natural meaning substitutable for patriarchal distortion."[44] Feminist critics must come to terms with the discursive construction of meanings and with the implications of that construction within structures of power and dominance.

Of particular epistemological interest are implicitly sexist and suppressive linguistic structures that inform basic metaphysical presuppositions and constructions of social reality. Merrill and Jaakko Hintikka, for example, contend that not even the basic ontological

---

[44]Nye, *Feminist Theory and the Philosophies of Man*, p. 178. I am indebted to Nye throughout this discussion.

assumptions of western philosophy are gender-neutral.[45] Rather, they project a demonstrably masculine ontology. Language is sexist, then, because of the ontology that is embedded in it and shapes its structure as much as its content.

The authors take psychological studies that reveal sex-linked differences among children even in quite simple cognitive responses as their point of departure. Such differences, they maintain, develop into pervasive cognitive orientations with significant ontological implications. For example, in experiments with collections of objects whose relations could have been variously construed, boys tended to bracket a truck, a car, and an ambulance, whereas girls bracketed a doctor, a hospital bed, and an ambulance. The Hintikkas claim that such behavior derives from a general masculine preference for dealing (whether as children at play or as adults doing philosophy) with separable, manipulable, independent, and discrete units. The authors contrast this preference with feminine concentration on relational characteristics and interdependencies. The prevalence in western philosophy of ontological models that postulate "a given fixed supply of discrete individuals, individuated by their intrinsic or essential (non-relational) properties" is a manifestation of that preference. Yet the Hintikkas contend that the material, inanimate, nonhuman world might be known quite differently were the dominant thought structures to reflect a primary concentration on relations, configurations, and interdependencies. Such an alternative would invite "comparisons of different worlds in terms of their total structure . . . [leading] . . . to entirely different identification methods, which are much more holistic and relational."[46]

The Hintikkas are in fact arguing that language is sexist because it expresses a masculine reality. Hence for the women in western societies, for whom these philosophical assumptions shape both thought and language, the structures and limits of their knowledge are derived from the experiences of a select, intellectually and socially privileged group of men: the philosophical system builders. This suggestion affords a partial explanation of the cognitive dissonance many female and feminist philosophers experience with the ontological divisions embedded in mainstream epistemology, both historical and current. If it is correct, their diagnosis of androcentricity in the fundamental conceptual apparatus of mainstream western philosophical

[45]Merrill B. Hintikka and Jaakko Hintikka, "How Can Language Be Sexist?" in Harding and Hintikka, eds., Discovering Reality.
[46]Ibid., p. 146.

thought makes it impossible to claim rational, objective necessity for those conceptual structures and the naming patterns they legitimate. Their 'maleness' does not invalidate the structures *tout court*, but it does locate their origins in the subjectivity of their male creators.

A cautionary note must again be sounded at this point. The Hintikkas' argument plainly assumes essential and universal female/male differences. Hence it plays into the terms of the tension in feminist thought that both recommends and resists appeals to essential gender differences. The examples they elaborate prompt an immediate recognition both of how small boys tend to play with toys and of how grown boys tend to play with philosophical concepts. There is evidence to show that girls—and women—often do it differently. So there is an initial presumption in favor of these conclusions. But the tension derives from a recognition that it is the behavior patterns of a group of affluent white American boys that the Hintikkas are interpreting as "typically male." Granted, these boys are statistically more likely to grow up to be academic philosophers than boys who are less securely positioned in the dominant culture. So the parallels that emerge are significant for the nature and structure of philosophical discourse. But it would be a mistake, without more evidence, to extend them further. The parallels the Hintikkas discern between gender-specific behaviors and ontological structures do suggest gender specificities in language and thought. But, like the early feminist linguistic analyses, they paint with a broad brush, drawing their distinctions between maleness and femaleness with insufficient sensitivity to discriminations that need to be made within and across the two categories. To endorse an essentialism at a metaphysical level such as they assume would be both contrary to experiential evidence and politically suspect. The specificity of their sample needs to be taken into account in assessing the support that it provides for the conclusion that language is sexist.

It would be another mistake to read the Hintikkas' conclusions about linguistic sexism as an argument for essentially distinct—and possibly incommensurable—male and female realities. It is true that impermeable conceptual boundaries often seem to separate women's and men's experiences, even within the limits of racial, class, ethnic, and other divisions. But it would be a defeatist move to maintain that these boundaries reflect essential differences. The changes feminists are working for, with notable success, would not be worth the struggle if their achievement would still leave women and men locked into separate conceptual structures. Women are often judged deviant or sick if they resist dominant definitions of their situations and experiences.[47] But a belief that there are separate male and female 'realities' which allows such women to count as 'normal' within *their own* reality is no solution. It might reflect a conviction that women's separate reality is of a significance equal to masculine reality, but different from it: hence that the two 'realities' are complementary. But such a conviction would reaffirm the biological determinism that declares all women irrational because they cannot conform to masculine rational standards. If their 'reality' is different, such failures to conform would not even be surprising. All of the evaluative dichotomies whose dissolution I have been advocating would be reinstated, and male/female complementarity would again recommend itself as the best form of social, political, and epistemological organization.

Avoiding the pitfalls of essentialism and the postulation of separate 'realities', the 1985 publication of *A Feminist Dictionary*[48] demonstrates that language can effectively be diagnosed as sexist. Yet the diagnosis creates politically powerful tools that do not play into the mystique of incommensurability and separate realities.

It is particularly astute of the authors to have named their book a *dictionary*, for the 'great', established dictionaries enjoy a special status in relation to language. Roy Harris notes that people commonly see a dictionary as a repository of verbal meanings par excellence, regarding it with a veneration and respect for authority that amounts almost to superstition. A dictionary stands as a repository of impersonal ideas expressed and owned by no one:[49] its authoritarian format obscures its human (hence fallible) origins. Indeed, Oxford philosopher Richard Robinson describes a dictionary as a table (like a mathematical table) "of eternal facts that were not made by men and cannot be unmade by them."[50] On this view the possibility of reading a dictionary as a history of usage in specific circumstances—where specific interests prevail—disappears from view.

Now Kramarae and Treichler argue in their introduction that the facts that most standard dictionaries record are facts "made by men," where 'men' is emphatically not the generic term that it apparently is for Robinson. It refers to *male* human beings only. Dictionary making per se is a sociopolitical activity, and their sociopolitical goal is to establish women as "originators of spoken or written language

[47]I discuss this situation at length in Chapter 5.
[48]Cheris Kramarae and Paula Treichler, *A Feminist Dictionary* (London: Pandora, 1985).
[49]Roy Harris, *The Language Makers* (Ithaca: Cornell University Press, 1980), see pp. 78, 130.
[50]Ibid., p. 140. The quotation is from Richard Robinson, *Definition* (Oxford: Oxford University Press, 1954), p. 36.

forms."[51] Hence they eschew the established practice of citing male sources for first usages; and their principles of selection are avowedly political, subversive, and often wonderfully witty. They illustrate by example the selectivity of dictionary making. Juxtaposing their dictionary with a standard one reveals the arbitrariness of a dictionary's authority and demonstrates how that authority is often claimed at the expense of women and other 'underclass' groups. They are amply successful in showing that 'received' language bears a masculine stamp. Yet for all that they celebrate 'the feminine', they avoid claiming discrete, separate, or essential male and female 'realities'.

The *Feminist Dictionary*'s discussion of 'sexism' is a case in point. The authors cite the *Macquarrie Dictionary* definition of 'sexism' as "the upholding or propagation of sexist attitudes," and its definition of a 'sexist attitude' as one that "stereotypes a person according to gender or sexual preference, etc.": definitions in which the word's specifically feminist origins *and* purposes are invisible. The *Feminist Dictionary* insists on the primary reference to women's experiences, defining 'sexism' as "a social relationship in which males have authority over females" (citing Linda Phelps) and tracing its coinage to a 1968 paper by Vanauken, "Freedom for Movement Girls—Now." The contrast demonstrates the term's political force in naming experiences "central to women's lives, which [were] wordless for many years."[52] Introducing the term into common parlance made it easier to recognize (= know) and conceptualize the experiences for purposes of constructing strategies of opposition and resistance.

The force of the term 'sexism' derives as much from its affinities with words that do not describe just those experiences, nor just describe women's experiences. This is the value of *not* developing the argument in terms of radically different male and female realities. Its cognitive and political force derives from its association with practices women *and* men call 'racist'. The implicit proposal that the analogies between the practices named by 'sexism' and 'racism', respectively, be taken seriously draws on a recognition of experiences familiar to both women and men, albeit differently, across other differences. The term performs the "double function" of pinpointing certain practices as discriminatory and aligning those practices with an acknowledged moral repugnance inherent in racism.[53] These moves would be nei-

---

[51]Kramarae and Treichler, *Feminist Dictionary*, p. 1.

[52]Ibid., p. 411.

[53]Grimshaw makes analogous points about the coinage of the term 'sexual harassment'; and 'double function' is her term (*Philosophy and Feminist Thinking*, pp. 87–88). In this discussion of 'sexism' I am indebted to Grimshaw.

ther possible nor intelligible on an assumption of discrete female and male realities or of the inherent incommensurability of female and male language. Kramarae and Treichler's linguistic proposals work subversively, against the grain of an established usage that purports to *know* what words need to be defined and what their accepted usages should be. Although their work is addressed to women, it acts as a biting internal critique of 'masculinist' assumptions per se.

Epistemologically, it is still true (as Kramarae observed in an earlier, coauthored article) that "there is a problem [for women] both of concept formation within an existing male constructed framework and a problem of language use in developing and articulating an authentic understanding of the world and one's relationship to it."[54] But the point does not hold equally for all women, and feminist critiques are effecting significant changes in the politics of discourse, making its hidden structures visible and devising strategies for resistance. Wittgenstein's contention that "*the limits of my language* mean the limits of my world" may have some truth to it,[55] but it does not exclude possibilities of expanding and altering those limits. Prior to the consciousness raising of 'second wave' feminism, even a woman of privilege might have accepted the limits of *his* language as the limits of her world and hence of her knowledge. Now it is increasingly possible for women, and other suppressed and marginalized speakers, to subvert and challenge patriarchal language so as to name their experiences, hence to construct knowledge from their perspectives. The subjective constraints that 'received language' imposes on possibilities of knowing are by no means absolute.

Linguistic restraints are not absolute, not carved in stone; but neither, Andrea Nye cautions, is it easy to erase them. Patriarchal language and logic are alarmingly adept at recouping rebellion and deviance, reclaiming authority over discourse that seeks refuge in the margins. Nye writes: "A woman's language, whether an independent woman's language or maternal semiotics, [becomes] the rediscovered underside of male logic and all that rationality imagines it must cover, reject, or fear. As such, it [continues] to be a language of the oppressed, a language without authority . . . which cries and communicates but cannot establish or prescribe."[56] Now there is a certain cons-

[54]Cheris Kramer, Barrie Thorne, and Nancy Henley, "Perspectives on Language and Communication," *Signs: Journal of Women in Culture and Society* 3 (Spring 1978): 644.
[55]Ludwig Wittgenstein, *Tractatus Logico-Philosophicus*, trans. David Pears and B. F. McGuinness (London: Routledge & Kegan Paul, 1961), #5.6.
[56]See Nye's chapter "A Woman's Language," in her *Feminist Theory and the Philosophies of Man*, p. 211. Nye's provocative analyses of French feminist and poststructuralist

tancy to this relentless recuperation of the marginal by the hegemonic center; this is Nye's point. But she argues that there is no necessity to it.

Poststructuralist "deconstruction[s] of the text of patriarchy" have, indeed, made visible "the conflictual and alienated sources of the philosophy of man." But the picture of language they paint is de-historicized to erect a putatively universal structural 'symbolic' from which there is no escape. Hence any move to create a "feminine counter-text" is bound, from its inception, to invite reclamation by the dominant discourse. By contrast, work on the *history* of grammar and of dictionary making has greater political potential. It reveals that grammar is not *discovered*, Nye contends, but is "an interested imposition on language of a certain kind of speaking."[58] Historical research of the 1970s, particularly in the relatively unknown work of Julia Stanley and Emile Benveniste, is a valuable resource for feminist projects because of its capacity to reveal the sources of the powers of language not just in an eternal (Lacanian) phallic signifier, but in the specific practices of "language makers."[58] Read dialectically with poststructuralist deconstructions of patriarchal texts, historical studies make possible engagement in discourses that might be able to articulate women's experience because their contents are not dictated by the 'Law of the Father'.

Nye intends her historical appeals to counter the tendency of Lacanians and Saussurians to posit language as an "absolute social beginning"—a structure into which one is born and remains caught with little hope of escape. She is looking for ways to resist the immobilizing implications of language understood as "a transcendent object posited beyond the unsatisfactory reality of linguistic and cultural diversity and change."[59] The question is whether, in Nye's critique of the recuperative power of structuralist analyses, she has painted herself into a corner where the project she proposes cannot be realized. Her point is to claim a space outside post-structuralist theory—to deny *its* hegemony, its universal relevance. Attempts *within* it to create a women's language are, she persuasively argues, likely to fail; so she looks again at the resources that are available beyond it. The question is how a historical project such as the one she advocates

---

language theory are too complex for summary, but I am indebted to her in my thinking here.

[57]Ibid., pp. 218, 214.
[58]I refer to the title of Harris's book, cited above.
[59]Nye, *Feminist Theory and the Philosophies of Man*, p. 216.

could address and challenge postmodern analyses. Postmodern theorists may still reclaim, marginalize those endeavors. The best possibility of success resides in pursuing historical studies assiduously to the point of making an irrefutable case for their constitution of a voice that can, indeed, show that language is mutable, refusable.

I have attempted to show that it is by no means fanciful to conclude that ideal objectivity is a refined, rarefied, and institutionalized manifestation of dominant western male subjectivity. But the *subjectivity* of knowledge would not pose such a threat to rationality were *it* not so distortedly construed. Discussions of objectivity, which claim in the name of impartiality that people are essentially and interchangeably *alike*, assume at the same time that subjectivity and its manifestations in experiences are inherently idiosyncratic—that there is no commonality. Claims that knowledge is both subjective and objective do not amount to challenging the unchallengeable when the subjective/objective dichotomy is dissolved into terms that shade into each other without obliterating one another.

The Sex/Gender System

The objective/subjective dichotomy occupies a central position in mainstream epistemology, marking off knowledge that is worthy of its title from less worthy contenders. The complex, genderspecific workings of that dichotomy show without doubt that the sex of the knower *is* epistemologically significant. The veneration of ideal objectivity and the concomitant denigration of subjectivity are manifestations of a 'sex/gender system'[60] that structures all the other inequalities of western social arrangements and informs even those areas of life—such as 'objective' knowledge—that might seem to be gender-free.

Harding describes this system as:

a fundamental variable organizing social life throughout most recorded history and in every culture today . . . it is an *organic* social vari-

---

[60]The label originates with Gayle Rubin, "The Traffic in Women," in Rayna Reiter, ed., *Toward an Anthropology of Women* (New York: Monthly Review, 1975). Teresa de Lauretis observes: "The sex-gender system . . . is both a sociocultural construct and a semiotic apparatus, a system of representations which assigns meaning (identity, value, prestige, location in kinship, status in the social hierarchy, etc.) to individuals within the society." De Lauretis, *Technologies of Gender* (Bloomington: Indiana University Press, 1987), p. 5.

able . . . not merely an "effect" of other, more primary, causes. . . . [It] appears to limit and create opportunities within which are constructed the social practices of daily life, the characteristics of social institutions, and all of our patterns of thought.[61]

This 'system' manifests itself differently in different social and political groups; it varies along economic, racial, religious, class, and ethnic lines. But some such system is in place in every known society, where it functions to produce relations of power and powerlessness. I have been arguing that knowledge does not transcend, but is rooted in and shaped by, specific interests and social arrangements. Hence it is scarcely surprising that epistemic structures encode and rely on a set of putatively 'natural' dichotomies that assume hierarchical relations of gender politics in the construction and dissemination of knowledge.

The withholding of authoritative epistemic status from the knowledge *women* have traditionally constructed out of their designated areas of experience affords a peculiarly salient illustration of gender politics at work.[62] 'Gossip', 'old wives' tales', 'women's lore', 'witchcraft' are just some of the labels patriarchal societies attach to women's accumulated knowledge and *wisdom*. Yet the knowledge in question stands up to the most stringent tests that even the objectivists require. It is testable in practice across a wide variety of circumstances. (Think, for example, of midwifery or cookery.) Its theoretical soundness is evident in its practical applications. Its objectivity is apparent from the fact that its creators and practitioners have to cope with the intractability of the people they know and the objects they know and use. Children improperly cared for will not thrive; plants will not grow in just any soil or location; water will not boil in a refrigerator. This knowledge is valid across a wide historical and geographical range when specific local variations are taken into account. I cite examples from practices commonly classified as trivial, women's work to show that the knowledge derived even out of such denigrated practices is wholly worthy of the name. Its subjugation and trivialization can be explained only in terms of the structures of power and differential authority encoded in the *purity* demanded by ideal objectivity. This knowledge cannot attain that standard, the supposition is, because it grows out of experiences, out of continued contact with the particularities of material, sensory objects—and it is strongly

[61]Sandra Harding, "Why Has the Sex/Gender System Become Visible Only Now?" in Harding and Hintikka, eds., *Discovering Reality*, p. 312.
[62]I discuss examples of this withholding in Chapters 5 and 6.

shaped by the subjectivity of its knowers: *women*. Hence, for a system that enshrines male subjectivity in the name of objectivity, while suppressing the products of female subjectivity with the accusation that they lack objectivity, knowledge of these kinds can count only as women's lore.

Academic disciplines cooperate in promoting these inequalities. Jane Martin observes that most disciplines—she names history, psychology, literature, fine arts, biology, and sociology—"exclude women from their subject matter, distort the female according to the male image of her, and deny value to characteristics the society considers feminine."[63] Jane Flax argues that philosophy in general and epistemology in particular are products of the "patriarchal unconscious" at work.[64] She is referring not just to specific male philosophers with peculiar psychological backgrounds and conditionings. Rather, she traces the maleness of philosophy to an ideology perpetuated in the raising of male children in affluent western families to produce adult men whose philosophy—like all of their activities—bears the marks of approved 'masculinity'. The ideal of objectivity that governs the mainstream epistemological tradition mirrors the self-sufficiency to which male children are nurtured. It depends on a denial of relatedness and dependence, which originates in the requirement that a male child separate from and deny his mother. The consequent self-sufficiency acccounts for the belief that reason must triumph over the senses, just as the male should govern the female, and sustains the reason/emotion, male/female, subjective/objective dichotomies. For Plato and Descartes, "reason emerges only when nature (the female) is posited as the other with an 'inevitable' moment of domination"; for Hobbes, Freud, and Rousseau, reason is a secondary process that emerges "under the authority and pressure of the patriarchal father."[65] These deep-seated forces establish and sustain the influence of the sex/gender system.

---

[63]Jane Roland Martin, *Reclaiming a Conversation: The Ideal of the Educated Woman* (New Haven: Yale University Press, 1985), p. 3.

[64]Jane Flax, "Political Philosophy and the Patriarchal Unconscious: A Psychoanalytic Perspective on Epistemology and Metaphysics," in Harding and Hintikka, eds., *Discovering Reality*.

[65]Ibid., p. 269. Flax's analysis of mother-dominated child rearing is initially persuasive in confirming stereotypical expectations for male and female children. Like many of the landmark writings from the early 1980s, it ignores historical, class, ethnic, racial, and cultural variations in family structures; and assumes that mothering takes place within a nuclear family. Flax takes no account of lesbian or homosexual parenting or of single parenting, implying that mothering is a constant, uniform practice. Hence she cannot show that child raising constructs gender differently to the extent that it is enmeshed in, constituted by, or subversive of systems of economics, politics, and power.

Feminist epistemologists can discern patterns that make it appropriate to ask of any ideal of objectivity, Out of *whose* subjectivity has this ideal grown? Whose standpoint, whose values does it represent? The point of the questions is to discover how subjective and objective conditions *together* produce knowledge, values, and epistemology. It is neither to reject objectivity nor to glorify subjectivity in its stead. Knowledge is neither value-free nor value-neutral; the processes that produce it are themselves value-laden; and these values are open to evaluation. The evaluative process is not a simple one, because there is no external vantage point from which to engage in it. An epistemologist has to devise ways of positioning and repositioning herself within the structures she analyzes, to untangle the values at work within them and to assess their implications. Feminists working in epistemology need to develop critical, analytical techniques that can break the thrall of an unworkable conception of objectivity, and to articulate viable, empowering epistemic imperatives and strategies.

CHAPTER THREE

Second Persons

Autonomy: The Received View

Assumptions about subjectivity and agency are implicit in analyses of epistemological and ethical issues. Although such assumptions are not always elaborated into a theory of 'human nature', they inform beliefs about which problems merit consideration, and judgments about the adequacy of solutions. Claims to the effect that the construction of knowledge should be an independent project, uncontaminated by the influence of testimony, opinion, or hearsay, presuppose cognitive agents who can know their environments by their own unaided efforts. Assumptions that knowledge, once acquired, is timelessly and universally true presuppose constancy and uniformity in subjectivity across historical, cultural, and other boundaries. Analogously, contentions that one should not be swayed by feelings and loyalties in moral decision making presuppose a 'human nature' amenable to guidance by reason rather than emotion, whose possessors can live well by acting as impartially as possible.

Although this is a book about *knowledge*, in this chapter I focus on a conception of 'human nature' that informs mainstream *ethical* theories. There are three principal reasons for doing so. First, the assumptions about subjectivity that inform standard ethical theories are continuous with those that inform mainstream theories of knowledge. Moreover, because ethics is about how to act, how to be a good person, conceptions of subjectivity and agency are closer to the surface, more visible, than in theories of knowledge, in which the knower is virtually invisible: his presence does not count. Hence an analysis of the assumptions that inform moral theories is equally pertinent to theory of knowledge. Second, epistemological issues are implicated in moral deliberation. Every such process has a cognitive core, for the quality of the deliberation and the conclusions—both theoretical and practical—it legitimates are shaped by an agent's *knowledge* of the situation, the problem, and the people concerned. That knowledge can be more or less adequate; it can yield a clear view of the situation and its implications; it can be vitiated by prejudice and bias or insufficient investigation. Hence the quality of the cognitive project in which it is based shapes moral thought and action. Third, and conversely, ethical issues are implicated in analyses of knowledge. I am interested in people's—in women's—efforts to know well, to make sense of their experiences, and to position themselves knowledgeably in the world and in their relationships and alliances. As I have argued in my *Epistemic Responsibility*, knowledge construction permits considerable freedom, within the minimal constraints I discuss in Chapter 2. And knowledge has political consequences: 'truths' have implications; they do not pertain in isolation. Hence ensuring the accountability of knowledge claimants requires imperatives of responsibility to regulate epistemic carelessness, dogmatism, and *akrasia*. These *epistemic* imperatives are closely analogous to moral imperatives because knowing well is a matter both of moral-political and of epistemic concern.

These imperatives derive their urgency from a conception of cognitive agency for which intersubjectivity is primary and 'human nature' is ineluctably social. The conception contrasts sharply with the ideology of self-sufficiency that informs standard ethical and epistemological theories and casts suspicion on interdependence. Feminist critiques of mainstream ethics and of epistemology have detected analogous flaws in the construction of subjectivity at their core; hence a parallel analysis is illuminating for both areas of inquiry.

I focus here on the ideal of 'autonomous man', conceived as nature's highest achievement, to reveal the ephemerality of this construct and show that such a conception is inimical to feminist thought. In this chapter I concentrate on the place of autonomous man in ethical theory, and in the following chapter I map out his place in theory of knowledge.

The autonomous moral agent is the undoubted hero of philosophical moral and political discourse:[1] the person—indeed, more accu-

---

[1]Often I refer to moral and political together or conflate them. My purpose is to show that feminist moral theory is political and that traditional moral and political

rately, the *man*—whose conduct and attributes demonstrate the achievement of moral maturity and goodness. Developmental and educational theorists counsel in favor of structuring the processes so that rational, self-conscious, autonomous *individuals* will be their products,[2] and the realization and maintenance of autonomy is a goal of moral and political life. Yet the construction of autonomy as an overarching ideal invites feminist challenge, not emulation. Its achievement would not signal arrival at a morally and politically via-ble stance. Positing achieved autonomy as the mark of moral maturity has had the effect of withholding approval from people whose con-duct, in fact, is often praiseworthy. Women, children, blacks, the aged and the ill are just some of many examples: people whose politically constructed and enforced lack of autonomy excludes them from full moral agency, rendering them dependent and subject to paternalistic control.

It may sound odd to urge *feminists* to challenge the hegemony of autonomy. Feminists have urged women to strive for autonomy, both as freedom *from* patriarchal oppression and as freedom *to* realize their capacities and aspirations. Nor could one minimize the effects of sub-ordination in smothering women's autonomy and agency. Struggles for autonomy have been central to feminist theory and action.[3] Mary Wollstonecraft's *Vindication of the Rights of Woman* can be read as a plea for female autonomy, albeit in a limited form by late-twentieth-century standards (and a form that requires a woman to be 'more like a man'). Present-day feminists have worked to elaborate and realize a viable autonomy as an emancipatory tool,[4] and it is politically urgent that feminists not simply renounce autonomy in favor of a caring, purely relational morality. Relationships without autonomy can be claustrophobic and exploitative. My point, then, is not to deny auton-omy a place on feminist agendas, but to argue that ideals of autonomy have generated an autonomy-obsession that serves no one well. Au-tonomy and dependence tend to be polarized as the terms of a stark

---

theories make identical assumptions about agency. To argue that moral and political theory could be separated would endorse a contestable public/private split that would perpetuate women's limited access to 'public' life.

[2]The writings of Emile Durkheim, Lawrence Kohlberg, R. S. Peters, and Jean Piaget are typical in this respect.

[3]According to Zillah Eisenstein it is a "universal feminist claim that woman is an independent being [from man]," a claim "premised on the eighteenth-century liberal conception of the independent and autonomous self." Eisenstein, *The Radical Future of Liberal Feminism* (New York: Longmans, 1981), p. 4.

[4]It is important not to minimize the success of these endeavors. As Lynne Segal notes, "the degree of independence and autonomy many women now experience was almost unthinkable to the eighteenth and nineteenth century feminist." Segal, *Is the Future Female? Troubled Thoughts on Contemporary Feminism* (London: Virago, 1987), p. 25.

dichotomy, so that self-reliance and reliance on other people are constructed as mutually exclusive and the achievement of self-reliance is thought to require a complete repudiation of interdependence.

As an antidote to autonomy-obsession, I shall develop an interpretive reading of Annette Baier's conception of 'second personhood' and compare it with Caroline Whitbeck's relational ontology and Sara Ruddick's 'maternal thinking'. I shall argue that there is no stark dichotomy between interdependence and autonomy, that they are neither oppositional nor mutually exclusive. The point is to effect an integration of autonomy and solidarity in which the quality of each is open to moral-political critique.

The writings of Immanuel Kant offer the clearest articulation of a position that accords autonomy pride of place. Here 'autonomy' refers to the exercise of the freedom of the will of a rational, self-conscious agent, to the self-determination of that will quite apart from any object willed. This conception of autonomy is implicit in the two pivotal claims (in the *Groundwork of the Metaphysic of Morals*) that the good will is the only thing good in itself and that duty must override inclination in moral deliberation and in action based on it.[5]

A reading of Anthony Trollope's novel *The Warden* illuminates some implications of Kantian, and Kantian-derived, autonomy, with its inflexible rule of duty over inclination. John Bold, a zealous young reformer, takes upon himself a mission of reforming the Anglican clergy, particularly its members who seem to be abusing the privilege of their office for unwarranted financial gain. He includes in his campaign the Warden of Hiram's Hospital, a man of impeccable moral character, whose prosperity is a consequence rather of good fortune than deviousness. Despite Bold's friendship with the Warden and his love for the Warden's daughter, he pursues his course singlemindedly. He asks: "Because I esteem Mr. Harding is that a reason that I should neglect a duty which I owe . . . ? or should I give up a work which my conscience tells me is a good one, because I regret the loss of his society?" And of Eleanor Harding, he claims: "if she has the kind of spirit for which I give her credit, she will not condemn me for doing what I think to be a duty . . . I cannot for her sake go back from the task which I have commenced."[6] So he embarks on a course of

---

[5]Kant writes: "The will is therefore not merely subject to the law, but it is so subject that it must be considered as also *making the law* for itself and precisely on this account as first of all subject to the law (of which it can regard itself as the author)." Kant, *Groundwork of the Metaphysic of Morals*, trans. and analyzed by H. J. Paton (New York: Harper Torchbooks, 1964), pp. 98–99.

[6]Anthony Trollope, *The Warden* (1855; New York: Washington Square, 1962), pp. 54–56.

action that will ruin Mr. Harding's reputation and undermine the man psychologically.

The Kantian net of universalizable principles is too coarsely woven to capture the moral significance of the fact that the Warden's wealth has not come to him by immoral or politically unacceptable means. The presumption that Bold's relationship to the Warden, and his consequent *knowledge* of the Warden's character and circumstances, creates in favor of appealing to *who* the Warden is, is erased in a deliberation guided wholly by 'universal' rules. There is no space to argue that this case is different because of who *this* man is, in his specificity and particularity. Hence the Kantian impartiality principle does not generate an instrument finely enough tuned to translate principle into morally sensitive practice. If wealth in the clergy is a mark of corruption, then it must always be so, without exception.

Bold's actions reveal both the strengths and the weaknesses of Kantian morality. There is no doubt that Kantian theory provides general guidelines for action in 'conflicts of interest'. People who aspire to moral goodness have to develop a strong respect for principle so that they can stand firm against emotional temptations, neither abusing nor misusing their station or privileges for the sake of familial and/or friendly allegiances. Such principled persons do not stoop to patronage, preferential treatment, or favoritism, but live as exemplars of the impartial practice dictated by the moral law within. John Bold is such a person. His principles are of the highest, adopted for the sake of goodness rather than personal gain. He adheres strictly and strongly to them, never permitting inclination (affection, friendship, love) to interfere with the performance of his duty.

But Bold's stance also illustrates the limitations of the Kantian position in which, to quote Robert Paul Wolff, "despite his overriding concern for moral matters, Kant seems never to have asked himself the fundamental question, What is it for one man to stand in a real relation to another man?"[7] The dismay that John Bold's actions occasion signals that there is something amiss in his refusal to acknowledge the moral requirements of relationships into which he has entered as freely as he has embarked on his reformist campaign. Yet a Kantian could applaud his conduct, for emotions (in this case, the affective ties of relationships), in Kant's view, are passively undergone. Because they have no rational source or component, they threaten autonomy. A truly moral agent is autonomous in reason,

[7]Robert Paul Wolff, *The Autonomy of Reason* (New York: Harper & Row, 1973), p. 15.

rationality; emotions, which he experiences merely passively, must be transcended.

Even in an analysis of Kantian morality which did not address its feminist implications, it would be difficult to show how anyone could live a morality that always exalts duty over the loyalties of relationships and alliances. Such loyalties may prompt 'conflict of interest' abuses, but it is odd that efforts to resolve them would simply assume that public projects (Bold's reformist undertaking) should, as a matter of course, prevail over private ones (his strong affectionate ties). This rule of conduct makes moral decision making simpler, but only at the expense of obscuring the complexity of the task of effecting a balance *between* claims of duty and inclination.

Feminist moral theorists have argued that Kantian theory constructs 'persons' not just as autonomous but as discrete *atoms*, who do not count intimate relationships among their central experiences. Such relationships are anomalous, irrelevant, and threatening to moral integrity. Even the 'respect for persons' formulation of the categorical imperative, with the principle that an action-governing maxim has to be universalizable and with its emphasis on rights and duties, requires moral decision makers to deny or override their 'special' personal relationships. Emphasis on the *rights* of autonomous individuals, together with the minimal significance accorded to the responsibilities of people to and for one another, produces a tension, for moral agents, between claims of impartiality and of particularity.

Viewed developmentally, it is curious that rights would command impartial respect. Learning about morality is learning about the responsibility, care, and concern one owes to, or might direct toward, specific other people. It is not easy to believe that such a training would 'naturally' generate an ideal of moral impartiality. Nor is it easy to understand how an impartial judgment could count as an agent's *own* judgment, or what acting upon it would show about her moral goodness. Yet it is not a mark of moral slovenliness to care about the quality of one's conduct: it is morally suspect not to.[8] Thus there is a sharp discontinuity between the formal requirements of Kantian morality and the experiences, insights, and intuitions that early socialization fosters in cultures in which training for 'moral goodness' is integral to child raising.

Although an ideal of autonomy does not figure so prominently in

---

[8]In my thinking about these points I am indebted to O. J. Flanagan, Jr., and J. E. Adler, "Impartiality and Particularity," *Social Research* 50 (October 1983): 576–596.

utilitarian as in Kantian ethics, there are comparable tensions for utilitarians between claims of impartiality and of particularity, and striking affinities between utilitarians and Kantians in their constructions of 'the moral agent'. Indeed, John Stuart Mill's belief in an individual's capacity to know and choose what is in *his* own interests, and his consequent arguments against paternalism, take for granted an autonomous moral agent who is just like the Kantian one. Prima facie utilitarianism looks preferable on questions of impartiality versus particularity. For a utilitarian, actions that benefit friends, relations, and political comrades might qualify as good because they increase the agent's pleasure, thus supporting an argument in favor of positive duties to benefit friends, allies, and relatives.

That support is only apparent, however. The utilitarian conception of persons as interchangeable units of moral action, benefit, judgment, and decision making derives from the individualism central to the liberal and the German romantic traditions. It, too, is based on a strong impartiality requirement that everyone must act to produce the greatest possible general utility. Concern for the benefits or harms of particular persons is merely incidental and primarily instrumental. Relationships per se have no intrinsic value; doing what benefits the agent's friends, colleagues, or country is wrong if it hinders the production of a greater good for a larger number of people. Indeed, a utilitarian might, paradoxically, find that producing benefit for strangers, or even for enemies, has to be judged more conducive to utility than any alternative course of action, even if his own displeasure at doing so will detract from the utility he can produce.[9] For orthodox utilitarians, if the total utility is great, the identities of the beneficiaries are insignificant.

Present-day autonomous man differs from the Enlightenment hero, celebrating his freedom to trust in the power of his own reason and ready to shed the constraints of heteronomy. A cluster of derivative assumptions now attaches to ideals of autonomy. Autonomous man is—and should be—self-sufficient, independent, and self-reliant, a self-realizing individual who directs his efforts toward maximizing his personal gains. His independence is under constant threat from other (equally self-serving) individuals: hence he devises rules to protect himself from intrusion. Talk of rights, rational self-

[9]In this discussion of utilitarianism I am indebted to Susan Sherwin, "Ethics: Towards a Feminist Approach," *Canadian Woman Studies/Les cahiers de la femme* 6 (Spring 1985): 21–23.

interest, expediency, and efficiency permeates his moral, social, and political discourse. In short, there has been a gradual alignment of *autonomy* with *individualism*.[10]

I have not presented a survey of the place of autonomy and its latter-day analogues in moral and political discourse, but it is worth adding that contractarian theories, both early and late,[11] assume, as Virginia Held notes, that the individuals who make and endorse social contracts are "male, adult, economically self-supporting, and psychologically self-sufficient."[12] Although Jean-Paul Sartre writes from quite a different tradition about *man's* existential choices, affinities with the self-making and separate self-sufficiency of the positions I discuss are evident throughout his writings.

I am not suggesting that there are philosophers who believe that people are, or could be, *wholly* autonomous and self-sufficient. Autonomous man is an abstraction: neither all men nor all avowedly autonomous men exhibit all of his characteristics all of the time. Nor are such characteristics the exclusive preserve of men. But autonomous man occupies the position of a character ideal in western affluent societies. Characterizations of this abstract figure lend themselves to a starkness of interpretation that constrains moral deliberation while enlisting moral theories in support of oppressive social and political policies.

Philosophers are increasingly aware of these flaws.[13] John Benson sees autonomous man as "distant and intimidating," engaged in "self-creation and persistent radical self-questioning."[14] Daniel Callahan

---

[10]Jane Martin finds this alignment already in Rousseau's writing. She notes that "until relatively late adolescence Emile's education is designed to give him virtually no knowledge of others or even of himself in relation to them. . . . Emile is supposed to exist for himself alone" (*Reclaiming a Conversation*, p. 56). This lack of knowledge, in Martin's view, equips Emile poorly for his role as a citizen.

[11]I refer to the social contract theories of Hobbes, Locke, and Rousseau, and John Rawls's more recent version in *A Theory of Justice*. For a study of the implications of contractarianism for feminist political theory, see Carole Pateman, *The Sexual Contract* (Stanford: Stanford University Press, 1988).

[12]Virginia Held, *Rights and Goods* (New York: Macmillan, The Free Press, 1984), p. 75. Lynne Arnault argues that R. M. Hare's 'universal prescriptivism' works with an identical conception of subjectivity. See Lynne S. Arnault, "The Radical Future of a Classic Moral Theory," in Jaggar and Bordo, eds., *Gender/Body/Knowledge*.

[13]Many of the articles in Thomas C. Heller, Martin Sosna, and David Wellbery, eds., *Reconstructing Individualism: Autonomy, Individuality, and the Self in Western Thought* (Stanford: Stanford University Press, 1986), challenge the place of autonomy in western cultures.

[14]John Benson, "Who Is the Autonomous Man?" *Philosophy* 58 (1983): 5. Benson notes that, while an excessively heteronomous person can be described as credulous,

criticizes the assumption in medical ethics, that respect for patient autonomy must override practitioner paternalism, for its implication that obligation is binding only when it is autonomously contracted into: a belief that "shrivel[s] our sense of obligation" toward one another and impoverishes health care by taking as the norm "physicians who, far from treating us paternalistically, treat us impersonally and distantly, respecting our autonomy *but nothing else*."[15] Nancy Hartsock's feminist critique is directed at the construction of 'rational economic man' as an agent who is an autonomous, "independent, frequently isolated, and presumably hostile being . . . whose very humanity is based on [his] independence from the wills of others."[16] Hartsock shows that economic and political exchanges have become a model for human relationships which legitimates competition and exploitation as primary forms of interaction.

It may be that no theorist who counts autonomy as a pivotal ideal intends to advocate it to the exclusion of community and interdependence. But in practice, values generated in relationships and community are frequently represented as intrusions on or threats to autonomy. It makes a structural difference whether theory construction moves from autonomy to community or in the reverse direction. Often theorists who see autonomy as a primary, fundamental trait posit a contradiction between self-sufficiency and interdependence, on the assumption that a person has to buy interdependence at the *cost* of some measure of autonomy. Theorists who start from communality and interdependence can accommodate the requirements of autonomy better than theorists for whom autonomous existence is the 'original position' can accommodate the requirements of community. This discrepancy may simply reflect the fact that lives begin in interdependence, hence that communality-based positions map more readily onto 'natural' developmental patterns, whereas individualistic starting points are 'artificial'. For whatever reason, relational positions yield constructions of subjectivity that escape many of the negative consequences of autonomy obsession, while retaining an explanatory power at least as promising.

---

gullible, compliant, passive, submissive, overdependent, or servile, it is difficult to find a term for excessive autonomy. He proposes 'solipsism' or 'arrogant self-sufficiency'.

[15]Daniel Callahan, "Autonomy: A Moral Good, Not a Moral Obsession," *Hastings Center Report* 14 (October 1984): 41.

[16]Nancy Hartsock, *Money, Sex, and Power* (Boston: Northeastern University Press, 1986), p. 38.

Second Persons

Autonomy-oriented theories rest on a cluster of assumptions about subjectivity that are as much prescriptive as descriptive. A descriptive premise, which casts human beings as creatures capable of sustaining self-sufficient existence, acquires prescriptive dimensions in an attendant assumption that the *telos* of a life is the realization of self-sufficiency and individuality. Such a stance yields the sparsest of pictures of subjectivity. When it can count as adequate, even for theoretical purposes, to regard persons simply as bearers of rights or as rational, self-conscious agents, it is small wonder that a picture emerges of separate and oppositionally divided individuals, clutching their rights jealously to them and looking on their fellows not only as other but as alien, threatening those rights by their very existence.

Concentration on the *otherness* of other people has several consequences. First of all, its oppositional tenor casts people not only as different one from another, but as essentially opaque to one another. Rather than starting from a recognition of the existential primacy of social dependence, individualistic ontology and the moralities derivative from it take isolation and separation as the undisputed starting points of moral-political deliberation. At the same time, and paradoxically, such theories concentrate so much on formal sameness in their stripped-down versions of 'selfhood', that people—whether as bearers of rights or as rational, self-conscious agents—emerge as interchangeable units, anonymous beings who can rely on formal, simplistic, moral decision-making procedures. Assumed formal sameness and interchangeability impede the development of conceptual tools for coping with politically and morally significant differences. Hence the best that such theories can allow is a pale, pluralistic liberal toleration: a bare recognition of difference-in-isolation, which may be tolerated, but requires neither understanding nor care.

Against this backdrop it is easy to see why interdependence and cooperation come across as less valuable than separateness. They entail a compromise of autonomy and self-sufficiency; a failure of self-reliance. In a society comprised of a random assembly of such discrete, separate individuals, interdependence is at best *manageable* if carefully regulated; at worst it is straightforwardly menacing. This conception of people as essentially separate and self-contained implies that they are not only opaque to one another, but also alien and alienated one from another even in their (atomistic) sameness.

Feminist critiques of individualism have tended either to argue for reconstructions of subjectivity oriented toward granting to such 'feminine' values as caring and connectedness the place that autonomy occupies in individualistic thinking; or they have worked within the influence of postmodernism to derive conceptions of multiple or fragmented subjectivities, discursively constituted by and positioned within the political, racial, economic, sexual, ethnic, class, and cultural spaces of twentieth-century societies. Linda Alcoff locates an 'identity crisis' in feminist theory in a tension between these tendencies.[17] The crisis is at once about the theoretical identification of feminisms and feminist values, problems, and strategies and about claiming an identity as a feminist, politically engaged subject.

Taking the 'cultural feminist' path involves subscribing to an ideology of female nature or essence, where essence is defined by sex-specific characteristics, and patriarchy amounts to the suppression of essential femininity. Feminists endeavor to preserve yet revalue biological/gender differences, arguing that patriarchal power has to be deterred from its projects of denigrating or obliterating the feminine values that should, instead, become the principles of social reconstruction. Yet in their celebration of women's natural attributes, cultural feminists work with a "homogeneous, unproblematized, and ahistorical conception of woman."[18] Hence the political power of their analyses is inadequate to the specific historical situations in which feminist agendas have to be created and enacted.

Theorists who take the poststructuralist (or posthumanist, post-essentialist) direction argue that subjectivity is a construct, hence not a locus of fixed intentions, natural attributes, or a privileged, self-actualizing consciousness. 'Woman' is a fiction that feminists need to deconstruct, and the same is true of gender differences. Because there is no essential core, there is no repression: there is no whole, authentic, repressed self dormant beneath sociocultural accretions. The traditional moral attributes of the humanistic subject, who is allegedly possessed of a free will, are constructs of the same humanistic discourse that constructs that subject himself. The only way to break out of the structure of humanistic thought, then, is to assert "total difference," Alcoff notes. Yet this move, too, is problematic. Feminists cannot claim a place outside sociocultural-ideological constructive processes, from which to affirm feminine specificity, to make demands in the name of 'women', to name and contest oppression, for

[17]Linda Alcoff, "Cultural Feminism versus Post-Structuralism: The Identity Crisis in Feminist Theory," *Signs: Journal of Women in Culture and Society* 13 (Spring 1988): 405–436.

[18]Ibid., p. 413.

every such move threatens to deconstruct itself on its own terms. As Alcoff trenchantly poses the question: "If gender is simply a social construct, the need and even the possibility of a feminist politics becomes immediately problematic. What can we demand in the name of women if 'women' do not exist and demands in their name simply reinforce the myth that they do?"[19] The terms of the 'identity crisis' do not force a choice between these positions so much as they require critical analyses of the implications of both.

My continued engagement with problems of moral philosophy in the rest of this chapter—like my engagement with theory of knowledge in the rest of this book—locates my critique, albeit ambivalently, in dialogue with a residual humanistic subjectivity, yet a subjectivity that would be largely unrecognizable to its humanist ancestors. Its postessentialist cognizance of its specificity, its locatedness, make it impossible for it to take up a humanistic 'view from nowhere'. It is a situated, self-critical, socially produced subjectivity, yet one that can intervene in and be accountable for its positioning.

I shall elaborate Baier's conception of 'second persons' to trace a path through some of the spaces that neither essentialist nor postessentialist theories have closed off. The central claim of her article "Cartesian Persons" poses a sharp contrast to autonomy-obsession. Baier observes: "A person, perhaps, is best seen as one who was long enough dependent upon other persons to acquire the essential arts of personhood. Persons essentially are *second* persons."[20] Implications of this claim in several of Baier's other essays add up to a repudiation of individualism in its ethical and epistemological manifestations, which is less an explicit critique than a demonstration of the communal basis of moral and mental activity. It is possible to endorse Baier's 'second persons' claim without renouncing individuality, if 'individuality' is not equated with 'individualism': she shows that uniqueness, creativity, and moral accountability grow out of interdependence and continually turn back to it for affirmation and continuation.

Despite the predominance of individualism and autonomy-centered theories, there are historical precedents for relational constructions of subjectivity. Hegel, in the *Phenomenology of Mind*, assumes interdependence both at the level of consciousness and in the social sphere. Marx argues that human beings are constituted by his-

[19]Ibid., pp. 417, 420.

[20]Annette Baier, "Cartesian Persons," in her *Postures of the Mind: Essays on Mind and Morals* (Minneapolis: University of Minnesota Press, 1985), p. 84. The other essays I allude to are in this volume. I raise some of the issues I discuss here in my review of Baier's book in *Dialogue* 26, 1 (1987): 201–207.

torical and material circumstances: constituted as *class* members and not primarily as individuals. And Bradley maintains that it is only as a social being, a member of a community, that a person is recognizably a human, moral self. In feminist literature, Chodorow's and Gilligan's relational accounts of the psychological construction of human selves have been enormously influential. Chodorow rejects autonomous individualism for a 'relational individualism' derived from object-relations theory, in which the self is "intrinsically social . . . because it is constructed in a relational matrix and includes aspects of the other."[21] In *In a Different Voice*, Gilligan endorses Chodorow's position, but in a later piece she argues against the tendency of object-relations theory to represent the mother as an attachment figure seen primarily through the eyes of a child—a tendency that minimizes the mutuality of relationships.[22] Despite the criticisms it has prompted, Gilligan's and Chodorow's work has been a valuable resource for feminist reconstructions of subjectivity. It is important to deemphasize the object-relations and mother-blaming aspects of the latter and the essentialism of both, to focus upon the 'second person' dimension of relational subjectivity, if the work is to realize its emancipatory potential.

For Baier, moral analysis begins from a recognition that the "good and hopeful aspects of our condition, as much as the evils, stem from the fact of interdependence." Moral philosophy should promote responsible, worthy alliances and relationships, for self-realization can be achieved only relationally. Hence, with Hume, Baier rejects the possibility of a purely intellectual morality, urging the importance of educating the emotions and passions. She is less concerned to construct a universal, impartial moral theory than she is to cultivate abilities to think well about "human active capacities for cooperation."[23] Moral analysis should concentrate on virtues teachable by word and deed, hence shareable, and constitutive of evolving moral practices. These processes are more important than the development of deductive moral *systems* in which less general principles derive from more general ones.

Analogously, in epistemic activity, 'personal' knowledge depends on common knowledge. Even the ability to change one's mind is learned in a community that trains its members in conventions of

[21]Nancy Chodorow, "Toward a Relational Individualism: The Mediation of Self through Psychoanalysis," in Heller et al., eds., *Reconstructing Individualism*, p. 204.

[22]Carol Gilligan, "Remapping the Moral Domain: New Images of the Self in Relationship," in ibid., p. 245.

[23]Baier, *Postures of the Mind*, pp. 231, 218.

criticism, affirmation, and second thinking. Being self-conscious means knowing oneself to be a "person among persons," and "realization, if professed, is essentially shared. . . . *Realize* is used when I speak as a member, not an outsider."[24] The cooperative moral and epistemic practices Baier analyzes would escape the defensiveness of traditional morality that are implicit, in a different guise, in mainstream epistemology.[25]

Feminist interpretations of Baier's views will vary according to their reading of "the essential arts of personhood." There are many such arts, dependent on the kind of personhood that is expected to emerge. Female and male personhood are by no means equivalent either (abstractly) with one another or in different classes, races, and cultures. Women's continued oppression, however it is contextualized, can be attributed in large measure to the tenacity of a stereotyped ideology of 'femininity'. And the structures of child-raising practices, at least in (normative) affluent, heterosexual, western nuclear families, foster marked differences in female and male personhood. Readings of the 'essential arts of personhood' have to be sensitive to these points.

Baier's readers need not assume that a 'complete', unified personhood is the goal of instruction in these arts. In fact, her position makes it easy to defy any assumption that self-sufficient, universal Man could remain the undisputed hero of moral discourse. Her claims force theorists to examine the implications of an interdependence that is continuous, if variously located and elaborated, throughout people's histories, manifesting itself in patterns of reciprocal influence. Shifting configurations of relationships, and constant reassimilations, reinterpretations, reconstructions of personal histories, commonly in dialogue with other 'second persons', demonstrate the inadequacy of conceptions of unified, transparently self-conscious selves immune to contradiction and ambiguity, revealing no gaps in self-awareness.

I spell out these points to dispel any misconceptions that reference to the 'essential' arts of personhood might occasion. Baier's point, as I read it, is that these arts are essential to being a person *simpliciter*. Yet she is no essentialist, either in the open-textured conception of 'personhood' she articulates or in her conception of the 'arts' that a moral agent has to acquire. Her analysis is bound neither by a monolithic construal of self-realization nor by parochial ideals of 'human good-

---

[24]Ibid., pp. 89, 32.
[25]I discuss the epistemological implications of these points in the next chapter.

ness'. Hence the analysis can address the specificities of subjectivity across a range of sociocultural and political locations. Showing how persons *are* essentially second persons has the heuristic value of with-holding endorsement of the autonomy, self-sufficiency, and/or self-making that moral philosophers consider integral to an attainment of mature agency. If persons are essentially second persons, there can be no sense in assuming that they grow *naturally* to autonomous self-sufficiency, only then—perhaps cautiously, incidentally, or as an afterthought—to participate in intimate relationships. 'Second per-sonhood' becomes one of the givens that I discuss in Chapter 2, one of the objective conditions for the construction of knowledge and morality. A human being could not become a person, in any of the diverse senses of the term, were she or he *not* in 'second person' contact from earliest infancy. The example of the Wild Child of Aveyron, which I discuss in my *Epistemic Responsibility*, illustrates this point. His complete lack of 'second person' interaction prevented him from developing a recognizably 'human' agency. Autonomy and self-sufficiency define themselves against a background of second person-hood.

Baier argues that constructions of subjectivity derive from their initial formations in childhood, where a cultural heritage is transmit-ted "ready for adolescent rejection and adult discriminating selection and contribution"; she points out that "gods, if denied childhood, cannot be persons" and that "persons are the creation of persons."[26] The closeness of the relationships in which these creative processes occur in (privileged) infancy and childhood underlines the curious-ness of expectations that a training in the arts of personhood will mature into self-sufficient, autonomous adulthood. The expectations posit a sharp discontinuity between developmental processes and their alleged 'products', implying that there is a point in a life history at which development is completed. These presuppositions leave no space for the disruptions, decenterings, and contradictions that re-quire constant learning and relearning of the 'arts of personhood'. It is not easy to resist the conclusion that the constructors of autonomy-centered theories must be free to remain aloof from child-raising la-bor, and to ignore its implications in their histories and in structuring relationships. The fact that, in western affluent societies, such people are usually men, is further evidence in support of the claim that the theories bear an unmistakably androcentric stamp.

Although Baier characterizes 'second persons' descriptively, not

[26]Baier, *Postures of the Mind*, pp. 85, 86.

prescriptively, her account is normative in its recommendation that philosophers acknowledge that the good and helpful aspects of human lives, as much as their evils, derive from interdependence. 'Second person' thinking presupposes relationships qualitatively different from the ones implied in third-person talk *about* people. 'Second persons' engage with one another and care about the quality of that engagement—whether in fondness or in fury. A Sartrean constitution of other persons as starkly 'Other', as *en soi*, shows by contrast what I mean. In feminist literature, Marilyn Frye points to a sharp antithesis to 'second personhood' in the arrogant (masculine) eye, which "gives all things meaning by connecting all things to each other by way of their references to one point—Man"; she claims that, for most people, a woman existing outside the field of vision of that eye "is really inconceivable."[27] Jessica Benjamin echoes these points: "The repudiation of recognition between persons and its displacement by impersonal objective forms of social intercourse is the social homologue of the male repudiation of the mother."[28] Imposing meaning on someone else's existence from a position removed from it and ignorant of, or indifferent to, its specificities is at the furthest remove from second-person relations in their normative dimension. Impersonal interactions often mask a similar ignorance and indifference in their disinterested neutrality.

Baier makes few specific claims about *who* the second persons are who will help children acquire the sociocultural qualifications for membership in specific groups, nor are caregiver-child relationships privileged in her analysis. 'Second person' patterns of dialogue and relationship occur across the sociopolitical map. Such patterns of dialogue cannot presuppose equality between interlocutors, especially in parent-child contexts. Yet in some contexts, a project of consciously working toward promoting encounters that are hospitable to second-person dialogue can undermine intransigent inequalities. Possibilities of such dialogue exist in employer-employee, bureaucrat-client, doctor-patient relationships; across collegial and familial relationships, and in chosen personal relationships.[29] The practice of 'second

[27]Frye, *Politics of Reality*, p. 80.

[28]Jessica Benjamin, "The Bonds of Love: Rational Violence and Erotic Domination," in Hester Eisenstein and Alice Jardine, eds., *The Future of Difference* (New Brunswick, N.J.: Rutgers University Press, 1985), p. 64.

[29]A consciously adopted 'second person' pattern of action as a political strategy is elaborated in Beatrix Campbell's report of the Cleveland (Yorkshire) child-abuse cases. Campbell describes the formation, by the Leeds police force, of a team to deal with sex crime, in which the members of the team set out to develop cooperative strategies with one another and with the professionals on whom they needed to depend. Their suc-

person' discourse has the emancipatory potential to open up freer discursive spaces than those constructed and constrained by the objective, impersonal forms of address characteristic of the anonymous 'public' activities of late capitalist societies. In claiming this promise for discursive strategies, I am not ignoring the intrication of discourse and forms of address within power structures that cannot be overthrown singlehandedly or all at once. Neither, though, would it be reasonable to minimize the local successes that feminists have achieved in the micropractices of restructuring personal, social, and political institutions and relations. Many of these reconstructions start from a working hypothesis that persons are, essentially, second persons. The legacy of feminist consciousness-raising practices informs that hypothesis and often confirms its validity.

Baier takes into account the place of parenting in the construction of 'second person' subjectivity. Yet she neither identifies mothering/child raising as the 'essence' of femaleness, and hence of *value* in private life, nor does she project maternal values onto social life, as Alcoff's 'cultural' feminists often do. By contrast with the maternalist positions I shall analyze, it is worth noting that the structure of Baier's analysis—at once formal and engaged—allows it to extend into a political discourse that avoids the immobilizing implications both of cultural and of poststructuralist thinking, while keeping open a space for effective agency, alliances, and relationships. Second-person discourse can be productive across contexts in which the identities of the interlocutors vary widely: they can be groups, institutions, practices, as well as particular subjects.

Mothers and Friends

Baier's discussion of 'second persons' dovetails in some respects with Whitbeck's characterization of subjects as "relational and historical being[s] whose creativity and moral integrity are both developed and realized in and through relationships and practices." Specific relationships and practices position each life at a nexus of many other lifelines and experiences, partially separate and partially interrelated and interdependent. Creativity and integrity are interactive and mutually constitutive. People are never quite what they were or will be,

---

cess, contrasted with the ineptitude of their Cleveland counterparts, seems to have had everything to do with the forms of dialogic interaction they developed. See Beatrix Campbell, *Unofficial Secrets* (London: Virago, 1988), esp. pp. 103–111.

in the multiplicity of the relationships—economic, social, political, and environmental—that engage them. Self-other relations are played out "between beings who are in some respects analogous . . . [where] the scope and limits of that analogy . . . are something to be explored in each case," as they work to achieve the best understanding possible between beings who are "distinct and different *in some respect.*"[30] Relationships are neither essentially oppositional nor polarized. They develop "through identification and differentiation, through listening and speaking with *each other*, rather than through struggles to dominate or annihilate the other,"[31] as autonomy-centered theories suppose.

Whitbeck's analysis of relational ontology counts among the landmarks of American feminist thought of the early 1980s. Yet its commitment to the project of enabling 'private-sphere' female values to inform 'public life' places it squarely within the terms of the tensions I have been discussing, particularly in the 1990s, when a sensitivity to differences has proliferated well beyond the distinctions for which she meant to make space. That commitment is especially apparent in Whitbeck's endorsement of Ruddick's belief that 'maternal thinking' can serve as a model of self-other relationships, and Whitbeck's partial incorporation of that putative paradigm into her own position.[32]

Ruddick's conception of 'maternal thinking' is, prima facie, both appealing and compelling, a fact to which the widespread influence of her work attests. Even feminists who are critical of its substance (and I count myself among them) have derived their articulations of problems, complexities, and ambiguities from within the conceptual space she has opened up.[33] Moreover, the guiding force behind her analyses of maternal thinking has emancipatory implications, for her expressed intention is to "honor the fact that even now, and certainly

[30]Caroline Whitbeck, "Feminist Ontology: A Different Reality," in Carol Gould, ed., *Beyond Domination* (Totowa, N.J.: Rowman & Allenheld, 1983), pp. 66, 75.

[31]Ibid. The suggestion that individuals might otherwise be engaged in struggles to annihilate one another may sound excessive. Yet the (figurative) annihilation of another person in a contest, sporting event, or business deal, and the (literal) annihilation of an enemy are continuous, and each area of discourse assumes the same kind of 'personhood'.

[32]See Sara Ruddick's article "Maternal Thinking," which I cite in Chapter 1. When Whitbeck wrote her article, Ruddick's book—*Maternal Thinking*—had not yet appeared. My comments assume the publication of both the article and the book.

[33]My disagreements are elaborated in my "Autonomy Reconsidered," *Atlantis* (Spring 1988), and "Second Persons," in Marsha Hanen and Kai Neilson, eds., *Science, Morality, and Feminist Theory* (Calgary, Alberta: University of Calgary Press, 1987). Ruddick has given 'maternal thinking' a more nuanced articulation in her book.

through most of history, women have been the mothers."[34] Capitalist industrialized societies are fundamentally dependent on women to reproduce the labor force, both in the classical Marxist sense of feeding and restoring them for each day's work and in the feminist sense of reproducing the species.[35] Yet women's labor is accorded no monetary value, and minimal social recognition and esteem. Because birth and childraising are constructed in the dominant ideology as purely instinctual processes, no thought is given to the distinctive—and generalizable—modes of *reason* that must inform their effective performance. The kinds of knowledge that a mother needs to mother well rank along with the epistemologically unworthy items of wisdom and folklore for which mainstream theorists of knowledge have no time.

Ruddick's claims for 'maternal thinking', then, are at once political and epistemological. Basing her case on the premise that "distinctive ways of knowing and criteria of truth arise out of practices,"[36] Ruddick presents a detailed analysis of mothering as a paradigmatic practice. It is her contention that the epistemological moves that good mothering requires, and the attitudes that it fosters, have a scope of application and relevance well beyond the boundaries of the practice itself, just as scientific thinking stretches well beyond the confines of the laboratory. The political thrust of the argument, then, is that the epistemic values maternal thinking engenders have the capacity radically to restructure the relationships of human subjects to their human and natural environments, away from exploitation, toward preservation. In honoring mothers' work, feminists have realized, as Jane Martin puts it, that "intelligence and a certain stability of character are seldom considered maternal qualities, yet they are as important to child rearing as to other activities." She argues that "reason and self-control" have as vital a part to play in the "educative aspects of mothering"[37] as they do in any of the activities traditionally valued in patriarchal societies. In Ruddick's book, 'maternal thinking' becomes the basis for 'a politics of peace'.

In taking issue with Ruddick's position and Whitbeck's endorse-

[34]Ruddick, *Maternal Thinking*, p. 44.

[35]For a now-classic analysis of women's reproductive labor see O'Brien, *Politics of Reproduction*.

[36]Ruddick, *Maternal Thinking*, p. 13. I analyze the epistemological implications of her book in greater detail in my review essay "Will the 'Good Enough' Feminists Please Stand Up?" where I also discuss Spelman's *Inessential Woman*. The essay will appear in *Social Theory and Practice*, Spring 1991.

[37]Martin, *Reclaiming a Conversation*, p. 99.

ment of it in its earlier version, I am not denying the explanatory potential of developmental analyses. In citing Baier's claims for 'second personhood', I have declared the implausibility of believing that there could be a 'natural' state of separateness that needs to keep infringements on it carefully controlled.[38] Left on their own to develop autonomous self-sufficiency, protected from interference, infants and children would simply not survive. So there is something persuasive about the contention that analyses of subjectivity and moral agency need to take into account the constitutive roles of care, responsibility, and trust in mothering and child development. My problem is to see how such insights could warrant granting 'maternal thinking' or its close analogues (for example, family living) paradigmatic status.[39] There are better reasons against than there are in favor of this move. Not least among them is the fact that participation in nurturing and mothering activities, and the social ideologies and institutions that support them, have been instrumental in maintaining women's subordination, oppression, and economic dependence, not just because they have been assigned to women as their sphere, but because they have been managed by patriarchal expertise and constructed as a site for blaming women when anything, at any point in her/his life, 'goes wrong' with the child.

Ruddick's analysis of mothering is problematic, in fact, on a point that initially looks like as one of its strengths. She draws a painstaking, detailed picture of the day-to-day practicalities of a mother's life, complete with its failures and successes. Hence she anchors her analysis firmly within women's experiences and reads those experiences as authoritative sources of knowledge. Feminists have been rightly insistent and articulate about the need to take women's experiences seriously, to refuse the patriarchal, paternalist constructions that (male) experts are accustomed to impose on such experiences, thus taking them out of women's control. Adrienne Rich's book *Of Woman Born: Motherhood as Experience and Institution* is written precisely to reclaim motherhood as experience—and a source of women's strength—from 'expert' projects to construct it as an institution, scien-

[38]Hartsock observes: "We are born helpless and begin life within a relation that can only with great difficulty and distortion be described as an exchange relation—that between mothers and children." Hence it is absurd to think that "individuals are fundamentally isolated . . . and that initial contacts [are always] . . . based on opposing interests." Hartsock, *Money, Sex and Power*, p. 41.
[39]See Whitbeck, "Feminist Ontology," p. 75. Neither Whitbeck nor Ruddick claims explicitly that these practices have paradigm status. But the generalizability claims that they make carry paradigmatic implications.

tifically controlled, offering minimal scope for the 'maternal thinking' that Ruddick advocates.[40]

The problem is that Ruddick concentrates on motherhood as experience at the expense of developing an adequate analysis of it as institution—'institution' understood both as the domain of medical practitioners and as the social construction of mothering practice as it is implicated in the wider socioeconomic-political-racial structures of the society in which it occurs. This criticism applies more strongly to the article than the book. In the book, Ruddick is more aware of the significance of her location in shaping her account of mothering. Hence she acknowledges that her conception of 'maternal thinking' derives from the practices of the affluent, educated, American middle classes. Yet she engages in very little analysis of how that location works to construct mothering as an institution with a peculiar set of demands and frustrations. She gives scant attention to the psychological pressures and ambivalences that operate differently for women in specific sociocultural-economic circumstances. My problems with maternal thinking derive mainly from these features of the analysis.

Some of the ambivalences women experience are occasioned by changing conceptions of 'the proper way to care'—of how to be a 'good enough' mother—that emanate from the expert pronouncements of the (male) authorities who dictate the social norms of maternal practice. Contradictory directives about scientific and regulated, versus permissive and constantly attentive, caregiving fly in the face of the stereotype-informed belief that caring is, at bottom, a natural female capacity. When that belief confronts the equally strong stereotype-informed belief that women have no authority to implement their natural capacities, it is small wonder that maternal practice is often experienced as a site of conflict more bitter than any Ruddick describes. Mothering is not simply a natural response to children's needs; nor are 'children's needs' transparently and unequivocally observable. They, too, are ideologically constructed—and often highly contested—in historically, economically, culturally, and racially various forms. At one historical period or cultural place children need constant contact and attention; at other places they need to be left alone except at carefully monitored feeding times. In industrialized societies, only a certain class and group of mothers can be counted on to follow the dominant ideological pronouncements: namely, affluent

[40]Adrienne Rich, *Of Woman Born: Motherhood as Experience and Institution* (New York: Harper & Row, 1976).

women who can do the caring themselves or pay less affluent women to do it for them. Yet *their* practices constitute the norm.

Maternal thinking as Ruddick articulates it, and Whitbeck (partially) endorses it, has the effect of confirming traditional stereotypes of women—and of men. In its essentialist tendency to universalize women's 'special' qualities, it glosses over the reasons, quite apart from maternal connectedness, why women have developed these qualities fairly consistently in certain classes of western societies. The secondary place that even affluent women occupy and the limited options available to them in such societies have required women to be, and often to mother, in conformity with sexual stereotypes simply to survive. Skills that women develop in contexts of excessive dependence and in situations of relative powerlessness are at best equivocal in their political promise.[41]

The veneration of mothering practices in fact works to suppress and/or condemn ambivalences characteristic of mother-child relationships, often despite Ruddick's endeavors, especially in the book, to take ambivalence into account. The "angers and ambivalences of maternal love"[42] she refers to appear to cluster around a common, constant, core 'self'. Yet her emphasis on mother love as constitutive of maternal thinking often minimizes the power of the darker psychic forces that shape these relationships, not only when one member is really a child, but throughout their various lifetimes. Such forces are palpably at work in most parenting relations. Even in the best and most secure ones they are apparent, if minimally. Their starkest manifestations in child abuse suggest—though these would *not* be characteristic of the 'positive' maternal thinking Ruddick describes—that only a highly idealized style of mothering can generate the thinking that both Ruddick and Whitbeck find in it. The assumption of 'wholeness', 'togetherness' on the part of maternal caregivers implicit in Ruddick's analysis makes it difficult to accommodate the fact that a mother, too, is living out a particular moment of her psychic history, in which it is not always possible for her to act with the 'integrity' that maternal thinking requires.[43] Odds are against the assumption that a

---

[41]It is worth noting that 'affluent women' is a term with ambiguous reference. Class attribution on the basis of a husband's or father's class is at best tenuous, at worst deceptive. Unless women are economically self-sufficient, calling them middle-class or affluent merely includes them in the class of their more affluent partner. Such women often, in fact, are poor.

[42]*Maternal Thinking*, p. 237.

[43]Lynne Segal observes: "Mothers do not always embody conventional 'feminine' styles and behaviour for their children. The parallel between the social and the psychic is too tightly drawn in most of the fast-accumulating mother-daughter literature, with little

mother is, unequivocally, a more integrated being than a growing child: apart from all else, many mothers are young, and mothering is stressful. Assumptions about their maturity, autonomy, and wholeness require mothers to suppress their own insecurities, and to repudiate their developmental locatedness. Venerating connectedness, caring, and cooperation, and designating them *women's* values, makes it difficult for women to cope with conflicts and discords not just between women and their children, but also between and among women. Indeed, in suppressing the ambivalence common even in the exemplary relationships it extols, 'maternal' feminism relies on assumptions about human nature that are, in many respects, as reductivist, essentialist, and oppressive as those characteristic of autonomy-centered theories.[44]

This putative *repudiation* of self-sufficiency and oppositionality, then, is equally shaped by a paradigm of a unified and in some sense 'complete' subjectivity. Maternal thinking runs the risk of attempting to replace one unified individual/agent with another, who differs mainly in being collectively or altruistically, rather than individualistically, oriented. So although maternal thinkers reject autonomy-based conceptions of subjectivity, they do so by positing an ideal of 'wholeness' with prescriptive dimensions that have the potential to oppress women by inducing as much guilt as older, autonomy-prescriptive positions have done.

Feminist endeavors to revalue connectedness and caring nonetheless retain a strong appeal in disconnected and generally uncaring mass societies, governed by principles of instrumental reason. Hence wariness about the essentialism of these efforts is checked by a recurring recognition of the potential of these practices. Their elaboration requires a delicate balancing act, at once placing an appropriate emphasis on connectedness and caring, acknowledging the separateness of human subjects even in their interdependence, and taking into

consideration of all the external and internal factors which impinge upon and disrupt the 'ideal mother, ideal family' scenario." Segal, *Is the Future Female?* pp. 140–141.

[44]Mothering may sometimes work as Ruddick envisages: it would probably be a good thing for children, and even for mothers, if it did. Clearly, though, it would strain her analysis to try to show that it could apply to a mother who has "swapped one of [her children] for an alsatian dog" (Campbell, *Unofficial Secrets*, p. 144). Ruddick's thesis can afford the theoretical apparatus only for seeing this woman as an aberration from a norm. It is ill adapted to analyze the socioeconomic circumstances that produce such options. Nor can it deal with the more complex issue in which a presumption in favor of women being the practitioners of preservative love apparently requires *them* to preserve their children from sexually and punitively abusive fathers, condemns them for collusion if they do not, yet requires the fathers to take minimal responsibility for their actions. (This aspect of mothering is a constant theme in Campbell's study.)

account the fact that there are no unmediated relationships. Like the subjects who make them, relationships are located, and mediated by the structures of their location. Despite the perniciousness of autonomy-obsession, then, it is vital to draw prescriptive paradigms from practices that can promote the located and self-critical autonomy for which women must strive if they are to bring an end to their powerlessness.

It is not clear that maternal thinking can do what is required. In mothering relations throughout their duration, it is difficult to 'let go' of a child sufficiently to see her, or him, and act with her in full cognizance of her own agency; to resist treating her as a projection of her mother. Maternal thinkers' sometimes-excessive valuing of connectedness can represent such 'letting go' as neither right nor desirable. Moreover, in most feminist writing on motherhood, mothers are the 'persons' and children are the 'others'.[45] Hence maternal thinking could even provide a rationalization for inappropriate interference in a child's efforts to realize her own projects. Engaging with one's child as 'the person she or he is', however fluctuating her identity, requires more separateness than the early articulations of maternal thinking allow.

It is troubling, then, that in generating their views out of mothering practices—and even in arguing, as both Ruddick and Whitbeck do, that this kind of thinking is not open *only* to women *or* to mothers— 'maternal thinkers' privilege and sanctify this culturally overladen relation, which has been, at best, an ambiguous source of women's strength and has plainly been a constitutive force in the creation of 'autonomous man'.[46] In ideologically privileged middle- and upper-class western nuclear family structures, appropriate mothering is expected to inculcate in male children the capacity for separateness that dispassionate survival in a ruthlessly competitive market society requires. Fatherly participation, which has commonly been minimal, is directed toward reinforcing this masculine model. Only a stereotyped form of middle-class mothering, in a two-parent, heterosexual, and affluent family, really fulfills the requirements of maternal thinking. It is difficult to approve its characterization as 'maternal' when the use of the label requires so many disclaimers to extricate mothering practices from their embedded associations.

---

[45]See, for example, the essays in Joyce Treblicot, ed., *Mothering: Essays in Feminist Theory* (Totowa, N.J.: Rowman & Allenheld, 1984).

[46]See Dinnerstein, *Mermaid and the Minotaur*; Chodorow, *Reproduction of Mothering*; and Isaac Balbus, *Marxism and Domination* (Princeton, N.J.: Princeton University Press, 1982) for discussions of the contribution of 'mother-dominated' child raising to the creation of 'autonomous man'.

Some of Whitbeck's disclaimers reaffirm the potential of her relational ontology, despite her assertion that she takes the "practice of mothering and/or family living as paradigmatic."[47] She rejects the language of 'nurturing' because of its self-effacing, self-sacrificing female associations, and she explicitly dissociates her project from the practice of simply inverting patriarchal structures to affirm and celebrate 'the feminine'. Her observation that mothers learn from children just as children learn from mothers goes some way toward dealing with the problem of 'wholeness' as it is expected of maternal caregivers.

Given the force of these disclaimers, it is hard to see why maternal relationships, in particular, should be granted pride of place. It is possible to endorse Whitbeck's conception of the relational nature of subjectivity—which in this regard is close to Baier's—and to take her point that it is masculinist, patriarchal relations that are ordinarily modeled on individualistic, autonomy-oriented assumptions. It is plausible, further, to allow that a more promising conception of subjectivity can be derived from a "liberation of women's relationships and practices."[48] Yet it need not follow that mothering activity is the paradigmatic—and essential—practice.

Whitbeck's aim of constructing richer possibilities for subjectivity and agency out of relationships best and/or most commonly practiced by women would be better served by drawing on intimate friendships and close alliances. Such practices have the potential to yield a less culturally charged analysis. Friendships are created around an implicit recognition that persons are essentially (i.e., essential to their continued sense of self and well-being) 'second persons' throughout their lives. That men sometimes, too, engage in 'good' friendships—if perhaps (stereotypically) infrequently—counts further in their favor, as does the fact that friendship does not even implicitly exclude women who do not mother or who do not mother *well*. Nor does the rarity of the kind of friendship that fosters the "(mutual) realization of people"[49] detract from its potential. Such relationships are no rarer than clear and unproblematic mothering relations.

Without positing an essence of friendship or imagining it as a pure, unmediated relationship that escapes psychosocial structuring, one can note certain of its empowering features. Participants in a trusting, mutually sustaining friendship or alliance can effect and maintain a balance between separateness and appropriate interdependence. Es-

---

[47]Whitbeck, "Feminist Ontology," p. 75.
[48]Ibid., p. 79.
[49]Ibid., p. 65.

tablished friendships can cope, over time, with fluctuations in degrees of intimacy and levels of dependence and independence. That people commonly think of friendship as one of the finer relationships is apparent in observations that X is not just Y's mother, but also her friend; that A and B are not only lovers or spouses, but friends. By contrast with mothering, friendships can frequently admit of degree without engendering guilt, and they can develop out of parenting and other forms of caregiving without being essential to them or required of them. Caregiving relationships are not always friendships, but sometimes they are, and chances are that they are better thus. Friendship offers a fertile ground for the development of trust. In many ways it is more fertile than mother-child relationships, because in friendship, from the outset, there are symmetrical possibilities that rarely exist in quite the same way between mother and child, because of their obvious inequality, especially in the early years. Friendships can accommodate their own growth and can foster the growth of their participants, often by confronting ambivalences and ambiguities akin to those implicit in mother-child relations, but with the potential of being less emotionally fraught. Although intimate friendships have long been seen as women's practices, and devalued accordingly,[50] such friendships are also possible between men, and between women and men. Hence friendship can occupy the space claimed for the best forms of maternal thinking without requiring the strained rhetoric Ruddick has to develop to show how men, and childless women, can be mothers.

Friends are not interchangeable—neither are children or parents: it is not possible to substitute one friend for another and establish the same relationship. It is a paradoxical feature of individualistic thinking—in sharp contrast with 'second person' thinking—that it has no room for specificity and individuation. In its emphasis on

[50]Michel de Montaigne claims: "the ordinary capacity of women is inadequate for that communion and fellowship which is the nurse of this sacred bond; nor does their soul seem firm enough to endure the strain of so tight and durable a knot." Montaigne, "Of Friendship," in *The Complete Essays of Montaigne*, trans. Donald M. Frame (Stanford: Stanford University Press, 1965), p. 138. Vera Brittain observes that "the friendships of men have enjoyed glory and acclamation, but the friendships of women . . . have usually been not merely unsung, but mocked, belittled, and falsely interpreted." Brittain, *Testament of Friendship: The Story of Winifred Holtby* (London: Macmillan 1947), p. 2; quoted in Janice Raymond, *A Passion for Friends* (Boston: Beacon, 1986), p. 26. The friendship between Brittain and Holtby is also cited as an exemplary female friendship in Carolyn Heilbrun, *Writing a Woman's Life* (New York: Norton, 1988), pp. 99–108. Raymond notes that Freudian psychology views female intimacy as an insignificant prelude to full heterosexual maturity (see p. 224). Lillian Faderman attributes the denigration of women's friendships to the Freudian redefinition of proper heterosexual behavior for women and the labeling of women's intimate friendships as deviant and even pathological. Faderman, *Surpassing the Love of Men: Romantic Friendship and Love between Women from the Renaissance to the Present* (New York: Morrow, 1981).

impartiality and neutrality, it treats persons as indistinguishable and interchangeable: indeed, in the moral domain, it requires agents to overrule specific claims of loyalty and affection in the interest of treating all 'individuals' alike. One implication of 'mass society' is that specific and special interests often go unheard, despite the pain, discrimination, and oppression that such ignorings occasion. Yet there is no reason to believe that the claims of friendship will blind a responsible agent to considerations of fairness and justice; whereas, on the contrary, an impersonal obsession with fairness and justice, as matters for impartial adjudication, often blinds people to the specific concerns of particular persons and groups. In short, there is no prima facie reason against granting priority in moral deliberation to the quality of relationships.

In claiming that mothering (or parenting) does not count as an appropriate relational model, my interest is in *starting points*. My sense is that a better, clearer picture of the relational possibilities of parenting could result from deriving an understanding of such relationships from the features of a good friendship, rather than from working in the opposite direction. One of the most compelling reasons in favor of the friendship model is that friendships are not initially constrained by the complex power differential that must, of necessity, structure and limit their possibilities.

Aristotle develops the earliest-known extended philosophical treatment of friendship. It is clear that, for him, the capacity for friendship is as distinctive and constitutive a human characteristic as are rational and linguistic capacities. Yet individualistic theorists have neglected, and even on occasion denigrated, this aspect of Aristotle's thought. In just one notable example, W. D. Ross finds it "somewhat surprising" that Aristotle devotes two whole books of the *Nichomachean Ethics* to friendship: an anomaly Ross can explain only by noting that "the Greek word has a wider meaning than the English; it can stand for any mutual attraction between two human beings." On the whole, however, he finds the Aristotelian moral system "decidedly self-centred."[51] It is possible that Ross's Kantian orientation accounts for this reading of the friendship discussion. In any case, I draw quite different conclusions from those 'two whole books': I read them as integral to Aristotle's thoughts about virtue and happiness and about the persons who are capable of their achievement.[52]

"Surely it is strange," Aristotle writes, ". . . to make the supremely

---

[51]W. D. Ross, *Aristotle: A Complete Exposition of His Works and Thought* (1923; New York: Meridian, 1959), p. 223.

[52]In this reading I am indebted to Martha Nussbaum, *The Fragility of Goodness* (Cambridge: Cambridge University Press, 1986), esp. chap. 12, "The Vulnerability of the Good Human Life: Relational Goods."

happy man a solitary; for no one would choose the whole world on condition of being alone, since man is a political creature and one *whose nature is to live with others.*" The discussion in Books VIII and IX of the *Nichomachean Ethics* which leads up to this point makes clear that the finest and best form of 'living with others' is friendship. Indeed, even in the discussion of self-sufficiency in Book I, it is not a separate or radically independent self-sufficiency that Aristotle envisages. He derives the extension of the group that will constitute a man's self-sufficiency from the assertion that man is "born for citizenship."[53] His high esteem for friendship connects with the view that man is *essentially* a political creature. Aristotle could probably accommodate a claim about the existential priority of social, familial being as a preparation—or even as a precondition—for the actualization of a man's political nature, but only the latter has theoretical, philosophical significance for him. The point of being social is to be a member of the polis: to be a decision maker, with others, for the community.[54]

The pertinence of Aristotle's friendship discussion to my purposes derives from two interconnected considerations, which require modification because of a third, complicating factor. First, Aristotle makes friendship central to good character development, and second, the dependence of friendship on mutual acknowledgment of good character invokes important cognitive issues. Third, however, it is not possible, within the strict confines of the Aristotelian text, to claim that friendship of the best sort is possible for women—neither for women of his own class and time nor for women of the late twentieth century. Hence significant reconstructions are required if one is to read a less culture-bound, less androcentric *and* misogynist moral from Aristotle's account.

With respect to the first and second points, realizing the highest potential of moral character depends, for Aristotle, on granting due significance to love, friendship, and political associations. Friendship is "a virtue or implies virtue, and is besides most necessary with a view to living." It is more, even, than that: it is good for its own sake and noble; it is "a fine thing to have many friends; and . . . we think it is the same people that are good men and are friends."[55] The best friendship and love between men, then, is based on character and a conception of the good. There are men whom it is rational, reasonable to care for, to love, and to emulate, and Aristotle's claim is that good

[53]Aristotle, *Nichomachean Ethics*, trans. W. D. Ross, in *The Basic Works of Aristotle*, ed. Richard McKeon (1941; New York: Random House, 1971), 1169b18–21 1097b12.
[54]Joan Gibson clarified some of these points for me.
[55]Aristotle, *Nichomachean Ethics*, 1155a4–5, 1155a28–32.

friendship is possible in those (rare) circumstances where two such people find one another. Each esteems and loves the other for what that other is: for those dispositions and patterns of thought and action that are intrinsic to his being. Clearly, such a relationship is possible only if a man can know, respect, admire, and trust his friend. Indeed, on Aristotle's account, trust is central to friendship: without it, friendship can neither persist nor thrive. Trust enables a friend to learn from his friend's conduct, from a critical vantage point that is at once engaged and detached. Friendship thrives on possibilities of reliance on one another; hence it requires knowing each other's character and competence well. Otherwise it would not be so crucial either to personal well-being or to good political association. Hence forming good friendships requires a discerning cognitive capacity: it is a matter as much epistemological as affective. Friendship makes possible a peculiarly attuned knowledge and emulation of another person's character and creates a space where a friend can safely present his character and conflicts for guidance and wisdom. Friendship, for Aristotle, is based in mutuality, benevolence, and commitment,[56] in recognition of the other's separateness and independence—his appropriately understood self-sufficiency.[57]

Its cognitive dimension reveals friendship as a better exemplary relation than mothering. Friendship *requires* knowledge for its continuation: it would be impossible to sustain it in the absence of responsible mutual knowledge and trust. The relationship of mother and child, by contrast, persists, in one form or another, even when it is apparent that neither knows the other very well at all. This is one reason why a mother-child relation can be stultifying and exploitative.

Nonetheless, it is undoubtedly a manly relationship that Aristotle depicts; hence I have used masculine terminology to present it. It requires a 'generous' reading if it is to serve as a resource for feminist moral-political purposes.[58] Not only is it a manly relationship, but it is possible only for men who are citizens of the polis. Because friendship requires a common moral and legal status, it is not possible

---

[56]See ibid., 1166a1–10.

[57]This last claim may sit uneasily with Aristotle's view that friends find in one another "another self." I am reading the claim as a reference to mutual recognition of commonalities *and* differences. It might be truer to the text, however, to see friendship as a less differentiated relationship, in which both (alike) face toward the good in each other, and each sees himself reflected in the other. On this contentious point, I am opting for the more open reading of the relationship.

[58]Mary Dietz proposes a 'generous' reading of Aristotle, to which I am indebted here, in her article "Citizenship with a Feminist Face: The Problems with Maternal Thinking," *Political Theory* 13 (February 1985): esp. 27–30.

between masters and slaves, for they are neither equals nor mutually independent. Although the wife of a citizen is freer than a slave, she is inferior to her husband; hence any friendship between them can be only a pale imitation of the friendship between (male) equals.[59] The issue of friendship between women does not arise for Aristotle, but it is easy to extrapolate that, in his terms, the fact that women's reason is without authority shows that they are fitted neither to be political creatures nor, in consequence, to be properly virtuous. Given the links among virtue, equality, political being, and rational authority on which true friendship, for Aristotle, depends, it is clear that women cannot be friends in the fullest sense, either with one another or with men.

It is necessary to degender Aristotle's account to enlist it for feminist purposes. In what follows, then, I am reading *past* Aristotle's occlusion of the very possibility of female friendship, at least among free women. The task of presenting such a reading is made somewhat easier by the fact that the friends whose relationships he discusses do not manifest the most austere of twentieth-century masculine traits, nor are they autonomous men in any proto-Kantian sense. Greek friendship is at once a thoughtful passion and a bond that is superior to marriage. As such, it exemplifies relational possibilities that, according to Janice Raymond, can be "lived out by female friends in quite different ways."[60] Hence, although he writes *of* male friendships, the account is not *masculine* according to twentieth-century stereotypes. These are not self-actualizing agents, but political beings who realize their potential only in political, communal activity.

Pivotal to Mary Dietz's 'generous' reading of Aristotle is the claim that politics is not "tied to a particular "realm" . . . [but is] an activity that is primary to all other activities, be they public or private." Dietz argues that the Aristotelian view of politics as a sovereign and exclusive association extends the scope of political reference to include family practices and the relative claims of family members on an equal footing with social and economic issues and those more commonly associated with government. Hence she maintains: "Who we are allowed to be and what rights we are allowed to exercise, even in the supposed sanctity of the family, have always been and will continue to be governed by political determinations."[61] Her point is not a pessi-

---

[59]For a more extensive discussion of this point, see Spelman, *Inessential Woman*, pp. 39–41. Spelman notes that female slaves do not figure at all in the discussion: "by 'women' Aristotle means the female companion of a natural ruler, that is, a free woman, not a slave woman" (p. 41).

[60]Raymond, *A Passion for Friends*, p. 225.

[61]Dietz, "Citizenship with a Feminist Face," p. 27.

mistic, quasi-totalitarian one. Rather, she is arguing against maternal feminist appeals to a public/private distinction that protects the alleged sanctity of private values against the crassness of public, political exposure. Keeping 'the private' pure and sacred effectively immobilizes its occupants by maintaining their ignorance of the political forces that shape even their loving and caring.

Dietz's criticisms of maternal thinking as a basis for feminist political action turn on this last point. She argues—like Aristotle—that when the bonds of intimacy are extended to society as a whole, summoned in the service of political ends, the resultant denial of their inherent specificity destroys them. "The outside world can only taint or break, it cannot share, these bonds."[62] Mothers need to become politicized and act collectively as feminists, drawing on women's (historically apparent) distinctive organizational styles and modes of political discourse, not just on their ideal mothering skills. In political collectivity, women can work to secure policies that can, among other things, protect and preserve their children. They may be motivated as mothers, but they need to act as citizens.

Extricated from its entanglement in the sex-specific structures of citizenship in the polis, Aristotelian friendship can point the way to a relational analysis of subjectivity that is at once morally accountable, politically engaged, and located in 'second person' dialogues. To turn this extrication to feminist political ends without denigrating the intimate, often private nature of women's traditional friendship practices requires great care. The Aristotelian account articulates possibilities of political association and epistemic discernment which derive from good friendship. Feminists examining the history of women's friendships (to the extent that it has been recorded) find that affectionate relationships between women have often existed as "societies of consolation" and support in the crises of their lives. Yet confined, often, within the invisibility of their lives, women's friendships have been trivialized precisely because they do *not* reverberate on the public sphere or resonate within the realms of power, as the celebrated friendships between men have done.[63] It is important to retain a sense of the intensity of pleasure and affection, and of the sustaining practices that mark women's intimacy with one another, even in claiming those same friendships as a political resource. Dietz, in drawing on that resource, sometimes risks obscuring the extent of women's everyday joy in one another, in recreation and in work.

The fact that Aristotle defines friendship from the outset as a politi-

---

[62]Ibid., p. 32.
[63]I owe these points to Heilbrun, *Writing a Woman's Life*, p. 100.

cal relationship makes it possible to avoid the contortions that according 'maternal thinking' an analogous political significance would require. As a relation that is at once the locus for realizing intimate moral values, and sociopolitical values, friendship can be infused with greater, or lesser, intimacy. As a relation that depends on sensitivity and discernment, it lends itself well to epistemological elaboration.

Friendship and trust, for Aristotle, grow out of mutuality, out of "living together," not in the narrower sense that applies today to lovers, but in the broader sense of spending time in regular, familiar association, acquiring a full experience of one another's character and habits, knowing each other well. Because of its basis in *knowledge* of a friend's character, and hence of its potential for inspiration to moral growth, Aristotle remarks that: "the friendship of good men is good, being augmented by their companionship; and they are thought to become better too by their activities and by improving each other; for from each other they take the mould of the characteristics they approve—whence the saying 'noble deeds from noble men.'"[64] Wisely chosen friends enrich a person's life; unwisely chosen friends damage it.

The inspiration to emulate, Martha Nussbaum argues, comes more readily from personal intimacy and the admiration it fosters than from "more general social modelling." The intimate, engaged quality of a close relationship fosters a responsive understanding that is neither distanced nor purely intellectual, yet neither is it irrational. Nussbaum observes: "Frequently feeling guides attention and discloses to vision what would otherwise have remained concealed."[65] Feeling can, without doubt, blind a person to defects and dangers that she or he ought, with greater wisdom, to notice. But the issue here is not blind but *informed* feeling. Recognizing the cognitive value of friendship makes possible an acknowledgment of the extent to which friendship and love *can* reveal what is estimable—and infuriating, reprehensible—in another person.

The epistemic potential of friendship, as a locus for knowing other people well and for forming intelligent alliances, attests most plainly to the exemplary character of such relationships. In place of asserting a 'natural', 'found' sisterhood, appeals to friendship's epistemic dimension open up creative possibilities for achieving sound, morally and politically informed alliances, in which sisterhood, as Biddy Mar-

[64]*Nichomachean Ethics*, 1157b20, 1172a12–15.
[65]Nussbaum, *Fragility of Goodness*, pp. 363, 365.

tin suggests, "is achieved, not assumed; it is based on affinities and shared but not identical histories."[66] Alice Walker's conception of the "rigors of discernment" that such achievements demand;[67] Hannah Arendt's alignment of friendship with thinking, a considered thoughtfulness, mutual respect—her claim, for example, that "the dialogue of thought can be carried out only among friends"[68]— counter traditional associations of women's friendships with irrationality and triviality. At their best, women's friendships promote forms of solidarity that "are grounded not in claims to victimization but . . . in the convergence of shared perspectives, shared competences, and shared pleasures."[69]

Autonomy-oriented thinking concentrates on the blinding potential of loyalty and affection and yields an impoverished, wary conception of subjectivity. A relational, friendship-centered conception, by contrast, opens the possibility of granting moral priority to the very concerns about particular persons that impartiality-governed, individualistic moralities often obscure. Aristotle has no place, for example, for an impartiality principle of the kind that has figured in subsequent ethical theory. He believes, rather, that "injustice increases by being exhibited toward those who are friends in a fuller sense; e.g. it is a more terrible thing to defraud a comrade than a fellow-citizen, more terrible not to help a brother than a stranger, and more terrible to wound a father than anyone else."[70] These claims accord well with many feminists' everyday prephilosophical intuitions about the moral claims that affection and loyalty exert. But Aristotle's point is *not* that because close personal relationships demand so high a standard of justice, involvement, and benevolence, then impersonal relationships merit only minimal concern. Rather, it is that a high standard of justice is integral to a good life; the demands of love and friendship, which build on it, impose a still higher standard. In thoughtful, discerning relationships a person will not exercise loyalty blindly or whimsically, nor allow her fiercer loyalties to obliterate her broader commitments and allegiances.

The life of a person enmeshed in these affectionate and dutiful demands will be more complex and ambiguous than the life of a rule

[66]Biddy Martin, "Lesbian Identity and Autobiographical Difference[s]," in Bella Brodzki and Celeste Schenck, eds., *Life/Lines: Theorizing Women's Autobiography* (Ithaca: Cornell University Press, 1988), p. 96.
[67]Quoted in Raymond, *Passion for Friends*, p. 112.
[68]Hannah Arendt, *The Life of the Mind*, vol. 1, *Thinking* (New York: Harcourt, Brace, Jovanovich, 1978), p. 189.
[69]Martin, "Lesbian Identity," p. 92.
[70]*Nichomachean Ethics*, 1160a4–6.

utilitarian, who can follow a single moral line. But the capacity to engage self-critically and dialogically in relationships makes such complexity manageable, and the rewards are great. A morality based on justice—an elaborated neo-Kantianism—would no more suffice for feminist purposes than it does for Aristotle, who regards justice as a derivative mode (as the example of John Bold also suggests). For Aristotle, "when men are friends they have no need of justice, while when they are just they need friendship as well."[71] The autonomous moral agent would do well to read his Aristotle!

Aristotle apparently sees some aspects of the love appropriate to friendship in the love of a mother and child. Some of the same feelings are evidently at work, and similar moral and ontological considerations pertain. For example, a friend is one "who wishes his friend to exist and live, for his sake; which mothers do to their children."[72] In fact, ideal mother love may even be capable of engendering a special kind of friendship. Still, in view of the asymmetries and complexities inherent in the unequal power relation between parent and child, good friendship is better able to reveal how persons are, essentially, second persons. The point is not that unequal status and power always preclude friendship: student-teacher, patient-doctor, client-therapist, *or* parent-child relationships are sometimes, simultaneously, friendships. But this analysis reveals some of the features those relationships must have if they are to deserve the title.

Friendships are chosen relationships, just as partners to these—unequal—relations can choose to be friends. Friendship is not inherently gender specific, unlike maternal thinking, which, despite all disclaimers, retains its gendered associations. Nor are the fraught and oppressive aspects of 'the family' so integral to its potential. When a friendship threatens to manifest these features, it requires extensive negotiation to sustain it. A family relationship persists, through manifold distortions and abuses. Friendship is descriptively and evaluatively appropriate to designate an exemplary, constitutive relationship with close, intimate, and wide political scope. Finally, and particularly noteworthy, is the careful, reciprocal, nonimperialistic nature of the knowing on which good friendship depends. This exemplary 'second person' way of knowing another person affords a

---

[71]Ibid., 1155a26–27.

[72]Ibid., 1166a4–5. Nussbaum writes of the relationships "*that would not be classified as friendships*" which are included in the extension of the Greek term *philia* (commonly translated 'friendship', though not by her) and claims that "the love of mother and child is a paradigmatic case of *philia*." Nussbaum, *Fragility of Goodness*, p. 354, emphasis added.

preliminary model for a restructured subject-object relation that could displace ideal objectivity and move toward a reconstruction of cognitive activity and epistemic goals.

Moral Practice

It may be no coincidence that, in Trollope's novel, it is a woman— his sister—who dissuades John Bold from the dogged pursuit of his reformist project, urging him to acknowledge the moral claims of his loves and allegiances. Out of just such an apparently coincidental gender differentiation in moral response Carol Gilligan has developed the thesis that, in moral matters, male and female agents speak in different voices.[73] Indeed, if 'the John Bold dilemma' were presented to Gilligan's subjects, male responses might resemble Bold's own; female subjects might attend to the issues his sister finds more important.

Gilligan's project is to reinterpret Lawrence Kohlberg's measurements of moral maturity. She contends that the tendency of female subjects consistently to score lower on these tests than male subjects results not from a defect in female moral reasoning, but from a systemic problem with the tests themselves. Critical rereadings reveal that differences between standard 'female' and standard 'male' responses to the tests derive from markedly different conceptions of subjectivity and of self-other relations. These differences do not turn wholly on divergent evaluations of autonomy, yet the subjects who achieve the highest scores consistently value the *autonomous* endorsement of universalizable moral principles. These subjects are consistently male. Female responses tend to manifest a concern with relationship, connectedness, and caring. Gilligan believes that women's statistically greater tendency to respond thus can be explained in terms of the structures of mother-dominated child-rearing practices. Marking these two moral voices as 'masculine' and 'feminine' is not a matter of biological necessity, for both 'voices' are available to women and men alike.

---

[73]The position I refer to is developed in *In a Different Voice*. I introduce it with the claim that women and men speak in different voices, rather than adhering to Gilligan's formulation, in which *women* speak in *a* different voice—from men's. The rephrasing is important, first, because it catches the symmetry of difference. If women speak in a different voice from men, then men speak in a different voice from women. Second, and concomitantly, it refuses the assumption that the male 'voice' constitutes the norm, from which the female voice deviates. In discussions of political differences, the dominant voice commonly counts as the norm, from which the muted voice is marked as different.

Gilligan does not elaborate a 'feminine' alternative to traditional, autonomy-oriented moral and political theories, nor do the theoretical underpinnings of her work permit such a development.[74] Her principal contribution to the deconstruction of autonomous subjectivity is in the evidence she produces to demonstrate the arbitrariness of psychological assumptions that autonomy is a 'natural' end product of human development. Hence the hegemony of autonomy-centered moral positions is revealed as an assumed, not a natural, hegemony. It is by no means clear that Gilligan's findings point toward the development of a moral *theory* that grants center stage to the 'different' voice whose worthiness they affirm. Despite her insistence that this is a voice in which all can speak, its stereotypical female associations are so strong that granting it the main, or even an equal, speaking part would amount to a celebration of 'the feminine', with its implications of essentialism and complementarity intact. In Gilligan's analysis the question is not raised as to how the politics of discourse might construct different possibilities for female and male voices in different class, racial, cultural, ethnic, and economic contexts, in different age groups, or in the context of different sexual preferences.

Any simple celebration of 'female values' that aims to revalue them yet leave them intact ignores both the circumstances of oppression that have constructed them and the constraints that commonly attach to them. 'Connectedness' is a salient example. Even for privileged women, concentration on family and community has limited their ability to contest exploitation and has contributed to their powerlessness and oppression. Efforts to juxtapose a new ethics of caring and responsibility against a traditional ethics of rights and justice perpetuate dichotomies between duty and inclination, public and private, reason and emotion, and lead easily into a belief that the former, female morality expresses the lesser, parochial concerns of women; the latter, male morality addresses the more serious, global concerns of men. Hence women can, again, be charged with the moral guardianship of society, left to take care of its softer, more emotional requirements, which are merely supplemental to the 'real' business of morality.

A serious obstacle in the way of claiming a hearing for Gilligan's 'different' voice is that the claim has to be made from a position of relative powerlessness. When and how the voice can be heard, then,

---

[74]Gilligan's work has, nonetheless, been the catalyst for an enormous amount of scholarship in moral philosophy. One representative collection is Eva Kittay and Diana Meyers, eds., *Women and Moral Theory* (Totowa, N.J.: Rowman & Littlefield, 1987).

is often not within the power of its possessors to decide. Indeed, to go back a step further, the very 'needs' of which and terms in which the voice has learned to speak in western patriarchal societies are themselves constructed in situations of dominance and oppression. Hence critical moral analyses need to begin not with values and principles in the abstract, but with culturally situated social, political, and moral relations and the patterns of power and subordination they legitimate. Evidence from studies of American minority groups, for example, associates the development of a 'caring' morality more closely with marginal social status than with gender difference tout court. Joan Tronto proposes, therefore, that "if moral difference is a function of social position rather than gender, then the morality Gilligan has identified with women might better be identified with subordinate or minority status."[75] Moralities that derive from marginal, oppressed status are not for that reason alone of questionable political worth: often they work effectively as survival mechanisms. The point of articulating their derivation is to understand the cognitive and evaluative mechanisms that inform them and to develop strategies of social intervention that can permit an intelligent assessment of their potential.

There is no doubt that the displacement of the autonomous moral agent leaves a gap. It is not so clear, however, that the best move is to produce an alternative moral *theory*, in which lesser principles derive from more general or universal ones, in a deductive theoretical structure. Perhaps the most radical effect of feminist moral critiques is their demonstration that moral theories close off more possibilities of discernment and action than they create. A more productive route is to claim broader scope for engaged yet thoughtful *practices*, whose value is obscured by theories that pose as products of analysis but serve, rather, to foreclose it. The point, as Baier puts it, is to examine different ways of *being* moral agents: to work toward developing teachable and liveable moralities, sensitive to the sociopolitical contexts in which people need to live well and to sustain their relationships.[76]

Some of Gilligan's subjects, in their approach to moral dilemmas, engage in a style of deliberation markedly different from that common to the rubric of Kantian or utilitarian morality. Both in what they perceive as relevant and in their apprehension and structuring of experiences, these subjects adopt a deliberative posture analogous to

[75]Joan Tronto, "Beyond Gender Difference to a Theory of Care," *Signs: Journal of Women in Culture and Society* 12 (Summer 1987): 649.

[76]Annette Baier, "Doing without a Moral Theory," in *Postures of the Mind*, p. 232. My thoughts in this paragraph are prompted by Baier's discussion.

(Aristotelian) practical reasoning (*phronesis*). Their decision making is marked by a thoughtfulness that contrasts sharply with the Kantian concentration on achieving a principled moral stance, which carries over into Kohlberg's work. But this is not the standard utilitarian contrast. The concern at its core is less with consequences than with the *implications* of her actions and motives, both for the other people to whom the moral agent is accountable and who are affected by or implicated in her actions, and for herself.

To discern these implications, a person has to position herself critically within a situation, in relation to its various aspects, so as to take imaginative account of as many of these implications as she can, while not destroying her capacity to act. Annette Kuhn's provocative phrase, "passionate detachment,"[77] captures the epistemic posture that makes such deliberation possible. Like the attitude of a good therapist to a client—a kind of objective sympathy, a mode of participation without intervention, of compassion without passion—such knowing is at once involved and appropriately distanced. It requires a kind of perception that is, to quote Nussbaum, "both cognitive and affective at the same time . . . [that] consists in the ability to single out the ethically salient features of the particular matter at hand . . . in appropriate emotional response as much as through intellectual judgment."[78] A moral agent positions and repositions herself within a situation to become clear about what is at issue and to examine possible courses of action—always within the situation, for no removed, God's-eye vantage point is available.[79]

A cluster of 'traditionally female' values may indeed prove to be worthy guiding and/or regulating principles for practical deliberation: trust, kindness, responsiveness and responsibility, honesty and care could figure prominently. But in some circumstances it would be more appropriate to act in accord with efficiency-maximizing and autonomy-promoting values. Hence it is equally important, for this reconstructed moral standpoint, to ensure that the values and regulative principles invoked are appropriately responsive to the context.[80]

---

[77]See Annette Kuhn, *Women's Pictures: Feminism and Cinema* (London: Routledge & Kegan Paul, 1982), chap. 1.

[78]Nussbaum, *Fragility of Goodness*, p. 364.

[79]I introduce the ideas of 'positioning' and 'repositioning' in my "Experience, Knowledge, and Responsibility," in Morwenna Griffiths and Margaret Whitford, eds., *Feminist Perspectives in Philosophy* (Bloomington: Indiana University Press, 1988); reprinted in Ann Garry and Marilyn Pearsall, eds., *Women, Knowledge, and Reality: Explorations in Feminist Philosophy* (Boston: Unwin Hyman, 1989).

[80]Held maintains that the moral deliberation she advocates in *Rights and Goods* "can be plausible only if one's conception of morality includes both deontological and tele-

The Aristotelian orientation of this approach prevents its deterioration into an opportunistic situationism. Modes of deliberation vary qualitatively, according to the character and cognitive capacities of the deliberator, and are constantly available to critical evaluation. Hence a deliberative morality is at once open-textured, dialogic, and open to criticism, self-criticism, and debate. It leaves scope for trial and error, for showing that certain practices are not conducive to the production of social institutions and sociopolitical environments where people can live well. It requires a finely tuned moral-political awareness to avoid, at once, extreme relativism, conservatism, and mere tolerance. Held proposes that moral inquiry needs "something comparable to but not the same as the encounter with experience by which scientific theories are tested."[81] In such testing procedures, some practices will emerge as more appropriate than others, better able to promote empowering relationships and alliances, less liable to marginalize and oppress. Often it is easier (on an analogy with a falsifiability theory) to discern the *in*appropriateness of certain practices than it is to discover which ones, unequivocally, are best. Finding out how people should act now, in these circumstances, is like unraveling a detective story: often it is abundantly clear how things could not/should not be long before anyone knows how they were or should be.

Moral agents always make choices from specific positions vis-à-vis other persons, within specific environmental circumstances. There is no transcendent vantage point from which to judge them. Hence moral deliberators have to maintain a continuity with moral histories and experiences that are filtered out by ideal, impartial theories for which autonomy itself, in another connotation, entails freedom from the contingencies of circumstance. Although a critical, deliberative morality is a more modest option than theory construction, it has a greater potential to accommodate the subtleties of the experiences of real, gendered, historically located subjects, for whom the traditionally autonomous, impartial moral agent is a seriously flawed character.

---

ological components and allows for different resolutions of tensions between egoistic and communal claims in different domains. A pure Kantian, a pure utilitarian, a pure egoist, and a pure communitarian would find the analysis . . . hard to reconcile with his or her morality." Held, *Rights and Goods*, p. 35.

[81]Ibid., p. 59.

CHAPTER FOUR

The Autonomy of Reason

Cognitive Autonomy

Epistemological analogues to the role of autonomy in received conceptions of moral agency are apparent in a set of assumptions to the effect that knowers, like moral agents, are autonomous, self-sufficient individuals. Although autonomy does not have precisely the same connotations in its ethical and its epistemic senses, or in its Cartesian and its positivistic senses, the conception of subjectivity presupposed in these contexts is virtually identical. The effects of these presuppositions, in theory of knowledge, are analogous to their effects in moral philosophy. Yet once the implications of autonomous epistemic agency are critically examined, the conclusion suggests itself that persons are as essentially 'second persons' in epistemic activity as they are in moral activity.

Beliefs that knowers can and should be self-sufficient, and that objects of knowledge are independent and separate from them, yield a composite picture of knowledge in which autonomy is a privileged value. A dominant feature of this picture is the assumption that knowledge is a *product* of inquiry that stands alone in the sense that details of the processes of its production are irrelevant to its structure, content, and/or evaluation. This assumption connects with the view that knowledge worthy of the name is timelessly and placelessly true, and that its objects are independent in the senses both of being disconnected from knowing subjects and of being inert in and unaffected by the knowing process. Empiricist theorists, in particular, believe that perception and memory play a significantly greater role in knowledge acquisition than testimony, where 'testimony' is construed quite broadly to include everything that a knower learns from other people rather than by his own independent efforts. 'Testimony' covers a wide range, from parental and classroom instruction, to acquiring information from other people in any number of contexts, to learning from media reports, textbooks, and learned articles. In contrast with Baier's claim about the dependence of individual memory on group memory, empiricists hold that memory, like perception, functions individually and independently. Hence cognitive interdependence can be acknowledged only with respect to reliance on testimony. But testimony is accorded minimal significance—and dependability—as a source of knowledge. A distrust of testimony, which is often equated, evaluatively, with opinion or hearsay, works to denigrate interdependence and to reinforce a belief in epistemic self-reliance that is implicit in most received theories of knowledge.

Theorists who adhere to this 'autonomy of knowledge' persuasion[1] maintain that knowledge properly so-called transcends experience, whose particularity can only sully and muddle its purity and clarity. Hence they posit a rift between practice and theory which privileges theory over practice. This rift is particularly evident in the method of abstracting simplified (hence clarified) exemplary knowledge claims to demonstrate the possibility, verifiability, and appropriate strategies for justifying knowledge claims. Epistemologists are rarely concerned that such samples should show how people know in their everyday lives. What matters is that a sample reveal the nature and conditions of knowledge through its exemplary nature. Indeed, it might be a mistake to locate a sample claim in the world, to contextualize it, because mixing it in with the muddle and contingency of real situations diminishes its clarity and results in theoretical inadequacy. The *individual*, autonomous knowers who produce such knowledge claims are the same abstract individuals who are the heroes of mainstream moral discourse. Their specificity and their cognitive 'location' count for nothing. Moreover, should such contextual issues threaten to intrude into epistemological discussion, that intrusion will have to be suppressed. These are the knowers who occupy the 'S' position in the 'S knows that p' rubric: the knowers whose vantage point is, at once, everywhere and nowhere. Their *autonomy* legitimates them as know-

---

[1]Harding uses this phrase in her article "Why Has the Sex/Gender System Become Visible Only Now?" She attributes it to David Bloor, *Knowledge and Social Imagery* (London: Routledge & Kegan Paul, 1977).

ers through a set of evaluative processes that gives them every reason to resist suggestions that, in knowledge, they could be essentially 'second persons'.

Whereas the autonomous *moral* agent makes his most unequivocal appearance as the hero of Kantian moral discourse, the autonomous epistemic agent is most strikingly visible as the pursuer of the Cartesian "project of pure enquiry."[2] A follower of Descartes's method is radically independent, adhering to the method in a process of solitary rational endeavor and embarking on that pursuit by freeing *him*self both from his previously accumulated beliefs and habits of mind and from the influence of his own physical being. This extrication accomplished, he works toward a subjective, individual certainty. As I note in Chapter 1, reason is autonomous in the Cartesian project in two senses. First, the quest for certain knowledge should be an independent one, undertaken separately by each rational being; and second, that quest is a journey of reason alone, unhindered—and hence also unaided—by the senses. Despite Descartes's acknowledgment of the benefits of cooperative scientific inquiry, and despite the fact that knowing exercises the faculty of reason that is common and alike in all knowers, his account of knowledge seeking is of an introspective activity that depends neither on the embodied nature of a knower nor on his (or her) intersubjective relations.

Construals of cognitive autonomy and self-sufficiency vary throughout the history of western philosophy both before and after Descartes—from Plato's insistence, in the *Republic*, that the last step toward knowledge of the unhypothesized hypothesis (toward "that which requires no assumption and is the starting point of all")[3] must be made by each would-be knower separately and singly, through to the primacy Bertrand Russell accords to knowledge-by-acquaintance. But through these variations runs a constant thread of belief in the importance of detachment, impartiality, neutrality, and cognitive self-reliance for knowers worthy of that name. Out of these beliefs emerges the stark conception of objectivity I discuss in Chapter 2. The interdependence of objectivity and autonomy will be apparent: only a knower who is autonomous in the self-reliant sense—and reliant on reason alone—could be as objective as that stark conception requires; and, conversely, such objectivity is achievable only by a knower who

[2]The allusion is to the title of Bernard Williams's book *Descartes: The Project of Pure Enquiry* (Harmondsworth: Penguin, 1978).
[3]Plato, *Republic*, trans. Benjamin Jowett, in *The Collected Dialogues of Plato*, ed. Edith Hamilton and Huntington Cairns (Princeton: Princeton University Press, 1961), 511b.

is autonomous in having achieved detachment and impartial neutrality in his epistemic activity.

Although Kant's epistemological project differs markedly from Descartes's, Kant is as committed as Descartes is to a conception of the autonomy of reason. This commitment is evident, particularly, in his separation of reason from the vagaries of experiences and in his intention to develop a theory of understanding *as such*—of what it is and how it must function if knowledge is to be possible at all. The point is not that Kant wants to arrive at an account of knowledge that is unconstrained by experience. Rather, he wants to establish the a priori conditions of experience and knowledge. To that end, he maintains that transcendental argument can lead to "knowledge which is occupied not so much with objects as with the mode of our knowledge of objects in so far as this mode of knowledge is to be possible *a priori*."[4] The knowing subject for whom such knowledge is possible is any being who can use the term 'I' to identify *him*self as the subject of experience, any being for whom the formal conditions of knowing can be established. Hence the analysis Kant offers is of the knowledge of a 'standard knower', undifferentiated from other knowers by any of his particular traits or by any of the contingent circumstances in which he might acquire his knowledge. With his doctrine of the transcendental self (the transcendental unity of apperception), Kant's concern is not to present a self-aware subject aware of his (or her) own nature, idiosyncrasies, and specificity, nor to define 'the self' as an entity *in* the world. He is interested in the self only as a limiting point of empirical knowledge. As an aspect of that self, then, reason is autonomous, as it is concomitantly in functioning independently of all particular circumstances, either personal or contextual. In all of these repects the Kantian knowing subject is identical with the Kantian moral agent—autonomous and impartial, his moral and epistemic consciousness alike determined by reason quite untainted by affectivity (inclination). Like the Cartesian reasoner, the Kantian epistemic agent is a subject whose physical embodiment plays a minimal role in his intellectual life.

Despite the avowed transcendental aim of his epistemology, Kant's Copernican Revolution in philosophy opens possibilities for interpretations of human knowledge which Kant himself probably did not intend. This opening is a consequence of his placing the knowing

[4]Immanuel Kant, *The Critique of Pure Reason*, trans. Norman Kemp Smith (London: St. Martin's, 1929), B 25.

subject at the center of the cognitive process, and of his conception of knowledge as a *creative* synthesis of the imagination. Because the imagination is active in its creativity, it is by no means fanciful to find in Kantian epistemology the scope for elaborating a position (albeit by diverging from Kant's initial aims) in which creativity admits of specific variations according to whose it is and when and where it is practiced. It is true that Kant posits ahistorical, universal categories of understanding and conditions of knowability. Yet, for him, the mind does not merely 'read off' what it is given, what is there in the world. The intellect is no passive recording instrument, but an active creator—constructor—of knowledge. Hence Kant prepares the way for analyses of knowledge as construct and for contextualizing epistemic activity so that the knower, and not just the known, comes under epistemological scrutiny.[5] In consequence of these Kantian moves, a theoretical space becomes available for acknowledging the epistemological significance of the question, Whose knowledge are we talking about?—a question that is central to feminist epistemological inquiry. In short, Kant's epistemology is a rich resource for analyses of knowledge that take human specificity into account yet, because of its dependence on formal conditions, does not reduce to stark subjectivism.

The 'autonomy of knowledge' credo is as strong in empiricism and positivism, both early and in their more recent variants, as it is in Cartesian and Kantian epistemology. Most of the attributes that implicitly characterize a knower in empiricist-positivistic theories of knowledge—implicitly, since knowers themselves rarely figure explicitly in the discussion—coincide with the attributes of an autonomous Kantian or Cartesian knower. Detached, neutral, objective observations, possible for all 'normal' knowers under 'normal' observation conditions, are the basis of empiricist-positivistic knowledge claims. Any knowledge worthy of the name is analyzable into simple observational components whose accuracy is demonstrable on the basis of a correspondence relation in whose terms perceptual observations are *caused* by corresponding items in the visual, or other perceptual, field. No questions arise as to the influence of prejudgment or emotions on the observational process, nor is it conceivable that observation could be value-laden. Observations are interchangeable and constantly replicable, for all knowledge is acquired by the same

---

[5]My *Epistemic Responsibility* takes this aspect of Kantian epistemology as its starting point.

methods. Hence it makes no difference who the knower is. The disparate, historically located embodiment of such knowers is irrelevant, for the assumption is that a knowledge claim can and should be analyzed and evaluated on its own merits. Knowers whose knowledge derives from such perceptual observations are the same abstract individuals whose utilitarian or contractarian *moral* judgments are based in impartiality and utility.

The pivotal place of the autonomy of reason in Descartes's philosophy may make it seem odd that Baier should develop her notion of second personhood with reference to *Cartesian* persons. Yet the notion is implicit and available for development in Descartes's own thought—specifically, in his observations about language and about the epistemic status of childhood experiences. If persons must be second persons even for Descartes, with his strong endorsement of the autonomy of reason, then it must follow that 'second personhood' is as essential as Baier believes.

Now there is no doubt that Descartes distrusts language as it contrasts with the certainty of pure thought. He states in the *Meditations* that "although without giving expression to my thoughts I consider all this in my own mind, words often impede me and I am almost deceived by the terms of ordinary language."[6] In the *Rules*, he remarks that "verbal questions are of such frequent occurrence, that almost all controversy would be removed from among Philosophers, if they were always to agree as to the meaning of words."[7] For Descartes, the route to certain knowledge would be easier and less hazardous were one never obliged to resort to speech, but could rely on reason alone. Nonetheless, Baier notes, when they move out of the theoretical mode, "Cartesian persons and embodied Cartesian thinkers *speak*."[8] As persons, if not as pure intellects, Cartesian thinkers engage in conversation. It is true, however, that Descartes does not consider language *essential* to thought. But behind this Cartesian disbelief lies not just a distrust of language, but a failure to notice how much that very distrust depends on language itself. Indeed, Alasdair MacIntyre suggests that it is just because his knowledge of languages (i.e., of French and Latin) is "invisible to . . . Descartes" that he overlooks the extent to which his radical doubting leaves undoubted those very languages whose structures order "both thought and the world

[6]René Descartes, *Meditations*, p. 155.
[7]René Descartes, *Rules for the Direction of the Mind*, in *Philosophical Works*, trans. Haldane and Ross, 1:51.
[8]Baier, "Cartesian Persons," in *Postures of the Mind*, p. 80.

expressed in a set of meanings."[9] His doubt is by no means as absolute as he believes. Hence Descartes fails to take into account the extent to which the languages in which he expresses his doubt are bearers of a tradition from which he has inherited the epistemological ideals that inform his quest for automous rational certainty and on which his radical doubting depends. The theoretical mode is dependent on habits and skills acquired in the speaking (embodied) mode, in a tradition that Descartes could have absorbed only as a second person, a person who conversed with and was taught by others.

Baier is well aware that Descartes would have accorded no more *epistemological* significance to childhood learning processes than he would have accorded to the capacity of language to shape the operations of reason. Descartes sees childhood as a stage of existence that sets up the "obstacles," such as docility, acceptance of authority, and a preoccupation with bodily appetites, "whose overcoming constitutes intellectual progress."[10] Descartes observes that "since we have all been children before being men . . . it is impossible that our judgments should be so excellent or solid as they should have been had we had complete use of our reason since our birth, and had we been guided by its means alone."[11] But Baier argues that it is precisely because people have been children, have not been guided by the pure light of reason, but have lived embodied lives, dependent on guidance from other people, that pure rationality has the appeal that it does for Descartes. She writes: "Without earlier confusion to reflect on, a Cartesian intellect would have no purpose. Its ends, like ours, are set by its beginnings."[12] Those beginnings could not have evolved into an adulthood in which their repudiation is possible had one not, in childhood, been a second person. There would have been no one to ensure the child's survival and growth, nor to teach him the languages whose structures mirror and are mirrored in rational thought. By highlighting these underelaborated aspects of Descartes's metaphysics of the person—by reading it 'against the grain'—Baier shows that even Cartesian persons, those most independent of knowers, are essentially second persons.

[9]Alasdair MacIntyre, "Epistemological Crises, Dramatic Narrative, and the Philosophy of Science," *The Monist* 60, 4 (1977): 458.

[10]Baier, "Cartesian Persons," p. 83.

[11]Descartes, *Discourse on the Method*, p. 88.

[12]Baier, "Cartesian Persons," p. 86.

Reason and Masculinity

The significance for feminist thought of the contention that autonomous reason is grounded, after all, in second personhood may not be immediately apparent. The point is not that women, with their essential connectedness, have always acknowledged the fact of second personhood, whereas men have denounced it in the name of masculine self-sufficiency; hence that communal, dialogic inquiry is a feminine mode, and its avoidance in the name of autonomy a masculine plot. Nor is it that there is a separate, female, 'second person' way of knowing that speaks in a different voice from male cognitive autonomy. Yet beneath such implausible simplifications is a subtler truth whose implications merit feminist attention.

Throughout the history of western philosophy there is a demonstrable alignment between the ideals of autonomous reason and ideals of masculinity. That alignment suppresses and even denigrates values and attributes long associated with 'the feminine' at the same time and in the same way as it devalues epistemic dependence in the name of cognitive self-reliance. Both philosophical discourse and the everyday ideology that bears its mark take universal, essential (though sometimes evolving) conceptions of masculinity and femininity for granted. There is no consideration of specific differences between men, except insofar as these can be counted as aberrations from the prevailing norm. Yet the ideals of masculinity that align with ideals of reason derive—locally, specifically—from the experiences of the men who construct the dominant theories of both. The conceptions of femininity that contrast with masculinity—and with reason—are the theoretical constructions of that same group of men. It is a commonplace of western philosophy and folklore, then, that women are irrational creatures, either inferior or utterly lacking in reason. Man may indeed be a rational animal, but the history of western thought makes it clear that 'man' in this context is not a generic term. Implicitly or explicitly, rationality is an attribute of masculinity.

A claim that men are rational beings, whereas women are not, is untenable by anyone who gives serious attention to the bias and false essentialism that sustains this folklore where it still enjoys credence. But there is, nonetheless, a problem about reason for women and for feminists. In *The Man of Reason*, Genevieve Lloyd traces the historical development of western ideals of Reason. Although variously articulated, these ideals are markedly consistent in defining themselves by

contrast with and exclusion of traits, values, and attributes unquestioningly marked 'feminine'. 'Feminine', in this context, refers not to
those derivative qualities that define present-day stereotypes of 'woman': qualities such as delicacy, seductiveness, empty-headedness, and
frivolity. Rather, in its early philosophical origins, it refers to a metaphysical principle that separates an entire aggregate of characteristics
attributable of entities in the world, both animate and inanimate, into
positive, masculine qualities and negative, feminine ones. In the
Pythagorean table of opposites, *maleness*, like limit, light, good, and
square, are associated with determinate form; *femaleness*, unlimited,
dark, bad, and oblong, with (inferior) formlessness.[13] Variations on
and derivations from these earlier principles inform subsequent philosophical analyses of the relative rational capacities of women and men
and feed ultimately into popular stereotypes of femininity (and masculinity) that are still in common currency, the best feminist efforts
notwithstanding.

Lloyd's claims require careful interpretation. Hers is not the facile
contention that what is true and rational for men is untrue and irrational for women—that reality, knowledge, reason, and rationality
divide neatly into 'his' and 'hers'. She is arguing neither that the
history of philosophy is "consistently and *obsessively devoted to* the
exclusion or transcendence of the feminine" nor that conceptions of
'maleness' have been historically and culturally invariant, as Susan
Bordo suggests.[14] Lloyd's point, as I understand it, is that in spite of
explicit avowals to the contrary (by such philosophers as Augustine
and Descartes), Reason nonetheless persists as an ideal that incorporates attributes valued as masculine and is defined in terms of them.
That incorporation is accomplished by suppressing traits that are devalued because of their associations with 'the feminine'. Far from
being products of an 'obsessive devotion' to devaluing femininity,
articulated ideals of Reason, often despite their author's expressed
intentions, attest to the cultural embeddedness of those early metaphysical principles and their latter-day variants and to their constitutive effects in philosophical thought. Nor has a constant 'male' principle or a constant conception of masculinity prevailed unaltered since
ancient times. Yet throughout (western) historical and cultural variations in conceptions of maleness, of masculinity, *and* of reason, there

[13]See Lloyd, *Man of Reason*. Lloyd discusses the Pythagorean opposites on p. 3 and
compares them with Philo's 'distinctions of existence' on p. 25.

[14]Susan Bordo, *The Flight to Objectivity: Essays in Cartesianism and Culture* (Albany:
State University of New York Press, 1987), p. 9, emphasis added.

is a remarkable coincidence among the definitions, symbolisms, and associations of masculinity and those of Reason, a coincidence too remarkable to be merely coincidental.

Reason is discursively constructed as an object of descriptive and normative analysis, in a philosophical discourse whose symbols and metaphors shape *and* are shaped by dominant conceptions of knowing. The alignment of Reason with masculinity is more than simply a matter of using a neutral, transparent symbolism that does not affect the 'actual' situations it symbolizes, nor is reason a 'natural' kind or item. Lloyd shows that ideals of Reason, throughout their shifting and evolving history, designate what it is to be a good knower, determine what counts as knowledge and as a proper object of knowledge—and prescribe the "proper relations between our status as knowers and the rest of our lives."[15] In short, these ideals have had a tacit yet constitutive effect on the shape of western metaphysics, epistemology, and ethics: an effect that has filtered through into popular conceptions of what knowledge is, who knowers are, and whose knowledge claims are authoritative.

Feminists cannot simply claim a place for women within the androcentric domains of Reason and rationality except by affirming women's right to inclusion within a *masculine* conception of Reason. Resistance against such a project is of a piece with feminist resistance to the exclusionary, immobilizing structures of dichotomous thinking. It does not signal an endorsement of the stereotype according to which those structures are inherently, naturally male and therefore only aberrantly, unnaturally female. There is no doubt that a false essentialism informs both male and female stereotypes. But hegemonic ideals of reason are constructed out of symbolisms, qualities, and modes of thought that map accurately onto, and are mirrored by, hegemonic ideals of masculinity. The constitutive elements of ideal masculinity are opposed in the manner of Aristotelian A/Not-A contradictories to the elements that generate received conceptions of femininity.[16] So there is no place on the terrain of Reason to which women can claim rightful occupancy.

The problematic of Reason, for feminists, plays into the tension I discuss in Chapter 3. Many feminists are convinced that traits associated with essential femininity—responsibility, trust, and a finely

---

[15]Lloyd, *Man of Reason*, p. ix.
[16]See my discussion of Nancy Jay's article "Gender and Dichotomy" in Chapter 1.

tuned intuitive capacity, for example—are *epistemically* valuable.[17] They contribute positively to emancipatory epistemic practices and can be turned effectively to political ends. Some of the same feminists explicitly dissociate themselves from the practices that ideal Reason/masculinity underwrites: adversarial, territorial, impartial epistemic practice is the most salient example. But within the terms of the Reason/masculinity construct, 'feminine' attributes are, in effect, attributes of unreason. Women have to eschew those qualities and practices to enter the domain of Reason: they must either repudiate their sense that experiences and emotional responses contribute to objective knowing or map out separate, 'women's ways of knowing', which qualify neither as authoritative nor rational within the dominant structures.

A set of traits that are discursively, ideologically constitutive of masculinity cannot simply shift or expand to incorporate women and retain their referential and evaluative scope. Women who seek inclusion will at best achieve the status of aliens, immigrants, whose presence is tolerated not on their own terms, but on the natives' terms. Their efforts to find a place within the discursive construct will be treated as outsider, imitative behavior, and discounted without disturbing the stereotyped boundaries of masculinity or of femininity. Consider autonomy. Its construction and valuation as a masculine character trait either effaces the very possibility of female autonomy or asserts that the autonomy women achieve is of different worth. Jane Martin observes that "when a woman displays . . . rationality and autonomy . . . she is derided for what are considered negative, unpleasant characteristics, even as her male colleagues are admired for possessing them."[18] Autonomy and rationality are not the gender-neutral traits many philosophers have assumed.

In short, dichotomously polarized terms are absolute and mutually exclusive opposites. Reason has no part of emotion, cognitive autonomy excludes all forms of dependence, both on other people and on the knower's own sensory, bodily apparatus. Entry into the domain of Reason requires a denial of epistemic value to affectivity in all of its

---

[17]Wendy Hollway records her conscious decision to resist her "horror of using the word 'intuitive'" to explore her intuition. She observes: "My intuition was not some primitive product of my feelings, in contrast to the use of reason (the significance it has through being associated with women). I *knew* which people . . . would be more likely to be aware of the issues that I was interested in." Hollway, *Subjectivity and Method in Psychology: Gender, Meaning, and Science* (London: Sage, 1989), p. 16, emphasis added.

[18]Martin, *Reclaiming a Conversation*, p. 32. Martin is referring to James Watson's depiction of Rosalind Franklin in *The Double Helix*.

forms, to cognitive interdependence, and to the particularities of experience, bodily existence, and practical activities.

Many feminist theorists are reluctant to subscribe to the view that affectivity, bodily specificity, intersubjectivity, and cognitive 'location' can have no part in informing the rational construction of knowledge. Their reluctance amounts neither to an acceptance of the stereotyped feminine associations of these and related factors nor to a contention that rational activity is for men only. Rather, feminists are caught between a recognition of the productive, emancipatory worth of cognitive postures commonly devalued as 'feminine' and a recognition of the source of those postures in the oppressive and exploitative positions reserved for women in malestream thought and the social structures it legitimates. They need at once to recognize the political potential of affirming an ideal of a distinctive alternative to the autonomy-of-reason credo—an alternative that can become a basis, a rallying point for resistance to the oppressive structures of Reason/masculinity—and to recognize the political dangers of such an affirmation in its tendency to confirm masculine suspicions about the inchoate emotivism of life 'down among the women'. It might be possible to construct such an alternative around a core of statistically common, distinctive experiences that need neither to be viewed as stable attributes nor to be coextensive with gender, race, or class identity. Yet taking on an epistemic identity explicitly structured by devalued female attributes—occupying a 'feminist standpoint'—risks perpetuating the traditional reasons for women's oppression; refusing to take on an identity risks having no platform for intervention, no rallying position from which to contest oppression. Out of the tension generated by these opposed risks, feminists need to articulate strategies for deconstructing and subverting sociocultural representations of femininity that construct it rigidly and stereotypically through a *devaluation* of women's traditional sources of strength. The emergent position needs to be gender-sensitive to avoid the false posturing of gender-neutrality that merely conceals androcentrism and sexism and often amounts to gender-blindness.

'Second person' thinking makes an important contribution to this project. Epistemological positions developed around a 'second person' conception of subjectivity represent the production of knowledge as a communal, often cooperative though sometimes competitive, activity. Either way, knowledge claims are forms of address, speech acts, moments in a dialogue that assume and indeed rely on the participation of (an)other subject(s), a conversational group.

These are not the monologic pronouncements that autonomous reasoners presume to make. Hence Baier's contention that even changing one's mind is possible only for a member of a community that trains its members in criticism, affirmation, and second thinking, and her claim that "realize" is a locution that signals membership rather than outsider status.[19] A knowledge claimant positions herself within a set of discursive possibilities which she may accept, criticize, or challenge; positions herself in relation to other people, to their responses, criticisms, agreements, and contributions. Indeed, within the 'second person' rubric, dialogue is primary, so that even thinking, that seemingly solitary activity, is constructed on a conversational model. Baier's characterization of changing one's mind accords with this point. Arendt refers to "the thinking dialogue between me and myself," observing that "the guiding experience in these matters . . . is friendship and not selfhood; I first talk with others before I talk with myself . . . and then discover that I can conduct a dialogue not only with others but with myself as well."[20] For the autonomy-of-reason persuasion, by contrast, these aspects of 'second person' subjectivity must be transcended in the project of attaining ideal objectivity.

There are resources available in an alternative, and often critical, movement in 'mainstream' epistemology itself, which feminists can tap. Remaining in dialogue with the 'mainstream' offers certain strategic advantages. First, it avoids the pitfall of advocating a separate, feminine epistemology, with its inevitable privatization, ghettoization, and consequent devaluation. Second, many of these critical movements have aims that are consonant, to an extent, with feminist critical aims. Hence there is no conceptual value in rejecting them for their androcentric origins, only to reinvent them as though for the first time. A critical awareness of their androcentric taint can enable feminists to make use of their productive insights while evading their capacity to replicate less productive practices.

Mainstream epistemologists are no longer unanimous in construing 'the epistemological project' as an attempt to discover the universal and abstract conditions of knowledge, as a quest for unassailable foundations, or as a knockdown refutation of skepticism. Some epistemologists go so far as to challenge the validity of epistemology as such; some are engaged in reevaluations of the claims of relativism, in advocating interpretation rather than analysis, and in understanding

[19]See my reference to these epistemic implications in Chapter 3.
[20]Arendt, *Thinking*, pp. 187, 189.

the place of knowledge in people's lives.[21] A revived interest in pragmatism, which appeals to Peirce's conception of a community of inquirers, presents a particularly salient challenge to Cartesianism and its successors.[22] In some of these projects, the picture of a knower as a solitary truth seeker is giving way to a conception of knowers as social beings and of knowledge seeking as a communal, dialogic activity marked by interdependence and intersubjective critique in which inquirers are, plainly, second persons.[23]

It is tempting to believe that these projects signal the end of Cartesianism and mark the ascendancy of a social, interdependent, located conception of subjectivity—to see a relocation of knowledge within social and political structures, which can displace the hegemony of the autonomy-of-reason persuasion. Philosophers are examining affinities between ethics and epistemology, and connections between knowledge and power. They are analyzing the role of received discourse and expertise in legitimating or suppressing knowledge.[24] Some are raising questions about the contribution of cognitive 'location'—racial, ethnic, cultural, class, gendered—to the possibility of knowledge acquisition and to the attribution of credibility and authoritative status. A shift from scientific to literary paradigms is increasingly apparent, especially among social scientists. There is often a presumption, if not an outright commitment, to taking 'second person' issues seriously. These critical interventions have neither achieved centrality nor replaced older epistemological paradigms. But their critique of the dominant paradigm—the autonomy-of-reason paradigm—is increasingly audible.

Feminists contribute a distinctive set of speaking parts to this new critical discourse, in voices that explicitly acknowledge their political commitment. That commitment is born of a growing realization of the effects of the autonomy-of-reason ideal in informing and legitimating

[21]For a discussion of contrasts between the 'received' view and some recent challenges, see Ernest Sosa, "Serious Philosophy and Freedom of Spirit," *Journal of Philosophy* 84 (December 1987): 707–726.

[22]For a work of disenchantment with the epistemological project, see Richard Rorty, *Philosophy and the Mirror of Nature* (Princeton: Princeton University Press, 1979). Rorty's *Consequences of Pragmatism* (Minneapolis: University of Minnesota Press, 1982) develops an interest in pragmatism that is evident in the earlier book. Bernstein's *Beyond Objectivism and Relativism* presents a sympathetic reinterpretation of relativism.

[23]See, for example, Barry Barnes and David Bloor, "Relativism, Rationalism, and the Sociology of Knowledge," in Martin Hollis and Steven Lukes, eds., *Rationality and Relativism* (Cambridge: MIT Press, 1982).

[24]Most noteworthy in this context is the work of Michel Foucault. See especially his *Power/Knowledge: Selected Interviews and Other Writings, 1972–1977*, ed. Colin Gordon, trans. C. Gordon et al. (New York: Pantheon, 1980).

cognitive politics and practices that disadvantage women, denigrate their epistemic practices, and contribute to their oppression. Feminist epistemologists need to demonstrate the role of gender as an analytic category that reveals the persistent significance, political and epistemological, of the sex of the knower. There is no doubt that they can find both scholarly and political allies in these critical interventions, which are continually disturbing the smoothness of the mainstream. But feminist epistemologists could not simply claim these projects as their own and argue that they only need slight adaptations to align with feminist purposes. For a start, it is by no means clear that all of these interventions entail a repudiation of individualism and autonomous agency. Few if any explicitly address the matter of a knower's bodily, sexual specificity, which determines her or his access to many kinds of experience and domains of discourse. Hence few of these critiques are explicitly gender-sensitive in the way that feminist epistemological interventions have to be. Feminist epistemological inquiry needs to focus on the effects of socially embedded 'gender orders' on the construction of knowledge.

The epistemological situation is analogous to the situation in moral discourse that prompted Gilligan's challenge to Kohlberg's theory of moral development.[25] For Kohlberg, women's deliberations fall into a shadowy realm of the not-properly-moral. Yet women's apparent failure to achieve autonomy and moral maturity on Kohlberg's scale is evidence of the crudity of the scale as a research instrument, not a demonstration of natural female inadequacy. Female subjects' tendencies to contextualize their responses by drawing on a cluster of experiential factors can as plausibly be read as evidence of moral strength and sophistication. There are notable epistemological parallels in women's alleged failure, according to the autonomy-of-reason standard, to qualify as fully fledged members of an epistemic community. The traditional moral and epistemic domains are alike in blocking women's access to the authoritative positions that cognitive and/or moral maturity makes available to its possessors.

Now the quality of an action is determined as much by an agent's knowledge of the circumstances and people involved as it is by the principles and standards she or he invokes. Parallels between gender-specific moral and epistemological presuppositions are most plainly visible in situations in which the cognitive content of a moral situation is at issue. But such parallels extend into a much broader epistemic context, revealing that the shape and content of mainstream

[25]See Gilligan, *In a Different Voice.*

epistemology—like that of ethics—has been dictated by a single voice that has claimed the central speaking part by drowning out more muted voices. Those voices speak 'without authority', often of concerns like those uttered in the 'different' voice Gilligan heard.

Stringent *epistemic* restrictions constrain the scope of two of the best-established moral philosophies that work with the conception of an autonomous, interchangeable, impartial moral agent. Rawlsian moral agents must achieve their impartiality by deliberating behind a 'veil of ignorance', and in the Kantian scheme, noumenal selves cannot be sufficiently individuated for their problems and concerns to be adequately understood. Kohlberg's work appears, prima facie, to avoid such restrictions, for he does, after all, deal with concrete examples. Yet even in the well-known Heinz dilemma, neither the motivations of the druggist as a 'concrete individual' nor the histories and broader circumstances of the other people involved are judged relevant to the conceptualization of the problem.[26] The example consists only in sparse abstractions from 'narrative histories' and motivations, which provide no basis for knowledgeable, properly informed deliberation and critique. Kohlberg's moral epistemology is no more adequate than that which underpins traditional moral theory. He does not make it possible for his subjects to know the actors in a moral drama well enough to judge them responsibly.[27]

Gilligan's subjects practice cognitive skills statistically atypical of men's moral deliberations. They are attentive to the details of situations and life histories, receptive to other people's experiences and constructions of meaning. Ironically, this cognitive approach—this attention to detail and particularity—prompts the conclusion that women are cognitively immature, for theirs is not the formal, detached stance that denotes Kohlbergian moral maturity. For their epistemic subtlety and sophistication to count as authoritative attributes, the standards would have to be redrawn to incorporate sensitivity and responsiveness as sources of effective epistemic agency.

Seyla Benhabib contends that it is vital to know other people as concrete—not merely as 'generalized'—others, for adequate moral judgment to be possible *simpliciter*. Her claim is not that requirements of generality or universalizability are illegitimate per se. She is

---

[26]I owe these thoughts to Seyla Benhabib, "The Generalized and the Concrete Other," in Seyla Benhabib and Drucilla Cornell, eds., *Feminism as Critique: Essays on the Politics of Gender in Late-Capitalist Societies* (Minneapolis: University of Minnesota Press, 1987), p. 88.

[27]I discuss an extended example of such cognitive inadequacy, with reference to Kantian moral theory, in my "Persons, and Others," in Judith Genova, ed., *Power, Gender, Values* (Edmonton: Academic Printing and Publishing, 1987).

not advocating a theory/practice dichotomy, in which the generalized other represents the theoretical side (where, alone, deliberation is possible), the concrete other the practical side. Nor is her implication that the concrete other is purely 'concretized' and idiosyncratic. The 'generalized' rubric, as it currently prevails, suppresses the peculiarities of real, 'concrete', specifically positioned subjects, but the concrete other can be analyzed in terms that derive from that rubric. General and more formal conceptions of subjectivity, interests, and locations—such as racial or ethnic membership, sexual preference, economic circumstances—provide frameworks within which analyses of concrete situations that involve specific persons take place. But formal conditions alone cannot afford a viable basis for moral deliberation. In Benhabib's view, "the recognition of the dignity and worth of the generalized other is a *necessary*, albeit not *sufficient*, condition to define the moral standpoint in modern societies. . . . the concrete other is a critical concept that designates the *ideological* limits of universalistic discourse. It signifies the *unthought*, the *unseen*, and the *unheard* in such theories."[28] The task is to effect a balance between two unworkable extremes: declaring the radical idiosyncrasy of every 'concrete other' or making the scope of identities and positions so broad, so general, that they obscure epistemically and politically salient specificities.

Continuities with Baier's conception of second persons and Whitbeck's of relational selves are apparent in Benhabib's observation that "the self only becomes an I in a community of other selves who are also I's. Every act of self-reference expresses simultaneously the uniqueness and difference of the self as well as the commonality among selves."[29] Commonality *in general* is claimed as a basis of reflection and deliberation with this conception of subjectivity, but particular, concrete commonalities need to be discerned. There is no justification for assuming commonality in any given instance, unless one knows enough about people, histories, and events to be able to judge that *these* people are 'likes' who should—and can—be treated alike, in this situation, in this respect.[30]

[28]Benhabib, "Generalized and Concrete Other," p. 92.

[29]Ibid., p. 94.

[30]Arnault remarks: "Because people may, and often do, dispute the definition of a moral situation, the universalizability requirement that we treat like situations alike can only be viable if the task of defining what constitutes a 'like' situation is articulated as involving the viewpoints of moral deliberators who are not solitary, disembedded, point-of-viewless beings but rather who are socially constructed, embodied members of historically changing groups with epistemologically distinctive vantage points." Arnault, "Radical Future," p. 197.

Benhabib's distinction between *substitutionalist* and *interactive* universalism is as useful for epistemological as for moral theory.[31] In substitutionalist thinking, a certain group—white, male, educated, usually propertied, and privileged adults—constitutes the paradigm of 'humanness' and hence of experience and agency. Differences among individual members of the group disappear in moral analysis to produce a smooth, homogeneous aggregate of easily replicable experiencers and bearers of rights. Principles and conclusions are equally relevant to any one of them. Interactive universalism, by contrast, takes differences seriously. It retains a presumption in favor of adherence to such principles as fairness and reciprocity, but argues that their scope always requires contextual interpretation. They may apply quite differently in different circumstances, depending on what is at issue and who is involved. In some circumstances, these principles pale in significance before a different kind of goal—one perhaps more concerned and caring, yet less fair; one that places trust above reciprocity.

Substitutionalism (interchangeability) in ethics has its epistemic counterpart in the 'S knows that p' formula, where both S and p are place holders. I have elaborated some implications of this status, for S, as it attests to the epistemological significance of the sex of the knower. Equally interesting implications of the place-holder status of p run parallel to substitutionalist moral discourse. In the selection of epistemological examples, the context in which p occurs is rarely relevant. Theorists assume that clear, unequivocal knowledge claims can be submitted for analysis only if they are abstracted from the confusions of context. Such examples, like the moral claims Benhabib discusses, are commonly selected (whether by chance or by design) from the experiences of a privileged group of men, regarded as paradigmatic for human rational endeavor.

Historically, the philosopher arrogated that privilege to himself, maintaining that an investigation of his thinking can reveal the workings of human thought per se. Berkeley remarks that it is "very obvious, upon the least inquiry into our own thoughts, to know whether it be possible for us to understand what is meant by the *absolute existence of sensible objects in themselves*, or *without the mind*." Locke writes: "If other men have either innate *ideas* or infused principles, they have reason to enjoy them . . . I can speak but of what I find in myself and is agreeable to those notions." Hume observes: "I never can catch *myself* without a perception . . . If any one upon serious

---

[31]Benhabib, "Generalized and Concrete Other," p. 81.

and unprejudic'd reflexion, thinks he has a different notion of *himself*, I must confess I can reason no longer with him." Descartes writes: "I cannot doubt that which the natural light causes me to believe to be true, as, for example, it has shown me that I am from the fact that I doubt, or other facts of the same kind." What is striking about these claims is their common conviction that a philosopher can draw universal theoretical conclusions from observations of his own cognitive processes. A thinker whose thinking does not resemble the philosopher's is not thinking clearly or correctly.[32]

In Baconian, positivistic, and later (twentieth-century) empiricist thought, paradigmatic privilege belongs more specifically to standardized, faceless observers or to scientists. (The latter, at least, are also notoriously white and male, if not necessarily propertied.) Their simple observational experiences comprise the primitive building blocks from which knowledge is made. A noteworthy feature of those observational 'simples' is that they are caused, almost invariably, by medium-sized ordinary physical objects such as apples, envelopes, coins, sticks, and colored patches. Rarely if ever in the literature, either historical or modern, is there more than a passing reference to knowing other people as an exemplary form of knowledge. The references that do exist are usually to recognition (i.e., observational information) that this is a man—whereas that is a door or a robot. With respect neither to material objects nor to other people do formally paradigmatic knowledge claims convey any sense of how these 'knowns' might figure in a knower's life. Just as moral and cognitive agents reduce to "an empty mask that is everyone and no one" (to use Benhabib's evocative phrase[33]), so in S-knows-that-p epistemology, p is an empty container that is everything and nothing.

The epistemic restrictions that the use of this model entails suppress the context in which an object is known. They seem also to account for the fact that apart from simple objects—and even there it is questionable—one cannot, on this model, know anything well enough to do anything very interesting with it. One can only *perceive* it, usually at a distance. Perhaps in consequence of this practical restriction, this limited usefulness of the knowledge that this model can

[32]George Berkeley, *Principles of Human Knowledge* (New York: Scribners, 1929), part I, sec. 24; John Locke, *An Essay concerning Human Understanding* (New York: Dent, 1961), book II, chap. XI, 16; David Hume, *A Treatise of Human Nature*, ed. H. Selby-Bigge (Oxford: Oxford University Press, 1969), p. 252; Descartes, *Meditations*, p. 160. These historical examples are modified from my article "Importance of Historicism for a Theory of Knowledge," pp. 159–160.
[33]Benhabib, "Generalized and Concrete Other," p. 89.

account for, the domain that is excluded from acceptable moral discourse—that is, most of everyday experience—is likewise excluded from epistemological discourse. Just as the moral point of view, in Benhabib's analysis, is restricted to the generalized other, whose differences from other 'others' are smoothed out to achieve sameness of judgment, treatment, and evaluation, so knowledge is not of concrete or unique aspects of the world or society. It is of *instances* rather than of particulars: the norms of formal sameness obscure differences just as they do in the moral domain, and the idea that knowledge properly so-called must transcend or prescind from experience also places a knower—paradoxically—behind a 'veil of ignorance'.

In the historical examples I have cited, and likewise in more modern forms of empiricism, theories of knowledge (and hence also of Reason) are derived from the experiences of uniformly educated, articulate, and epistemically 'positioned' adults who introspect retrospectively to review what they must once have known most simply and clearly. Locke's tabula rasa is one model for such introspection to approximate; Descartes's radical doubt is another. Yet this is a curious form of introspection, for it consistently bypasses the epistemic significance of early experiences with other people, with whom the relations of these philosophers must surely have been different from their relations to objects in their environment. Indeed, as Benhabib observes in another context, it is a strange world from which their picture of knowledge is derived: a world in which "individuals are grown up before they have been born; in which boys are men before they have been children; a world where neither mother, nor sister, nor wife exist."[34] Whatever the differences that child-raising practices may, historically, have exhibited, evidence implicit in (also evolving) theories of knowledge points to a noteworthy constancy. In the separated adult stage that childhood emerges into, the knowledge that enables a knower to give and withhold trust as a child, and hence to survive, is passed over as unworthy of philosophical notice. It is not easy to resist the conclusion that theorists of knowledge must be childless or must be so disengaged from the rearing of their children as to have no awareness of children's cognitive development. Such disengagement, throughout a changing history and across a wide range of class and racial boundaries, has been possible primarily for men; hence the androcentric derivation of autonomous Reason is scarcely surprising. In this context, the value of Ruddick's 'maternal

[34]Ibid., p. 85.

thinking' is, in fact, apparent. People who have participated in the practices that inform such thinking could not easily ignore the role of knowing and being known by other people in a child's cognitive development. Nor could they readily denigrate the role of such knowledge throughout a personal epistemic history or subscribe wholeheartedly to a conception of autonomous reason.

What, then, are the feminist implications of the autonomy-of-reason ideal? Philosophers have isolated the autonomous use of reason as its best—and often its only legitimate—use. That isolation has been achieved by the exclusion, from prevalent constructions of Reason/masculinity, of character traits and experiences deemed inimical to reason's proper functioning. By no means coincidentally, those very suppressed traits constitute the conception—the ideal—of femininity that has prevailed both in popular and in academic discourse. The resultant suppression of 'the feminine' mirrors and is mirrored in the oppression of women in patriarchal societies.

Epistemological Consequences

With reference to moral autonomy, I noted that, in the radically individualistic conception of subjectivity that informs the traditional discourse of moral agency, personal relationships are accorded no significance as constitutive, primary human experiences. They are depicted as anomalous events, threatening to moral integrity. Hence the autonomous moral agent is a person whose cherished self-sufficiency is constantly under threat, who must guard against the possibility of intrusion by erecting a barrier of rights and rules around himself. For such a person, dependence, cooperation, and relationship are risky undertakings. Wariness about their inherent risks blinds him to their "good and helpful aspects."[35] The resultant modes of existence are those forms of impersonal, objective social intercourse whose origins Benjamin connects with the male repudiation of the mother.[36] The epistemological counterparts of these impersonal social modes are apparent in defensive epistemic postures and in the persistent temptations of skepticism. Most notably, these impersonal modes structure a subject-object relation manifested at once in a wariness of epistemic dependence and in a suppression of 'the feminine'. These features derive, alike, from the conception of knowers as soli-

[35]This is Annette Baier's phrase, which I quote in Chapter 3, p. 83.
[36]See Chapter 3, above, p. 86.

tary, separate, and perpetually subject to epistemic threats and risks against which they have to protect themselves by their own efforts.

Defensiveness

Defensiveness in epistemic practice is manifested both in the distrust of testimony I have discussed and in a need to produce definitive cognitive claims that one can, above all, defend against challenges and counterclaims. Descartes's distrust of testimony is evident in his project of systematic methodological doubt, which derives from his conviction that rationality, almost by definition, depends on reliance on one's own judgment. Equally striking are Kant's statement of his first maxim of human understanding, according to which one must "think for oneself," and his connection of the "need of being guided by others" with *prejudice* and a kind of blindness "in which superstition places us."[37] Given the enormous influence of these two thinkers in the construction of dominant ideals of rationality and knowledge, it is small wonder that a distrust of testimony occupies a central place among the epistemic ideals of western philosophy. Its centrality accounts for the fact that theorists of knowledge tend to forget just how small a portion of knowledge is, or could be, a product of simple observation or independent reasoning. The examples commonly adduced as epistemic paradigms obscure the extent to which people are dependent, at a fundamental level, on other people—parents, teachers, friends, reporters, authorities, and experts—for what they, often rightly, claim to know. An imaginative review of what the reader would claim to know at this very moment should reveal how little of that knowledge has been, or could have been, acquired from her or his own perfectly solitary efforts.

The persistence of the 'romantic ideal' of intellectual autonomy makes it necessary, rather, to argue, as John Hardwig does, for the importance of epistemic dependence to the very possibility of being a rational epistemic agent. Hardwig's telling example of an article in *Physical Review Letters* cowritten by ninety-nine authors shows that epistemic dependence is a fact of cognitive life even in physics, that 'special' form of inquiry from which ideals of objectivity derive. Hardwig observes that the experiment reported in the article *could not* have been performed by one scientist, or by a small group without becoming obsolete by the time of its completion. Moreover, many of the

---

[37]Immanuel Kant, *Critique of Judgement*, trans. J. H. Bernard (New York: Hafner, 1972), pp. 136–137.

coauthors would not know how some of the results were achieved, even though they relied on them in producing their own contributions. Hardwig cites the experiment not as an anomaly of scientific practice, but to support his claim that analogous situations pervade epistemic lives—that *"rationality* sometimes consists in deferring to epistemic authority"—a point that, he notes, "will strike those wedded to epistemic individualism as odd and unacceptable, for it undermines their paradigm of rationality."[38] Yet Hardwig is urging more than mere tolerance of epistemic dependence. He is claiming that the Peircean conception of the *community* of inquirers as the primary knower, in which individual knowledge is derivative, is the most plausible one, in view of the role of circumspect reliance on testimony as a *condition* of responsible knowing.[39]

A shift toward granting due significance to cognitive interdependence reveals that the art of discerning whom one can trust is one of the most essential arts of personhood: an art that cognitive agents are continually learning and modifying. The matter of determining what human sources of knowledge are trust*worthy* is vital to responsible knowing. The construction of knowledge is an intersubjective process, dependent for its achievement on communal standards of legitimation and implicated in the power and institutional structures of communities and social orders. The intricacies of the politics of knowledge in any community and the status of cognitive authorities and of 'state of the art' knowledge need, contrary to the autonomy-of-reason view, to be counted among the conditions that make knowledge possible.[40]

Malestream philosophical methodology is shaped, nonetheless, by an adversarial paradigm defined in terms of rational autonomy and defensiveness. This is the paradigm Moulton documents, with its capacity to limit the scope of inquiry and to foreclose possibilities of understanding. In philosophy practiced under its aegis, "the only problems recognized are those between opponents, and the only kind of reasoning considered is the certainty of deduction, directed to

[38]John Hardwig, "Epistemic Dependence," *Journal of Philosophy* 82 (July 1985): 343.
[39]See ibid., p. 349.
[40]The cooperative function of an epistemic community is elaborated in Thomas Kuhn, *The Structure of Scientific Revolutions*, 2d ed. (Chicago: University of Chicago Press, 1970); differently articulated, it is a central theme in the work of Foucault. See also chap. 7, "Epistemic Community," of my *Epistemic Responsibility*. Helen Longino, in *Science as Social Knowledge: Values and Objectivity in Scientific Inquiry* (Princeton: Princeton University Press, 1990), which I read after this book had gone to press, develops a contextual empiricism for which scientific inquiry is a social, not an individual, process.

opposition."[41] Its analogues are discernible across many areas of inquiry, in narrowly defined research projects within any discipline, whose primary intention is to provide an unassailable solution to a closely circumscribed problem. Inquirers who engage in their projects defensively and adversarially are at some pains to deny cognitive interdependence. It is hard to believe that communication figures prominently among their goals.

Now it is important to acknowledge that the adversarial method is generated out of an aspect of philosophical practice that is, prima facie, commendable: the practice of developing well-argued accounts of well-defined and carefully chosen problems. Like the desire for autonomy, the underlying motivation is intellectually quite respectable. It goes awry when it turns from a quest for the most plausible line of inquiry into an obsession with defending a position. An adversarial posture is often manifested in a need to be right rather than creative or insightful, or in a reluctance to entertain alternative possibilities. Moulton argues that mainstream professional philosophy is governed by this paradigm. Nor is it surprising that such a philosophical style should gain ascendancy in societies in which esteemed men of privilege inhabit a public world dominated by political, military, commercial, and scientific competition. It is no wonder that such men would adopt a philosophical idiom based on the language of war. But the consequence is that knowers are jealously protective of their own territories of personal expertise. This protectiveness operates as a constraint on philosophical dialogue, creativity, and understanding which serves no one's purposes well.

Skepticism

On the starkest construal, the autonomous reasoner is utterly alone in his cognitive endeavors, with no community of like-minded inquirers to inspire or stabilize his efforts, to reaffirm his intuitions, or to reassure him in moments of doubt. He can trust no one to check the veracity of his perceptions; there is no one to whose perceptions he can appeal to determine whether he is deluded, or dreaming, or the dupe of an evil genius. Everything is up to him. In a situation of such solitary confinement, it is hardly surprising that he might experience constant anxiety and that skepticism would be a persistent and unnerving temptation. Richard Bernstein describes this state of mind as

[41]Moulton, "Paradigm of Philosophy," p. 157.

"Cartesian Anxiety," to indicate not that it originates with Descartes, but that it is well portrayed in the journey of the soul Descartes describes in the *Meditations*. That nightmarish journey is driven by an overwhelming awareness of human finitude and fallibility, in a desperate search for security. It is a quest for "some fixed point, some stable rock upon which we can secure our lives against the vicissitudes that constantly threaten us. The specter that hovers in the background of this journey is not just radical epistemological skepticism but the dread of madness and chaos where nothing is fixed, where we can neither touch bottom nor support ourselves on the surface."[42] It ends only in Descartes's declaration of dependence on an omniscient and beneficent God who will keep his anxiety at bay.

Feminist epistemologists have written very little about the problems of skepticism, but Bordo and Scheman both interpret Cartesian skepticism not simply as a methodological device, but as evidence of Descartes's experience of a genuine epistemic threat.[43] In both readings, Descartes's skepticism is positioned at the intersection of a set of cultural phenomena to which his radical doubt is a response. And both theorists read late-twentieth-century child psychology onto medieval (Bordo) and Cartesian thinking in ways that are creative and provocative, if at times troubling. Both Bordo and Scheman view Descartes as the author of a skeptical orientation that he has bequeathed to his philosophical successors in the form of a tempting and problematic legacy.

In her psychocultural reading of the *Meditations*, Bordo examines the "epistemological uncertainty . . . [that constitutes] . . . a dark underside [of] the bold Cartesian vision." Historically, she believes, Descartes and his successors sought to control the insecurity by a 'flight to objectivity'. But that objectivity, for all its self-proclaimed absolutism, was quite tenuous, and the chaos of skepticism always threatened to overwhelm it. Bordo constructs an intricate set of connections among autonomy-obsession, masculinity, and this persistent threat of skepticism that haunts the quest for epistemic certainty. The Cartesian "masculinization of thought," she claims, "is one intellectual 'moment' of an acute historical flight from the feminine, from the memory of union with the maternal world, and a rejection of all values associated with it." Because, for Descartes, the mind provides "only the most fragile and fleeting contact with the world," the best hope for certainty and constancy is in the development of a "mas-

[42]Bernstein, *Beyond Objectivism and Relativism*, p. 18.
[43]See Bordo, *Flight to Objectivity*, and Scheman, "Othello's Doubt/Desdemona's Death" (esp. p. 128 n. 6).

culine" epistemology in which separation—autonomy—can be reconstructed as a position of control, and hence "detachment from nature acquires a positive epistemological value."[44] The moves by which this detachment is effected replicate psychological processes of male repudiation of the mother and identification—albeit remotely—with the father.

Ontogenetic-phylogenetic parallels between a sense of oneness with the universe characteristic of a medieval world view and a sense of oneness with the mother (or primary caregiver) that is recapitulated, in infancy, in each human life figure largely in Bordo's analysis. The move to independence and autonomy that male children of affluent white western societies are commonly expected to make produces a 'separation anxiety' that, she believes, mirrors and is mirrored in a historical severance from unity with the world. Bordo locates the cosmic occurrence of that severance in a cluster of historical events. In "the epistemologically undermining effect of the Reformation," with the claims it advanced for "the authority of inner conviction," she sees a reason for a resurgence of skepticism in a more radical form than any of its earlier appearances. Once the practice of appealing to a transcendent God for absolute assurance has been challenged, a knowledge seeker is thrown back on his own resources, unable any longer to rely on "the authority of doctrine."[45] Other contemporaneous cultural events make epistemic certainty still more elusive. Bordo cites the discovery of the telescope as a demonstration at once of the fallibility of the senses and of the spatial and cultural specificity of the perceptions that had been thought to provide immediate knowledge of 'reality'. She contends that voyages of discovery to the New World occasioned a new awareness of the parochialism of conceptions of 'human nature' and of ideas, experiences, and values. And she argues that the discovery of perspective in art, which locates the viewing subject outside and in a certain relation to the world depicted in a painting, disrupts a sense of oneness, of fixed and knowable positioning in a hierarchy, that is present in medieval art.[46]

For Bordo, in short, Cartesianism signals the emergence of a subjectivity in philosophy, whose tendency to initiate a slide into subjectivism and, ultimately, into skepticism can be stopped only by taking refuge in perfectly guaranteed objectivity. Subjectivity is, in fact, coextensive with the cognitive 'location' of the knower, whose recognition reveals his capacity to "bestow false inner perceptions on the outer

[44]Bordo, *Flight to Objectivity*, pp. 4, 9, 18, 108.
[45]Ibid., pp. 38, 39.
[46]Ibid., pp. 62–68.

world of things."[47] The knower makes a new appearance, then, as a source of error, illusion, specificity, and (potentially) false perspective. Ideal objectivity alone is powerless to stop the slide.

Now ontogenetic-phylogenetic parallels are notoriously troublesome. They risk constructing earlier phylogenetic stages as naive and childlike, inviting a dismissive, patronizing attitude. Interpretations of a 'spirit of the age' are at best selective and at worst superficial, glossing over differences in people's histories to present a dubiously unified picture. They often rely on or construct a false essentialism. Disagreements among historians attest to some of these problems. To cite one example, there is a tension between the attunement and oneness with nature that Bordo sees in medieval art and Kenneth Clark's claim that, until the fourteenth century, nature was so frightening and dangerous that artists could cope with it only in paintings of idealized, enclosed, and therefore protected, gardens. Clark emphasizes the role of perspective in creating a "landscape of fact," mathematically delineated and hence able to convey *certain* knowledge of a nature now less frightening, more knowable.[48] Perspective offers the certainty of one and only one spot from which an accurate, true picture can be seen and gives access to mathematically correct relationships within it.

These points do not outrightly contradict Bordo's claims about the distanced, disconnected subject-object relation that perspectival observation endorses. People might, at once, feel both in tune with and apprehensive about the unpredictable forces of nature. But Bordo's accounts of attunement and perceptual distance underpin more global theses about human relationships to the world. She is constructing parallels between the disappearance of a medieval world view and the making of masculinity in present-day child-raising practices. Lack of historical unanimity and divergent psychological theories, conceptions of 'masculinity', and good child raising enjoin care in endorsing her conclusions.

Bordo draws on a wide range of cultural and historical accounts of the constitution of medieval and early modern thought to support her claim that there is an organic mode of medieval thought that is displaced in detached, mechanistic conceptions of nature. Feminist philosophers may take issue with her decision to appeal more to cultural and psychological than to philosophical sources, for the latter could contribute significantly to her project. The rediscovery of classical skepticism in the late Renaissance, and the nominalist and realist

---

[47]Ibid., p. 51.
[48]Kenneth Clark, *Landscape into Art* (Harmondsworth: Penguin, 1956), p. 35.

debates of that era, together with a move away from logic- (and hence certainty-) based linguistic philosophy, toward less certainty-guaranteeing forms of argumentation, practical reasoning, and rhetoric, must all have been catalysts of the displacement she analyzes. Her analysis could have benefited from their inclusion.[49]

Scheman likewise finds sources of Cartesian skepticism in the Reformation, in voyages of discovery, and in the birth of the new science. She writes: "The accommodation to scepticism is historically uneasy, poised between nostalgia for a (mis)remembered world of unquestioned certainty and stability and the hope that scientific rationality will bring the world under our practical and epistemic control." That accommodation is "engendered," Scheman believes, in a repudiation of the engulfing, submerging power of that early world which echoes and is echoed in a male child's repudiation of maternal power—an inevitable repudiation "in a world in which men are expected to dominate . . . women—whose bodily presence reawakens infantile experiences of dependency and symbiotic intimacy."[50] Descartes provides a clear example. Epistemic dependence, for Descartes, was as intolerable and unreliable as sensuous immersion in objects in the world. Hence he needed to claim, and continuously reclaim, God-guaranteed certainty in his own self-reliant existence, to keep skepticism (tenuously) under control.

Bordo's readings of twentieth-century developmental psychology, and especially of Piaget, are consistent with Scheman's depiction of cultural patterns that foster separation in male children and encourage connectedness in female ones. Yet these patterns do not work in the same way for all children or all parents, and neither Bordo nor Scheman takes their historical, class, and cultural specificity very seriously into account. Statistically, there is no doubt that masculine separateness and female connectedness are the positional norms for men and women in the privileged classes, races, and sexual persuasions of the western world. What is at once compelling and vexing about the points at which Bordo's and Scheman's analyses intersect is that the pictures they (variously) draw of a one-time connectedness and growing separation in the history of thought do resonate powerfully—and creatively—with conceptions of ideal, anxiety-ridden masculinity and idealized, connected femininity. Hence both interpretations count, innovatively and heuristically, as contributions toward establishing gender as an analytic category of philosophical

---

[49]These points were explained to me by Joan Gibson.
[50]Scheman, "Othello's Doubt/Desdemona's Death," pp. 114, 117.

inquiry by proposing that gender structures inform an epistemological process—that is, the emergence of Cartesian skepticism—that
would appear *not*, prima facie, to be a gender-related process in any
sense of the word. They locate the construction of a skeptically threatened subjectivity in social, historical, and cultural contexts that open
new possibilities for critical engagement with the evident androcentricity of malestream philosophy, however elusive its sources.
This is the compelling aspect.

The vexing aspect derives from the tension that has been playing
and will continue to play throughout the issues I engage with in this
book. Each analysis is constructed around troubling essentialist assumptions, which contrast masculine and feminine epistemic postures, and mechanistic and organic cosmologies, as parallel and intransigent polarities. Hence Bordo's and Scheman's accounts risk
replicating the effects of the male/female opposition not just as a
historical event, but as an ongoing sociocultural-psychological pattern
that contains within itself all of the available possibilities.

Now there is no doubt about the hegemonic historical force of that
dichotomy, nor about the need to understand it well in order to develop strategies to subvert it. Both Bordo and Scheman contribute inven-
tively to that part of the project. For their analyses—variously—to
realize their promise, they would both need to contextualize their
appeals to present-day theories of psychological development as sites
of the production of male/female differences. Locating those processes so closely within nuclear family structures and the 'mothering'
practices they are built on assumes patterns of interaction that are too
sparse and specific to be cast as the producers of gender identity.
Family structures are themselves constructed within regimes of economy, politics, and power, just as skepticism is a product of cultural
and historical forces that shape the Cartesian *cogito*.

One of the most interesting insights that these analyses produce is
a recognition of how sophisticated and difficult an achievement radical skepticism is. Epistemologists who present it as an abyss on
whose edge every knower struggles to maintain a precarious balance
rarely acknowledge its difficulty. Autonomy-obsession glosses over
the developmental processes that make radical skepticism extremely
unlikely: the *vital* implication of the fact that persons are, essentially,
second persons. Development from infancy into adulthood depends
unequivocally on interdependence, for all of the familiar biological—
and even psychological—reasons. Undoubtedly, as people mature,
they often realize that they have been, and continue to be, too depen-

dent, too trusting. Other people are frequently unreliable; they can deceive a person, injure her, let her down; people sometimes wonder whether they 'really know' anyone. Nor can one count, unequivocally, on not letting oneself down, on knowing oneself, or avoiding self-deception. Yet without other people, no one would *be* to doubt and be aware of her or his fallibility. A doubt that doubts the conditions of its own possibility is even more radical than Cartesian doubt: it verges on irrationality. So a simple move from a judicious recognition of fallibility to the nihilism of skepticism is too swift: it can be made only by ignoring the very forces that have shaped it. Were autonomy-obsession displaced, and the pervasiveness of second-person relationships fully acknowledged, temptations to skepticism might not be so strong.

The Subject-Object Relation

The subject-object relation that the autonomy-of-reason credo underwrites is at once its most salient and its most politically significant epistemological consequence. The relation pivots on two assumptions: that there is a sharp split between subject and object and that it is a primary purpose of cognitive activity to produce the ability to control, manipulate, and predict the behavior of its objects. Such a relation is taken for granted in hegemonic conceptions of the nature of scientific practice. Indeed, Evelyn Fox Keller suggests that professional science tends to attract people—generally men—for whom an objectivist ideology, "the promise of cool and objective remove from the object of study,"[51] provides emotional comfort.

The established subject-object relation in epistemologies that aspire to the scientific ideal is a distanced, neutral, separated one, and in all of these aspects it is asymmetrical. The subject is removed from, detached from, positions himself at a distance from the object; and knows the object as other than himself. Unidirectional observation is the primary subject-object relation—a relation best maintained vis-

---

[51]Evelyn Fox Keller, *Reflections on Gender and Science* (New Haven: Yale University Press, 1985), p. 124. Keller analyzes autonomy as an epistemic value and a regulative scientific ideal.

Wendy Hollway notes that "scientific *practice* is the product of a history in which science has developed in tandem—as simultaneous cause and effect—with a certain subjectivity characteristic of that subset of white men who have been the scientists." Yet she cautions that "there is not a one-to-one correspondence between scientific practices and the psyche of the practising scientists" (*Subjectivity and Method in Psychology*, p. 119). I return to this point in the next section of this chapter.

à-vis medium-sized objects in the physical world or microscopic objects available for scientific observation, quantification, and measurement. The paradigmatic status of this relation in theory of knowledge derives in large part from the paradigmatic status of physics and, as in idealized conceptions of physics, from a belief in observational 'simples' as models of what is knowable. Theorists of the autonomy-of-reason persuasion assume that neither the subject nor the object will be changed or otherwise affected in an act of knowing. *Understanding* the object of inquiry, where it figures at all among epistemic concerns, is of minimal significance. In fact, a subject's demonstrated ability to manipulate, predict, and control the behavior of his objects of knowledge is commonly regarded as the evidence par excellence that he knows them.

Vision is the privileged sense in the construction of this subject-object relation. Visual metaphors—knowledge as illumination, knowing as seeing, truth as light—shape hegemonic conceptions of knowledge just as surely as masculine metaphors shape hegemonic conceptions of reason. Vision has so well established a role in mainstream thinking about the nature of knowledge that its aptness is rarely questioned. With its roots both in Platonic philosophy and in the sophisticated development of optics in the early modern scientific era, it is no wonder that vision would have emerged as a model both of knowing per se and of the best and most natural relationship between knower and known. Even philosophers such as Aristotle, who discuss touch as a source of knowledge, take vision as the model in whose terms touch can be understood. For Descartes, who contributed to the science of optics and for whom vision figures preeminently as a source of sensory experience, the choice of this model is not surprising. But the (often unspoken) assumption that vision can set the standards for perceptual accuracy, knowledge, representation, and theories of mental imagery is less plausible. Rather, the privileging of vision structures the conceptualization of problems of knowledge in ways that are more matters of happenstance and historical accident than of necessity.

The primacy accorded to vision reinforces and is reinforced by the subject-object relation taken for granted in most traditional theories of knowledge. The relations between knowers and the known implied both in visual metaphors and in the privileging of vision among the senses are intricate and even paradoxical. Evelyn Keller and Christine Grontkowski note, "Vision connects us to truth as it distances us from the corporeal." In Platonic philosophy, the eye, the sun, and light are used "both metaphorically and directly, to establish the characteristics of intelligibility," which culminates in contemplation of the

Forms (= things that are seen).[52] From Plato, through to Descartes's faith in inner perception and the natural light of reason, to modern scientific confidence in the knowability of nature, vision is a constitutive and constant metaphor in western conceptions of knowledge.

For autonomous knowers, Keller and Grontkowski suggest, vision "most readily promotes the illusion of disengagement and objectification" because it is perception at a distance: hence it requires a separation between subject and object, while conveying the impression that this separation is natural and necessary. Standard philosophical theories of vision represent it as a 'bare', primitive, quasi-foundational, innocent mode of perception, which provides direct, untainted access to reality. Hence they obliterate all traces of the developmental, constructive processes—of the learning—that is implicated in even the most apparently simple forms of seeing. They ignore the extent to which even seeing is culturally, historically, and ideologically shaped. They abstract both perceiver and perceived from the circumstances and conditions that, at any moment, *make* perception what it is. Whether a philosophical theory is constructed from the vantage point of the 'inner' eye—the eye of the mind—or the outer eye of natural vision, the outcome, in mainstream theory, is some version of the detached (and hence *objective*) relation of knowing subject to objects of knowledge. Descartes even severs all connections between intellectual 'seeing' and physical perception in his mind/body dualism. Hence he can claim to achieve a rational autonomy understood as freedom from the deceptions of physical, sensual dependence. For both Newton and Einstein, knowledge par excellence is a form of seeing either as God himself saw or through pure thought; hence, in Keller and Grontkowski's words, "the world is severed from the observer, illumined as it were, by that sense which could operate, it was thought, without contaminating."[53]

A dual sense of vision is operative, then, in the history of philosophy. Vision at once severs the object from the subject through perceptual distance, and connects subject and object across a perceptual distance. Paradoxically, the connection is a distanced one; ideally, it will touch neither the knower nor the known, but will leave both just as they were. Vision, according to Keller and Grontkowski,

> by virtue of its apparent atemporality, both invites and lends itself to an atemporal description of truth and reality . . . there is little question

[52]Evelyn Fox Keller and Christine Grontkowski, "The Mind's Eye," in Harding and Hintikka, eds., *Discovering Reality*, pp. 209, 211.
[53]Ibid., pp. 213, 218.

that its . . . disengagement from action, experience, and dynamic interaction invites and lends itself to a model of truth which transcends the
more body bound, materially contingent senses. . . . the possibilities of
perspective it grants us, and the gain the visual sense derives from
distance further contribute to a model of truth based on distance between subject and object, knower and known.[54]

There is no doubt that this is the vision of the autonomous epistemic
agent and that his knowledge claims aspire to that ideal, restrictive
objectivity I discuss in Chapter 2.

Missing from Keller and Grontkowski's analysis of the role of vision in the production of knowledge is any examination of the part
this detached subject-object relation plays in elaborating structures of
power and control.[55] It is an incontestable fact that vision, for all its
detachment, is a remarkably effective instrument of control. Its effectiveness is most infamously illustrated in Sartre's *Being and Nothing-
ness* and *No Exit*, where he represents human relations as situations in
which one conscious subject objectifies the other through his or her
gaze, thereby casting the other in the mode of being of the *en soi*,
ontologically of a status no different from that of a physical object.
The power of vision, of the gaze, is overwhelming and immobilizing
in the Sartrean account. It is no less so—and no less paralyzing—in
Frye's stark description of the activities of arrogant (male) perceivers
who "organize everything seen with reference to themselves and
their own interests . . . [thereby coercing] the objects of [their] perception into satisfying the conditions [their] perception imposes."[56]
The coercive and punitive gaze, thus variously described, is a counterpart, in a knower's relations to other people, of the distanced
subject-object relation traditionally considered appropriate for the
achievement of valid (= objective) knowledge. For women, none of
this language is stark enough to capture the objectifying effects of
vision as an instrument of knowledge. As Donna Haraway observes:
"The eyes have been used to signify a perverse capacity . . . to distance the knowing subject from everybody and everything in the
interests of unfettered power."[57] Catharine MacKinnon points out

[54]Ibid., pp. 219–220.
[55]Keller engages with questions of power in "The Gender/Science System: or, Is Sex
to Gender as Nature Is to Science?," *Hypatia: A Journal of Feminist Philosophy* 2 (Fall 1987):
37–49, but not with reference to the power of the gaze.
[56]Frye, *Politics of Reality*, p. 67.
[57]Donna Haraway, "Situated Knowledges: The Science Question in Feminism and
the Privilege of Partial Perspective," *Feminist Studies* 14 (Fall 1988): 581.

that feminists are only beginning to understand the relationship between vision as *appropriation* and as objectification.[58]

In the variations Foucault composes on Jeremy Bentham's *Panopticon*, he constructs a vivid analysis of the interweavings of a more generalized vision and visibility with knowledge and power. The Panopticon (= the all-seeing) is both prison and metaphor. As a prison, it consists in a building in the form of a ring, in whose center is a tower with windows opening onto the inside. The cells that comprise the ring have windows on both the inside and the outside, so that their inhabitants, illumined from behind, are perpetually visible to the overseers in the tower, with the result that "daylight and the overseer's gaze capture the inmate more effectively than darkness [in a dungeon], which afforded after all a sort of protection." As metaphor, the Panopticon represents the political power of a surveillance "both global and individualising,"[59] which systematically denies to bodies, individuals, and things the protection of privacy, secrecy, darkness. Power can be focused in the central observation point that is at once the source of knowledge and of control. Analogies suggest themselves with Orwell's Big Brother, whose gaze is all-seeing and all-knowing, or with an all-powerful God who, as all-seeing, is able to know even the darkest secrets of a sinner's heart.

Foucault writes of a power exercised "by virtue of the mere fact of things being known and people seen in a sort of immediate, collective and *anonymous* gaze." In the Panopticon, "*each person*, depending on his place, is watched by all or certain of the others. [It is] . . . an apparatus of total and circulating mistrust, because there is no absolute point."[60] Hence it would be a mistake to read him as saying that the central tower is *the* privileged locus of power: there is no absolute, sovereign locus. The viewed view the viewer with a gaze just as powerful: viewed and viewer are interchangeable, and power is everywhere, and nowhere in particular.

Now Foucault does not engage with issues of gender, class, race, or other forms of privilege. Were he to do so, it might be less easy for him to maintain—as he apparently means to—that visual positions are randomly distributed throughout societies. The Panopticon im-

[58]Catharine A. MacKinnon, "Feminism, Marxism, Method, and the State," in Sandra Harding, ed., *Feminism and Methodology* (Bloomington: Indiana University Press, 1987), p. 150 n. 4. MacKinnon quotes Susan Sontag: "The knowledge gained through still photographs will always be . . . a semblance of knowledge, a semblance of wisdom, as the act of taking pictures is a semblance of wisdom, a semblance of rape."

[59]Foucault, "The Eye of Power," in *Power/Knowledge*, pp. 147, 146.

[60]Ibid., pp. 154, 158, emphasis added.

age, and the more extensive analyses of surveillance in his studies of prisons, hospitals, and asylums, produce an apparatus for understanding knowledge-vision-power relations that feminists can use for their own purposes, as long as they read past the absence of gender. Foucault dislocates power from a unitary, sovereign place in order to show that the occupants of the tower are there more by chance than by natural right. Hence he makes a place for circulating relations of control and refusal, for subversive positions, subjugated knowledges, local resistances. Yet at any historical moment there are asymmetries: the occupants of the cells may not be without power, but they are clearly not as powerful as the viewers in the tower, for their vision is more severely limited by the structure of their location.

Yet Foucault's image of shifting centers of vision and control maps readily onto empiricist-positivist presuppositions that vision is alike in all 'normal' observers in standard observation conditions, presuppositions that derive from an equivalent failure to take account of the asymmetry of viewing positions. In his Panopticon image, social life is a configuration of anonymous, impartial surveillance and control, in which the occupants of the cells are in the position of the underclass groups in Harding's analysis.[61] Their controlled perspective could be justified by an empiricist conception of mind that attests to their passivity and malleability. The shifting, impersonal workings of power-knowledge, and the subject-object relations they legitimate, point to the constraining sociopolitical implications of autonomous, objective reason.

Re-visions

Objectivist discussions of vision rarely mention one of its aspects that develops in infancy, is crucial to infant development, and figures prominently in personal relationships. That aspect is direct eye contact between people: a symmetrical act of mutual recognition in which neither need be passive and neither in control. Such contact is integral to the way people position themselves in relation to one another and signify the meaning of their encounters. Through it, they engage with one another, convey feelings, and establish and maintain, or renegotiate, their relationships. From earliest infancy, the recognition of intersubjectivity in such contact is integral to knowing one another, to

[61]See my discussion of Harding, "Social Function of the Empiricist Conception of Mind," in Chapter 1, above.

communication, trust, sympathy, and reliance. Where such contact is not possible, people need to be especially creative in making relationships. When people are at pains to avoid eye contact, they confirm its power and significance. This "primitive and universally formative" experience of "locking eyes" is a model, Keller and Grontkowski note, for the communicative and connective (as contrasted with the distancing, objectifying) aspects of vision.[62] Accounts of knowledge that accorded *this* visual mode due significance might subvert the traditional subject-object relation. There would be more room for reciprocal subject-object relations, responsive to differences and idiosyncrasies. Subject-object relations thus restructured could produce epistemological positions that would accord better with feminist purposes.

It is by no means fanciful to imagine such a conception of relations extending from personal relationships to the wider animate and inanimate world. R. G. Collingwood describes an *artistic* seeing that is closer to the personal than to the distanced mode. In a painter's vocabulary:

Seeing . . . refers not to sensation but to awareness . . . [it] includes . . . much that is not visual . . . an awareness of 'tactile values' or the solid shapes of things, their relative distances, and other spatial facts which could be sensuously apprehended only through muscular motion . . . an awareness of things like warmth and coolness, stillness and noise . . . . it is a comprehensive awareness . . . a total imaginative experience.[63]

Brought to bear on observations of the natural world, this kind of seeing could signal a more respectful relation with nature, a greater care for its peculiarities, than objective observation permits. An awareness of the kind Collingwood describes is integral to present-day ecology movements, whose continuity with some aspects of feminist theory is well known.[64] It has the potential to mitigate against treating nature as simply 'out there', remote from human purposes and projects but available for manipulation, prediction, and control.

In fact, some phenomenologists work with a conception of the relations between knowers and 'the world' which has more in common with Collingwood's "awareness" *and* with ecological thinking than it does with an objectivist subject-object relation. Martin Heideg-

---

[62]Keller and Grontkowski, "Mind's Eye," p. 220.
[63]R. G. Collingwood, *The Principles of Art* (Oxford: Clarendon, 1938), p. 304.
[64]I elaborate some implications of that continuity in Chapter 7.

ger's phenomenological analysis of Being-in-the-world and Maurice Merleau-Ponty's description of the human body as an "expressive space" are two cases in point.[65] For Heidegger, *Dasein* (= the human being) is characterized, essentially, by Being-in-the-world. He[66] is no transcendent, purely rational creature, but a being immersed in the world. His modes of being (*existentiale*) are differentiated through the relations they reveal: to Others, to natural and material entities. Likewise, for Merleau-Ponty, the fact that human beings are "through and through compounded of relationships with the world"[67] provides the starting point for his analysis of perception—an engaged, not a distanced, sensory mode, which enlists a perceiver's whole sensory apparatus.

For Heidegger, philosophy takes its point of departure, then, from the fact of human existence in a concrete, matter-of-fact, daily world: a world that Dasein encounters through *things*, objects that he comes across in his everyday existence. Objects in the world may be 'present-at-hand' to Dasein, out there, available for scientific study and theoretical speculation. They may, by contrast, be 'ready-to-hand' as equipment, as entities with which he has 'concernful' dealings, hence as entities that he *knows* quite differently from those that he studies from a distance. Using a piece of equipment, a crafted, constructed tool, is the model for the relation at issue here. It affords a knowledge quite different in scope from that of detached, observational knowledge. Heidegger maintains, "No matter how sharply we just *look* at the 'outward appearance' of things . . . we cannot discover anything ready-to-hand. . . . But when we deal with them by using them and manipulating them, this activity is not a blind one; it has its own kind of sight, by which our manipulation is guided." Dasein's most authentic modes of being in the material world, then, involve an intimate, hands-on knowledge of particulars, which are so closely connected with him that they virtually become, in their usage, parts or extensions of his body. Heidegger illustrates this point with the example of a craftsman using a hammer, thus conveying the idea of knowing things through working with them, through practical involvement, in which work, praxis, has a function of discovery, revela-

[65]See Martin Heidegger, *Being and Time*, trans. John Macquarrie and Edward Robinson (New York: Harper & Row, 1962); and Maurice Merleau-Ponty, *The Phenomenology of Perception*, trans. Colin Smith (London: Routledge & Kegan Paul, 1962), p. 146.
[66]I use the masculine pronoun intentionally here. Like the man of reason, Dasein is unequivocally male.
[67]Merleau-Ponty, *Phenomenology of Perception*, p. xiii.

tion.[68] This notion of Dasein's relational positionality with respect to things, persons, language, works of art, and more complex artifacts and aspects of nature extends throughout Heidegger's oeuvre. Just as primordially as human beings are in the world, so too they are with others: others encountered not merely as present-at-hand, but as beings who are themselves present as Dasein and who are objects of their solicitude. The felt presence of others opens the possibility for an authentic mode both of being and of speaking which can escape the leveling-off effects of idle talk and undifferentiated objectification.

Heidegger's use of the terminology of "attentive dwelling within the sphere of things," his discussion of art (especially Van Gogh's painting of the peasant shoes) as "the disclosure of what the equipment . . . is in truth," his conception of the earth as a "sheltering agent,"[69] and his evocation of *dwelling* in the earth in the sense of preserving it from exploitation[70] speak of relationships between Dasein and the world in which predictability and control are pale substitutes for understanding and concern. Merleau-Ponty brilliantly complements this picture in his example of an organist learning to play a new, unfamiliar organ. The moves the organist makes to acquaint himself with the instrument include no reasoned analysis of its features, no drawing up of a chart or plan. Rather, they demonstrate how the *body* is "mediator of a world." The organist "sits on the seat . . . gets the measure of the instrument with his body, *incorporates within himself* the relevant directions and dimensions, settles into an organ as one settles into a house."[71] It is his body that understands, absorbs significance and meaning, and undertakes its projects with a *felt* understanding. For Merleau-Ponty, it is inconceivable that meaning should be derivable from "an act of thought . . . the work of a pure *I*," nor could bodily experience be explained as "the work of a universal constituting consciousness."[72]

Now there is no sense in which Heidegger and Merleau-Ponty could be declared protofeminists, nor is my discussion meant to claim them as feminist sympathizers. There is no place for women in either philosopher's work. Dasein is a self-authenticating being whose projects and equipment—with the possible exceptions of needles and the

---

[68]Heidegger, *Being and Time*, pp. 98, 101.
[69]Martin Heidegger, "The Origin of the Work of Art," in *Martin Heidegger: Basic Writings*, ed. David Farrell Krell (New York: Harper & Row, 1977), pp. 155, 164, 169.
[70]Martin Heidegger, "Being Dwelling Thinking," in ibid., p. 328.
[71]Merleau-Ponty, *Phenomenology of Perception*, p. 145, emphasis added.
[72]Ibid., p. 147.

peasant woman's shoes—belong entirely to the world of men. His orientation toward death has been the subject of feminist criticism,[73] and his being with others is a gender-neutral (= gender-blind) companionship in which love, intimate friendships, and familial relationships do not figure at all. Merleau-Ponty's perceiving subject is implicitly male. Although his chapter "The Body in Its Sexual Being"[74] does deal at some length with the example of a girl forbidden to see the young man with whom she is in love, Merleau-Ponty does not even address the possibility that a person's 'sexual being' would be quite differently realized in a female and in a male body.

Nonetheless, there are convergences between my project and certain aspects of these philosophers' thought, convergences that open possibilities of dialogue between feminists who take issue with the dominant epistemological discourse, and phenomenologists. Several of these convergences are worthy of note. Both Heidegger and Merleau-Ponty (i) reject the autonomy-of-reason model, arguing that all knowing is permeated with mood, feeling, sensibility, affectivity. They (ii) ground their analyses in experience, in praxis and embodied existence; hence the examples of knowledge to which they appeal are of knowledge in use, useful knowledge in the everyday world. They (iii) concentrate on *particular* experiences, specific modes of existence, from the conviction that it is in particularity and concreteness that generality—essence—can be known. They (iv) do not privilege vision: perception engages all of the senses; objects are known by touch, holding, sensing their whole presence. Indeed, perception also engages a 'sixth sense' that Oliver Sacks (following Sherrington) calls 'proprioception': the sense of themselves through which people "feel [their] bodies as proper to [them] . . . as [their] own"[75] and position themselves in the world through an awareness of the shape, capacities, and sociocultural inscriptions of their bodies. Finally, (v) they offer an account of being in the world which resonates with the activities of moral and epistemic subjects who know and understand by positioning and repositioning themselves within a situation in order to understand its *implications* and see in those implications contextualized, situated reasons for action. In all of these convergences, there are resources for feminist critical rethinking of the suppression of such

[73]See Mary O'Brien, "Resolute Anticipation: Heidegger and Beckett," in her *Reproducing the World: Essays in Feminist Theory* (Boulder, Colo.: Westview, 1989), for an excellent example of such criticism.

[74]Merleau-Ponty, *Phenomenology of Perception*, pp. 154–162.

[75]Oliver Sacks, *Man Who Mistook His Wife for a Hat*, p. 42.

modes of perceiving and knowing by the dominant paradigm, with its veneration of rational autonomy and its privileging of vision.

These phenomenological discussions speak of and from an established philosophical discourse informed by alternative constructions of the subject-object relation. This is not the mainstream discourse in whose terms Anglo-American epistemology and philosophy of science are predominantly discussed, and purists might find it illegitimate to introduce it into a book that engages primarily with mainstream epistemology. But part of the project of feminist critique is to uncover the suppressions and exclusions that received ways of thinking have effected and to challenge disciplinary, methodological, and ideological boundaries. Feminist critique is creative in making space available for crossing boundaries; in defying territoriality.

It is surprising that mainstream epistemology pays so little attention to touch, which figures at least as prominently as vision in everyday, subjective experience. Although people can and do survive well without sight, survival is next to impossible for a person with no sense of touch, unless she or he has constant, vigilant support from others and hence not even minimal autonomy. Touch is a source of knowledge at once more detailed and more stable than vision. With tactile confirmation, people are more secure in trusting their visual perceptions. Touch is integral to close relationships, in establishing and sustaining their intimacy, as is hearing, especially in its *listening* dimension. Heidegger claims that 'listening to' is fundamental to being open to and being with Others, and that authentic listening is possible only when one understands.[76] Gilligan writes of the importance, in breaking the spell of autonomy, of conceiving identity formation in terms of dialogue, in which listening and responding are paramount. That listening has both moral and epistemic dimensions is apparent in the sudden awareness that someone is *not* listening, an awareness that extends "across examples that range . . . from a problem in international politics to conflicts in personal relationships, making the public as well as the private dimensions of attachment or interdependence clear."[77] An epistemological recognition of the constitutive valence of second-person relationships and of the knowledge on which they depend would more clearly reveal the formative epistemic role of touch and hearing and displace objectivist vision from its

[76]Heidegger, *Being and Time*, pp. 206, 208.
[77]Gilligan, "Remapping the Moral Domain," in Heller et al., eds., *Reconstructing Individualism*, p. 250.

privileged epistemic position. Touch and listening are possible only for explicitly situated knowers.

Keller and Grontkowski conjecture that the transition in ancient Greece from an oral to a literate culture produced other shifts: "from identification and engagement to individualization and disengagement, from mimesis to analysis, from the concrete to the abstract, from mythos to logos."[78] They speculate that traditional metaphysical dichotomies were reinforced and recreated in the shift, with the consequence that analysis, disengagement, and logos gained (or regained) ascendancy. The contention that the ascendancy they imagine is a result of historical happenstance, not natural necessity, opens gaps in the seamless surface of received discourse, which claims to represent the natural, inevitable order of things.

Epistemological positions—'styles of reasoning'[79]—that appeal to touch, listening, and engaged modes of vision are taken up at points in the work (and in studies of the work) of three women scientists: Anna Brito, Rachel Carson, and Barbara McClintock. Certain characteristics of their (various) positions merit analysis, both for the commonalities in the practice of these scientists—who were not, apparently, influenced by one another—and for the epistemological styles that feminists have found significant in it. In Brito's work with lymphocytes and McClintock's work with maize, Jane Martin discerns a 'different style' of doing science—a style marked by an affection, attention, and involvement commonly characteristic of close personal relationships.[80] In Carson's later writings, Vera Norwood detects an overriding concern for a "right" understanding, whose rightness consists in a respectfully constructed epistemic relation between knowing subjects and their natural environments.[81]

Several features differentiate these scientists from malestream 'normal science'. Their work is marked by (i) a respect that resists the temptation to know primarily in order to control. Carson observes: "The 'control of nature' is a phrase conceived in arrogance, born of the Neanderthal age of biology and philosophy, when it was supposed that nature existed for the convenience of man."[82] The work is

---

[78]Keller and Grontkowski, "Mind's Eye," p. 209.

[79]I borrow this phrase from Ian Hacking's "Language, Truth, and Reason," in Hollis and Lukes, eds., *Rationality and Relativism*.

[80]Jane Roland Martin, "Science in a Different Style," *American Philosophical Quarterly* 25 (April 1988): 129–140.

[81]Vera Norwood, "The Nature of Knowing: Rachel Carson and the American Environment," *Signs: Journal of Women in Culture and Society* 12 (Summer 1987).

[82]Rachel Carson, *Silent Spring* (New York: Fawcett, 1962), pp. 261–262, quoted in Norwood, "Nature of Knowing," p. 756.

(ii) oriented toward letting the 'objects' of study speak for themselves; hence it is wary of imposing preconceived ideas and theoretical structures. Yet this openness is not theory-neutral. Rather, it is an attitude aware of the constraints of theory-ladenness and thus governed by reflexive, self-critical imperatives. The approach is (iii) nonreductive, adding to the first two features a recognition of an irreducible complexity in nature. (Norwood repeatedly remarks on Carson's wariness of epistemological hubris.) In all of the features there is (iv) a sense of the knowing subject's position in, and accountability to, the world she studies. That sense manifests itself in a mode of observation that is immersed and engaged, not manipulative, voyeuristic, or distanced. These positions entail a repudiation neither of the power of vision nor of empirical observation as a source of knowledge. But they presuppose a mode of observation that departs, qualitatively, from ideal observational objectivity. These scientists entertain no illusions that observation could be neutral or unbiased; rather, they emphasize the value of learning to see well. (Norwood refers to Carson's desire to teach the next generation "adequate seeing."[83]) Finally, and implicated in all of these features, is (v) a concern to understand difference, to accord it respect, hence to overcome temptations to dismiss it as theoretically disruptive, aberrant, cognitively recalcitrant. For mainstream philosophy of science, "the uniqueness and complexity of individuals are viewed as problems to be overcome by science not as irreducible aspects of nature."[84] By contrast, the practice of these three women honors individuality and uniqueness just as much as it works toward a general, theoretical understanding. Their concern with concrete particulars and with the dependence of general knowledge on knowing those particulars well is an epistemological correlative of Benhabib's conception of the relations between the generalized and the concrete other.

In McClintock's work, Keller finds a subject-object relation, "premised on respect rather than domination,"[85] in which respect for difference in her specimens shapes the research and the conclusions she draws. McClintock does not equate difference with aberration; rather, she focuses on it, peruses it. For her, differences and idiosyncrasies in her specimens are theoretically fascinating and revealing, not frustrating. She is guided by a conviction that it is possible to weaken presumed boundaries between subject and object. Hence her goal is

---

[83]Norwood, "Nature of Knowing," p. 757.
[84]Martin, "Science in a Different Style," p. 130. I am indebted to Martin in my thinking here.
[85]Keller, *Reflections on Gender and Science*, p. 135.

to understand, not to manipulate, predict, or control the genetic pat-
ternings of her maize. Her commitment to constructing a reciprocal
subject-object relation is at odds with a belief that things are best
known from an appropriately objective distance. McClintock speaks
of her need to "listen to the material," declaring that she knows every
plant intimately and finds it "a great pleasure to know them."[86]
Would it be merely fanciful to say that her research practice depends
on a 'second person' engagement with inanimate specimens? There is
no doubt that it is ecologically oriented, based as it is in a 'feeling' for
what the gene is to the cell and what the cell is to the organism as a
whole. However one describes the feeling—whether in terms of
friendship, intuition, or sympathy—it is antithetical to the distanced,
autonomous position of ideal ethical and epistemological objectivity
and continuous with the discourses of friendship, relationship, and
interdependence. In view of her dissociation of her life and work
from "all stereotypic notions of femininity,"[87] it would be a mistake to
interpret McClintock's epistemic position as an intentional celebration
of 'feminine' values. But she shows in her professional practice that it
is possible to make space in scientific research for suppressed practices and values that, coincidentally or otherwise, are commonly associated with 'the feminine'.

Brito's accounts of her work with lymphocytes tell an analogous
story of friendship and love when she speaks of her need, as a scientist, to "identify totally" with what she is doing, of the need to "*be* a
tumor" if one really wants to understand about a tumor. In her attention to detail, Brito is explicitly antipathetic to Baconian, Cartesian,
and Lockean projects of seeking universal, governing laws.[88] She
contests prevailing conceptions of nature as dumb, needing to be
tortured to reveal *her* secrets, and Brito's avowed identification with
nature renders metaphysical assumptions of an *external* world problematic. Claiming that "the nearest an ordinary person gets to the
essence of the scientific process is when they fall in love," Brito explains: "You, the scientist, don't know you're falling in love, but
suddenly you become attracted to that cell, or to that problem. Then
you are going to have to go through an active process in relationship
to it, and this leads to discovery."[89] In 'received' conceptions of scientific practice, "personal feelings and relationships are taken to be

[86]Ibid., p. 164.
[87]Keller, "Gender/Science System," p. 42.
[88]June Goodfield, *An Imagined World* (Harmondsworth: Penguin, 1982), pp. 226, 228.
[89]Ibid., pp. 228–229.

impediments to objectivity, not ingredients of discovery,"[90] Martin observes: intimations of affection and love would be more embarrassing than illuminating. Yet for McClintock and Brito, such feelings and relationships are integral to science.

A similar relational orientation is evident in Carson's work. Yet her reservations about 'connectedness' help to check possible (romantic) imbalances in readings of Brito's and McClintock's expressed attitudes. The Goodfield and Keller narratives of these scientists' relationships with their objects of study highlight an apparent dissolution of the rigid boundaries commonly assumed between subject and object. But the merging between subject and object that Brito, especially, claims to achieve is as troubling as it is salutary in its refusal of boundaries. There are too many echoes, here, of the rhetoric of love— usually of a man for a woman—that urges her to merge with him and hence to submerge her subjectivity, to deny her agency, and thus to disappear into the relationship. Translated into epistemological terms, such a loving attitude risks obscuring the extent to which objects of study are indeed separate from a researcher and recalcitrant to a whole range of cognitive structurings.[91] Objects of scientific investigation are as much sources of surprise, frustration, and unexpected discovery as they are of predictability and potential control: in this they are very like people.[92]

Carson's work is marked by a more conflicted, and hence differently nuanced, construction of the relationship between subject (natural scientist) and object (nature). In some places, "nature is described as a mother creating a home for her children," yet in other places Carson is clearly more concerned with ways in which "the natural world does not function as a home *or* household for its human children." Norwood observes that, for Carson, "the sea is no beloved mother, passively accepting, absorbing and redirecting the changes her children go through . . . [it] is 'other' than humankind."[93] A sci-

---

[90]Martin, "Science in a Different Style," p. 130. Keller notes: "From reading the text of nature, McClintock reaps the kind of understanding and fulfillment that others acquire from personal intimacy." Keller, *A Feeling for the Organism: The Life and Work of Barbara McClintock* (New York: Freeman, 1983), p. 205.

[91]In recognition of this separateness and recalcitrance, I argue, in Chapter 1, that radical relativism is not a viable epistemological stance.

[92]Haraway remarks: "Accounts of a 'real' world do not . . . depend on a logic of 'discovery' but on a power-charged social relation of 'conversation'. . . . In some critical sense that is crudely hinted at by the clumsy category of the social or of agency, the world encountered in knowledge projects is an active entity." Haraway, "Situated Knowledges," p. 593.

[93]Norwood, "Nature of Knowing," pp. 744, 748, 753.

entist has to take that 'otherness' into account if her knowledge is to be 'true to' her object of study. Perhaps the sea is not a mother, but it can, for Carson, be a rewarding, awesome, albeit unruly, and always surprising acquaintance. The difference between these two constructions attests to the epistemological advantage of drawing on friendship rather than mothering, as a relationship that depends on knowledge that is neither distanced nor engulfing, neither detached nor imperialistic.

Carson's project is to eschew mechanistic thinking, to emphasize the organic interconnections of human and other forms of organic life, and to undermine the arrogance of scientific and epistemological projects directed toward achieving control over nature. Yet for all that she thinks in terms of an organic oneness of life forms, she notes an equally compelling "lack of connection between humans and all the nonhuman natural world," a sinister side to connectedness, which becomes apparent "as we come to understand the webs of death interwoven with the webs of life." For Carson, it is as important to recognize the extent to which the natural world resists epistemic pattern making as it is to look for simplicity and regularity; as necessary to see the environment as "new, astounding, unusual" as to tame it; as vital to recognize flux and surprise as regularity and stasis. She sees epistemological hubris in complacent approaches to the environment, which value labeling and categorizing over "adequate seeing and feeling."[94] In these aspects of Carson's position, Norwood discerns an epistemological sophistication that often goes unnoticed.

My contrast of Carson's work is meant to highlight her concentration on the separateness that—perhaps paradoxically—makes good connections possible, not to minimize its continuity with the work of Brito and McClintock. This paradoxical dimension underlines the aptness of a personal-relational model of subject-object relations. An epistemology that draws on knowing other people well has to find a balance between the limits and the potential of such knowledge. It needs to guard against imperialism—against the potential for harm in impositions of one person's understanding, patterns, and descriptions on another person's experiences and self-perceptions. It has to be fallibilist, open to revisions and renegotiations in claims to knowledge. It must be sufficiently complex to take account both of commonality and of ineluctable difference, separateness, and resistance to being swallowed up in a relationship, subsumed under a description; it must be cognizant of the power that is claimed with every

94Ibid., pp. 753, 754, 757.

knowledge claim and hence accountable for the political implications of exercising cognitive agency. Like nature, friends are both resistant to their friends' pattern making and receptive to it. Extending to the natural world the model of knowing other people which establishing and sustaining a friendship requires could make possible a subject-object relation that is neither engulfing nor reductive, neither aggressively active nor self-deceptively passive—yet engaged and responsive, not neutral.

Now is there anything specifically female about these women's epistemic practices? What can be attributed explicitly to their femininity rather than, coincidentally, to their idiosyncrasies and social positions? The questions are not easy to answer. Consider, for instance, Stephen Jay Gould's observation that "McClintock's style of doing science is not uncommon; it just isn't widely used in her own discipline,"[95] and his claim that he himself—with many other good scientists—uses just such an approach. His point is clearly not to assert that he does science 'like a woman' or in a feminine style: it is to deny that there is anything distinctively 'feminine' about it, to claim it as part of 'normal science'. Keller herself cautions that "the suggestion that women . . . will do a different kind of science simultaneously invokes the duality of sex, and undermines (or proposes the undermining of) our confidence in the privileged attachment of science to nature."[96] Keller does not dispute the efficacy of scientific methodology nor the impressiveness of science's accomplishments. Yet neither does she query the 'maleness' of scientific practice. Arguing that concepts of "rationality and objectivity, and the will to dominate nature," at once inform a particular vision of science and the institutionalization of a definition of manhood, Keller nonetheless maintains that "because science as we know it developed only once in history, the notion of a 'different' science is to a considerable degree a contradiction in terms."[97] The claim is contentious, because there is no such single entity as 'science as we know it'. Even 'normal science' is a heterogeneous enterprise, both synchronically and diachronically.

Yet Keller wants to argue simultaneously that privileged white men are drawn to science because of particularities of their upbringing and consequent psychosexual development, *and* that women can do the same science as men, even though they may do it differently. The

[95]Stephen Jay Gould, review of *A Feeling for the Organism*, by Evelyn Fox Keller, *New York Review of Books* (March 1984). Cited in Martin, "Science in a Different Style," p. 130, and in Keller, "Gender/Science System," p. 41.
[96]Keller, "Gender/Science System," p. 45.
[97]Keller, *Reflections on Gender and Science*, p. 64.

problem is that the construction of gender she derives from object-relations theory posits fixed, static, developmental differences between women and men, with sex as the single differentiating cause. It is not easy to see, on Keller's view, how a woman could practice 'normal science' without abdicating femaleness: hence her socio-professional position looks like an aberration, a deviation from the pattern normatively constructed by object-relations theory. Neither is it easy to account for diversity in men's scientific practices. In short, for Keller, a female scientist lives a perpetual identity crisis, and a male scientist operates only within an unrealistically narrow range of positional options.

To profit from Keller's pathbreaking insights, yet avoid these constraints, Wendy Hollway draws on a Kleinian construction of psychological development, in which emphasis is displaced from childhood to more widely distributed—'second person'—intersubjective moments. Hollway resists the discourse of individuals and ideology to focus on the construction of subjectivity as a "product of positions in a potentially infinite number of discourses and related practices, many of which confer meanings very different to 'woman' as it is signified in scientific discourse."[98] Neither science nor any other discourse in which people are positioned is unitary, nor are patterns of gendered subjectivity frozen in their postoedipal configurations. Hollway's analysis does not minimize the conservatism of socially approved female and male child raising in constructing people's options, nor does it trivialize the contradictions that many women experience in their efforts to 'be' scientists, particularly in their confrontations with the dominant discourses of scientific institutions. Rather, Hollway aims at producing an explanation adequate to the complexities of multiple subjectivities and to diversity in scientific practice, in which both women and men have varied relations to the dominant discourse. Whether those different relations affect how they *do* science is a matter for case-by-case analysis, in which gender cannot be the sole explanatory factor. At issue are the political structures of 'science' and 'society' and the different positions that differently gendered people occupy—differently. The question comes back, then, to the problematic of knowledge and subjectivity, to questions about how the subjectivity of scientists contributes to the objective construct called 'science'. These are questions of gender, because there are no ungendered scientists. They are not about gender alone,

[98]Hollway, *Subjectivity and Method in Psychology*, p. 117.

but about gender as it constructs and is constructed in relations of politics and power.

There is no doubt that people for whom science does offer the "cool and objective remove" that protects them against anxiety tend to be defensively attached to the dominant mode of scientific practice, resistant to alternative styles and/or subject-object relations. Undoubtedly, it is their "production and reproduction of the discourse which has been the historical vehicle for science to become what it is."[99] But this historical result is not biologically determined, nor has it produced a unified, seamless scientific practice: gaps can be created— and widened—within it without destroying its attachment to nature. This creation is as much political as it is epistemological, for there is no politically neutral community or group of inquirers: any that claim neutrality are merely reaffirming the power of the status quo.

Whatever its gendered derivations, there is a curious gap in Gould's argument that McClintock's method is just like his own—a gap that matches a gap in mainstream epistemology. Gould's conception of epistemology does extend beyond the standard one, to incorporate "intuition, insight, and concrete knowledge of particulars."[100] Yet it has no place for the intimacy and friendship that, on McClintock's account, characterizes her relationship with her corn. Hence Gould's declared affinity with McClintock requires no compromise, on his part, of the reductivism integral to the epistemology he takes for granted. To give appropriate credence to McClintock's presentation of her practice, it is necessary to allow that there is either *more* than knowledge at issue in her relation to her maize or a *kind* of knowledge that differs markedly from standard scientific objectivity: a multifaceted, more complex, more textured knowledge.[101]

Gould's contention that these aspects of McClintock's knowing are unworthy of epistemological notice is of a piece with his denial that her femaleness is significant for her epistemic position. In fact, precisely those "elements of McClintock's and . . . [Brito's] style [that] are associated with women and femininity"[102] are the ones he finds trivial, irrelevant. His description plays directly into the questions

[99]Ibid., p. 120.
[100]Martin, "Science in a Different Style," p. 134.
[101]I am indebted to Jane Martin, again, in my thinking here.
[102]Martin, "Science in a Different Style," p. 135. Martin notes that "the genderization of what according to our accepted definitions qualify as non-epistemological elements of the different style does not constitute a barrier to their acceptance as legitimate elements of scientific method or research simply because science itself is genderized" (p. 136).

about the nature of epistemology with which feminists are engaged. Malestream epistemology draws its boundaries so as to exclude from the proper exercise of autonomous reason the very traits and styles that McClintock and Brito declare integral to their own scientific practice. Gould's response to the challenge that the successful deployment of a 'different style' appears to pose is to keep the boundaries of epistemology intact by banishing the differences to an extraepistemological realm. Many feminists, by contrast, respond by calling for a more generous, more honest epistemology that takes into account the range of capacities, discursive positions, attitudes, and interests that contribute to the construction of knowledge. A refusal to rethink the boundaries has the effect of suppressing and denying status to women's constructions of their experiences and agency in a manner that is of a piece with women's suppression/oppression under patriarchy.

The point is not that science is simply a masculine enterprise and should for that reason alone be discredited. Scientific practice is often not explicitly sexist, even though it plainly is both patriarchal and androcentric, in consequence of the institutions in which it is practiced, and the practitioners from whose observations it is produced. Feminist critiques of science cannot simply advocate a rejection of received scientific method. Rather, their aim is to develop critical analyses of the presumptions that sustain scientific androcentrism, to examine the location of science within sociopolitical-economic *and* gendered structures, and to uncover the exclusions and suppressions that are consequent on a concurrence with its dominant ideology.[103] Autonomy, anonymity, and ideal objectivity are normatively legitimated by that ideology. Yet as Brito observes, "anonymity is an *achievement*, a real achievement, of the enterprise. It provides a comfortable framework in which we are all *equal* and our agonies are hidden from the public gaze. There are no personal traits being revealed, or insecurities. It is all one security."[104]

It would be foolish for feminists to direct their critiques toward a simple withdrawal of respect for scientific achievement or a repudiation of its paradigm-governed (in the Kuhnian sense) structure. If they were to make such a move publicly yet unilaterally, they would merely confirm the persistent belief that women can neither do nor

---

[103]Keller maintains that "the practice of science is in fact quite different from its ideological prescriptions . . . [and that] actual science is more faithfully described by the multiplicity of styles and approaches that constitute its practice than by its dominant rhetoric or ideology." *Reflections on Gender and Science*, p. 125.

[104]Goodfield, *An Imagined World*, p. 236.

understand science anyway, so it is no wonder that they are "against" it. What better evidence could there be of female irrationality?

In practical terms alone, women need science for the freedoms it can offer them. Privileged, affluent women can make use of the technological advances, achieved out of scientific discovery, to free themselves of much of the domestic labor that used to constitute women's lot. Increased contraceptive possibilities and medical care have changed women's lives across a wider social spectrum, in decreasing unwanted childbearing, reducing infant mortality, and making disease and death more manageable. Many of the opportunities for work, travel, entertainment, and education that economically advantaged women can enjoy are made possible by science. There is no need to detail the achievements of 'science' further to make the point. Like every activity and institution, science is as political as it is 'beneficial'—and it is, in consequence, unevenly beneficial and often harmful, for all of the reasons feminists are learning to see and many more that they presumably have not yet seen. Only the very affluent can reap the fullest benefits science and technology produce, and even then many affluent women do not have access equivalent to that of their male 'equals', for reasons both political and economical. Many less affluent and racially and culturally marginalized women *and* men suffer directly or indirectly in processes of scientific experimentation and production. Scientific achievement is at once wonderful and awful: it can never be evaluated merely as knowledge for its own sake, for there are always political implications. Yet feminist philosophers of science maintain that androcentric science is often 'good science' in its "scrupulous adherence to scientific methodology."[105]

The purpose of feminist critiques is to reveal the limitations of the methodology, to open possibilities of "theoretical and methodological pluralism."[106] Such efforts could locate specific puzzles and their solutions within sociopolitical-environmental analyses that would reveal the interrelation of apparently separate and isolated areas of inquiry, both in their potential for mutual illumination and in their multiple effects. Feminist critiques do not just create a requirement of *adding* 'new' or 'different' problems to scientific theory and practice, any more than feminist thought, more generally, would fulfill its

---

[105]This is Elizabeth Potter's phrase, in "Modeling the Gender Politics in Science," *Hypatia: A Journal of Feminist Philosophy* 3 (Spring 1988): 20.

[106]I owe this phrase to Alison Wylie, in her article "Gender Theory and the Archeological Record," in Margaret Conkey and Joan Gero, eds., *Women and Prehistory* (Oxford: Blackwell, in press).

purposes simply by adding women to malestream discourse. They require scientists—and knowers in general—to become accountable, in both their theory and their practice; to recognize that 'normal science', in its current form as a body of knowledge consists, as Ruth Hubbard argues, in a "set of descriptions put forward by the mostly white, educated, Euro-American men who have been practicing a particular kind of science during the past two hundred years."[107] Accountability entails acknowledgment of the roles of subjectivity and context in the construction of knowledge: these cannot be stripped away, but need to be analyzed and evaluated. Crucial to the process, then, is a reinsertion of the experimenter as a specifically located, gendered, self-conscious subject into every account of scientific inquiry, so that 'S' can no longer pose as a faceless abstraction in an 'S knows that p' rubric that requires him to take no responsibility for his knowing and allows him to disappear behind his 'findings'.[108] Hubbard proposes that, in philosophy of science, the social sciences rather than physics could become models for analysis. There, context stripping is impossible. In theory of knowledge, as I have been arguing, knowing other people could displace 'S knows that p' paradigms. There, too, context stripping cannot be tolerated, and a knower is always accountable.

Knowing Other People

Now it is not possible simply to turn to mainstream social science for models of knowledge that permit us to understand people or for models that can serve as paradigms for the construction of knowledge per se. Large areas of social scientific inquiry adhere to the positivist/empiricist ideals of objectivity and neutrality, contending that the production of covering laws is the only legitimate scientific goal. Quantification is still esteemed as the best method for achieving certain knowledge; qualitative research is still frequently marginalized and dismissed as 'unscientific'.[109] Feminist critiques of mainstream

[107]Ruth Hubbard, "Some Thoughts about the Masculinity of the Natural Sciences," in M. Gergen, ed., *Feminist Thought and the Structure of Knowledge*, p. 10.

[108]Hence Haraway argues for situated, embodied knowledges and against "various forms of unlocatable, and so irresponsible, knowledge claims. Irresponsible means unable to be called into account." Haraway, "Situated Knowledges," p. 583.

[109]Hollway cites the inscription on the facade of the Social Sciences Research Building at the University of Chicago, which reads: "IF YOU CANNOT MEASURE, YOUR KNOWLEDGE IS MEAGER AND UNSATISFACTORY." Hollway, *Subjectivity and Method in Psychology*, p. 88.

social science have demonstrated its persistent androcentrism and frequent sexism.[110] The positivist/empiricist observational model is best adapted to study interchangeable objects whose behavioral patterns can be measured and mapped, predicted and manipulated. So it can study human beings only by assimilating them to objects that respond predictably to certain stimuli, cluster together in certain ways, repel each other under specifiable circumstances, and are immune to or susceptible to precise kinds of pressures, reactions, attractions. Hubbard's observation that context stripping is impossible in social science is more prescriptive than descriptive: in positivist/empiricist social science, it is the rule. She is right, nonetheless, to declare it impossible, prescriptively, for there is no doubt that it is impossible to know, to understand people out of the contexts that construct and maintain their subjectivity.

Consider the 'S knows that p' rubric, where p does not stand for a green patch or an apple but for another person. To make the substitutions work, one has to alter the formula a little, either by contracting it into 'S knows P' (Susan knows Pat) or by expanding it into 'S knows that P is . . . , or can . . . , or does . . . ' (Sue knows that Pat is manipulative, or can help out, or listens well). The contractions and expansions cannot compensate for the restrictions inherent in these minimal claims. Such one-liners do not even begin to provide a basis for judging a person or for making decisions that could affect the course of her life. That such variations on an 'S knows that p' model could count as the basis not only of social scientific conclusions but also of moral deliberation is not as far-fetched as it might seem. Kohlberg's Heinz dilemma is a case in point: all S knows is that p is a druggist, a sick wife, or a man who cannot afford to buy a drug. She or he knows nothing about the circumstances that create the dilemma. Is the druggist charging an unreasonable price or a fair one? What are these people's social and financial resources? Is there no one they can call on? Are they racially or economically marginalized, and hence extraordinarily bereft of social resources? Can they not borrow the money, ask for credit? Are they an autonomous man-wife unit in solitary confrontation with the druggist? It is not easy to see, even in a

[110]Some now-classic feminist critiques are Rayna Reiter, ed., *Toward an Anthropology of Women*; Naomi Weisstein, "Psychology Constructs the Female," in Vivian Gornick and Barbara K. Moran, eds., *Woman in Sexist Society* (New York: Basic, 1971); Jean Baker Miller, *Toward a New Psychology of Women* (Boston: Beacon, 1976); and Dorothy Smith, *The Everyday World as Problematic* (Toronto: University of Toronto Press, 1988). For a more comprehensive list, see Alison Wylie, Kathleen Okruhlik, Leslie Thielen-Wilson and Sandra Morton, "Philosophical Feminism: A Bibliographic Guide to Critiques of Science," *Resources for Feminist Research* 19 (June 1990), 2–36.

research or a classroom setting, how anyone could respond to the dilemma without knowing more about the story. Notorious illustrations of the pedagogical use of such a minimalist moral epistemology are kidney-machine or lifeboat dilemmas, in which students of moral philosophy learn that a five-year-old boy, a brilliant scientist, and a seventy-year-old woman need dialysis or are on board a sinking ship. There is only one machine/one lifeboat; who should be saved? Nor are reductive examples of this sort restricted to classrooms and philosophy texts. Press and media discussions of sensitive and complex issues such as abortion, euthanasia, or birth control commonly rely on equally minimal epistemological content as the basis for generating 'informed opinions' about matters that are literally vital. The very possibility of constructing a knowledgeable position on any of these issues is obstructed by the summary, stereotype-dependent information that poses as knowledge of what is at issue. The knowledge claims invoked—statistical evidence about the frequency of abortion, for example—and the scope claimed for them attest to the continued hegemony of a neopositivistic commitment to the 'unity of knowledge' project, whose aim is to show that the experimental, observational methodology and the models of knowledge of natural science are appropriate for the human sciences: it is to establish social scientific inquiry on a 'properly scientific' basis.

There may be some truth to Jane Martin's claim that, "were McClintock and Anna [Brito] social scientists, their concern for concrete individuals and their experiences of merging with the things they study would be considered normal by at least some metatheorists of their domain."[111] But in positivist/empiricist social science circles, they would as readily be marginalized and dismissed as eccentric as they have been by natural scientists. Feminist critiques are directed against those social sciences in which their scientific 'styles' are by no means routine. Feminists are not alone in developing critiques of 'scientific' social science,[112] but their analyses focus on the effects oppressive to women that follow from the persistence of the reductive, ideal-

[111]Martin, "Science in a Different Style," p. 130.

[112]A landmark criticism of the application of natural scientific methodology to social science is Peter Winch, *The Idea of a Social Science and Its Relation to Philosophy* (London: Routledge & Kegan Paul, 1958). Winch extends his analysis to an anthropological context in "Understanding a Primitive Society," *American Philosophical Quarterly* (1964), reprinted in Bryan R. Wilson, ed., *Rationality* (Oxford: Blackwell, 1971). Other articles in the Wilson volume address the issue of understanding other people's experiences from their point of view (of participant observation), rather than as detached observers of specimens of behavior. The discussion is continued in Hollis and Lukes, eds., *Rationality and Relativism*. See also the Wylie et al. bibliography.

objectivity model in social science, and on the political implications of androcentric and sexist social scientific practice.

The aspect of positivist/empiricist social science most pertinent to the present discussion is its tacit assumption that the best and most natural line of reasoning in epistemological theory construction is *from* knowledge of simple physical objects *to* other kinds of knowledge. The work of Carson, Brito, and McClintock gives a glimpse of the differences it could make to knowledge of physical, natural 'reality' if the line of reasoning were drawn in the opposite direction, *from* the knowledge integral to good personal relationships *to* the natural world. It is probably not appropriate to advocate such a redirection for all areas of scientific or social scientific inquiry, and it is just as necessary to guard against allowing the redirected approach to become reductive in its own terms, losing sight of the independence of objects of knowledge and discounting the claims of an appropriately conceived objectivity. Nonetheless, knowledge constructed in an interpersonal mode opens possibilities of insight and understanding sufficient to warrant claiming its epistemic significance well beyond the traditionally constructed 'personal' domain.

The problem is to show how a 'second person' relationship characteristic of friendship can inform a reconstructed subject-object relation between knowers and the known, and how the 'second person' knowledge integral to such friendships can have paradigmatic import when the object of study (the known) is inanimate. The case has to be made by analogy and not by requiring scientists to convert from being objective observers of, to being friends with, the chemicals, particles, cells, planets, rocks, trees, and insects they study. There are obvious points of disanalogy, not the least of which derives from a traditional belief that it is *possible* to know the subject matter of science, whereas it is never possible really to know other people. The persistence of the problem of 'other minds' in malestream philosophy attests to the strength of that belief. But this apparent disanalogy appears to prevent the analogy from going through partly because of presuppositions built into empiricist-objectivist theories.

According to the stringent paradigms based in positivistic conceptions of the nature and scope of physics, science can produce knowledge that is certain in the sense that it is established, universally and uncontrovertibly, for all time. Whether or not such pure and perfect knowledge has ever been achieved is an open question: a belief in its possibility guides and regulates mainstream theory of science and a good deal of scientific practice. The presumption that knowing other people is difficult to the point of near-impossibility is established by contrast with those paradigms, whose realization may be possible only in contrived, attenuated physical science instances. By *that* standard, knowing other people, however well, does look like as pale an approximation as it was for Descartes, by contrast with the 'clear and distinct ideas' he was otherwise able to achieve. The question is why *that* standard, which governs so minuscule a part of the epistemic lives even of members of the privileged professional class and gender, should regulate legitimate uses of the label 'knowledge'. The rarity of its achievement should prompt denials of its paradigmatic validity.

Were the positivist-empiricist standard to be displaced by more complex analyses of the extent to which knowledge claims are provisional and approximate, knowing other people would not seem so different after all. Current upheavals in epistemology suggest that displacement projects are already under way. Not the least important for the topic at hand is the growing appeal of hermeneutic, interpretive, literary methods of analysis and explanation in the social sciences. The skills involved in using these methods are not so different from the interpretive skills that the maintenance of good friendships requires. Whether their appeal extends to the natural sciences is not clear. But the point of the challenge is also to locate natural scientific inquiry differently, to recognize it as a sociopolitical-historical practice in which knowing who the scientist is can reveal important epistemological dimensions of her or his inquiry. Even if knowing other people cannot (yet) be the model, it is no longer possible to argue convincingly that such knowledge cannot be part of scientific inquiry.

A more stubborn point of disanalogy may appear to reside in the fact that chemicals and plants and rocks cannot reciprocate in the ways that friends can. There will be none of the mutual recognition and affirmation between scientist and specimen that there is between friends. But after Heisenberg's formulation of the 'uncertainty principle', it is no longer possible to assert unequivocally that objects of study are inert in and untouched by the observational processes even of physics. Once that point is acknowledged, it is no longer so easy to draw rigid lines separating responsive from unresponsive objects. Moving to a framework of 'second person' knowledge does not, per impossibile, require scientists to begin talking to their rocks and cells or to claim that the process does not work because the rocks fail to respond. It calls, rather, for a recognition that rocks and cells, and scientists, are located in many relations to one another, all of which are open to analysis and critique. Singling out and privileging the asymmetrical observer-observed relation is but one possibility. It invites too-ready knowledge claims of a sort that friendship could not allow. A recognition of the space that needs to be kept open for reinterpretation, of the contextualizing that adequate knowledge requires, becomes clearer in the light of the friendship analogy. Though the analogy between the two kinds of knowledge can never be perfect, it is surely no more preposterous to argue that people should try to know physical objects in the nuanced way that they know their friends than it is to argue that they should try to know people in the unsubtle way that they claim to know physical objects.

The question as to whether 'second person' knowledge of other people can acquire paradigmatic status cannot be answered once and for all, particularly at this early, critical moment. Case-by-case analysis can create presumptions in its favor, a point I mean to illustrate with my discussion of Carson, McClintock, and Brito. The fact that social scientists are increasingly drawn to interpretive rather than positivistic models may have the repercussions for natural science that Hubbard and others hope. Kenneth Gergen envisages scientists engaging in a "craft labor" that depends on a "direct immersion in nature, a working with or a coordination of actions with one's surroundings,"[113] which emphasizes the role of practical activity. Just how he believes that this project could be carried out is not yet clear: it awaits case-by-case analysis.

In social scientific practice that adheres to a positivist/empiricist credo, it is difficult to understand how the knowledge constructed could ever qualify as *knowing* other people. Of psychology, Hollway notes, "Ideas of mind, self and subjective experience have remained outside mainstream psychology . . . in its efforts to ally itself with natural science."[114] In its devotion to quantitative methodology, mainstream psychology continues to reveal its commitments to a scientific methodology and to puzzle its critics about how it can hope, by those methods, to understand people. In sociology, anthropology, economics, political science, and history, analogous debates persist, to greater or lesser degrees, about the possibility of being properly scientific, as opposed to the need to understand and engage with human subjects on their own terms.

Challenging the hegemony of prevalent methodological orthodoxies calls for imagination and a respect for autobiographical accounts and observations, even when those accounts appear to require rein-

[113]Kenneth Gergen, "Feminist Critique of Science and the Challenge of Social Epistemology," in M. Gergen, ed., *Feminist Thought and the Structure of Knowledge*, p. 41.
[114]Hollway, *Subjectivity and Method in Psychology*, p. 89.

terpretation. Imagination is essential to the openness that seeing things from someone else's point of view requires. Yet openness has to be tempered with respect so a knower can guard against imposing her beliefs that she knows just how it is for another person. It is important not to curtail possibilities of negotiation and reassessment, not just to slot events and other people's experiences into ready-made categories. Categories are both enabling and constraining; without them, conceptual thinking and language would be impossible; but their application risks blotting out the complexities of the very phenomena and experiences they purport to represent.

Clinical psychology provides pertinent illustrations of this point. In *The Man Who Mistook His Wife for a Hat*, Oliver Sacks observes:

> There is no "subject" in a narrow case history; modern case histories allude to the subject in a cursory phrase ("a trisomic albino female of 21"), which could as well apply to a rat as a human being. To restore the human subject at the center—the suffering, afflicted, fighting, human subject—we must deepen a case history into a narrative or tale; only then do we have a "who" as well as a "what," a real person, a patient, in relation to disease—in relation to the physical.[115]

Sacks's dialogues with his clients show that "it is possible to be objective and subjective at the same time, that the gulf between the psychical and the physical can somehow be bridged."[116] Full narrative concentration on the circumstances of a 'concrete other' does not interfere with drawing general conclusions: on the contrary, it renders them more adequate. Sacks demonstrates the effectiveness of a narrative case history approach in disrupting the constraints of categories and dichotomies.

Crucially at issue in Sacks's work are questions about the nature and extent of a practitioner's claims to know other people well enough to draw conclusions and make recommendations that affect their capacities to live well. The crippling and undermining potential of a failure to know is illustrated in May Sarton's story of Caroline Spencer,[117] an elderly, intermittently confused patient in a nursing home, who is reduced by her 'keepers' to the sum of her moments of

[115]Sacks, *Man Who Mistook His Wife for a Hat*, p. xiv. I cite this passage in an earlier version of this discussion in my "Stories People Tell," *New Mexico Law Review* 16 (Fall 1986).

[116]The wording is Charles Rycroft's in his review of Sacks's book, in *New York Review of Books* (March 13, 1986), p. 11.

[117]May Sarton, *As We Are Now* (New York: Norton, 1973). This novel is the subject of my analysis in "Persons, and Others."

confusion. They ignore all manifestations of her lucid, creative, and self-aware cognitive agency. Treating her as merely a senile patient, positioned in a routine and a set of expectations that make of her a simple category, they can forget that she is the subject of her own experiences.

I cite these 'cases' to illustrate the value of case-by-case analysis in revealing how constructions of reality, and of the relation of thought to reality, can hold knowers captive. John Wisdom contends, "At the bar of reason, always the final appeal is to cases."[118] His point, as Roger Shiner reads it, is that "judgements about particular cases are the foundation of reason itself."[119] Case-by-case argument, for Wisdom (following Wittgenstein), is crucial to philosophy's primary therapeutic task: relieving 'mental cramp'. The tenacity of entrenched pictures of reality derives from the philosophical predilection for generality that gives only perfunctory attention to particular cases, which Benhabib discusses with reference to the moral domain. Wisdom argues that concentration on cases does not impede systematic procedure: on the contrary, it yields systematic accounts that are more adequate to their subject matter. The practice of setting one case beside another, together with appealing to contrast, paradox, metaphor, and even poetry, produces an epistemological picture that has room for specificity and historical process. That picture contrasts markedly with the more common, "static frozen pictures" that suppress particularity in the interests of generality, reinforcing the belief that substitutionalist thinking has no place for detail and specificity. Shiner rightly maintains that a mistaken preoccupation with science, where neutral detached theory is possible, leads philosophers "to despise the particular case."[120] Although detached neutrality is a contested possibility even in science, the self-presentation of science takes it for granted. The low esteem accorded to case studies (such as those that characterize the work of Brito and McClintock) is one of the consequences.

In the 'cursory phrases' with which standard case histories refer to people as 'cases', as in Caroline Spencer's story, only a minimal effort is made to know a person: one or two objectively observable features classify her, sum her up. Missing is any recognition of the patient as a subject with a history and experiences, whose view of her own situa-

---

[118]John Wisdom, *Paradox and Discovery* (Oxford: Blackwell, 1965), p. 102. Quoted in Roger Shiner, "From Epistemology to Romance via Wisdom," in *Philosophy and Life: Essays on John Wisdom*, ed. Ilham Dilman (The Hague: Martinus Nijhoff, 1984), p. 291.
[119]Shiner, "From Epistemology to Romance," p. 291.
[120]Ibid., pp. 302, 306.

tion is as worthy of analysis as the objective 'expert's' view of her. Sacks's case history analysis—like Wisdom's case-by-case approach and the narrative strategies of novels and biographies/ autobiographies—facilitates a reconstruction of people's histories and circumstances as an interplay between 'expert' representations and a subject's construction of her experiences. Hence both for social theory and for knowing people in more everyday contexts, these approaches create possibilities of *being* subjective and objective at the same time— subjective in taking account of the specificities of subjectivity, objective in drawing more general conclusions, showing how stories fit into broader schemes, while leaving conclusions open to modification and reinterpretation.

Just such a style of reasoning is characteristic of a female contribution to moral analysis that philosophers have neglected. In representations of personal relationships and intricate, restrictive social structures, nineteenth-century female novelists reveal a capacity to write sophisticated moral philosophy long before they could claim positions as professional philosophers. The abstract construction of moral experience and agency of standard moral theories cannot yield a moral epistemology sufficiently sensitive to engage with families, friendships, and personal histories, nor to situate them in the circumstances that produce them. But novels locate moral analyses and deliberations in textured, detailed situations in which a reader can, vicariously, position and reposition herself to understand some of the implications, for people's lives, of moral decisions, attitudes, and actions. A novel, therefore, Edward Mooney suggests, is less likely than standard moral theories "to run roughshod over the moral subtleties of personal and familial relationships, and their roots in trust, affection, and sympathy."[121] The same philosophical intransigence that sustains the autonomy-of-reason persuasion denies the relevance of literature and narrative to philosophical inquiry and justificatory procedures. Narrative is too specific; it dwells on particulars and admits affective concerns at every turn. Therefore, the argument goes, it can only confuse the pursuer of objective knowledge.[122] My claim is that inquiry—both moral and epistemological—needs narrative to supply the particulars upon which analysis has to be based.

[121]See Edward Mooney, "Gender, Philosophy, and the Novel," *Metaphilosophy* 18 (July/October 1987): 245. Mooney makes no mention, however, of the sociopolitical factors that determine women's position as novelists, nor does he take account of the narrow, patriarchally determined options that their 'moral philosophies' detail.

[122]For an interesting counterargument pertinent to the present discussion, see David Polkinghorne, *Narrative Knowing in the Human Sciences* (Albany: State University of New York Press, 1988).

Rethinking the epistemic basis of the practices that depend on knowing other people—intimate relationships, alliances, clinical and legal practice, social scientific inquiry, and moral analysis—and breaking out of embedded categories and labeling practices is not easy. It is difficult for an inquirer to become aware of what Wittgenstein calls the "pair of glasses on [his/her] nose through which [s/he] see[s] whatever [s/he] look[s] at."[123] The process involves facing uncertainty, approaching the world with blurred vision. Often, one must learn to see all over again, an endeavor that requires training in imagination and sensitivity. A challenging aspect of this project is learning to *listen responsibly* to stories people tell about their experiences, even though the stories may not be *true*. Indeed, a first step is to abandon the presupposition that people have uniquely privileged access to the truth about *their own* experiences. So the task of redirecting one's vision involves paradox after paradox. Not only does it require suspending old ways of seeing, but it often demands a willingness to see less rather than more clearly. Not only does it call for abandoning categories and theories in favor of the complexity of experiences, but it insists on a recognition that first-person narrative accounts may *not* afford immediate access to the truth. Even an account of my own experiences, told as honestly as I can tell it, is but one account among many. The insightful dialogue of knowledgeable friendship often constructs an understanding of one or both of the friends' 'own' experiences which she/they could not have achieved alone. Analogously, psychotherapeutic practice is premised on a belief that people often do not understand their experiences. Sometimes it is successful in constructing alternative interpretations, whose resonance or dissonance, for both participants, can be tried out, negotiated, reconsidered. Yet neither the subject that tells stories nor the subject about whom they are told is a fixed or transparent entity, and changes accompany every telling.

Not even the limitations of full narrative constructions can gainsay the fact that minimalist, reductive epistemologies are of minimal value. For ease of analysis, manipulation, and/or prediction, reductivists focus on as few salient features of a subject or a situation as will allow them to categorize and judge. Clean, uncluttered analyses are valued more highly than rich, multifaceted, but messy and ambiguous, narratives. Reductivist analyses interpose theoretical tenets and presuppositions *between* subject and object, creating and maintaining a rift, a

---

[123]Ludwig Wittgenstein, *Philosophical Investigations*, trans. G. E. M. Anscombe (Oxford: Blackwell, 1951), #103.

dichotomy. They inhibit the construction of knowledge and belief out of an interplay of subject-and-object, interconnected and reciprocally influential. Too much structure, too rigidly defined, closes off more possibilities than it opens. Where inquiry aims to know other people, categorization cannot substitute for understanding. Noticing that "pair of glasses on our nose," attempting to do without them, can facilitate the "adequate seeing" that for Carson is indispensable to knowing well.

I have claimed that parallels between moral and epistemological analysis are clearest in situations in which the epistemic basis of *moral* deliberation is at issue, but that those parallels extend into epistemology per se. The relevance of narrative to epistemology proper may not be so obvious as its relevance to *moral* epistemology. But my claim is that once epistemologists recognize the locatedness of all cognitive activity in the projects and constructions of specifically positioned subjects, then the relevance of narrative will be apparent as an epistemological resource. The model of the autonomous Cartesian knower has worked to obscure that significance.

Questions about the quality of cognitive agency—about its 'locatedness' and vested interests—*cannot* arise within Cartesian analysis. A disembodied, autonomous reasoner must treat all knowledge claims alike. He cannot have a passion for truth, nor (in his empiricist guise) can he think about understanding except as an accumulation of more and more justified knowledge claims. Hence narrative accounts of his projects might be of mild historical interest, but they would be of no epistemological significance. Mainstream epistemology can deal with such matters only by relegating them to a pre- or extraepistemological context of discovery.

Feminist readings of Brito's, Carson's, and McClintock's stories are part of a proliferation of feminist critiques of science, all of which show beyond a doubt that the contexts of discovery and justification—either in science or in the construction of 'everyday' knowledge—cannot legitimately be held apart. Science is made by scientists, knowledge by knowers. Hence it cannot be free of subjective interests, values, commitments, and needs. Theoretical presuppositions, vested interests, and the selective focus of research methodologies determine the outcome of the discovery process. (Bleier remarks that "scientists cannot simply hang their subjectivities up on a hook outside the laboratory door."[124]) There can be no sense to the claim that, in the context of justification, all of these impurities are

[124]Bleier, "Lab Coat," p. 63.

filtered out to produce neutral, interchangeable results. Evaluation can approach adequacy only when the putative division between the two contexts is deconstructed.

Kohlberg's work illustrates this point. So long as he focused only on processes of justification—categorizing results and deriving law-like patterns—the invisibility of female subjects at the highest levels of moral achievement was itself invisible. But when Gilligan analyzed the discovery process, revealing the underrepresentation of women in the sample, with its consequences that categories and laws were derived solely from male experience, the flawed nature of the theory was glaringly apparent. An analysis of the context of justification alone would not have revealed the problem. Once it is granted that processes of discovery shape the entire process of knowledge construction and evaluation, the effectiveness of narrative accounts in illuminating the nature and status of knowledge per se demands to be taken seriously.

Despite the continued hegemony of the autonomy-of-reason model in mainstream epistemology, some philosophers have noted how narratives can locate knowledge construction in specific contexts and subjectivities. According to MacIntyre, a dramatic narrative can reveal that an epistemological crisis "is always a crisis in human relationships."[125] Hence the neutral-observer-confronting-neutral-data model must give way to a conception of knowledge seeking as a process specifically located within historical, social, and cultural concerns. In my *Epistemic Responsibility*, I draw on the story of nineteenth-century biologist Philip Gosse to argue that an epistemic character flaw can vitiate cognitive practice. Gosse's excessive integrity and religious zeal conspire to produce in him a dogmatism that prevents his evaluating Darwinian theory neutrally. He positions himself so that he cannot see and evaluate the evidence for the theory that was producing a revolution in his own area of expertise. His story poses serious questions about the credibility of the observational model of knowledge acquisition at the heart of empiricist thinking. The fact is that often an observer simply cannot see what is in front of him. Addressing a related point, Scheman, in her article on the engendering of skepticism, achieves her most telling effects in drawing analogies between Cartesian skepticism and Othello's growing skepticism, which results, ultimately, in Desdemona's death. Scheman's interweaving of Cartesianism with the dramatic narrative reveals the pull of skepticism not just as a philosophical exercise, but as a serious

---

[125]MacIntyre, "Epistemological Crises," p. 455.

subjective temptation. Her readers gain a new perspective on its possible implications for cognitive agency.

Resituating epistemological inquiry as a practice, an event in people's histories, cuts through suppositions that scientists—or any other cognitive agents—can simply use language transparently to convey their objective results. Paying heed to literary texts, to scientific treatises *as* literary texts, Bleier claims, forces a recognition of "the degree to which . . . scientific writing itself participates in *producing* the reality [scientists] wish to present." Referring to the "multiplicity of meanings" of a scientific text, Bleier argues that, "as literary criticism has 'debunked the myth of linguistic neutrality' in the literary text, it is time to debunk the myth of neutrality in the scientific text."[126] The point is not to advocate a reversal of the unity-of-knowledge project, requiring a narrative context before any knowledge claim can be evaluated. Such a reversal would be as ludicrous as the practice of stripping epistemological significance from the context of discovery. Narrative accounts are valuable in their insistence that knowledge is a human construct, hence that it is possible to evaluate it better when one understands the construction process. Narratives fill in gaps left by reductive analyses. In consequence, they are less liable to suppress the experiences and material, local conditions that make knowledge possible.

Looking at the picture of philosophically orthodox knowledge 'against the grain' reveals that it relies for its 'hard-edged' quality as a finished product on erasing all traces of the cognitive activities of 'second persons'. Feminist-informed shifts in perspective look beneath the finished surface to assess the processes, false starts, errors, and insights that have produced received conceptions of knowledge construction, epistemology, philosophy of science, and scientific practice itself. It is not clear how 'second person' analyses will change moral and epistemological discourse. But the lines I have been following reveal some implications for subjectivity and cognitive agency of the autonomy-obsession that has been constitutive of malestream philosophy. At the very least, such analyses show that one of the most essential arts of personhood is learning how to achieve an appropriate interplay between autonomy and communal solidarity in epistemological and moral theory and practice.

126Bleier, "Lab Coat," p. 61.

CHAPTER FIVE

Women and Experts:
The Power of Ideology

Knowing Women

So far in this book I have been examining the construction of knowledge as philosophers commonly conceive of it. I have argued that prevalent conceptions of knowledge incorporate implicit beliefs about subjectivity and cognitive agency which pivot around two assumptions: that knowers are male and that their cognitive activity should model itself on a 'pure' version of the methodology of natural science, developed in physics. Paradigmatic instances of knowledge are drawn from observational knowledge of medium-sized physical objects, with the consequence that a distanced, often controlling and manipulative relation of subject to object is the accepted relation. The subject is neutral, purely rational, and detached in his disengaged observation of the object; the object remains inert in and unaffected by the knowing process.

The medium-sized physical object paradigm is not the only one available to theorists of knowledge. I have suggested that epistemological analyses might have taken their point of departure from knowing other people, deriving conceptions of the nature of knowledge, and of an appropriate subject-object relation, from such knowledge.[1]

[1]There are other alternatives to the physical science paradigm. Hermeneutics and deconstruction concentrate primarily on textual interpretation: the potential of an interpretive epistemology to extend beyond literary criticism is apparent, for example, in interpretive social science and in critical legal studies. Collingwood's theory of historical knowledge as paradigmatic offers another possibility, which I evaluate in my "Collingwood's Epistemological Individualism," *The Monist*, 72 (October 1989): 542–567.

I have cited developmental and other evidence that recommends this line of reasoning.

Cogent reasons for considering the viability of such a model derive from examining the consequences, for knowledge of other people and for situations in which that knowledge is deployed, of the positivistic project of achieving a unification of science. According to the positivistic ideal, all scientific inquiry—including inquiry in the human sciences—should be conducted on the model of natural scientific inquiry, especially as it is practiced in physics. As Rudolf Carnap expresses this point, "*every sentence of psychology may be formulated in physical language . . . all sentences of psychology describe physical occurrences, namely, the physical behavior of human and other animals . . . physical language is a universal language.*"[2] Otto Neurath reiterates the point, with reference to sociology, in his observation that once the unification of science is achieved, "there will no longer be a special sphere of the 'psychical.'"[3] Thus knowledge of other people—at least propositional claims worthy of the label 'knowledge'—would be based in empirical observation of patterns of behavior and physiological manifestations, which are knowable to the extent that they are amenable to quantification or to codification in terms of laws, probabilities, and/or rules.

The unification-of-science project is continuous with the (Humean) empiricist theory of mind, whose consequences for underclass groups, as Harding analyzes them, I discuss in Chapter 1.[4] With its emphasis on passivity and manipulation, the theory endorses a research methodology that immobilizes and even obliterates the 'subjects' it studies, rendering them as personally invisible, as faceless, and as interchangeable as the place holders in the 'S knows that p' formula. Postpositivist empiricist epistemology still dominates Anglo-American philosophy and social scientific practice, downstaging the critiques of constructivists, Marxists and socialists, structuralists, hermeneuticists, and other scholars engaged in 'successor epistemology' projects. The ongoing debate in the social sciences about the relative

[2]Rudolf Carnap, "Psychology in Physical Language," in A. J. Ayer, ed., *Logical Positivism* (New York: Macmillan, Free Press, 1959), p. 165, emphasis in original.

[3]Otto Neurath, "Sociology and Physicalism," ibid., p. 298.

[4]In the Editor's Introduction to *Logical Positivism*, Ayer notes the positivists' affinity with Hume's well-known dictum: "If we take in our hand any volume; of divinity or school metaphysics, for instance; let us ask, *Does it contain any abstract reasoning concerning quantity or number?* No. *Does it contain any experimental reasoning concerning matter of fact and existence?* No. Commit it then to the flames: for it can contain nothing but sophistry and illusion" (p. 10). Quotation from David Hume, *An Inquiry concerning Human Understanding* (Indianapolis: Bobbs-Merrill, 1955), p. 173.

merits of quantitative and qualitative research methods frequently comes out in favor of the former. This continued hegemony of positivistic, quantitative methods explains the attractions of Stanley and Wise's subjectivist reconstruction of social reality. Despite the problems with their project, which I discuss in Chapter 2, Stanley and Wise's critical opposition to the imperialism of positivistic social science is understandable and instructive.

The persistent appeal of quantitative methodology, even in the social sciences, has its source in the historical assimilation of people to objects in the empiricist project and its latter-day variants, in which knowledge of controllable, manipulable, predictable objects is constitutive of the 'received' conception of knowledge per se. My contortions in Chapter 4 in modifying the 'S knows that p' formula to accommodate instances where p is a person indicate that the model is transferable to the study of human beings *only if* they are objectified. Just how things could be different if knowing other people counted as paradigmatic knowledge is difficult to surmise, but there are indications in Brito's, Carson's, and McClintock's 'personal' engagements with nature. It is clear that alternatives need to be constructed if social scientists are to desist from assimilating the people they study to physical objects. In such assimilations, subjectivity vanishes in the knowledge that purports to explain it.

In this chapter, I examine institutionalized, 'public' knowledge that derives out of a continued endorsement of some versions of the unity-of-science/unity-of-knowledge projects. In particular, I consider the effects of complex institutional patterns of knowledge about people in legitimating the networks of authority and expertise that sustain asymmetrical, oppressive social and institutional power structures. There is no doubt that the division of intellectual labor essential to the functioning of mass technological societies underwrites patterns of epistemic privilege which have oppressive and disempowering effects in the lives of both women *and* men. The rhetoric of the 'little man', the faceless cipher who has no say in the sociopolitical shaping of his destiny, is as well known as (and is longer-lived than) the discourse of women's oppression. But women's oppression is my subject here, and women's disempowerment by structures of authority and expertise constitutes a special case, even with its variations across the axes of race, class, ethnicity, sexual preference, and age.

Although 'the ordinary man' and 'the ordinary woman' may indeed be similarly immobilized by the sociopolitical structures of mass societies, there is a crucial asymmetry in their situations. A man can be marginalized in consequence of his class, ethnicity, or race, his character, economic circumstances, age, sexual preference, or educational 'inadequacy'. But it is rare, in male-dominated societies, for him to be marginalized primarily because of his maleness. A woman, by contrast, is disempowered in the face of authority and expertise because she is female, in ways that cut across and inform all of the other socially disadvantaged positions she occupies: as a member of an oppressed class, race, or ethnic group; as economically or educationally 'inadequate'; as old, unmarried, overweight, or psychologically unbalanced.[5] There is no doubt that femaleness is differently articulated and operative across other marginalizations: it is no constant, stable ingredient to 'include' with such other ingredients as, for example, color, wealth, and age. But gender is always a determining ingredient in the way lines of power and privilege are drawn, and it is always asymmetrically determinant for women and for men. Recognition of this aspect of women's oppression led feminists of the 'second wave', initially, to see women as a class and to analyze their oppression as a form of class oppression. This mode of analysis has fallen into disfavor as it has become apparent that its propensity to obscure differences outweighs its advantages. Yet there is a truth at its core that is still politically significant.

Questions about knowledge are implicated in all aspects of women's oppression. In previous chapters I have examined the received conceptions of knowledge in mainstream philosophy to demonstrate the myriad ways in which the sex of the knower matters in epistemological discourse, despite appearances and allegations to the contrary. The epistemology I have been discussing is principally preoccupied with formal questions. My argument now is that it is equally important to address questions of content and that the applicability of formal principles varies according to the content of the knowledge under analysis. The inadequacy of the 'S knows that p' formula for knowing other people is one illustration of this point.

In this chapter, then, my concern shifts to the content of ordinary and institutionalized knowledge of/about women: to representations of women both in everyday, 'man in the street' knowledge and in the structures and institutions of knowledge *about* people. A range of conceptualizations of 'woman's nature' informs media depictions of

---

[5]Frye writes: "Whatever features an individual male person has which tend to his social and economic disadvantage (his age, race, class, height, etc.), one feature which never tends to his disadvantage in the society at large is his maleness. The case for females is the mirror image of this. Whatever features an individual female person has which tend to her social and economic advantage (her age, race, etc.), one feature which always tends to her disadvantage is her femaleness." Frye, *Politics of Reality*, p. 31.

women's activities, medical judgments about women's health, educational claims about women's intelligence, historical analyses of women's experiences, philosophical conceptions of female subjectivity, and psychological prescriptions for normal womanhood. In all of these domains—and in analogous ones I have not named—'knowledge' of what a woman is and can do derives as much from stereotypes, ideology, folklore, prejudice, and intractable misconceptions as it does from efforts to understand how women experience their subjectivity and agency in concrete, specifiable circumstances. Rarely are stereotypes of women open to renegotiation in the light of evidence that challenges them at their core. Discounting this 'knowledge' as mere error is not particularly effective, for it is so embedded in dominant social and ideological structures that more than a denial is required to dislodge it. Frequently, women themselves endorse it as unthinkingly as men do.

The intransigence of the institutionalized structures of power/ knowledge that define what it is to be a woman, and are stubbornly deaf to criticism, blocks women's access to the authority they require to take responsibility for their circumstances.[6] Enmeshed in such structures, women find themselves thwarted in their efforts to achieve the level of cognitive and moral autonomy that is crucial to their social empowerment. Many women live as self-fulfilling prophecies, adhering to the options constructed by 'experts' who allegedly know them better than they could hope to know themselves. Indeed, it is ironic that everyone can be an expert about women—about what they are and what they can be or do—except women themselves, whose self-presentation is often discredited by people who claim to know better in the name of a higher expertise.

To understand the implications of these structures of knowledge for women's lives, it is necessary to expand the analysis of second personhood I develop in Chapter 3. There I argue that the biological necessity of interdependence renders implausible the goal of self-sufficiency implicit in the ideas of agency that inform malestream ethical theories. I concentrate on the relational construction of subjectivity and specifically on the import of friendships and parent-child relationships. In Chapter 4, taking issue with the 'autonomy-of-

---

[6]The power/knowledge reference is to Foucault; see his *Power/Knowledge*. The power Foucault locates in the power/knowledge complex is not the hegemonic, sovereign power of a political tyrant. It manifests itself, rather, in the 'totalizing' effects of established discourse, which suppresses other ways of thinking, rendering them invisible. There is neither a single locus nor an identifiable agent of power, yet power is at once constitutive of subjectivity and of possibilities of action and critique. (See my discussion of the power of vision, in Chapter 4.)

reason' ideal, I argue that persons are as essentially 'second persons' in cognitive as in moral agency. My emphasis, in both chapters, is on the *enabling* aspects of interdependence; my focus on the personal sphere intends to reclaim locatedness and 'concreteness' as the starting points of analysis and the places where its theoretical conclusions have to be tested.

The danger of thus focusing the inquiry, though, is that it may seem not to escape the imbalance it is designed to redress. Speaking sometimes as though second persons could be abstracted from history, society, class, race, and culture, it risks conveying the impression that relationally constituted subjects emerge from relationships with self-determining possibilities not significantly different from those of the autonomous moral or cognitive agent. Hence the complex configurations of social, cultural, psychological, and ideological structures, which continually shape and reshape self-definition, tend to be obscured. In turning, now, to an examination of structures of authority and expertise, and the 'knowledge' that secures their sociocultural status, I am trying to give a fuller picture of some of the more impersonal, and often less benign, aspects of second personhood: to extend its implications more fully into the sphere of political analysis.

There is no mysterious gap between representations of 'woman' in received knowledge and folk wisdom, and what she *really* is, such that if certain misconceptions were stripped away, her 'true nature' would be revealed. Simone de Beauvoir's frequently cited dictum aptly captures what I mean: "One is not born, but becomes, a woman . . . it is civilization as a whole that produces this creature, intermediate between male and eunuch, which is described as feminine."[7] There is no primeval, natural, free, and unconstrained woman, whose pristine and integrated self is buffeted and fragmented by external social pressures that render her susceptible to epistemic dependence. A woman is constituted, in her subjectivity, by the positions she occupies, the prescriptions, ideologies, myths, and other cultural constraints that structure the pressures she experiences, throughout her life, to be a good woman. It is not possible to strip away those accretions in the hope of finding a core, real self underneath: subjectivity *is* the 'accretions'. Like reason, as I characterize it in Chapter 4, subjectivity is no naturally occurring entity like a rock or a tree.[8] As Marxist and postmodernist thinkers argue, albeit from divergent starting points, a human subject is a cultural product. Nor

---

[7]De Beauvoir, *Second Sex*, p. 301.

[8]I am not forgetting that trees and rocks are produced out of natural processes. My point is that the construction of human subjectivity is a qualitatively different process.

is it possible to designate a point of origin for the process that produces prescriptive 'humanness' or prescriptive femininity. The authorities whose claims to know women grow out of the preconceptions I shall discuss are themselves, likewise, culturally constituted:
there is no neutral, unconstituted place from which to examine the
(ongoing) constitutive process. So this matter is not a simple one of
unmasking a conspiracy and attributing blame, but a complex one of
analyzing the constructs in whose terms women make their identities, in order to assess women's capacities for achieving control over
the oppressive aspects of those constructs.

There is no point in embarking on such an assessment unless one
can assume that people can intervene in their lives and take charge of
the processes that shape them. Indeed, the idea of autonomous agency is appealing precisely because it promises maximum intervention
and control. In its liberal articulations it appears even to eschew biological determinism and to offer individuals the freedom to make of
themselves what they will. Both Marxists and postmodernists insist,
however, that these are false promises, that choices are themselves
constructed by sociocultural-economic circumstances in which people
are inextricably enmeshed. Many feminists have received these insights enthusiastically, for they accord with a sense that many women
have of being caught up in and propelled by structures of power and
constraint against which they are virtually helpless. Autonomous,
individualistic endeavor—which is, in any case, only remotely accessible to women—cannot effectively resist those structures. These considerations may seem to render the constructive, agentic powers of
second personhood useless in any domain *but* the personal. Critics
may argue that the value of the conception is obliterated by the "impersonal objective forms of social intercourse" of which Benjamin
writes,[9] which take on a life of their own and deny all political significance to the "recognition between persons" integral to second personhood. Hence the role of second personhood as constitutive of
subjectivity may appear trivial. Yet recalling experiences of how people are, developmentally, second persons and seeing friendships as
empowering relationships may make it possible to circumnavigate
some of the neodeterministic implications of postmodern, deconstructed subjectivity.

Because it rejects the humanistic picture of a unified self definable
in terms of essential attributes and because of its postulation of a
multiple, fluid subjectivity, Alcoff claims that postmodernism offers

[9]Benjamin, "Bonds of Love," p. 64, cited in Chapter 2, above.

feminists a promise of a rich and extensive "'free play' of a plurality of differences unhampered by any predetermined gender identity."[10] This promise of freedom explains its initial appeal. Nonetheless, in place of the old essentialism, it risks positing a new form of determinism in which human agents are swept along by a tide of discourse that they are powerless to resist. Hence their 'agency', in effect, seems to count for naught. This facet of postmodern subjectivity must give feminists pause.

Aware of these problems, Alcoff explores a subtle way of reconceptualizing subjectivity, particularly female subjectivity, in terms of 'positionality'. A subject's identity would be understood as "relative to a constantly shifting context, to a situation that includes a network of elements involving others, the objective economic conditions, cultural and political institutions and ideologies, and so on." Female subjectivity is a relational construct, but it is neither immobilized nor stabilized, as it is in the impersonal structures of androcentric discourse, where it is defined *in relation to* a single, undisputed norm: masculinity. In fact, 'positionality' explicitly resists taking any one position as referent, be it the position of the masculine norm; of white, middle-class feminism; of female separatism; or whatever. The point is not to advocate quiescent liberal tolerance, however. It is to analyze, assess, assume accountability for the positions one occupies, while engaging in critical dialogue with, or resistance against, occupants of other positions, in cognizance of their political implications. Identity forms and reforms, according to Alcoff, in contexts of "concrete habits, practices, and discourses,"[11] which are at once fluid, unstable, yet amenable to quite precise, determinate articulation at specific historical sites and moments. These articulations—say, a woman's narrative of her experiences as a heterosexual feminist activist, working for better daycare—are open to social and political critique, remapping, renegotiation. Yet they designate positions that are, at the same time, sufficiently stable to permit active political involvement. Positions are at once loci for the active construction of meaning—meaning that is neither simply discovered nor imposed, but constructed—and foci for sociopolitical critique. The positionality proposal draws on specifically located beginnings in and elaborations of the second-person relationships that are pivotal points in any life history. It creates a political space for reinterpreting and engaging

---

[10]Alcoff, "Cultural Feminism," p. 418.
[11]Ibid., pp. 433, 431. I discuss the implications of positionality further in Chapter 7.

critically with the forms of authority and expertise that circumscribe women's control over their lives.

Authority and Expertise

The structures of power-knowledge in western societies, within which women must claim their identity and power, are historically rooted in an ancient, taken-for-granted biological determinism. One of its earliest articulations, in which it has undeniable epistemological import, is in the passage from Aristotle's *Politics* that I cite in Chapter 1. With reference to the human soul, Aristotle observes that "the slave has no deliberative faculty at all; the woman has, *but it is without authority*, and the child has, but it is immature."[12] In this chapter and the following one, I analyze persistent variations on this representation of 'woman' as a creature whose deliberative faculty—her capacity to think, judge, and know—is *without authority*. The fixity of this conception yields the political consequence that women frequently find themselves in positions of reliance on 'experts', even when they have good reasons to believe that they *know* as well as, or better than, the experts do. In this chapter, I show how convictions about their rational incapacity structure women's constructions of their own psychological well-being: matters that concern each woman most directly and about which she would expect to be in a good—if not perhaps the best—position to speak with authority. In the next chapter, I show how this same assumption can vitiate women's efforts to achieve authoritative cognitive status in aspects of their work in which, on the basis of their experience, *their* expertise should be acknowledged.

There is nothing contentious about the assertion that there are close connections among knowledge, expertise, and authority. People commonly assume that knowledge is the basis of expertise and that expertise confers authority on its possessors. A person of recognized expertise, in a social/epistemic community, is usually in a position to have his (and sometimes her) pronouncements respected and to be consulted as an authority when expert advice is required. Expert endorsement cannot confer truth on knowledge claims, yet arguments in favor of taking certain claims seriously derive reasonable support from references to the expertise of the authorities who endorse them.

[12]Aristotle, *Politics* I, 1260a, emphasis added.

Consider debates about the efficacy of vitamin C in curing or preventing colds. To date, its powers have not been definitively established, but when doctors of known expertise and authority testify in its favor, the credibility index rises. Hearing the detractors, people want to know about their credentials, as indicators of how seriously their claims to expertise can be taken.

This state of affairs is simply part of the division of intellectual labor essential to the smooth functioning of complex epistemic communities. The advantages of the division clearly outweigh its disadvantages, for no one *could* acquire all of the specialized knowledge a person would need in order never to be reliant on someone else's expertise.[13] Such reliance is evident when people make major purchases and in the opinions that inform their decisions to vote, to see a play or a film, to support or protest against technological developments, and to refrain from taking certain medications. It would be impracticable to condemn it. Yet it is an ongoing problem for cognitive agents, both individually and collectively, to ensure that their reliance is neither naive nor ill-informed. Because people often have no choice *but* to consult 'experts', the process of learning whose pronouncements are properly authoritative and deserving of credence is crucial to the development of a capacity to know well and to the establishment of a person's status as a responsible member of an epistemic community. Concentration upon individual, putatively autonomous knowledge claims that derive from 'direct' contact with the world obscures the role of these credibility-discerning and -establishing activities. Theorists of knowledge often forget how small a portion of their knowledge people gain by first-person experiential means. In fact, people are fundamentally dependent on one another—on their parents, children, teachers, students, friends, on reporters, authorities, and experts—for what they, often rightly, claim to know.

It is as important, then, for a would-be knower to be able to recognize when *someone else* knows and can be trusted as it is to be able to demonstrate that she herself is knowledgeable and can do certain things reliably and well. In fact, the issue of establishing and relying on authority and expertise, morally, politically, and epistemically, turns on questions about how to be appropriately judicious and circumspect in granting and withholding trust. Like all cooperative en-

---

[13]I discuss some implications of this division of labor more fully in my *Epistemic Responsibility*, chap. 9. For an instructive discussion of feminist implications of the division of intellectual labor, see Kathryn Pyne Addelson, "The Man of Professional Wisdom," in Harding and Hintikka, eds., *Discovering Reality*. Nelson has an extensive analysis of Addelson's article in chap. 4 of *Who Knows*.

terprises, the division of intellectual labor depends on the coopera-
tors' ability to *trust* one another to play their parts responsibly. Baier
observes, "We inhabit a climate of trust as we inhabit an atmosphere
and notice it as we notice air, only when it becomes scarce or pol-
luted."[14] In situations of unequal power, people may, indeed, need to
learn to notice it: to trust themselves to claim validity for their experiences and to be critical where they sense that they have placed their
trust unwisely. It is not easy for a woman who has minimal faith in
her deliberative capacities to adopt such a critical stance.

The problematic of trust plays into the tensions I discuss in Chapter 3—the tensions generated out of efforts at once to assert constancy
of traits and attributes—of 'character'—and to escape the rigidity and
politically vexed implications of unified, humanistic subjectivity with
its attendant essentialist problems. A conception of multiple, fluid,
continually repositioned subjectivity sits uneasily with claims that it is
both possible and politically crucial to know people well enough to
trust them. This unease at the crux of 'the identity crisis in feminist
theory' signals the recognition of a paradox that has always to be
renegotiated: subjectivity is neither stable nor unified, yet it is impossible to affirm political identities and allegiances in the absence of
reliability, accountability, and trust. The friendships on which the best
political alliances are modeled can neither be created nor sustained
without trust. Friendships do not do well when the friends are required frequently to prove their trust, yet excessive demands of consistency and rigid predictability can damage friendships irreparably.
Likewise, in larger alliances, it is important to maintain a steady assumption of trust, yet not to assume so rigidly that there are no
means of accommodating the contradictions of multiple subjectivities.

The appropriate move, as I see it at this stage in the development
of feminist thought, is not to dissolve these paradoxes by opting for
one of the two 'sides' unequivocally. It is, rather, to develop creative
strategies for maintaining the tension between them: placing trust
where practical deliberation suggests that it is reasonable to place it,
with these people, in these circumstances; recognizing that it may,
ultimately, be necessary to revise one's judgment—and that decisions
to trust are indeed poised unsteadily between incompatible beliefs
about subjectivity *even though* trust, to be worthy of the name, needs
to be placed firmly and with conviction. Uncomfortably as these
recommendations may sit with the expectations of principled deci-

[14]Annette Baier, "Trust and Antitrust," *Ethics* 96 (January 1986): 234. My thinking
about trust has benefited from Baier's work on the subject.

siveness of standard moral theories, they have a certain phenomenological, experiential appeal. Many people conduct their relationships quite well on the basis of the practical reasoning on which these processes depend: often their lives are neither chaotic nor ossified, and they retain definite capacities for action.

Trust involves making oneself vulnerable, granting other people access to, and even control over, valued aspects of one's life, conferring on them the power as much to damage, destroy, or misuse those things as to take care with them. People trust one another with their intimate secrets, with the power to intervene in their mental and physical health, with the health and well-being of people they love, and with their most valued possessions, to mention only a few of the areas where trust extends. It is a risky business, whose very imperceptibility enhances the risks. Conferral and acceptance of trust require second-person interdependence in its most open and most fragile aspect.

This fragility is most apparent in unequal relationships. Inequalities result from the differences in people's capacities to consent to trusting relations: infants and children, the senile, the very sick, people who are illiterate or linguistically marginalized often cannot give informed consent, yet trust may be essential to their survival. The persistent 'infantilization' of privileged white women in patriarchal societies, in the name of their delicate natures and deficient deliberative capacities, renders them fundamentally unequal to 'the man of reason' and often meekly acquiescent in the unwitting and unquestioned trusting that is expected of them.[15] Such relationships show clearly that the contractual morality of the autonomous moral agent is inadequate to grasp the complexities of trust. The rhetoric of voluntary agreement cannot account for the politics of trusting. As Baier puts it: "Men may but women cannot see morality as essentially a matter of keeping to the minimal moral traffic rules, designed to restrict close encounters between autonomous persons to self-chosen ones. Such a conception presupposes both an equality of power and a natural separateness from others, which is alien to women's experience of life and morality." The power differentials that construct women's political and social positions show that it is rational to trust only "in the absence of any reason to suspect in the trusted strong and operative motives which conflict with the demands of trust-

---

[15]It is important to bear in mind that 'woman's nature' is a class- and race-specific phenomenon: poor women, unmarried women, and the women of color or of marginalized ethnic groups, who are expected to do hard physical labor, are represented as much less delicate.

worthiness as the truster sees them."[16] Trust-based relationships lend themselves readily to the forms of exploitation to which women of all classes, races, ages, and persuasions have long been subject.

Issues of the politics of knowledge are variously implicated in conferring and withholding trust. Knowing other people is central among them—knowing people well enough to trust them wisely, to be sensitive to their trust, and to take account of the responsibilities that trusting enjoins. Being sufficiently self-aware to acknowledge one's capacity to participate in relationships that require trust is equally crucial. This form of epistemic power is not readily won by 'underclass' persons. (The consciousness-raising strategies of the 1970s were designed to enable women to claim it.) As long as women's visible behavior conforms to social expectations, the assumption is that they have consented to occupy the places that silence and oppress rather than empower them. It is vital for women to learn how to evaluate the 'experts'' expertise, to recognize what makes a doctor, teacher, therapist, colleague, or friend worthy of trust. In areas where an expert's authority is a product of education and training, it may be necessary to learn enough about the subject matter (say, medical options) to understand and accept or reject expert advice. No one can become an expert in every area of specialization; many women, with encouragement and support, can become well enough informed to know where it is reasonable to place their trust. Only by so doing can they resist the disempowering effects of authority and expertise. Women have to challenge and reconstruct the meanings of expertise if they are to take control of their lives.

Placing trust wisely in situations of unequal power requires learning to differentiate *authoritative* manifestations of epistemic authority from merely *authoritarian* ones. The distinction turns upon the competence, the informed and hence justified position of an authoritative expert, contrasted with the *power* of an authoritarian knower to claim credibility on the basis of privilege alone or of ideological orthodoxy, rather than on a basis of responsible epistemic practice.[17] Power may also be a product of authoritative knowing, but it is more likely to be earned than arbitrarily claimed. An authoritative knower is often diffident about his or her degree of expertise, fallibilist, and prepared to reconsider or even to reserve judgment. Authoritarian knowers, who have more reason to be diffident, often are less so. Learning to recog-

---

[16]Baier, "Trust and Antitrust," pp. 249, 254.

[17]I am drawing here on an earlier discussion of this distinction in my "Simple Equality Is Not Enough," *Australasian Journal of Philosophy* 64 (suppl.) (June 1986): 48–65.

nize justified authority, then, is complicated, for high-ranking positions of authority can be won through ideologically sanctioned exploitative maneuvers almost as readily as they can be achieved in consequence of careful knowing. By the same token, low(er)-ranking status is not, unequivocally, a sign of ignorance or lesser reliability. In its extreme form, authoritarianism becomes "the domination of the ignorant masses by a powerful elite."[18] Even its less extreme forms have this potential.

For women, learning to place their trust wisely is doubly complex because of the tenacity of beliefs about their lack of rational capacity which still echo Aristotle. These beliefs sustain men's paternalistic control over women's lives. Women's lack of authority in their own 'deliberative faculties' apparently makes it right and proper for men, who by nature do have such authority, to allow women to benefit from it. Reasons in favor of this relationship are all the more cogent for men whose deliberative faculties have been honed in professional, 'scientific' training. Yet the fallibility both of the 'arts' and of the 'experts' whose authoritarian practices I discuss below reveals the necessity for circumspection in seeking their help.

The difficulty of fulfilling this requirement is exacerbated by a further consequence of women's alleged lack of deliberative authority. In Aristotle's scheme, an aspiring virtuous young man discerns the nature of moral and intellectual virtue by observing the conduct of virtuous citizens in the polis. He learns goodness by emulating the good, wisdom by emulating the wise. Yet these possibilities are not available in the same way for women. Not even the wives of politically visible men have access to the public spaces where virtuous conduct presents itself for emulation. Women's lives do not afford access to a community with whom they could evaluate the models, even if they could observe them; nor can they act publicly in places where their conduct, too, could count as a paradigm of virtue. Nonetheless, the fact that women in the Greek polis were credited neither with moral nor with intellectual virtue is persistently explained on the basis of their deficient reasoning powers rather than their social position. In the 1990s women are still largely invisible as moral and intellectual authorities, notwithstanding Rosi Braidotti's optimistic claim that "the presence of real-life women in positions of authority and knowledge is opening up new possibilities for self-image and identi-

[18]This is Ursula Le Guin's phrase, in *Language of the Night*, quoted by Hilary Rose in "Dreaming the Future," *Hypatia: A Journal of Feminist Philosophy* 3 (Spring 1988): 120.

fication in women."[19] They are few in number, and it is still too easy to dismiss them as the exceptions that prove the rule.

The notorious scarcity of intellectually authoritative women imposes a subtle constraint on women's resistance to paternalism. Historically, there are notably few exemplary female knowers: no female Newtons, Descartes, or Darwins (though now we have Barbara McClintock). Hence women commonly have access only at second hand to ideals of cognitive authority. They frequently have to approach such ideals through a translation process that must traverse or circumnavigate the dogma according to which these possibilities are closed to women.[20] The problem is that for a woman to believe in her competence to evaluate and challenge authority she needs faith in the credibility of her judgment. Circumspection is a luxury reserved for people who have succeeded in achieving the conviction that people like themselves *can* plausibly claim authority. So although I am not urging that people can model their aspirations only on the achievement of people just like themselves, I am suggesting that a sense of cognitive dissonance constrains their aspirations when women *always* have to define their cognitive standards according to possibilities only rarely available to people like themselves. People learn about their possibilities, initially, from observing what people 'like them' (whatever the extension of that phrase) can do. They do not jump from rooftops expecting to fly, because they learn that that is not a human possibility. Analogously, people acquire a sense of how people like themselves can think and act, a sense that they ingest to the extent that it can determine their position on the epistemic map.

Logically, every way of thinking, kind of creativity, and level of intervention and challenge is as open to women as it is to men. Such an assumption is integral to the autonomy-of-reason view that reason is alike in all men. But realizations of logical possibility are thwarted in practice, for women, by the tenacity of structures informed by essentialist conceptions of 'woman' that deny credibility to their projects. It is not enough for a woman simply to refuse the essentialism

[19]Rosi Braidotti, "Ethics Revisited: Women and/in Philosophy," in Carole Pateman and Elizabeth Gross, eds., *Feminist Challenges: Social and Political Theory* (Sydney: Allen & Unwin, 1986), p. 51.

[20]Elisabeth Young-Bruehl remarks: "So great . . . is the weight of prejudice about women's abilities and achievements as thinkers that we often look to the lives of thoughtful women with questions not about how they thought of their thinking but with questions about how they thought at all, how they managed *not* to be as this great weight of prejudice prescribed." Young-Bruehl, "The Education of Women as Philosophers," *Signs: Journal of Women in Culture and Society* 12 (Winter 1987): 207.

and act according to her own lights, with the full authority of a competent knower, in the expectation of public acknowledgment. Communal standards of received discourse work as much to constrain as to facilitate and legitimate cognitive pursuits, and selves are socially constituted. Hence there is no unconstrained place in a woman's psyche from which she can affirm her *real*, authoritative self simply by thrusting aside the practical and ideological constructs that have produced her (present) position. Women are not trapped without recourse in the Aristotelian mold, but resisting its tenacity, breaking out of its constraints, requires more than a simple decision to evade its influence.

Although the advantages of a division of intellectual labor cannot be denied, then, many women in male-dominated societies are too heavily reliant on experts. Where expertise poses as absolute authority and is supported in its pose by institutional and professional structures and affiliations, it is difficult for women to challenge its verdicts, to seek open-ended, interpretive advice, to displace pronouncements from 'on high'. Women's increasing engagement in consumer movements and in self-help medical and legal groups is an important step in enabling them to take power and responsibility into their own hands. The engagement works precisely because of its solidarity in collectivity, its structural opposition to oppressive structures. Women who have lived in situations of excessive heteronomy need to be able to claim greater autonomy in order to gain freedom from the paternalistic oppression of masculine expertise. That ability can be achieved only by working collectively to reshape the stereotype-informed structures that erode their capacity to claim authoritative status.

Stereotypes and Ideology

Epistemologically, stereotypes—whether of women, blacks, the working classes, or the elderly—are both puzzling and paradoxical. Stereotype users are usually convinced that they *know* that women—or blacks, or the working classes—are just as the stereotypes say, even when they are confronted with more than enough empirical evidence to undermine their convictions. On any test of justification or adequacy, stereotypes would come out poorly, except perhaps on a crude coherentist test, where they might cohere well with assumptions about women, and women and men, that they themselves reinforce. They are the most inadequate of claims to know other people.

Yet when the complexity and ambiguity of claiming to know another person is smoothed over by the epistemological assimilation of people to objects, the crudity of stereotypes is obscured. It might even seem that it is no more significant to claim that a woman's nature is determined by her biology than it is to claim that a table's 'nature' is determined by the materials from which it is made. Yet there is a major difference. In 'S knows that p' statements about women, the p place is held by a condensed theoretical construct—'woman'—whose sociocultural-political dimensions need to be articulated and analyzed. 'Woman' and 'table' are asymmetrical labels; people can be stereotyped, material objects cannot.

Although stereotypes are crude epistemological tools, a facility in their usage often masquerades as knowledge. Yet stereotypes generate both epistemic indolence and epistemic imperialism—patterns scarcely indicative of good knowing. Indolence is evident in a user's conviction that he knows what he is talking about to the extent of claiming absolution from any requirement to know it better. Such absolution encourages intellectual *akrasia*, an entrenched reluctance to inquire further lest one have to "reconsider a range of treasured beliefs."[21] Imperialism is manifested in a conviction that the stereotyped category is summed up, that the putative knower has put his or her mark on it, labeled it for what it is, and claimed it as part of his or her stock of cognitive possessions. There is an arrogance at work here which claims a right to be heard as an authority about the object of the stereotyping. That arrogance feeds into the totalizing effect of a stereotype, in which the stereotyped, generalized 'other' subsumes every concrete 'other' absolutely, making of stereotypes loci of power and control. To borrow a formulation of Andrea Nye's, a stereotype acquires the status of a form of language that claims for itself "the authority to tell us who we are and what we may do."[22]

According to the principles of informal logic, stereotypes amount at once to hasty generalizations, and to illegitimate appeals to authority. Both in stretching accidental characteristics to sum up all people of a certain 'sort' (be they women, or blacks, or even men) and in posing as finished products, not open to amendment, stereotypes are like judgments based on hasty generalization. Yet a stereotype will not derive solely from the process of simple enumeration from which hasty generalizations ordinarily are constructed. Stereotypes are as

[21]I take this phrase from Amélie Rorty, "Akratic Believers," *American Philosophical Quarterly* 20 (April 1982): 179.
[22]See Andrea Nye, "The Unity of Language," *Hypatia: A Journal of Feminist Philosophy* 2 (Summer 1987): 96.

much the products of accumulated cultural lore as of inductive evidence based in limited experience. They are the engrained and tenacious products of acculturation processes that continually confirm their legitimacy.

Stereotypes of 'woman' pose as knowledge of who women essentially are, of what they are like, and hence of how they should appropriately be placed and treated in society. (The passive voice signals women's powerlessness in societies in which their place is not chosen, but assigned by the speakers of the dominant, stereotype-informed discourse.) Stereotypes construct women as 'generalized' objects of knowledge that are often sharply discontinuous from women's self-conceptions and -understandings.[23] Yet they are so efficacious in sustaining the construct that women are often constrained to adjust their self-conceptions to align with the stereotype-informed conception of their 'real' nature. Hence stereotypes inform and legitimate structures of authority and expertise in mutually reinforcing processes of confirmation and fulfillment. Women do not simply don a stereotype as they might a costume or a role: this is not a matter of superficial overlay. They are encoded by, marked with stereotypes, from earliest infancy. They learn to suppress suspicions that there is something amiss, to blame themselves rather than the stereotype when their experiences suggest that the 'fit' is less than perfect. Stereotyped conceptions of 'woman's nature' count among the most intransigent features of the sociopolitical-epistemic structures that shape and restrict women's lives, inducing them to acquiesce in those restrictions.

A simple repudiation of stereotype-imposed restrictions is not so easy, though. The very possibility of knowledge depends on categories and systems of classification: a language comprised only of particulars could neither be spoken nor understood. Nor is it easy to see how one could take the initial steps toward knowing someone without a preliminary category-guided set of moves, if only to situate her for purposes of opening an exchange. So categories—even stereotypes—perform a useful preliminary function in relationships. But any aspiring 'second person' relation sets out at once to correct for the stereotype, to discard it.

Categories and classifications resemble stereotypes in many respects: they, too, derive from cultural traditions; they generalize and abstract from experience. Categories and classificatory schemes differ

---

[23]The allusion is to Benhabib's article, "Generalized and Concrete Other," which I discuss in Chapter 4.

most saliently from stereotypes in their open-ended, 'fallibilist' possibilities, which contrast with the dogmatic rigidity of stereotypes.
That difference may be more ideal than real, for categories and
classifications have a tendency to ossify and become closed. It is
worth emphasizing, however, for cognitive agents can control the
process: even though they need categories, they can learn to resist
stereotypes. Consciousness raising is partly about this kind of resistance. Stereotypes afford the very starkest illustration of essentialism at work, showing how it precludes knowing people well and
legitimates their objectification.

The affinity between stereotypes and dogmatism is no accident.
Historically, the term 'stereotype' was adopted expressly to convey a
rigidity of mind and narrowness of perception. It referred originally
to a form of printing and rigid duplicating. In 1922 Walter Lippmann
appropriated it for social science, to refer to "pictures in our heads."
He argued that "the 'real' environment is altogether too big, too complex and too fleeting for 'direct acquaintance'" and that stereotypes
serve "to preserve us from all the bewildering effects of trying to see
the world steadily and see it whole."[24] From this description, stereotypes sound like necessary devices for coping adequately with the
world. But coping adequately depends on knowing well, on trying to
see things 'steadily' and 'whole', however approximate the results
may be.

Stereotypes, for Lippmann, offer control where there might only
be chaos and confusion. They promise fulfillment, Nye observes, of
an ancient philosophical "dream of oneness, order, and harmony, of a
clarity of thought which would reduce diversity to overriding design
or principle."[25] The unity-of-science project is one aspect of that
dream. Nye detects a "unity of language" project that is a complementary or derivative aspect: it accounts for the appeal—and the
tenacity—of stereotypes.

On Nye's account, it is hardly surprising that the stereotype's assumed position as knowledge of how women *are* renders it immune to
counterevidence. The philosophical unification of language—and
hence of the knowledge assumed to be embedded in it—is produced
out of a refusal to hear what others say, how they perceive themselves

[24]Walter Lippmann, *Public Opinion* (1922; New York: Free Press, 1965), quoted by
Hilda Kuper, "Colour, Categories, and Colonialism: The Swazi Case," in *Colonialism in
Africa 1870–1960*, vol. 3, *Profiles of Change: African Society and Colonial Rule*, ed. Peter
Duignan and L. H. Gann (Cambridge: Cambridge University Press, 1971). The fact that
an evaluation of stereotypes is central to feminist critiques of anthropological work in
Africa needs no explanation. (Helen Callaway brought this article to my attention.)
[25]Nye, "Unity of Language," p. 97.

192 What Can She Know?

and conceive of their experiences. All of this unruly particularity is encompassed and tamed within the authoritarian, dominant discourse. The rational ordering of that discourse, like the stance of the stereotype-informed autonomous reasoner, is achieved by suppressing particularity and diversity. Nye notes: "Instead of expressing personal experience, language must be grounded in authoritarian, impersonal truths." Stereotypes are *applied* to the social world—to other people—just as formal logical structures are applied to the physical world, to eliminate flux and contingency and to make possible a knowledge characterized, above all, by definiteness and fixity. Nye maintains that "the unification of language rests on and begins from the position that there is *no way* to understand what others feel or understand as uniquely their own."[26] Such a conviction is plainly compatible with the individualism I discuss in Chapters 3 and 4, for which persons are opaque to one another, and self-other relations are hostile and divisive. Such conceptions of subjectivity and relations do not require their adherents to know one another any better than stereotypes permit.

Like categories and other classifications, stereotypes abstract from 'reality' to create fixed points in its complexity and fleetingness, ways of finding one's way around. They are not easily undermined, because they are often accurate, at least to some extent. They function as cluster-concepts, so that the reality component at their core lends them an unwarranted credibility. But this is the accuracy of a caricature, not of a portrait, and it yields the kind of truncated picture that a caricature does. The problem is not that caricatures tell no truths, nor that they tell only partial truths where genuine truths would somehow be 'whole'; it is that caricatures control perception unduly. It was probably not easy to talk to Charles de Gaulle without focusing on his nose, even though interviewers knew that he was *more* than his nose. Caricatures make it difficult to see that 'something more'; they shrink one's perceptual possibilities.

Morally, a caricature is more benign than a stereotype, for there is a grammar of caricature creating and viewing which makes it possible to 'correct for the context'. A caricature proclaims its own partiality: someone who recognizes a politician from it knows the rules of the game. But stereotypes tend to be presented 'straight', to give 'the facts', to sum up just how people of a certain narrowly designated sort are, and to fit this person into that slot without remainder, obscuring any other view of her. They conceal their own partiality,

[26]Ibid., pp. 99, 105, emphasis added.

and the element of truth that they capture compounds the concealment. In the rigidity of a stereotype, there is none of the play and
interplay between speaker/writer/artist and audience that there is in
the creation and interpretation of a caricature.[27]

Functionally, a stereotype is like a Kuhnian paradigm: exceptions
tend to be discounted as aberrant rather than to threaten the stability
of the stereotype.[28] Stereotypes are strengthened and more firmly
entrenched on the basis of confirming instances, yet they are not
significantly weakened by seemingly contradictory ones. In fact, they
are curiously elastic even in their rigidity: they stretch and shift to
accommodate contradictions and reestablish themselves. Hence it is
not easy to undermine them.[29] As with unified meanings in general, a
'namer' has a good deal at stake in keeping labels intact to control the
complexity, fleetingness, and incipient chaos of the experienced
world. A detached knower needs common meanings, Nye observes,
for "as long as names are allowed to shift and mutate, they will not be
understood and the speaker, removed from ordinary discourse, will
remain alone."[30] When the conservation of such 'common meanings'
appears to be a requirement for keeping a social order intact, then
counterevidence is the more assiduously suppressed, whether consciously or otherwise. Cynthia Russett shows that, in the nineteenth
century when claims for sexual and racial equality were being pressed
on all sides, threatening social upheaval, scientists devoted themselves to demonstrating the 'naturalness' of the old order. "Scientists
responded to [the] unrest with a detailed and sustained examination
of the differences between men and women that justified their differing social roles." Among the many results of this examination was the

[27]Consider the contrast between stereotypes and archetypes. Whereas an archetype
opens a range of interpretive possibilities, a stereotype has just the opposite effect. It
closes off interpretation, conceals complexity and ambiguity.

[28]See Kuhn, *Structure of Scientific Revolutions*, for an account of the role of paradigms
in normal science. I discuss this feature of stereotypes at greater length in Chapter 6.
De Beauvoir's discussion of myths of femininity shows that they operate very much as
stereotypes do. She writes: "As against the dispersed, contingent, and multiple exis-
tences of actual women, mythical thought opposes the Eternal Feminine, unique and
changeless. If the definition provided for this concept is contradicted by the behavior of
flesh-and-blood women, it is the latter who are wrong: we are told not that Femininity
is a false entity, but that the women concerned are not feminine" (*Second Sex*, p. 286).

[29]Both women who do and women who do not fit stereotypes are oppressed by
them. An apt illustration of how women remain "caught in the stereotype" comes from
a British newspaper account of a woman trade union member's complaints about
sexual harassment. This woman "was not taken seriously by some of those in authority
because she was single, middle aged, and ordinary looking." Ann Smedley, "Faint-
hearted Progress," *The Guardian*, June 18, 1985, p. 22.

[30]Nye, "Unity of Language," p. 106.

construction, by nineteenth-century psychologists, of a "feminine psyche very much in accord with prevailing cultural views of womanhood—gentle, emotional, nurturant, weak-willed, and dependent."[31] Dislodging stereotypes of woman turns people's lives upside down: for the men who occupy positions in the power structure that are threatened by this upheaval, the experience is not pleasant.

It would be a mistake, though, to claim that stereotypes and paradigms are perfectly analogous. Kuhn argues that it is impossible to engage in normal science in the absence of a paradigm; and yet it is both possible and morally-politically imperative for knowledge of other people to get free from the constraints of stereotypes. Nonetheless, two points of comparison attest to the aptness of the analogy. Consider first the *power* exerted by both paradigms and stereotypes. The intrication of knowledge and power is now (especially following Foucault) a philosophical and political commonplace, and the entrenched institutional and disciplinary power of a paradigm can confer legitimacy on aspiring scientific endeavor or relegate it to the limbo of unacceptability. Stereotypes function in the same way in designating legitimate, as opposed to aberrant, female conduct and social positioning. Their effect is as apparent in women's efforts to establish themselves in more public places as it is in dictates about how women should conduct the personal, more 'private' aspects of their lives.[32]

Second, consider the process of paradigm change. In Kuhn's view, scientific revolutions occur when the explanatory power of a paradigm is exhausted or when it encounters so many insoluble puzzles that it can no longer sustain its hegemony. A point comes when the paradigm has been subjected to so many strains that it must give way to a new paradigm, with greater explanatory power; though sometimes there is a period of interregnum before a new paradigm is articulated and established. This aspect of the paradigm-stereotype analogy gives feminists reason for optimism. Stereotypes of woman are going through a period of strain such that there are good reasons

[31]Cynthia Eagle Russett, *Sexual Science: The Victorian Construction of Womanhood* (Cambridge: Harvard University Press, 1989), pp. 10, 42.

[32]As Katherine O'Donovan shows in *Sexual Divisions in Law* (London: Weidenfeld & Nicholson, 1985), gender ideology, encapsulated in stereotypes, structures the public/private dichotomy and dictates the boundaries of each of its 'sides'. Law both creates and sustains the dichotomy in its decisions about what behavior is amenable to public intervention and what should remain unregulated. See my review of O'Donovan's book in *Canadian Journal of Women and the Law* 2, 1 (1987): 190–198.

to hope that they will give way to new constructions and representations. To this end, feminist critical inquiry has to be sustained.

The most persistent stereotypes of 'woman' (= middle-class white women) amount, in fact, to variations on the Aristotelian theme of woman's lack of deliberative authority. Subjective and emotional in their judgments, scatter-brained, politically immature, financially irresponsible, and constitutionally delicate, women are incapable of sophisticated, abstract thought. Their minds are forever occupied with trivia; their conversation is largely gossip, itself construed as trivial.[33] Women should be allowed neither to engage in serious professional occupations nor to perform hard physical tasks; they should participate neither in the 'processions of learned men', the professions of hardheaded men, nor the sports of athletic men. Their role is to bear children and to maintain the 'home', man's haven in a heartless world. Stereotype-derived 'knowledge' about what women *are* is both prescriptively and descriptively hegemonic. Despite their obvious inadequacy, these stereotypes define what it is to be a 'good' woman, contribute to keeping women in their proper place, and provide reasons for condemning women as deviant who attempt to defy their prescriptions.

Despite their putatively universal scope, however, most of these standard stereotypes—like the Aristotelian claim—apply to the traits and conduct of the (heterosexual) mothers, daughters, sisters, and wives of the men of the dominant social groups. Working class, black, Hispanic, and other marginalized women are differently stereotyped, sometimes in terms of animality, closeness to nature, wanton sensuality. It is in the interests of the stereotypers not to rule out the participation of these women in hard physical work nor to discourage them from performing sexual services. The pieces of all of these stereotypes are movable across class and racial boundaries, according to the shifting requirements of the stereotyper. Many men want their wives to be all at once.

My point in focusing on stereotyped conceptions of woman's nature that masquerade as knowledge is not the purely empirical one that authorities and experts have just not looked carefully enough, that their observations are systematically skewed, whereas more careful looking would correct their errors and produce a more accurate

---

[33]Patricia Meyer Spacks reclaims gossip as a cultural form that has the "capacity to create and intensify human connection and to enlarge self-knowledge," in her *Gossip* (New York: Knopf, 1985), p. 19. She characterizes gossip as a "mode of exchange [which] involves the giving and receiving of more than information" (p. 21).

view of 'woman'. An empiricist analysis of this 'knowledge' cannot account for its persistence in the face of an accumulation of evidence that clearly discredits it. According to the empiricist model, a normal observer in normal observation conditions should be able to perceive correctly and hence to know. Such possibilities do appear to exist if a sufficiently simple example, like knowing that there is a book on the table, is treated as paradigmatic. In such examples, the acculturation process that makes observational claims possible has receded from view, creating the impression that no judgmental background is implicated in the making of a knowledge claim.

Stereotypes are at once invested with power from, and a source of power for, ideologies that underwrite a social-structural differential in the distribution of power and oppression, according to a sex/gender system that ensures the superiority of (certain) men and the inferiority (albeit variously) of women. In linking stereotypes with ideology, my intention is not to appeal to ideology conceived as a (Marxian) superstructure that generates after-the-fact conceptions to legitimate an economic (or other sociopolitical) arrangement. The linkage is more aptly conceived with an ideological structure like Antonio Gramsci's "common sense": an embedded, uncritical, mainly unconscious set of perceptions and understandings of the world which constitute a 'common' framework in a given era, culture, or social space. Gramsci allows the appropriateness of calling such an embedded philosophical orientation 'an ideology', so long as the word is used "in its highest sense of a conception of the world that is implicitly manifest in art, in law, in economic activity and in all manifestations of individual and collective life."[34] I use 'ideology' as a working concept to connote a set of beliefs, values, and representations that need to be explained with reference to the interests or position of some social group, a set of meanings in terms of which people live their sociocultural situation. Such meanings are implicated in the construction of subjectivity and the reproduction of power relations; in Michele Barrett's words, they "succeed insofar as [they] can produce acceptance of existing power structures as 'natural.'"[35] Ideological sociopolitical apparatuses, and the stereotyping practices that they produce, are intricated with power relations and interests that shape social realities so that they are accepted as naturally as, say, geological reality.

---

[34]Antonio Gramsci, *Selections from the Prison Notebooks*, trans. and ed. Quintin Hoare and Geoffrey Nowell Smith (New York: International, 1971), pp. 322, 328.

[35]Michele Barrett, *Women's Oppression Today: Problems in Marxist Feminist Analysis* (London: Verso, 1980), cited in Kramarae and Treichler, *Feminist Dictionary*, p. 206.

Neither the role of ideology nor the interests it sustains are always explicit or conscious. Hence its manifestations have to be uncovered and discovered. For the unmasking process, early second-wave feminists adopted the Marxism-derived term 'consciousness raising', to make the point that women's unconscious acquiescence in the structures of patriarchy amounted to a 'false consciousness' like that of the proletariat under capitalism. Yet Foucault sounds a cautionary note: he distrusts the term 'ideology', for "it always stands in virtual opposition to something else which is supposed to count as truth":[36] it presupposes the existence of a free, unconstrained place where the pure, unconditioned, and unmediated truth is available. For Foucault, there is no such place. Cognizant of the impossibility of dislocated argument, yet asserting the power of interrogation and refusal, Teresa de Lauretis advances a counterproposal: "The subject that I see emerging from current writings and debates within feminism is one that is at the same time inside *and* outside the ideology of gender, and conscious of being so, conscious of that twofold pull, of that division, that doubled vision."[37] That division opens a space for agency, for developing strategies of reconstruction and resistance.

From the fact that no unmediated, dislocated truths are available, it does not follow that no truths, values, or interests are better than others. Nor is the point that ideological positions and frameworks are pernicious; it is only that they require critique and demand accountability. Debate is not foreclosed in analyses of ideology, but reopened to address issues that are at once subtle and complex. Critique may have to proceed case by case, however. Science, as I argue in Chapter 4, may *not* be specifically sexist, even though it is commonly androcentric. Its androcentricity may inform and be informed by stereotypes of class and/or race, which also have to be uncovered and analyzed. Ideological commitments are differently manifested across domains of discourse, disciplines, and cognitive projects.[38]

The omnipresence of stereotypes and ideology demonstrates the necessity of developing a critical, self-reflexive 'history' of beliefs and practices to understand the persistence of stereotype-informed beliefs that fly in the face of empirical evidence. Explanations that draw straightforward causal connections, in which beliefs are simply *caused by* the evidence and formed in a tabula-rasa-like open mind, are

[36]Foucault, *Power/Knowledge*, p. 118.
[37]De Lauretis, *Technologies of Gender*, p. 10.
[38]I owe this point to Alison Wylie, "Gender Theory and the Archeological Record."

seriously inadequate. In their self-presentation as ideology-free, they make an implicit claim that the critic of ideology occupies an ideology-free space from which she or he can mount a critique. Appealing to a liberalist/empiricist understanding of ideology as inherently pernicious and irrational, and to the assumption that ideologies produce only blind and fanatical ideologues, such critics succeed in concealing the interestedness of their own positions, perhaps even from themselves. Feminist critiques of patriarchal ideologies which proceed from an explicitly asserted feminist standpoint must demonstrate that ideologically informed positions are not, as a matter of course, irrational and dogmatic,[39] and must show that ideological commitment and realism are not mutually incompatible.

Jon Elster's historical reconstructions of the tendencies of the oppressed to believe in the justice of the oppressive social order are instructive. He notes that the ideological beliefs of both the oppressed and the oppressors become (asymmetrically) self-fulfilling prophecies, fostering realizations of the constructs of self that the ideological structures impose (for the oppressed) and legitimate (for the oppressor). Yet the causal connections between such beliefs and the practices they inform is convoluted: it often turns out that the beliefs do not serve the interests of their shapers, even when they are the "ruling or dominant group."[40]

The construction of such "irrationally caused beliefs"—of bias, stereotypes, and ideologies—cannot be explained away as simple inferential errors, for then believers who were shown their errors would just repudiate them. But stereotypes and ideology do not evaporate so readily. Psychology and affect evidently contribute to their persistence, objectivism notwithstanding. Members of oppressed groups tend to adjust their wants to align with socially sanctioned possibilities, to gain relief from the tensions and frustrations (the cognitive dissonance) of having wants they cannot satisfy. Hence oppressed people tend to derive their sense of how things should be and how they should behave from their 'found' positions in structures that come to be, in Wittgenstein's terms, constitutive of the background against which they distinguish true and false.[41] Acquies-

---

[39]Susan Griffin engages with this problem in her now-classic article "The Way of All Ideology," in Nannerl O. Keohane, Michele Rosaldo, and Barbara Gelpi, eds., *Feminist Theory: A Critique of Ideology* (Chicago: University of Chicago Press, 1982).

[40]Jon Elster, "Belief, Bias, and Ideology," in Martin Hollis and Steven Lukes, eds., *Rationality and Relativism* (Cambridge: MIT Press, 1982), pp. 130–133.

[41]See Ludwig Wittgenstein, *On Certainty*, ed. G. E. M. Anscombe and G. H. von Wright, trans. Denis Paul and G. E. M. Anscombe (New York: Harper Torchbooks, 1971), #94.

cence in such ideological structures—in which lower classes, women, blacks affirm the justice of their position, believe that they are placed where they deserve to be—cannot be explained away as 'false consciousness'. Frye's image of the prevailing winds that cause the trees to bend in a certain direction—some more than others, because some are older, some more flexible, some more sheltered by other trees—offers a better understanding. In adjusting their wants, the oppressed develop a leaning posture that can accommodate and be more comfortable with the winds.[42]

Stereotype-informed conceptual structures generated out of these psychological-affective influences prevent their adherents from seeing their oppression and marginalization. Women who acquiesce in stereotypes by adhering to their prescriptive import (unwittingly) promote the illusion that they are *voluntarily* occupying their rightful place. Elster observes that a gender-, race- or class-related vulnerability to "fallacies, inferential errors, and illusions"[43] ensues, which is inexplicable on a simple empiricist model of a neutral observer whose beliefs and actions are directly *caused* by data received from the experienced world.

Now Elster's appeal to psychological and affective mechanisms of belief construction is compatible with aspects of feminist critiques of the autonomy-of-reason model. In this respect it is rare in the literature of mainstream epistemology, and it is for its rarity that I cite it. There is a continuity between his analysis and feminist projects of relocating knowledge within the complexities of lives and histories in order to understand how an individual subject's psychic mechanisms can be shaped by an oppressive social order, to the extent that she *cannot* see her situation "steady and whole." The inconceivability, for an oppressed person, of taking things into her own hands, of *asserting* her authority in the face of stereotypes that deny it, is not surprising. Espousing an ideology that rationalizes her inferiority, adopting a position of meekness, may be better than enduring the frustration of simultaneously knowing and refraining from knowing her strengths and capabilities.

Its focus on *individual* psychic mechanisms makes it difficult for feminists wholly to endorse Elster's position, however. He is writing from an instrumental point of view, in which the wants and interests of a rational, self-sufficient, and self-actualizing agent are the taken-for-granted model: the interests of an agent who *can* only be male.

[42]Frye, *Politics of Reality*, p. xii.
[43]Elster, "Belief, Bias, and Ideology," p. 137.

Elster's ideologue is an ahistorical being. The analysis takes no account of his historical situatedness—of the 'baggage' of acculturation that he inevitably brings to any knowing—and of the subtler power structures in which his projects inevitably are caught.

My contention that there is no ideology-free place may appear to imply that the only available epistemic choices are among greater or lesser *evils*. Yet neither quietism nor nihilism are the inevitable consequences. Hans Georg Gadamer's hermeneutic of the role of prejudice in the development of understanding presents a more promising option. For Gadamer, 'prejudice' has no inherently pejorative import: he uses the term interchangeably with 'prejudgments' to affirm its ubiquity and inevitability, hence to reclaim its cognitive centrality. Prejudices are preconditions for understanding as such. They "are not necessarily unjustified and erroneous, so that they inevitably distort the truth. . . . They are simply conditions whereby we experience something."[44] Prejudices, or prejudgments, determine the range of interpretations available at any historical moment. Hidden prejudices obstruct understanding; prejudices revealed, brought to judicious awareness, make knowledge and interpretation possible. They are empowering, not immobilizing. The task of uncovering prejudices, of distinguishing between legitimate and illegitimate tyrannical ones, is integral to cognitive practice.[45] Feminist inquirers resistant to the blinding effects of ideology can draw on its enabling potential to engage in feminist-informed inquiry with critical self-awareness.

Now stereotypes, in their rigidity, immobilize the stereotyped; yet according to Gadamer, prejudgments are an essential prerequisite of knowing. Subjectivity and agency are culturally, materially, historically constituted: knowers cannot leave their prejudgments behind to enter a condition of epistemic purity. Only an autonomy-of-reason fanatic could insist otherwise. Knowers are not mutely propelled by background prejudices, stereotypes, and ideologies unless they abdicate claims to agency. Yet neither are knowers free to negate the influence of preconceptions with a simple refusal. The emancipatory strategy is, rather, to acknowledge and analyze them, to deconstruct them if need be, and to work at turning them into the transformative resources that politically sound commitments require. The choice is

[44]Hans Georg Gadamer, "The Universality of the Hermeneutical Problem," in his *Philosophical Hermeneutics*, trans. David E. Linge (Berkeley: University of California Press, 1976), p. 9.
[45]In thinking about this matter, I have benefited from Jim Wong's unpublished paper "A Fusion of Horizons: Hermeneutics and Epistemic Responsibility."

not between crudely stereotyping and naively denying the existence of preconceptions. What, then, is the solution?

It could take up its starting position in a dialogic practice, a mutual, reciprocal interpretive critique. A dialogue that promotes the dissolution of dogmatisms requires an informed sensitivity to other people's situations, a responsive recognition of their specificities.[46] In these aspects, it is the antithesis of monologic, imperialistic stereotyping and labeling. It does not aim at empathy, if empathy entails arrogating another person's feelings to oneself, claiming to feel exactly what she feels. Nor does it aim to 'apply' one person's standpoint or criteria to another person's circumstances. Its purpose, rather, is to *interpret* and reinterpret, from a commitment to acquiring a critical understanding of commonality and differences. (Stereotypes close off interpretation: hence they need to be deconstructed.) 'Historical' analyses can enable people to understand their prejudgments and to evaluate them critically. Gadamer characterizes the best outcome of such processes as a "fusion of horizons" in which in a conversation one discovers "the standpoint and horizon of the other person, [and] his ideas become intelligible, without our necessarily having to agree with him."[47] The process is at once respectful and critical of the prejudgments of its participants: it is a productive second-person process.

In Chapter 7 I take up and elaborate the reconstructive, empowering potential of a conversational, dialogic model of inquiry that owes a debt to Gadamerian hermeneutics, with its ideal of achieving a fusion of horizons. My proposal departs from Gadamer's in two crucial aspects, however. For the potentially engulfing, merging potential of a fusion of horizons is not unequivocally desirable, and Gadamer does not take power into account, either as a given or as a goal.

Intricate structures of power are at work throughout any social order to legitimate knowledge and the institutional practices it informs. Foucault's conception of the power/knowledge connection opens a line of corrective inquiry to the Gadamerian failure to take account of the power mechanisms that constrain or facilitate dialogue. The totalizing, controlling power of discourse that gains institutional hegemony—in medicine, psychiatry, criminology, psychology, or

---

[46]See Hans Georg Gadamer, *Truth and Method*, trans. Sheed & Ward, Ltd. (New York: Seabury, 1975), p. 272.
[47]Ibid., p. 270.

sociology—is sanctioned by social regimes and deployed to control and discipline populations. By establishing what counts as normal, such discourses construct criteria for discerning deviances that become sites of investigation, surveillance, and treatment. In Victorian England, for example, marriage and motherhood became both the social and the medical norms of female existence. Lynda Nead notes, "Deviation from these norms results in disease and . . . social deviancy for women is also defined as a medical abnormality."[48] Stereotypes of 'woman' are at once generated and nourished by patriarchal ideology[49] *and* inform the rhetorical machinery that perpetuates that ideology. Their conservative, controlling function as loci of power reveals the efficacy of the power-discourse-knowledge nexus in keeping women in their rightful place.

Now the power at work in such discourses is not the usual, sovereign political power, uniformly superimposed on a subservient population. Power is manifested in local 'truths', prescriptions, and prohibitions; it is not exercised by or against specific individual subjects, but manifests itself in impersonal structures of legitimated knowledge. Power is apparent as much in exclusions as in inclusions. Certain descriptions preclude other descriptions: stereotypes of 'woman' efface the very possibility that women could have authoritative capacities of agency and resistance. There is a coordinated growth, then, in the Foucauldian conception of the human sciences. The human sciences construct the knowledge base on which social practices and institutions build, while those same practices and institutions confer legitimacy on social scientific discourse in mutually reinforcing, yet shifting, discontinuous processes. Strategies of resistance to such totalizing mechanisms as stereotypes are needed to refuse their repressive effects, to crack their veneer of completeness in order to lay claim to the possibilities they obliterate.

The power of stereotypes and ideologies is implicated in the myriad micropractices that are constitutive of more formal, institutional power structures. Stereotypes are everywhere and nowhere. Their origins are obscure: gesturing toward them in analyses of age-old

[48]Lynda Nead, *Myths of Sexuality: Representations of Women in Victorian Britain* (Oxford: Blackwell, 1988), p. 26.

[49]Parallels between the stereotyping of women and stereotypes of blacks, Jews, 'foreigners', Asians, the elderly, the working classes are too familiar. Women stereotype other women: feminists stereotype nonfeminists and vice versa; heterosexual women stereotype lesbians and vice versa; and all of these practices are disempowering both for the stereotyper and for the stereotyped. Men, too, are the objects of stereotyping, yet these practices are not sustained by social structures comparable to those that sustain the stereotyping of women.

attitudes and practices is the only possibility. They are not readily falsifiable either in theory or in practice, as demonstrably erroneous theories ultimately are; nor can their acquisition be explained on standard philosophical models of knowledge acquisition. Yet stereotypes and their analogues are embedded—often unconsciously and nearly imperceptibly—in the theories, practices, and attitudes of the authorities and experts whose influence in women's lives feminists are interrogating and working to negate.

Vulnerability and Credulity

James Thurber's fable "The Unicorn in the Garden" is an instructive tale, though for reasons that no doubt differ from his reasons for recounting it.[50] A man looks up from his breakfast to see a unicorn in the garden. He is both excited and delighted, but when he tells his wife, who is still in bed, she comments coldly: "The unicorn is a mythical beast." The man insists; she is convinced that he must be crazy. Yet when the police and a psychiatrist arrive, in response to her summons, and challenge the man to confirm his report of seeing a unicorn in the garden, he replies that he reported no such thing: "the unicorn is a mythical beast." So his wife is pronounced "crazy as a jay bird" and taken away cursing and screaming to be shut up in an institution, while the husband lives happily ever after.

Now Thurber draws from this story the moral "Don't count your boobies until they are hatched"; Martin Hollis, who cites it in support of his critique of 'strong programme' relativism, maintains: "It seems patent that the truth of the various beliefs makes all the difference. If there actually was a unicorn in the garden, his belief is not certifiable. If he actually said there was, her belief that he did needs no psychiatrist to explain it. The psychiatrist intervenes only when beliefs are false or irrational." His point is to argue that there are facts of the matter which determine the credibility of his—the man's—position against the obvious irrationality of hers—the wife's; to show that it is by no means "a matter of indifference whether to send for a zoo-keeper or a psychiatrist."[51]

Hollis's is one plausible reading of the Thurber story. But another, equally plausible one bears on the issues of authority, expertise, and

---

[50]"The Unicorn in the Garden," in James Thurber, *Further Fables for Our Time* (New York: Harper & Row, 1939), p. 65.

[51]Martin Hollis, "The Social Destruction of Reality," in Hollis and Lukes, eds., *Rationality and Relativism*, pp. 76, 77.

power at work in this incident. Can it be just a coincidence that it is the man who is believed and the woman who is pronounced crazy? Perhaps, but it is unlikely. It would be a better world—one where gender politics were more equitable, and objectivist theories of knowledge might more straightforwardly apply—if it were possible to conclude with confidence that a psychiatrist intervenes only when beliefs and actions are consistently false, erratic, or irrational by an external and apolitical standard. But the politics of madness plainly contributes to the outcome here, as it does in too many analogous instances for feminists to be sanguine about concurring with Hollis's faith in the epistemic warrantability of psychiatric judgment.

In the Thurber fable, action is taken on the basis of a judgment according to which *one* first-person experiential account is granted greater credibility than another. It is by no means clear how standard epistemology, with its distrust of experiential evidence and its commitment to impartiality, can evaluate such situations. Hollis, in common with the objectivists to whom he declares his allegiance, is convinced that the rationally informed expertise of the psychiatrist equips him to judge, reliably, *which* accounts are true. Established claims to authoritative expertise, in present-day western societies, are commonly articulated against the background of just that regulative ideal of a neutral, detached, impartial scientific knowledge, in whose acquisition political and other 'subjective' factors are scrupulously eliminated. Hollis plainly believes that the judgment that dispatches the woman to the "booby-hatch" is neutrally derived and factually based in just these senses.

Thurber's story is only a fable, written to amuse. But his wit gains in pungency and bite from its resonance with real events. In the same week that the press reports Soviet acknowledgments of the political misuse of psychiatric committal of just the sort depicted in Solzhenitsyn's novel *The First Circle*, it tells of an eighty-two-year-old American woman released after nearly six decades in a mental hospital, with an official claim that she "never belonged in an institution." It is true that this woman had been having "nervous spells" when she was interviewed for admission, but the interview—at least as it is reported—scarcely seems to justify committal. Responding to the psychiatrist's question about the difference between a cow and a horse, she said, "You milk a cow, but you can't milk a horse"—adding, "You're not making as big a fool of me as you think." The diagnosis was "psychosis, equivalent of epilepsy."[52]

[52]Toronto, *The Globe and Mail*, Associated Press release (November 24, 1987).

Now the juxtaposition of these two examples shows that it would be facile to represent the politics of madness as a simple masculine conspiracy to suppress allegedly irrational female behavior. At least as many male as female Soviet dissidents have been held in psychiatric institutions. In western societies, too, one can read of men's unjustified committals. Yet in most instances, committal is linked with 'underclass' status and unequal power and authority relations, recalling Harding's allegations about the social consequences of the empiricist theory of mind.[53] There can be no dispute about psychiatry's aptness as an instrument of coercion and control. Indeed, in broader social contexts, Hollis's faith in the translucency and neutrality of psychiatric judgment is evidently misplaced. Such judgments are mediated as much by interests, bias, ideology, and prescriptive, stereotype-derived thinking as they are by immediate confrontations with 'the evidence'.

There is no doubt that psychiatric practice is constituted within the spaces made available by a sex/gender system that is intricated with structures of racism, classism, heterosexism, and numerous other forms of oppression. The fact that there are consistently more psychiatric and therapeutic interventions in women's lives than in men's lives is now well documented. Often, it is true, women themselves *seek* psychiatric/therapeutic help and intervention; hence, according to the common wisdom, they choose it freely. But the freedom of such choices is highly contestable, given the structural, ideological assumptions encoded in western societies about women's 'natural' tendency to mental imbalance. In their appeal to a self-actualizing conception of autonomous subjectivity, representations of their choices as 'free' mask the extent to which choices are structurally constituted. The fact that there *are* gender-specific mechanisms at work here—as there are in the concentration of 'expert' control over femininity in all of its permissible manifestations, contrasted with lesser control over the construction of masculinity—is not open to dispute. Women, as they are positioned in western, science-venerating cultures, are widely and unduly dependent upon expert (masculine) intervention.[54] That dependence is apparent even in their childbearing and -rearing practices, which the same ideological constructions of femininity designate as their essential functions.

[53]See my discussion of her article in Chapter 1.
[54]It would be a mistake to claim that male 'experts' are alone in controlling women and other 'underclass' groups. Female medical practitioners, psychotherapists, and other authorities often conform to the male-practitioner model. I write here of a dominant pattern.

Writing about "the scientific answer to the Woman Question, as elaborated over the last hundred years by a new class of experts—physicians, psychologists, domestic scientists, child-raising experts," Barbara Ehrenreich and Deirdre English note a striking similarity in the relationship between women and experts, and traditional patriarchal constructions of the relationships between women and men. In the mid-nineteenth century, women began to respond with dependency and trust to a group of experts whose authority "rested on the denial or destruction of women's autonomous sources of knowledge."[55] English and Ehrenreich connect the rise of specialized, professionalized forms of expertise with the growth of the market economy set in motion by the industrial revolution and with consequent redrawings of boundaries between 'public' and 'private' spheres. They link women's loss of control over the productive processes that passed into the factory system with a "commodification" of women's traditional arts and skills and their displacement from authoritative social positions.

Expert authority established itself in a series of curious epistemological moves. A growing veneration of science led to concerted endeavors to construct a scientific basis for hitherto local, 'craft-like' skills, arts, and wisdom. Women's healing arts, their midwifery skills, their household management and child-raising techniques all became objects of scientific study. Claiming a closer connection between knowledge and human interests than an objectivist philosophy of science would allow, English and Ehrenreich note that "the new scientific expert . . . became an authority . . . [whose] business was not to seek out what is *true*, but to pronounce on what is *appropriate*."[56] The questions, Appropriate for whom? by what criteria? and to what end? point consistently, in their answers, to the desirability of maintaining women's dependence on masculine authority. Such dependent relations are instituted, allegedly, for women's own good. But it is not easy to believe that this 'good' is really 'their own good' as authoritative women would articulate it.[57]

Ehrenreich and English document the intervention throughout women's lives of "the ideology of a masculinist society, dressed up as

[55]Barbara Ehrenreich and Deirdre English, *For Her Own Good: 150 Years of the Experts' Advice to Women* (New York: Doubleday, 1978), p. 4.
[56]Ibid., p. 28.
[57]In *Madness and Civilisation* (trans. Richard Howard [London: Tavistock, 1967]), Foucault writes: "The doctor's intervention is not made by virtue of a medical skill or power that he possesses in himself and that would be justified by a body of objective knowledge. It is not as a scientist that *homo medicus* has authority in the asylum, but as a wise man . . . as a juridical and moral guarantee" (p. 270).

objective truth,"[58] which draws sustenance from entrenched stereotypes of women. The authors discern a correlation between an increase in these interventions and the end of a practical and social
authority women had been in a position to claim in their healing arts,
midwifery, and domestic production. Susceptible to the rhetoric of a
new scientific era that promised so much, and rendered increasingly
passive by the growing mystification of expertise, women were induced to acquiesce in an ideology that reaffirmed their incapacity to
think for themselves by signing over responsibility for their well-
being to the experts.

A complex, reciprocal interplay between upper-middle-class privilege and the masculine superiority of its practitioners constructed the
new science of medicine as an authority over women's lives. The
doctor acquired a mystified prestige from his training in an esoteric
scientific knowledge to which women had little or no access. Knowledge itself, increasingly, became a commodity of privilege. With the
rise of the middle classes and the establishment of (middle-class)
women's private domestic realm, the prestige of science extended
rapidly into the domains of housework and child rearing. House-
keeping was reconstructed as a full-time profession, to create, for
women, the illusion that this was a serious, all-consuming activity
that needed all of their talents and energies. Women began to draw
"prodigiously on the advice of male experts in an attempt to lay the
basis for a *science* of childraising and a *science* of housework."[59] The
rhetoric of 'scientific' housewifery, when science is mystified and venerated, points to the conclusion that any woman who ignores scientific expertise to rely on her experiences, intuitions, and skills is vio-
lating a fundamental epistemic imperative. When possibilities of
being a 'good enough' woman and mother depend on relinquishing
trust in their own skills in favor of a more distinguished expertise, it is
not surprising that women would do what was expected of them.
According to the experts, a woman's power had to be channeled away
from any temptation she might have to participate knowledgeably in
esoteric public knowledge and channeled toward concentration, in
the 'home', on her husband and child.[60] There, too, her power had to
be carefully controlled and her decisions managed—from the relationships she should appropriately establish to the detergent she
should buy. Lurking beneath these complex and interwoven prescriptions is a stereotyped conception of women as unbalanced and funda-

[58]Ehrenreich and English, *For Her Own Good*, p. 5.
[59]Ibid., p. 142.
[60]See ibid., p. 190.

mentally out of control, and of motherhood and femaleness as pathology. According to Dr. Joseph Reingold of the Harvard Medical School, "maternal destructiveness [is] built into the female psyche . . . it [arises] from a fundamental horror at being female, which [is] the 'basic conflict of the woman's personality.' "[61]

The conflation of femininity with pathology is a constant thread running through expert endeavors to control women—to channel their sexuality to conform with male expectations and heterosexual norms, to direct their projects even within their designated domestic sphere, and to shape their psyches to align with masculine constructions of good womanhood. All of these projects derive from a highly contestable *knowledge* base, constructed as much by stereotypes and ideology as by observation, objective judgment, or fact. Their effects are most strikingly visible in conceptions of female madness; and this is no surprise in view of the fact that women throughout the nineteenth and twentieth centuries—and especially at periods of social upheaval—have been represented as potential hysterics, constantly on the verge of madness. In the remainder of this section, therefore, I focus on madness as at once a symptom and a metaphor of women's oppression, centering my analysis on two studies of women and madness in which the *epistemological* claims are most clearly visible: *The Female Malady* by Elaine Showalter and Jill Matthews's *Good and Mad Women*.[62] These studies confirm the power of stereotypes and patriarchal ideology in shaping women's options and ensuring their docility and credulity.

I am interested in the epistemological implications of these studies, but my purpose is not to derive standard malestream conclusions about the nature, justification, and warrantability of knowledge claims. Rather, I want to highlight their demonstrations of the place of ideology in the production of knowledge, the relations of power and knowledge, and the construction of expertise and authority. The practices these studies detail show beyond doubt that, behind the mask of objectivity and value-neutrality that mainstream epistemology presents to the world, are complex structures of vested interest, dominance, and subjugation. In earlier chapters I have analyzed the effects of these structures in formal epistemological constructions; here I demonstrate some of their specific manifestations in 'received', expert knowledge. In displaying the stereotype-perpetuating power of em-

---

[61]Cited in ibid., p. 234.
[62]Elaine Showalter, *The Female Malady: Women, Madness, and English Culture, 1830–1980* (New York: Penguin, 1987); Matthews, *Good and Mad Women* (cited in Chapter 2).

pirical scientific investigation, carried by the rhetoric of what "science has proved" about women's natural inferiority to men and about the proper treatment of women's unhappiness, anxiety, and depression, these studies contribute tellingly to discrediting the self-proclaimed disinterestedness of scientific inquiry and ideal objectivity.

In the late 1860s Seymour Haden, speaking to the British Obstetrical Society, declared that, as practitioners among women, obstetricians "have constituted ourselves . . . the guardians of their honour. . . . We are, in fact, the stronger, and they the weaker. They are not in a position to dispute anything we say to them, and we, therefore, may be said to have them at our mercy."[63] Quoting Haden, Showalter observes that although the management of women's minds was carried out more subtly in the lunatic asylums of the time, "it too expressed the power of male psychiatrists over definitions of femininity and insanity . . . women's training to revere such authority in the family often made them devoted and grateful patients of fatherly asylum superintendents."[64] Such were the sexual power relationships in Victorian medicine.

Showalter's central theme is the "equation between femininity and insanity that goes far beyond statistical evidence or the social conditions of women"—the notion of madness as "the essential feminine nature unveiling itself before scientific male rationality."[65] In like vein, Matthews argues that the gender order of any society, social group, or culture creates an ideology of femininity with which it establishes what it means to be a good woman and requires women to approximate that ideal. The ideology is bizarre and ultimately crazy-making, for it has no definite or constant content. As with the stereotypes at work within it, there is no empirical, objective evidence to attest to the ideal's basis in women's 'nature' or experiences. Wild fluctuations in prescriptions for being a good woman map more readily onto perceived (patriarchal) necessities to curb and control women's self-perceptions than onto women's demonstrated capacities. 'Femininity' as a concept is an empty shell. It purports to capture the essence, the absolute meaning of female being, yet it is open to infusion with content by whatever authority conjures it into use. Hence "every woman's body and life, everything she does . . . become the objects of a struggle for control by competing

---

[63]Quoted in Showalter, *Female Malady*, p. 78.
[64]Ibid. The image of obedience to the father is drawn, again, from two-parent, patriarchal family structures.
[65]Ibid., p. 3.

forces, each force proclaiming itself the upholder of the true ideal of femininity."[66]

In the case notes of female psychiatric patients and in manifestations of the ideal of femininity in constructions of women's sexuality, work, and mothering in twentieth-century Australia, Matthews, like Ehrenreich and English, discerns a structural configuration in which professionals and experts become the overseers of the gender order, while assignments to the category of madness or goodness become instruments for controlling women by maintaining that order. Diagnoses of madness often incorporate—if indeed they do not focus solely on—madness as a deviation from a social norm. Thus, for example, one nineteenth-century treatise, *The Functions and Disorders of the Reproductive Organs*, contends that women are not *normally* "troubled" with sexual feeling, though it acknowledges "the existence of sexual excitement terminating even in nymphomania, a form of insanity which those accustomed to visit lunatic asylums must be fully conversant with"—suggesting to Nead that "desires which are defined as commonplace in men are treated as a form of madness in women."[67] Analogously, Showalter records the Darwinian belief that mental breakdown occurs when women attempt to defy their essential nature, seeking alternatives to their maternal function and resisting the idea that they exist to help and serve men.[68] Like the 'experts' whose ascendancy Ehrenreich and English document, Darwinian psychiatrists extended their authority to "the courtroom, where they made pronouncements on the family and the education of youth . . . the bedroom, where they defined acceptable sexual behaviour; and . . . the state, where they proposed mental hygiene as the model of social discipline."[69] In all of these places, women's vulnerability increased with their rhetorically induced willingness to trust in the authority of scientific expertise.

Epistemologically, the most striking conclusion that feminist work on women and madness supports is that madness itself is a largely undefined experience or state. With every major shift in the sociopolitical-economic climate, new definitions are constructed and new research projects developed to demonstrate their accuracy. It is impossible to specify objective criteria by which women are, con-

[66]Matthews, *Good and Mad Women*, p. 8.
[67]Nead, *Myths of Sexuality*, p. 50. The book quoted is by William Acton, published in London in 1857.
[68]Showalter, *Female Malady*, p. 123. See Russett, *Sexual Science*, for a fuller discussion of Darwinian constructions of 'normal' femininity.
[69]Showalter, *Female Malady*, p. 105.

sistently, diagnosed mad (or sometimes sane) or objective social norms whose transgression inevitably invites the diagnosis. It is difficult for a woman to *know* how she should be in order not to be declared mad, and to *know* the criteria by which she is ultimately diagnosed. It is not easy for women to make other people realize that they *know* something about the processes of their own lives, and for women to believe that authorities and experts really *know* enough to justify their authoritarian positions.

First-person experiential evidence is consistently undervalued and paternalistically reinterpreted in these diagnoses. *The Yellow Wallpaper* by Charlotte Perkins Gilman is a classic illustration. Gilman's efforts to construct as 'objective' as possible an account of her suffering, for her consultation with Dr. S. Weir Mitchell, who was to supervise her "rest cure," drew only scorn from the great man. Mitchell indicated his utter lack of interest: from his patients he did not require information—based even on their own experiences. He wanted complete obedience, based on *his* construction of their experiences. Equally poignant is the case of Camille Claudel, whose sculptures were overshadowed by those of her teacher and lover, Auguste Rodin. In consequence of having "placed herself beyond the pale of sanctioned femininity," Claudel suffered humiliation and retribution that prompted her withdrawal "into an increasingly alienated state." Her committal to a mental hospital for thirty years, on the basis of a medical certificate that her brother obtained against her will, leaves open the question "whether or to what extent Claudel was insane."[70] Her pleas for freedom were dismissed. In these situations, as in countless others, control is exercised over 'patients' rendered doubly vulnerable and passive, both by their suffering, whose genuineness defies endeavors to reconstruct it, and by an authoritarian expertise with scant discernibly objective basis.

Madness, Showalter declares, is "the impasse confronting those whom cultural conditioning has deprived of the very means of protest or self-affirmation." She observes that photographs of mad women in nineteenth-century medical texts reveal that "doctors imposed cultural stereotypes of femininity and female insanity on women who defied their gender roles"[71]; Matthews describes a psychiatric patient who "attempted throughout her life to be a good woman as was demanded by various people important to her, but she was con-

[70]The quotations are from Anne Higonnet, "A Woman Turned to Stone," *Women's Review of Books* 5 (September 1988): 6.
[71]Showalter, *Female Malady*, pp. 5, 86.

fronted by a series of incongruous meanings which she could not reconcile."[72] Women's efforts to be *good* women, according to fluctuating ideological requirements, too often fail. Inconsistent and contradictory demands built into stereotyped constructions of femininity contribute to the futility, desperation, and confusion that characterize women's diagnoses as mad, both historically and still today. Such diagnoses provide the rationale for women's admissions and readmissions to (institutional) psychiatric care, where they have to learn to be 'good' according to yet another standard to secure their release.

Now critics—especially those of an individualist, self-realization persuasion—might wonder why women do not reclaim their divergent experiences as evidence of superiority or heightened sensitivity, rather than acquiescing in diagnoses of mental instability or madness. The answer is distressingly simple: the structures of madness are already in place to account for those experiences. Foucault's (admittedly gender-blind) tracing of linkages between madness and animality, in which passion is the declared basis of madness, reveals that it is no wonder that women would constantly doubt their sanity.[73] The characteristic diagnostic signs of 'madness', in the grayer areas this side of psychosis, and features of the stereotypical construction of women's nature in hegemonic discourse, are remarkably congruent.

The mind/body, culture/nature, reason/passion dichotomies that inform the construction of rationality as a regulative ideal parallel the male/female dichotomy, both descriptively and evaluatively. In each pair, the second term (body, nature, passion, and female) is accorded lesser value and stands for the less controllable member.[74] Women's greater closeness to nature, it is claimed, causes their 'animal' (= passionate) natures consistently to overrule their rationality. Hence it is no surprise that Foucault's description of madness can be read, equivalently, as a description of femaleness: "The animality that rages in madness dispossesses man of what is specifically human in him; not in order to deliver him over to other powers, but simply to establish him at the zero degree of his own nature. For classicism, madness

---

[72]Matthews, *Good and Mad Women*, p. 7.

[73]See Foucault, *Madness and Civilisation*. It should be noted that Foucault's analyses in *The History of Sexuality*, vol. 1, *An Introduction* (trans. Robert Hurley [New York: Vintage, 1980]), of "the hysterization of women's bodies" acknowledge the gender-specificity of hysteria. The process, he notes, "involved a thorough medicalization of their bodies and their sex, [and] was carried out in the name of the responsibility they owed to the health of their children, the solidity of the family institution, and the safeguarding of society" (pp. 146–147).

[74]See my discussion in Chapter 2.

in its ultimate form is man in immediate relation to his animality, without other reference, without any recourse." Foucault observes that "unchained animality could be mastered only by *discipline* and *brutalizing*."[75] The same is clearly true of deviant, defiant, or passionate femininity.

Foucault writes of "the savage danger of madness" and its relation to "the danger of the passions and their fatal concatenation." He maintains that passion creates the very possibility of madness and that "moralists of the Greco-Latin tradition . . . chose to define passion as a temporary and attenuated madness."[76] Given the ideological alignment of women—essentially and naturally—with passions and animality, it is small wonder that madness should seem to be their natural lot. Conceptions of knowledge that derive from the assumption that knowers are perfectly rational cannot cope with *unreason*. They are unable to deal with the unruly aspects of human nature (= animality, passion) which, on Foucault's account, slide so readily into madness. The achievement of such rationality depends, in short, on the suppression of passions and animality. They must be relegated to an extrarational realm, attributed to lesser beings, contained within inferior doxastic modes. Hence it is no coincidence that women, whose lack of rational authority leaves them at the mercy of their animal natures, should become the lepers, scapegoats, of science-venerating societies. Their suppression enables rational man to disown the psychic mechanisms that threaten his rational purity.

These analyses of the social and scientific construction of madness are nothing short of bizarre, however, in a science such as medicine, with its claims to have a basis in empirical observation. They are particularly odd by the standards of the empiricist theory of knowledge that medical science commonly takes for granted. Empiricists, avowedly, put great store in first-person perceptual and observational reports, maintaining that a 'privileged access' to one's own experiences confers on such reports a special claim to credibility. For an empiricist such as Bertrand Russell, for example, 'knowledge by acquaintance' of one's sensory intake is accorded *foundational* status in a system of knowledge.[77] Although it would be an exaggeration to describe most people as empiricists in their everyday lives in just the sense Russell intends, there is considerable folk wisdom embedded in

[75]Foucault, *Madness and Civilisation*, pp. 74, 75.
[76]Ibid., pp. 85, 89.
[77]See Bertrand Russell, *The Problems of Philosophy* (Oxford: Oxford University Press, 1912); and "Knowledge by Acquaintance and Knowledge by Description," in his *Mysticism and Logic* (London: Allen & Unwin, 1917).

the contention that I can know what I am feeling and experiencing better than anyone else can. Hence it is not difficult to imagine the damage done by a systematic denial of these claims on the part of established and powerful experts, whom a woman has been trained to respect and trust. Epistemologically, these problems demonstrate the inadequacy—indeed, the absurdity—of a (scientistic) epistemological picture that claims a basis in experience, yet systematically discredits women's first-person narratives.[78]

In the current post-Kuhnian philosophical climate, in which a constrained relativism has gained a measure of epistemological respectability, 'objectivity' itself is a seriously contested concept. In theory of knowledge it is no longer an outright heresy to read 'objective' as a fluctuating designation. Sociologists of knowledge, such as David Bloor (and Barry Barnes), maintain that "objectivity is social," that "the *impersonal* and *stable* character that attaches to some of our beliefs . . . derives from these beliefs being *social institutions*";[79] and Jurgen Habermas claims an intricate connection between 'objective' knowledge and human interests, referring to the "critical dissolution of objectivism."[80] My critique of ideal objectivity in this book highlights feminist reasons for its contestedness.

Foucault's analyses of the intrications of power and knowledge challenge all of the pretensions of ideal objectivity. Taking his point of departure not from the seemingly exact and politically neutral science of physics, but from the normalizing power structures that generate and are generated by psychiatric knowledge, Foucault demonstrates the instability of claims to scientific objectivity. The arbitrariness of the assumption that physics can be a model of knowledge is just one consequence. Psychiatric knowledge works quite differently, yet Foucault's investigations do not point to the conclusion that psychiatry is aberrant measured by the 'normalizing' standard of physics. Rather, his readers cannot fail to suspect that physics is the aberration: physics yields an excessively optimistic belief in the possible *purity* of knowledge, with psychiatry as a poor contender by contrast. Foucault urges that, at least in the human sciences, it is only at one's peril that one ignores gaps and discontinuities in scientific knowledge or "the politics of the scientific statement."[81]

---

[78]I discuss another aspect of this denial in Chapter 6.
[79]David Bloor, "A Sociological Theory of Objectivity," in S. C. Brown, ed., *Objectivity and Cultural Divergence* (Cambridge: Cambridge University Press, 1984), p. 229.
[80]Jurgen Habermas, *Knowledge and Human Interests*, trans. Jeremy J. Shapiro (Boston: Beacon, 1971), p. 212.
[81]Foucault, *Power/Knowledge*, p. 112.

My point is not that objectivity is a myth, hence that the absence of objective criteria for diagnosing female madness—or goodness—is of no consequence. The unattainability of perfect, ideal objectivity does not annul the requirement for feminists, as for all inquirers, to be realists and to occupy as objective a standpoint as possible. As I have argued in Chapter 2, if there were *no* objective social facts—if it were impossible to take a realist position with respect to sexism, classism, racism, heterosexism, about all forms of suffering, marginalization, and oppression in capitalist, patriarchal societies—there could be no feminist or other emancipatory politics. Documentations and analyses of oppressive practices could simply be dismissed. It is not true that all knowledge claims are equally negotiated, that none are objective, even though divergent constructions of many situations are possible. Situations, structures, practices, and oppressions are there to be analyzed and subjected to critique; there are better and worse, more or less objective, ways of confronting them.

Reclamations

Wittgenstein's observation that "knowledge is in the end based on acknowledgement"[82] encapsulates the problematic of this chapter. Yet the capacity to gain acknowledgment is gender-related in ways that Wittgenstein himself would not have envisaged, and its gender-specificity is multidimensional. Like any other knower, a female knowledge claimant has to claim acknowledgment from other participants in a form of life. But advancing such claims is as much a political action as it is a straightforwardly epistemological one. Before she can so much as seek acknowledgment, a woman has to free herself from stereotyped conceptions of her 'underclass' epistemic status, her cognitive incapacity, and her ever-threatening irrationality. She has to achieve this freedom both in the eyes of other people, who too often deny her capacity by refusing to listen or give credence, and from her own standpoint, shaped as it also is by stereotype-informed assumptions that neither her experiences nor her deliberative capacities are trustworthy sources of knowledge. Politically, spaces have to be created where a woman's knowledge can be judged sufficiently authoritative to deserve acknowledgment, and the spaces have to be constructed variously, to respond to differences between and among women. The creation of such spaces depends on the collective and

[82]Wittgenstein, *On Certainty*, #378.

mutually enabling efforts of women who can trust themselves to know,[83] and to know that they know.

In this instance, a simple perceptual example can show what is at issue. Consider one of the most common 'S knows that p' examples: say, Sara knows that the cat is on the mat.[84] Now suppose that Sara's claim "the cat is on the mat" is contradicted by everyone around her: by people she knows and loves, who live in the house where the mat is located; by passing strangers; and by 'vision experts' summoned to check her perceptual powers. All of these people consistently insist that there is no cat on the mat. How long would Sara be able to defend the veridicality of her perception if *everyone* else, both now and over time, attested to the mat's emptiness? I suggest that she would soon begin to suspect she was hallucinating and to be disturbed about it, even if her visual observations check out positively with her other senses: she can touch the cat, hear it purr. Even the simplest of observational knowledge claims depend, more than people ordinarily realize, on corroboration, acknowledgment, either in word or in deed. When someone is in doubt about what she hears or sees, she is as likely to call on someone else to confirm her impression as she is to check it by any other means—and to call someone else again, if there is still no agreement. If everyone else consistently walked around the mat, Sara might never even have wondered; if everyone walked across the cat, she would have been perturbed much earlier.

Now suppose Sara's cat-on-the-mat experience is generalized throughout her perceptual life: in innumerable instances she has strong and persistent perceptions that no one else has. These experiences are vivid and in every respect indistinguishable from her perceptions that seem quite 'normal', in the sense that requiring acknowledgment for them does not so much as arise. It is hard to imagine how anyone could live with a generalized conviction of her perceptual idiosyncrasy without becoming wholly bewildered, distraught, and confused; nor how she could ever allude to those experiences without being judged at best peculiar, at worst quite mad. Sara would rapidly lose the capacity to trust her own observations (or, if

[83]The phrase is a variation on the title of Barbara Houston and Ann Diller's article "Trusting Ourselves to Care," *Resources for Feminist Research* 16 (September 1987): 35–38. Houston and Diller aptly comment that it would be "a mistake to think we can never trust ourselves, for that would be to succumb to a victim stereotype of women which is . . . falsifying of our experience" (p. 36).

[84]The example is frequently used in Foley's *Theory of Epistemic Rationality*, which is typical of 'state of the art' epistemology.

these peculiarities were hers from birth, she would never acquire that capacity). It is unlikely that her friends or associates would take her observational claims seriously—either her idiosyncratic ones or her 'normal' ones.[85]

It is instructive to engage seriously with this seemingly fanciful scenario, to think one's way into it, to imagine how it would be, minute by minute, to live it. My point is that it is not so fanciful. It generalizes readily to women's epistemic lives per se: ironically, it may not happen so often with their everyday perceptual experiences as it does in their more complex cognitive projects. But it happens frequently with respect to projects even slightly more complex. Consider the denigration of women's intuitions, arts, skills, and everyday practices, or the frequent, scornful dismissals of women's complaints of sexism or sexual harassment. The irony is that, because it is easy to argue that both women and men see cats on mats pretty much indistinguishably in similar circumstances, it appears to be nonsensical to suggest that women's knowledge claims frequently are suppressed for want of acknowledgment. Yet women are often, both metaphorically and literally, driven crazy by their incapacity to gain any greater acknowledgement for their knowledge (which, on one level, they *know* must be valid) than Sara can for her claim that the cat is on the mat.[86] These are not isolated, hallucinatory experiences. They are sufficiently pervasive for women, finally, to fear that they may be wrong after all, that they have missed the important point, and that the experts—who determine the norm from which women's perceptions diverge so radically—*must* be right.

With reference to women and madness, I drew attention to the ease with which self-doubt is created and feeds into a woman's special vulnerability, born of excessive dependence. There is a noteworthy connection between the production of that dependence and vulnerability, and the *cognitive posture* experts assume in relation to their clients/patients. Showalter documents the reluctance of Victorian

---

[85]As Wittgenstein remarks, "If I were contradicted on all sides and told that this person's name was not what I had always known it was (and I use 'know' here intentionally), then in that case the foundation of all judging would be taken away from me." Wittgenstein, *On Certainty*, #614.

[86]Adrienne Rich's "gaslighting" image is especially apt here. She writes: "Women have been driven mad, 'gaslighted,' for centuries by the refutation of our experience and our instincts in a culture which validates only male experience. The truth of our bodies and our minds has been mystified to us. We therefore have a primary obligation to each other: not to undermine each others' sense of reality for the sake of expediency; not to gaslight each other." Rich, "Women and Honor: Some Notes on Lying (1975)," in her *On Lies, Secrets, and Silence: Selected Prose 1966–1978* (New York: Norton, 1979), p. 190. Naomi Scheman reminded me of this passage.

asylum superintendents to listen to their patients "to find out how they felt and why," noting Charcot's manner of staring intently at hysterical patients while paying "very little attention to what they were saying." She remarks on Freud's excessive haste in imposing "his own language on [Dora's] mute communications." Instructively, she contrasts these postures with the approach of Josef Breuer, who "respected the intelligence of his hysterical female patient, encouraged her to speak, and then listened carefully to what she said."[87] The difference, as I see it, turns on acknowledgment. There is no more effective way to create epistemic dependence than systematically to withhold acknowledgment; no more effective way of maintaining structures of epistemic privilege and vulnerability than evincing a persistent distrust in someone's claims to cognitive authority; no surer demonstration of a refusal to know what a person's experiences are than observing her 'objectively' without taking her first-person reports seriously.

The epistemic-political challenge for women, then, is to devise strategies for claiming their cognitive competence and authority, their knowledgeability, and their right to know. Moving toward the development of such strategies may require taking responsibility for oneself, refusing epistemic oppression. But the means of so doing cannot be those of the autonomous, self-sufficient knower, for acknowledgment persistently withheld obliterates self-affirmation, sooner rather than later. Such strategies have to be mounted in *collective* social critique and active constructions of meaning, engaged in by women who can see and understand how power confers the status of knowledge on products of inquiry better characterized as conjectural, hypothetical, working theories; and how knowledge itself confers and is conferred by power, perpetuating these complex social structures. Women's successes in forming health collectives and in seeking access to feminist therapy and legal advice show that such power can become accessible also to the oppressed, who need no longer occupy the position of victim and suppliant, in thrall to expert mystification. Although victory is by no means total, women's achievements in refusing to occupy oppressed positions are noteworthy.

Foucault observes (in 1976) that he has "a sense of the increasing vulnerability to criticism of things, institutions, practices, and discourses. A certain fragility has been discovered in the very bedrock of existence—even, and perhaps above all, in those aspects of it that are most familiar, most solid and most intimately related to our bodies and to our everyday behaviour."[88] Women have been able to exploit

[87]Showalter, *Female Malady*, pp. 61, 154, 160, 157.

this vulnerability in breaking the hegemony of authoritarian expertise. Their projects acquire increased momentum from academic and
grass-roots critiques of scientific hegemony, which enable feminists to
"fight science with science." Those critiques are central to the project
of reevaluating the position and power of science in western societies
and of articulating critical analyses of scientific pretensions to discover the "nature of human beings" or to act as a "neutral arbiter" in
social debates.[89] The challenge is to achieve a proper balance between
skepticism and credulity. Too stringent a skepticism can thwart a
woman's chances of obtaining the authoritative help she needs, yet
excessive credulity generates a disempowering vulnerability. Women
can learn, collectively, to give and withhold acknowledgment and
hence to claim power for their knowledge. Michele Le Doeuff's wry
observation that "knowledge about women has always been masculine property"[90] begins to read like an observation that *belongs* in
the past tense. When women can be confident that it no longer holds,
they may be in a position to agree with Hollis that a psychiatrist
intervenes "only when beliefs are false or irrational." Until then, it will
be hard to know whether the man saw a unicorn in the garden or not.

Typically and stereotypically, women of the affluent classes are
trained from childhood to be more trusting than men. Hence they
tend to place their trust in people who present themselves as authorities, whereas men might, autonomously, resist. That such trust-
ingness is a primary source of women's vulnerability counts as a
cogent reason why an appropriate autonomy has to persist as a feminist goal, its tendencies to excess notwithstanding. Too much trust in
experts—too little trust in themselves and their collective strength—
renders women acquiescent and passive. For Baier, when trust manifests itself as "faith in the competence of the powers that be, then
readiness to trust will be seen not just as a virtue of the weak, but
itself as a moral weakness, better replaced by vigilance and self-
assertion, by self-reliance or by cautious, minimal, and carefully monitored trust."[91] This 'moral weakness' has stereotypically been construed as desirable for women, in affirmation of their diminished
deliberative capacities. Only in continuous refusal do women claim
the power to assume authoritative, expert status on their terms.

---

[88]Foucault, *Power/Knowledge*, p. 80.
[89]The phrases are from Londa Schiebinger, "Women and Science," *Signs: Journal of Women in Culture and Society* 12 (Winter 1987): 328.
[90]Michele Le Doeuff, "Women and Philosophy," *Radical Philosophy* 17 (Summer 1977): 7.
[91]Baier, "Trust and Antitrust," p. 242.

Claiming epistemic empowerment need not—and probably cannot—be a global project. In fact, articulated as a global imperative it produces more despair than hope. Women cannot refuse all reliance on expertise at once. The prospect is so daunting that few would be prepared to embark on it. But neither is expertise a neutral entity, part of 'the nature of things': it is constituted and impeded by social structures, mediated by power relations, and open to deconstruction and revision. Impressive feminist successes show that such revisioning can be achieved, piecemeal, but with widening spheres of influence.

Projects disruptive of the discourse of expertise have drawn on dialogic, conversational models, informed by assumptions of second personhood. They depend on responsible knowledge of other persons or an openness to the possibility of knowing them well enough. Thus they are continuous with the consciousness-raising groups of the 1960s and 1970s in which, through processes of mutual—tu quoque—recognition, women learned how to acknowledge their experiences. The friendship/second-personhood model enables women to recognize their commonalities and differences, to trust themselves and one another, to know hitherto suppressed truths about their social positions. This trust can develop into the power women need to reposition themselves in relation to authority and expertise. As Juliet Mitchell asks: "What can you do but disrupt a history and re-create it as another history?"[92]

No discourse is perfectly homogeneous, whatever its totalizing effects; if it were, change would be impossible, for a discourse would maintain absolute thought control. There are always recessive resources to be tapped, new structures to be constructed. Elisabeth Young-Bruehl observes that "all of the voices or purposes that are our minds must be heard in order for us to achieve not *an* identity but a more communicative form of life in the possibility of conversational reconciling, both in ourselves and with others."[93] Breuer's willingness to listen to his female patients and to take their stories seriously attests to one such possibility; R. D. Laing's project of making madness intelligible as a *strategy*—"a form of communication in response to the contradictory messages and demands about femininity women faced in patriarchal society"[94]—opened further possibilities.

The fact that crazy-making ideological control has by no means vanished from the social map shows that the processes set in motion

[92]Juliet Mitchell, "Femininity, Narrative, and Psychoanalysis," in her *Women: The Longest Revolution* (London: Virago, 1984), p. 288.
[93]Young-Bruehl, "Education of Women as Philosophers," p. 219.
[94]Showalter, *Female Malady*, p. 222.

by consciousness raising have not run their course, although note-worthy progress has been made. The demand for feminist therapists—therapists who will negotiate the terms of client-therapist dialogue to take participants' experiences and ideological orientations seriously, starting from a presumption of veridicality—has not gone unanswered. (There is reason to hope that Mary Daly's cynical designation of a therapist as "the/rapist" has lost some of its force.) Such relationships require a presumption in favor of taking first-person narratives seriously, even if the accounts need later to be amended, reinterpreted, studied for gaps and moments of self-deception. That presumption stands as a safeguard against precipitous incredulity, even on the part of an expert.

As P. Susan Penfold and Gillian Walker observe, an emphasis on "maintaining and enhancing [a] woman's power and responsibility"[95] is central to the democratic practices of a feminist therapy that validates women's assumption of responsibility for their own lives. British art therapist Diana Halliday conjectures that she sees more women than men in her practice because too few men are prepared to take the responsibility for themselves that entering a therapeutic relationship involves.[96] In this dimension, feminist therapy practice departs radically from the entrenched belief that women are intellectually and emotionally incapable of knowing their interests, let alone negotiating ways of having those interests met. Women's medical self-help groups and health collectives, women's insistence that they *know* how best to express their sexuality, and women's collaborative child-raising endeavors are forms of mutual acknowledgment in which expertise and authority are claimed in conversation, openness, and mutual responsibility. A positive connotation of 'responsibility' is invoked here: not the responsibility that is thrust on women for all of the problems and failures of their families' lives, but an active acknowledgment of the presumptive validity of a woman's perceptions, experiences, and capacities.

[95]P. Susan Penfold and Gillian Walker, *Women and the Psychiatric Paradox* (Montreal: Eden, 1983), p. 233.
[96]Diana Halliday, personal communication.

Credibility:
A Double Standard

The Double Standard

The 'double standard' whose political and epistemological effects I explore in this chapter is vividly illustrated in the conduct of the 1984 Grange Inquiry into infant deaths from cardiac arrest at Toronto's Hospital for Sick Children. Calling the inquiry "the highest-priced, tax-supported sexual harassment exercise that we've ever witnessed," Alice Baumgart observes, "When lawyers, who were mostly men, questioned doctors, the questions were phrased in terms of what they *knew*. When nurses were on the stand, the question was, 'Based on your *experience* . . .' Experience in our society is considered second-class compared to knowledge. Nurses should not know."[1] Now this is neither a unique nor an isolated occurrence in the politics of knowledge. Baumgart's observation attests to the fact that, still today, many professional women can claim only a limited cognitive authority. She is drawing attention to a double standard, within the medical profession, that sustains a hierarchical positioning of male and female practitioners. The standard is upheld rhetorically by a distinction between knowledge and experience, in whose terms knowledge is valued more highly than experience and confers authority where experience cannot. Analogous exclusionary structures oper-

[1]Alice Baumgart, "Women, Nursing, and Feminism," *Canadian Nurse* (January 1985): 20–22. Baumgart continues: "In the health care system, doctors have been regarded as the only 'rightful knowers'. What the doctor-nurse game is really all about is that nurses know, but can't let the world know that they know"(p. 21).

ate throughout public knowledge to ensure women's confinement within narrowly circumscribed private spheres of knowledge and expertise. Latter-day variants of Aristotle's contentions about women's lack of rational authority shape women's professional lives and areas of earned expertise just as they construct the expert knowledge *about* women that informs the practices I discuss in Chapter 5.

Two complex structural patterns converge to contain women within undervalued cognitive domains and to thwart their efforts to gain recognition as fully authoritative members of epistemic communities. First is the tenacious cluster of stereotypes that underpin and reinforce sociocultural representations of women as scatterbrained, illogical, highly emotional creatures, incapable of abstract intellectual thought. Because their judgments are vitiated by an unpredictable subjectivity, women's claims to knowledge and expertise are accorded minimal credence. People 'apply' stereotypes as proof that they *know* what women are like and what they can(not) do. Since stereotype-governed 'knowledge' is often supported by accredited experimental research, unmasking stereotypes for their crudeness as epistemological tools and submitting the sustaining evidence to critical examination are ongoing tasks for feminist political analysis.

Second, and interwoven with this epistemological pattern, is the curious distinction Baumgart notes between knowledge and experience. The distinction has the effect of discrediting putative claims to knowledge that fall outside the purview of a narrowly stipulated scope of the term, for which knowledge properly so-called must transcend the particularities of experience. The consequent designation of what *counts* as knowledge generates an awkward double bind for many professional women, with regard both to the 'raw materials' for the construction of knowledge and to their self-presentation as knowers. According to the stereotypes, women have access *only* to experience, hence not to the stuff of which knowledge is made. The very same stereotypes represent women as incapable of acquiring the methodological tools prerequisite for all potential knowers. These structural patterns again demonstrate the arbitrary and exclusionary nature of standard conferrals—and withholdings—of the honorific label 'knowledge' on cognitive products.

Questions about objectivity are still the central issue. Evidence that confirms the aptness of stereotypes is often derived by methods and from sources that appear to comply with acceptable standards of objective inquiry. Yet the ideal of objectivity is informed by methodological assumptions whose stringency at once disqualifies much of common, everyday, prephilosophical knowledge and obscures the subjective factors that shape 'objective' confirmations of stereotypes. A further reassessment of ideal objectivity as a guiding epistemological precept is implicated in this discussion of credibility. In the next section of this chapter, then, I extend my critique of stereotype-based 'knowledge' about women through an analysis of its effects in women's professional lives. In the third section, I elaborate some techniques for circumventing oppressive, stereotype-informed structures, through a revisioning of presuppositions about objectivity and cognitive agency. First, though, I recapitulate my reasons for conducting the inquiry in terms of credibility and cognitive authority.

People have to know what the world is like just to survive: to know how best to respond to and interact with the physical environment and with other animate, intelligent, and sensitive creatures.[2] In the process, it is as important to learn who can be trusted and how a person can know that *someone else* knows as it is for a knower herself to know certain facts and to know how to do certain things. Knowledge is an intersubjective product constructed within communal practices of acknowledgment, correction, and critique. As I have argued, near-exclusive epistemological concentration on individual, putatively autonomous knowledge claims, caused by 'direct' contact with the world, obscures the constitutive role of communal, dialogic credibility-discerning and -establishing activities. So a critical analysis of epistemic communities is as vital an epistemological project as are analyses of perception- and memory-based knowledge claims aimed at discerning conditions of their possibility and justification. Yet trustworthiness, credibility, and authoritative cognitive standing do not always correlate straightforwardly with 'high-ranking' sociopolitical status, nor is it legitimate, unequivocally, to read 'low(er)-ranking', marginal status as a mark of ignorance or lesser reliability. The nurses at the Hospital for Sick Children illustrate this point. In unmasking the rhetoric in whose terms knowledge confers authority, but experience does not, Baumgart shows how women's assumed lack of rational capacity blocks their access to authoritative status in a professional domain where *their* expertise should be acknowledged.[3]

[2] I elaborate connections with ecology in Chapter 7.

[3] In her analysis of the Grange Inquiry, Elaine Buckley Day observes: "The proceedings began by hearing testimony from doctors who presented evidence in the capacity of expert witnesses. This was the manner in which their credentials were submitted before the Inquiry, and the spirit in which they were questioned. The nurses were called as witnesses because some of them had been present when infant deaths occurred, not because they were regarded as having any expertise." Day, "A Twentieth-Century Witch Hunt: A Feminist Critique of the Grange Royal Commission into Deaths at the Hospital for Sick Children," *Studies in Political Economy* 24 (Autumn 1987): 21.

Science Looks at Women, Women Look at Science

It is tempting to interpret the greater numbers of women entering the medical profession as doctors as evidence that stereotype-informed structures are not so tenacious as my appeal to the Grange Inquiry example suggests. But historical evidence that women were never entirely welcome in medicine and recent intimations that history is on the point of repeating itself enjoin caution. It is no coincidence, just as more women are entering medical school, that suggestions are beginning to appear in the press that there are too many doctors and that the schools may have to curtail admissions. Nor is it a coincidence that, as female doctors and medical students increase their numbers, there are indications that medicine is no longer as attractive to *men* as it once was. Correlations between numbers of female doctors and the diminished prestige of the profession in the Soviet Union are well known to feminists. Parallels to these situations give cause for alarm.

In the late nineteenth century, for example, women began to be successful in their attempts to enter medical school just when doctors were worrying about the depressed state of the profession.[4] Doctors feared that growing numbers of women would exacerbate the situation, producing still more doctors than the society could support and inducing female patients to desert economically threatened male practitioners to support their newly qualified sisters. What, then, was to be done? Mary Roth Walsh observes: "One solution was to prove that a woman's nature, far from being an asset in a medical career, was an insurmountable liability. Nowhere in the profession was there a greater urgency to promote this idea than among those men who specialized in gynecology and obstetrics, the areas where women physicians posed the greatest threat." The question was debated in all seriousness as to whether "the quirls of a woman's brain have any peculiarities which necessarily unfit her from profiting from the most advanced medical instruction";[5] and the efforts of highly trained scientists, whose expertise confers authority on their work, were directed toward producing an answer. In a parallel move, nineteenth-century doctors campaigned to disqualify female lay healers and midwives by producing "'scientific' evidence that woman's essential na-

---

[4]Male doctors in the United States did not themselves receive properly 'scientific' training until the last decades of the nineteenth century. See Edward Shorter, *Bedside Manners: The Troubled History of Doctors and Patients* (New York: Simon & Schuster, 1985).
[5]Mary Roth Walsh, "The Quirls of a Woman's Brain," in Ruth Hubbard, Mary Sue Henifin, and Barbara Fried, eds., *Biological Woman: The Convenient Myth* (Cambridge, Mass.: Schenkman, 1982), pp. 245, 244.

ture was not to be a strong, competent help-giver, but to be a *patient.*"⁶ It is not surprising, then, that just at the time (between 1870 and 1910) when women of the middle classes were achieving success in their campaign for access to higher education, the professions, and political rights, a curious 'epidemic' of hysteria, anorexia nervosa, and neurasthenia was diagnosed. In response, Showalter notes, "the Darwinian 'nerve specialist' arose to dictate proper feminine behavior outside the asylum as well as in, . . . and to oppose women's efforts to change the conditions of their lives."⁷

Just as madness is both a symptom and a metaphor of women's oppression, so women's efforts to achieve authoritative status in the medical profession are both symptomatic and symbolic of the suppression of female knowledge and expertise. Medicine is a peculiarly salient example, for it enlists caring and nurturing skills long associated with woman's *essential* nature. Yet the professionalization of medicine, together with its establishment on a scientific footing, produced an exclusionary structure in which such experientially based female skills had no place. In short, when women approached medical science intending to qualify as knowledgeable, authoritative practitioners, they found that medical science itself was constructing an imposing body of knowledge to show that they could not, in fact, *be* effective practitioners. Their essential nature precluded it.⁸

Historically, women's exclusion from authoritative positions as practitioners in other scientific domains was further rationalized on grounds of propriety. Margaret Rossiter reports that such claims as "it [is] unseemly for a woman to expose her talents outside the home, especially to a male audience, or to acknowledge, let alone enjoy, any compliments or recognition she might receive," and "members of the stereotypically delicate female sex might either be embarrassed at the scientific discussion of biological facts or divert stouthearted men

⁶The process is well documented in Ehrenreich and English, *For Her Own Good;* here I quote from pp. 102–103. See Russett, *Sexual Science,* esp. chap. 7, for an illuminating historical analysis of scientific demonstrations of women's unfitness for science and medicine.

⁷Showalter, *Female Malady,* p. 18. Showalter observes: "Darwinian psychiatrists insisted that (in Maudsley's words) 'there is sex in mind as distinctly as there is in body' . . . [and that] female physiology marked women 'for very different offices in life from those of men'" (p. 122).

⁸Dr. Edward Clarke's book *Sex in Education* was instrumental in shaping these conclusions. Drawing upon Helmholz's principle of the conservation of energy, Clarke argued that energy women would expend in acquiring an education would be drawn away from the energy they required to fulfill their natural—and hence essential— reproductive functions. See Sayers's discussion of Clarke's influence, in *Biological Politics,* pp. 8–22.

from the serious pursuit of science"[9] were granted considerable credence. Alternatively, it is simply stated as obvious that female minds cannot cope with science; and that if they try to, their possessors will become unfeminine.[10] Lest these postures be dismissed as merely ridiculous and antiquated, there is ample evidence to show that, despite shifts in overt behavior, within the scientific establishment, women continue to face similar obstacles. Those who persist and succeed are the exceptions who prove the rule.[11]

In short, women's efforts to defy stereotypes throughout the scientific professions replicate the situation in medicine. In 1968, women graduate students in science at Yale were told that they were being trained to be the wives and research associates of their male fellow students.[12] It is impossible to see much improvement over the situation of women astronomers at Harvard in the 1880s and 1890s, when Edward Pickering, an alleged champion of women's rights to higher education and employment, hired innumerable patient and *grateful* women for the painstaking (but publicly invisible) task of observing and classifying stellar spectra. His practice, on a microcosmic level, confirms received conceptions of woman's proper place in professional science per se, which were still in force at Yale in the 1960s and have by no means disappeared, despite notably increased numbers of women in science, engineering, and medicine.[13]

These examples illustrate women's double-edged relationships to the 'master discourses' of hegemonic scientific knowledge. Not only

[9]Margaret Rossiter, *Women Scientists in America: Struggles and Strategies to 1940* (Baltimore: Johns Hopkins University Press, 1981), pp. 74, 76.

[10]An awareness of these misconceptions prompts Katherine Hilbery, in Virginia Woolf's novel *Night and Day* (1919), to conceal her secret passion for mathematics. Such fears trouble Ann Veronica's father in H. G. Wells's novel *Ann Veronica* (1909), prompting him to protect her from the harmful effects of going up to London to study chemistry.

[11]The persistent need to struggle against such obstacles is documented in Anne Sayre, *Rosalind Franklin and D.N.A.: A Vivid View of What It Is Like to Be a Gifted Woman in an Especially Male Profession* (New York: W. W. Norton, 1975); and in Evelyn Fox Keller, "The Anomaly of a Woman in Physics," and Naomi Weisstein, "Adventures of a Woman in Science," both in Sara Ruddick and Pamela Daniels, eds., *Working It Out: 23 Women Writers, Scientists, and Scholars Talk about Their Lives* (New York: Pantheon, 1977).

[12]Vivian Gornick, *Women in Science* (New York: Simon & Schuster, 1983), p. 78.

[13]Ruth Bleier writes, as recently as 1986, that "while, over the past 10–12 years, feminists within science and without have been dissenting from and criticizing the many damaging and self-defeating features of science (the absolutism, authoritarianism, determinist thinking, cause-effect simplifications, androcentrism, ethnocentrism, pretensions to objectivity and neutrality), the elephant has not even flicked its trunk or noticeably glanced in our direction, let alone rolled over and given up." Bleir, "Introduction," in R. Bleier, ed., *Feminist Approaches to Science* (New York: Pergamon, 1988), p. 1.

is it difficult for women to claim acknowledgment as properly authoritative knowers, there is the further problem that 'received' (scientific) knowledge itself—particularly biological knowledge—exacerbates their difficulty. An impressive accumulation of 'expert' knowledge stands as evidence that women simply cannot do science. Just as Aristotle's theories about women's inferior rational capacities were reinforced by the biological beliefs that informed them, so, for all its greater sophistication, nineteenth- and twentieth-century biology still accords credibility to the determinism that, since Aristotle's time, has designated women's place in almost every social structure and has defined the positions that educated women can occupy in the professions.

Recent research into hemispheric and lateralized brain functioning lends support to these same conclusions, as I note in Chapter 1. Its inconclusive, ambiguous results notwithstanding, that research is used to demonstrate the truth of biological determinism. Its results are read, for example, as proof of male superiority in visuospatial and analytic skills, despite the facts, as Bleier observes, that "if it is true that women use the left as well as the right hemisphere for processing visuospatial information . . . there is no reason to believe that left hemispheric analytical processing is a disadvantageous complement to right hemispheric visuospatial processing. The only reason for believing this is that, presumably, men do not do it and women do."[14]

A range of evidence, both recent and historical, that reinforces feminine stereotypes while claiming to establish natural differences that dictate separate spheres of male and (inferior) female activity, is drawn from observations of animal behavior, particularly of the higher primates. It is by no means obvious that primate and other animal behaviors unequivocally reflect the behaviors—and divisions of labor—that are natural, and/or desirable, for human animals; nor is it clear that the selection of primates for study is theory-neutral. In a now-classic article, Naomi Weisstein notes that primates studied to demonstrate the 'naturalness' of male and female behavioral differences tend to be the ones that behave just as the biological determinists assume they should. Thus, she writes,

[14]Ruth Bleier, "Science and Belief: A Polemic on Sex Differences Research," in Christie Farnham, ed., *The Impact of Feminist Research in the Academy* (Bloomington: Indiana University Press, 1987), p. 120. Judith Genova aptly cautions that the conclusions such research claims to establish, and the authoritarian scientific voice in which they are promulgated, warn us that "the danger to women's lives has never been more threatening." Genova, "Women and the Mismeasure of Thought," *Hypatia: A Journal of Feminist Philosophy* 3 (Spring 1988): 102.

baboons and rhesus monkeys are generally cited: males in these groups exhibit some of the most irritable and aggressive behavior found in primates, and if one wishes to argue that females are naturally passive and submissive, these groups provide vivid examples. . . . *The presence of counterexamples has not stopped florid and overarching theories of the natural or biological basis of male privilege from proliferating.*[15]

Confirming evidence is selected from the data so that stereotypes are reinforced, yet the possibility that the gender differences thereby confirmed might be observationally, ideologically *constructed* rather than natural is not considered. Even plausible demonstrations of continuity between human and animal behavior rarely prompt the question whether dominance behavior in *animals* might be learned rather than biologically determined. Yet Sayers suggests that dominance hierarchies among baboons often appear to develop in response to a scarcity of food, space, and cover and to excessive threats from predators.[16] This suggestion would not explain *male* dominance, since female baboons would be equally interested in food, space, and cover, but it does highlight the limitations of the data. Dominance behavior in animals could as plausibly be read to demonstrate the environmental and cultural structuring of human female and male differences as to support biological determinism. It is highly *implaus*ible that the behavioral patterns of only one biological species would be constructed out of environmental necessity.

The reasoning that legitimates conclusions about 'natural' female and male differences on the basis of observed animal behavior is blatantly circular. The vocabulary of active/passive behavioral differences, derived from the privileged classes and races of hierarchically ordered human societies, is enlisted, without modification, to describe animal behavior. Descriptions and explanations, drawn initially *from* human behavior, become the premises of arguments that claim to demonstrate the 'naturalness' of stratifications in human societies, based on *their* alleged resemblance to group behavior in animals. The fact that designations of the 'natural' in animal behavior are informed by entrenched assumptions about active male/passive female *human* behavior disappears from view. Evidence that those assumptions are borne out in nature is read straight from the data, effacing the question as to whether the data themselves could be theoretical constructs

[15]Naomi Weisstein, "Psychology Constructs the Female," in Vivian Gornick and Barbara K. Moran, eds., *Woman in Sexist Society* (New York: Doubleday, 1974), p. 219, emphasis added.
[16]Sayers, *Biological Politics*, pp. 74–75.

of the investigator—whether they seem to be 'given' only because observation starts from the assumption that these are the patterns a well-informed inquirer must look for. Ignorant of the culture-boundedness of their own 'objective' observations, then, sociobiologists (the principal articulators of such arguments), Sayers observes, "often regard [their] assumptions as constituting independent evidence for the validity of their biological explanation of human sex roles."[17]

Darwinian theory is a striking example. It marks the end neither of anthropocentrism nor of androcentrism in biology; rather, it reinforces the active male/passive female stereotypes central to the structures of Victorian patriarchy.[18] Hubbard cites the darkly amusing example of Wickler's puzzlement over the fact that, among bighorn sheep, the sexes cannot be distinguished on sight. Wickler is troubled that "between the extremes of rams over eight years old and lambs less than a year old one finds every possible transition in age, but no other differences whatever; the bodily form, the structure of the horns, and the color of the coat are the same for both sexes." Hubbard continues:

> Now note: " . . . the typical female behavior is absent from this pattern." Typical of what? Obviously not of Bighorn sheep. In fact we are told that "even the males often cannot recognize a female," indeed, "the females are only of interest to the males during rutting season." How does he know that the males do *not* recognize the females? Maybe these sheep are so weird that most of the time they relate to a female as though she were just another sheep.[19]

[17]Ibid., p. 58. Haraway cautions: "Westerners have access to monkeys and apes only under specific symbolic and social circumstances. Although systematically obscured and denied in the ideologies of culture-free, objective science, these circumstances matter to the fundamental nature of the sciences produced. . . . A scientist is one who is authorized to name what can count as nature for industrial peoples. A scientist 'names' nature in written, public documents, which are endowed with the special, institutionally enforced quality of being perceived as objective and applicable beyond the cultures of the people who wrote those documents." Haraway, "Primatology Is Politics by Other Means," in Bleier, ed., *Feminist Approaches to Science*, p. 79.

[18]Russett remarks: "Darwin confidently affirmed the inferiority of the female mind. This was not a conclusion he could have arrived at as he arrived at differences in temperament between the sexes, on the basis of analogy with the lower animals. There was no evidence that female dogs were any less intelligent than male dogs, or female lions than male lions. Hence Darwin's resort . . . to the social argument from lack of female achievement." Russett, *Sexual Science*, p. 81.

[19]Ruth Hubbard, "Have Only Men Evolved?" in Hubbard, Henifin, and Fried, eds., *Biological Woman*, pp. 31–32.

When observation is informed by the assumption that active behavior is male, passive behavior female, then it is not surprising that
an autonomous reasoner might conclude that the Victorian stereotype
is biologically determined. Even algae can be seen to exhibit this
behavior. Apparent exceptions tend to be dismissed as aberrant,
rather than read as indicators of theoretical inadequacy.[20]

Biologically reinforced stereotypes are peculiarly tenacious deter-
minants of women's positions in epistemic communities. When so
many disciplines and institutions to which women seek entry have
persistent, constantly revived histories of producing (allegedly objective) 'knowledge' that demonstrates their natural incapacity to do so,
it is a monumental project just to establish the credibility needed to
challenge the knowledge. Indeed, merely posing the challenge can be
read as further evidence of feminine irrationality. When a woman
attempts to defy scientific 'knowledge' about her nature in order to
establish credibility for herself that the stereotypes pronounce unlikely, she meets every imaginable resistance. Such resistance is palpable in the treatment of the nurses in the Grange Inquiry. There, as
Baumgart observes, women are credited only with experience,
whereas men are assumed to have knowledge. By comparison with
the latter, the former is judged worthless. Investigators who attempt
to determine whether this credibility differential is a product of
chance or a consequence of women's nature tend to come down on
the side of nature and to support their findings with evidence, expertise, and authority.

The sexual politics that upholds the double standard at work in
interpretations of these findings is interesting. One would expect that
biological determinism, once demonstrated, would explain female
and male behavior symmetrically, if in terms of different characteristics. Yet a persistent belief that women are, somehow, *more* biologically determined than men is sustained by an equally persistent conviction that women—even women of the white middle classes—are
'closer to nature' than men. Their closeness to nature, it is assumed,
renders women passive with respect to their biology to an extent that
men, in general, are not. Whereas men—white middle-class men, at
least—can transcend their biology to become the creators and per-
petuators of culture, and hence of the knowledge and power that

---

[20]Ibid., p. 27. In a more recent article, Hubbard notes that "questionable experimental results obtained with animals," especially rats, are used as though they apply
without modification or remainder to human behavior. Hubbard, "Science, Facts, and
Femininism," *Hypatia: A Journal of Feminist Philosophy* (Spring 1988): 10.

shape culture and claim cultural recognition, women are essentially, immutably, determined by theirs. De Beauvoir endorses these assumptions in the contrasts she posits between a man's capacity "to express himself freely . . . [to find] more and more varied ways to employ the forces he is master of," and a woman's biological "enslavement" to the species.[21] That endorsement has been a source of unease for many feminists about her representation of female existence in *The Second Sex*.[22]

A similar double standard constructs interpretations of sex-difference research in articulations that often obscure the inherent *symmetry* of difference while legitimating unjustified evaluative inferences. If woman's nature is indeed 'naturally' different from man's, then man's nature is, by the same token, 'naturally' different from woman's. Yet no evaluative conclusions follow. Nonetheless, the results of research into male and female 'natures' are commonly read to demonstrate that *female* nature alone is different. Hence in Bleier's remarks about left hemispheric analytical processing, which I cite earlier, the implication is that male nature is *human* nature, whereas female nature is derivative, aberrant, and therefore inferior. Asymmetrical support, then, is declared for masculine superiority and female inferiority, for the 'complementarity' thesis that designates separate male and female spheres of activity, and for the 'naturalness' of the female of the species remaining at home with the children, engaged in passive, submissive, nurturing activities. The belief that it is more appropriate for women to be nurses than doctors is a variation on these themes.

These convictions seem to ensure that women's cognitive authority will remain as limited as it has been throughout the history of modern knowledge, in which, as I note in the previous chapter, outstanding, authoritative, paradigm-creating achievements rarely bear a woman's name. Boyle's law, Lavoisier's theorem, Einsteinian physics, Darwinian and Freudian theory are well known, but there are few noteworthy theorems, laws, or theories named for a woman.[23] In view of the

[21]De Beauvoir, *The Second Sex*, p. 28. In *Money, Sex, and Power,* Hartsock observes, in such Greek texts as the *Iliad,* the *Oresteia,* and Plato's *Republic* and *Symposium,* an "insistence that female existence (but not male) is defined by the body, and [a] presentation of mythic forces as fundamental threats to the political community" (p. 187).

[22]See Catriona Mackenzie's "Simone de Beauvoir: Philosophy and/or the Female Body" for an interesting analysis of de Beauvoir's *"constructivist* account of the female body" (in Pateman and Gross, eds., *Feminist Challenges*). See also the articles in Helene Vivienne Wenzel, ed., *Simone de Beauvoir: Witness to a Century,* published as *Yale French Studies* 72 (1986).

[23]The Cauchy-Kovalevskaia theorem in mathematics is an exception, but Sophia Kovalevskaia's struggles to gain recognition show that it is difficult to count her

authoritative function of paradigms in validating cognitive projects it is no wonder that the absence of female-created paradigms might look like proof that such high-quality research is beyond women's capacities.

There are explanations for this female absence, both in entrenched convictions that women's nature renders them unfit for high-profile intellectual activity and in histories of circumscribed access to educational, research, and employment opportunities, reinforced by a consistent, stereotype-governed ideology that affirms women's natural inferiority. These structural obstacles act as major impediments for women themselves, and for the dominant, standard-setting cultural groups, in acknowledging the value of their work. Even so simple an act as claiming their achievements as theirs, not to mention aspiring to establish paradigm, is a remote possibility. Epistemic communities confer credibility according to systemically engrained structural conceptions about the kinds of people who can reasonably claim the credibility at issue. When women have rarely belonged to that group, the presumption against acknowledging their innovative achievements is hard to dislodge.[24]

Many areas of inquiry and research where women have, in fact, made pathbreaking contributions are, either by default or by design, excluded from the domain of 'normal science'. In noting this exclusion, it would be a mistake to read it as evidence that women cannot do real science after all. Such a reading would affirm the role of institutionalized 'normal' science as the arbiter and standard setter, while continuing to marginalize women's projects and practices according to worn-out, erroneous gender-attributions. Most seriously, it would affirm the proclaimed neutrality of science while obscuring its political, exclusionary practices. There is more than a little truth in Ruth Ginzberg's contention that 'gynocentric *science*', which centers on women's traditional knowledge and skills, does exist—invisibly, because it has been labeled 'art', as for example, "the *art* of midwifery, or the *art* of cooking, or the *art* of homemaking." Had these 'arts' been developed in traditionally male practices they might have been earned the labels "obstetrical *science*, food *science*, and family *social*

---

achievement as a genuine challenge to the stereotype. See Ann H. Koblitz, *A Convergence of Lives. Sofia Kovalevskaia: Scientist, Writer, Revolutionary* (Boston: Birkhauser, 1983). Perhaps Barbara McClintock's Nobel Prize in genetics makes her a genuine exception, but the story of her long obscurity does not inspire confidence that change is occurring rapidly or significantly. See Keller, *Feeling for the Organism*.

[24] I owe some of these thoughts to Bleier, "Science and Belief," p. 112.

science."[25] The late-nineteenth-century scientific revolution established some erstwhile 'arts' on a scientific basis, medicine among them.[26] Critical analyses of the power structures that determine which 'arts' pass the tests for elevation to scientific status need to be skeptical about claims to detached objectivity in assessing the exclusionary criteria those tests entail.

The power of representations of their 'nature' to determine women's positions in epistemic communities—together with the dissonance between those representations and women's demonstrations of their (various) capabilities—forces a sustained critique of claims to objectivity and theory-neutrality in gender research, however respectable its methodology. Even scientists who are generally meticulous in their work and recognized in their fields tend to suspend critical judgment to ensure that their data fit a ruling paradigm for which "significant cognitive sex differences . . . may be attributed to biological sex differences in the development, structure, and functioning of the brain,"[27] Bleier maintains. That suspension of judgment cannot be explained on an empiricist model of inquiry, for it derives from the social-political construction of science, scientists—and sexism. For Haraway, it confirms the necessity to locate epistemological analysis within "the social relations of science and technology,"[28] to reposition the evaluative project of epistemology at the center of a cluster of questions about the sociopolitical identities and self-interpretations of putative knowers. Hence justification is an interpretive, dialogic, hermeneutic project that must draw on sources far broader than the common, neopositivistic techniques of objective, neutral, monologic

[25]Ruth Ginzberg, "Uncovering Gynocentric Science," *Hypatia: A Journal of Feminist Philosophy* (Fall 1987): 91–92.

[26]Shorter dates the conferral of scientific status on medicine at 1894, with the development of the diphtheria antitoxin, and he notes that a range of 'arts', "from meteorology to metallurgy to the study of handwriting to the study of the mind," has acquired a scientific basis. Shorter, *Bedside Manners*, p. 131.

[27]Bleier, "Science and Belief," p. 113. The language of reproductive biology is persistently drawn from the mythology of active male/passive female—characteristics that biologists have attributed even to the behavior of sperm and ovum. These assumptions are detailed in Nancy Tuana, "The Weaker Seed: The Sexist Bias of Reproductive Theory," and the Biology and Gender Study Group, "The Importance of Feminist Critique for Contemporary Cell Biology," both in *Hypatia: A Journal of Feminist Philosophy* (Spring 1988).

[28]Donna Haraway, "A Manifesto for Cyborgs: Science, Technology, and Socialist Feminism in the 1980s," *Socialist Review* 15, 80 (1985): 85. Haraway intends the phrase quoted here "to indicate that we are not dealing with a technological determinism, but with a historical system depending upon structured relations among people. . . . [It] should also indicate that science and technology provide fresh sources of power, that we need fresh sources of analysis and political action."

verification and justification procedures. The interpretive project has to be multidisciplinary in a strong sense of the term: at once historical, sociological, psychological, literary, political-moral, and epistemological in its endeavor to construct interpretive analyses of cognitive 'locations' and the (Gadamerian) prejudgments that hold them in place. It is a never-ending process; yet, informed by feminist commitments, it opens up effective strategies for interrogating the pretensions of paradigmatic value-neutrality which frame the scientific inquiry of the malestream.

Now Gadamerian hermeneutics is elaborated, initially, as a method of textual interpretation, but its pertinence to the analysis of *scientific* discovery has not gone unnoticed.[29] Moreover, after Kuhn, it is neither so startling nor so damning as it once was to contend that ideological commitments and observer bias shape *scientific* discovery. Even philosophers who dispute Kuhn's conclusions have to give serious attention to his claims for the constitutive influence of social, historical, cultural, and personal factors in scientific research. The unattainability of perfect objectivity and theory-neutrality in science and in the construction of knowledge is a point of ongoing debate, in tension with reaffirmations of claims to ideal objectivity.

Issues of gender, race, and class do not figure among the factors that shape 'normal science', for Kuhn. He challenges the assumption that 'bad science' necessarily results if scientific practice is shaped by values, interests, and commitments. Yet he does not consider the possibility that the most scrupulously orthodox scientific practice, whose results would qualify as 'good science' even under rigorous scrutiny, could be systemically sexist and/or androcentric. Even a theory that is "cognitively virtuous and is produced by men and women of good will"[30] can be constructed as a product of nonscientific convictions about the desirability of characteristics, attributes, social arrangements, or explanatory modes, which are informed by embedded androcentric and/or sexist prejudgments. Hermeneutic, analytic, interpretive analyses need to be directed toward interrogating these prejudgments. Hubbard's analysis of how active male/passive female principles structure observations at a pretheoretical level is a striking contribution to this project. Elizabeth Potter's proposal that Boyle's corpuscular theory is analogously infected by pre-scientific assumptions about the lifeless passivity of the basic ele-

[29]See esp. Rorty, *Philosophy and the Mirror of Nature*, and Bernstein, *Beyond Objectivism and Relativism*.
[30]I borrow this phrase from Potter, "Modeling the Gender Politics in Science," p. 28.

ments of reality is another. These assumptions were conservative of a patriarchal social order that mirrors and is mirrored by 'the natural order'. Both orders would have been threatened by a model of inquiry derived from the assumption that matter is alive and active. Yet that threat operates at a subterranean level that only an interpretive analysis of the context of discovery can discern. Hence "even good scientific theories, by all the traditional criteria, can be androcentric or sexist in the sense that a sexist or androcentric assumption constrains the distribution of truth values throughout the system."[31] Their androcentrism/sexism has to be unearthed and demonstrated.

Stereotypes of 'woman' comprise a cluster of analogous assumptions, embedded within the ideal of objectivity to which many inquirers claim adherence. In biology, which concerns me here, these assumptions tend to predetermine the conduct of research, even at the early stages of experimental design. In developing feminist critiques of science, it is as important to avoid crude, essentialist assumptions about a reified, monolithic 'science' as it is to challenge the essentialism that informs many areas of scientific inquiry. Manifestations of androcentrism and sexism vary across scientific practices: Hubbard and Potter analyze aspects of one such manifestation; Bleier's critiques of brain lateralization research focus on another. Feminist critics of science have to conduct their analyses case by case to produce adequately nuanced critiques of the practices they study. Although stereotypes are blatantly essentialist, even they work differently in different contexts. The context stripping that characterizes autonomy-of-reason thinking renders all of these similarities and differences invisible and hence insignificant. For these reasons, hermeneutic analyses of cognitive locations have always, also, to be self-reflexive, self-critical of their own located specificity.

I have drawn attention to certain functional similarities between stereotypes and Kuhnian paradigms. Like Kuhnian paradigms, stereotypes filter out counterevidence to minimize its undermining effects, yet they draw strength from confirming instances. In stereotype-governed knowledge claims, exceptions are discounted as aberrant. Stereotypes of 'woman' filter out evidence that women are not really—and certainly not all—like that. Analogously, the 'ruling paradigm' that locates sex differences in innate, immutable brain differences obscures their social, political, material, and environmental sources. These similarities account, in part, for the tenacity of stereotypes and paradigms.

[31]Ibid., p. 31.

Analogies between stereotypes and paradigms raise a set of moral-political questions about paradigms themselves. Paradigms, especially in the physical sciences, have made claim to value-neutrality, despite Kuhn's incorporation of the role of interests and commitments in the science practiced under their aegis. But the issue is at best contentious. Any assertion that social scientific paradigms could be value-neutral would be still more contentious.[32] Statistical analyses—say, of the incidence of alcoholism in suburbia—may approximate the objectivity of a positivistic unity-of-science model. But claims to value-neutrality are harder to sustain in the face of demonstrations of the extent to which the presence of a human observer influences the behavior of observed subjects, and of the ability of subjects to second-guess experimenters to produce, or refuse to produce, expected results. The manner of these influences varies with the preconceptions both observer and observed bring to an experimental situation.[33] But even in carefully controlled observational (= nonparticipant) experiments, in which an intentionally detached experimenter's reactions are neither visible nor conscious, his or her hypotheses and expectations can direct the subject's behavior, and hence structure the experimental findings.[34] My contention is that even in observational studies of overt behaviors, which presumably have the best possible claim to objective neutrality, that claim can be substantiated only in a highly selective reading of 'results'. The relevance of these points to research into women's 'nature' and behavior is evident: an experimenter's embedded, stereotype-informed expectations are demonstrably effective in shaping the performance of female subjects, even as they purport to furnish 'proof' of female inferiority. Such practical consequences render contestable any claims to value-neutrality with regard to the conduct and/or the application of sex-difference research.[35]

[32]For Kuhn, the social sciences are in a preparadigm stage; hence he argues that his analysis is not applicable to research in those disciplines. This claim has not prevented practitioners from applying his theories to social scientific inquiry, in which analyses in terms of paradigms are often, in fact, illuminating.

[33]Gilligan's work shows how the preconceptions of Kohlberg's conceptual framework influence conclusions about female moral maturity.

[34]Weisstein cites a classic example of IQ testing in which students whose teachers had been told that they were 'promising' showed remarkable improvement in later tests. The conduct of the teachers toward those they believed to be bright worked to 'make' those students test brighter. Weisstein, "Psychology Constructs the Female," p. 215.

[35]Alcoff observes that "the positivist conception of theory-choice as essentially empirically determined or at least value-neutral has come under enough . . . attacks in recent times to make it wholly unacceptable. . . . Pierre Duhem's . . . compelling arguments that all propositions in physics are empirically underdetermined and Thomas Kuhn's . . . description of the history of science as paradigm-guided have seriously

Bleier's arguments about how the existing ideology of sex differences informs brain research, like Weisstein's claims about the influence of the same ideology in psychological experiments, render implausible any suggestion that biological or psychological paradigms could be morally-politically neutral. Potter's analysis of Boyle's corpuscular theory suggests that not even paradigms in the physical sciences can claim moral-political innocence. Evidence for the political investedness of one kind of paradigm does not legitimate global claims about paradigms per se, but it forces the question, even at the level of theory and paradigm choice: Whose knowledge—whose paradigms—are we talking about? The nontheoretical, pre- or extrascientific factors that inform paradigm choice, on Kuhn's account, have no greater claim to neutrality than the unconscious factors that maintain stereotypes in place. Yet once in place, paradigms are commonly accorded a status outside the fray, like an invisible hand that shapes the course of events without, apparently, meddling in it. Their constitutive assumptions recede from view and need to be uncovered and analyzed, just as stereotypes do. Science conducted under the aegis of a paradigm cannot be effectively self-cleansing if the paradigm itself is immune from scrutiny yet derives from ideologically informed assumptions.

The critical and self-critical exercise of ferreting out assumptions, biases, and observation-governing expectations must, perhaps paradoxically, be engaged in from a recognition that the research under scrutiny may, indeed, have been conducted in accordance with accredited methodologies and with sincere convictions about its own objectivity and impartiality. There are few flagrant villains in the piece. Indeed, if there were, the critical task would be easier, for they could simply be stopped. But the autonomy-of-reason presumption endorses a process of context stripping that obliterates the implicatedness of subjectivity in the construction of objectivity and the knowledge produced under its aegis. Consider reproductive biology. Evidence of the fallibility and contingency of models and preconceptions throughout the history of science might have led researchers in this area to be surprised at the apparent constancy of the active male/pas-

eroded many philosopher's [*sic*] of science commitment to the positivist model. The fact that the evidence for these claims comes from physics and not the social sciences makes it even less likely that social science can claim adherence to an ideal of methodological objectivity that even physics must forego. . . . Mounting evidence of value-laden theory-choice throughout the sciences seems to substantiate the view that there is no value-free methodology, or at least not one that human scientists can realistically employ *in practice*." Alcoff, "Justifying Feminist Social Science," in Nancy Tuana, ed., *Feminism and Science* (Bloomington: Indiana University Press, 1989), p. 88.

sive female model—and to contest its capacity to account for the behaviour of unsocialized cells—when upheavals in the social, macrocosmic structures from which the model derives are putting it to the test. It requires an effort to persist in affirming natural female passivity in times of active feminist resistance to traditional social orders. That resistance might be expected to count as just the sort of persistent questioning and criticism from (an)other person(s) that prompts researchers to reexamine and reassess their cherished theoretical assumptions, to be self-critical and accountable to contradictory evidence.

But the point is not to accuse Aristotle, along with those of his successors who fail to question their presuppositions, of a conscious and careless sexism, holding them accountable for what, arguably, they *could* not have recognized. It is, rather, that now that feminists are constructing sophisticated and well-documented critical interpretations of the circumstances of paradigm and stereotype production, self-critical imperatives take on an increased urgency. Feminist critique needs to occupy a place as an experimental control in scientific practice so that every experiment, assumption, and discovery is analyzed for gender bias, and questions about the constitutive effects of gender arrangements are always posed.[36] The burden of proof falls on inquirers who claim gender-neutrality to demonstrate the validity of their claims. The positions and power relations of *gendered* subjectivity have to be submitted to scrutiny, piece by piece, and differently according to the field of research, in all 'objective' inquiry. This task is always intricate, because the subjectivity of the feminist inquirer is always also implicated and must to be taken into account. Whatever else this project achieves, the double standard that deprecates women's intellectual projects with arguments about women's immersion in experience and particularity, while honoring men's endeavors because they rise above experience and particularity, can no longer be upheld.

My diagnosis of the infectious character of sexual stereotypes and ideologies in sustaining that double standard within scientific inquiry and institutional practices has, to this point, been ambiguous and even paradoxical. I have noted Kuhn's failure to count androcentrism and sexism among the subjective constituents of 'normal science', while warning against temptations to essentialize science as a reified, homogeneous, uniformly oppressive institution. I have likened ste-

[36] I owe this point about feminist critique as an experimental control to the Biology and Gender Study Group, in "Importance of Feminist Critique for Contemporary Cell Biology," p. 61.

reotypes and ideologies to an invisible hand, arguing that they operate so imperceptibly that it is not easy to identify villains or to accuse philosophers and scientists of a conscious conspiratorial sexism; yet I have declared the impossibility of casting paradigms, ideologies, and stereotypes in a morally-politically neutral role in the construction of scientific and other knowledge. Hence I am, at once, maintaining that there is no place for attributions of individual responsibility and blame and arguing that practitioners must be held accountable, that without accountability no revolution can be made. These paradoxical consequences of my analysis are produced by the paradoxical situation with which I am grappling. It is true, at once, that the language of individual, autonomous agency is ineffectual as an analytic tool, in this context, and that real, specific practitioners—not just discourses, ideologies, or forms of life—are complicit and accountable. The paradox cannot, at this stage, be dissolved: it can only be articulated as subtly as possible, to make space for negotiating strategies.

Neither the hierarchical structuring of medical and other scientific practice, nor the resultant (gender, race, class, ethnic, and other) marginalizations and oppressions can be disputed out of existence. But individual practitioners work within practices in which criteria of good professional and intellectual conduct commonly generate ignorance of a range of moral-political implications, even as they require cognizance of others. Hence Cheshire Calhoun notes that "neither holding individuals responsible for their participation in oppressive social practices nor excusing them seems an appropriate response."[37] By contrast with ordinary villains who violate accepted standards of morally-politically correct action, practitioners of 'normal science' engaged in sex-difference research are often adhering to canons of good scientific behavior. It is true that the standards would collapse if no one adhered to them, but it is not clear *whose* adherence is primarily culpable.

Now movements of social resistance and critique—such as the women's movement—create "abnormal moral contexts," Calhoun observes, in which "a subgroup of society . . . makes advances in moral knowledge faster than they can be disseminated to and assimilated by the general public. . . . Because moral knowledge is not shared, the presumption that all agents are equally capable of self-legislation breaks down." The problem, then, is how to require accountability in situations—unlike those of traffic rules or licensing laws—in which there is no normal, communal expectation that peo-

---

[37]Cheshire Calhoun, "Responsibility and Reproach," *Ethics* 99 (January 1989): 391.

ple should *know*. Neither Kuhn nor Aristotle can be held culpably ignorant of the androcentric/sexist consequences of the central tenets of their theoretical positions: causing harm, Calhoun notes, "is not the same as being responsible for harm."[38]

Crucial to mounting an effective critical strategy is the recognition that there is no finally or definitively privileged point in the social construction of practices and actions. Although there is no doubt that institutions and accepted behavioral standards shape individual thought and action, there is equally little doubt that standards and institutions are themselves social constructs. They are conserved when individual participation is excused by pleas of ignorance, and contested when new standards gain a hearing. Despite the vulnerability of working as a relatively isolated seer in abnormal contexts and the uncomfortable fact that taking up a position as a reproacher places women again in charge of the education of the oppressor, the only alternatives—acquiescence or excusing on grounds of ignorance—create no space for debate, resistance, or change. The epistemic advantage feminists gain from learning to name oppressive practices creates conflicting, painful demands, but it opens a space for productive and constructive dialogue. It is a salient feature of Kuhnian paradigms that they do, ultimately, yield to excessive strains on their problem-solving, explanatory, and action-directing capacities. There is every reason to expect that stereotypes of women, the inadequacies of which are being demonstrated on all sides, will resemble paradigms in this respect, if political efforts to unseat them are sustained.

Knowledge and Experience

The distinction between knowledge and experience which determines the credibility of the Grange Inquiry participants is puzzling. The assumption that there is a sharp break between experience and knowledge, such that accumulated experience neither counts as knowledge nor is regarded as its source, is curious, if not paradoxical, in view of the persistent esteem accorded to empiricist methodology as productive of knowledge. Empirical investigation—that is, investigation based in sensory experience—is commonly touted as the most reliable source of knowledge. It is odd, therefore, that people whose *experience* is clearly recognized would not, on its basis, qualify as accredited knowers.

[38]Ibid., pp. 396, 392.

The explanation derives, in part, from a long-standing assumption that knowledge that deserves the label will *transcend* experience. It may indeed have its beginnings there, but knowledge properly so-called must leave the particularity and seductiveness of sensory and affective experience behind to approach the ideals of objectivity, rationality, and impartiality which continue to govern epistemological theory.

The knowledge/experience differential Baumgart reports is of a piece with the dichotomies that standardly mark crucial philosophical distinctions, which I discuss in Chapter 2. The mind/body, reason/emotion, public/private dichotomies, like the knowledge/experience dichotomy, all have epistemological implications. The male/female dichotomy runs parallel to them and is likewise marked evaluatively, not just descriptively. In each dichotomy, the lefthand term designates the more highly valued quality or attribute. The referent of the righthand term is not only devalued but outrightly denigrated. It is a pivotal philosophical assumption that mind and its (ordered) activities are superior to body and its (disorderly) experiences. From Plato's insistence that knowledge is achieved only through liberation from the deceptiveness of the senses, through Descartes's conception of the soul as pure intellect, to Kant's critique of pure reason, this is a persistent theme. The alignment of reason with matters of the mind, and emotion with bodily experience, derives from these presuppositions. Emotion invariably clutters and impedes the essential project of reason: the attainment of certainty in knowledge.

The theory/practice dichotomy is informed by these same assumptions and is peculiarly salient for understanding the power-knowledge implications of the Grange Inquiry. Theoretical knowledge ranks as the highest achievement of reason. It is abstract, universal, timeless, and True. To attain this status it must transcend the particularity of practice (praxis) with its preoccupation with the contingent, the concrete, the here and now. Yet in the real world, outside the philosopher's study, many kinds of experience earn their possessors authoritative status. Few would doubt that the acknowledged knowledge of the doctors in the Grange Inquiry is *informed by* experience. Were it purely theoretical, people seeking practical care would be foolish to have faith in medical expertise. The same is true across public and professional domains, in engineering, technology, business, or politics. Appeals to an expert's authority and knowledge take for granted their basis, and record of successful application, in experience. Nonetheless, the nurses' experience is not credited as the basis of knowledge in the way that the doctors' experience is.

Even when empiricist *theories* of knowledge prevail, then, knowledgeable *practice* constructs positions of power and privilege that are by no means as impartially ordered as strict empiricism would require. Knowledge gained from practical (untheorized) experience is commonly regarded as inferior to theoretically derived or theory-confirming knowledge, and theory is elevated above practice. Differential rankings of academic and research disciplines attest to these differences: distinctions between 'pure' or 'hard' as opposed to 'applied' or 'soft' sciences, the (one-time) prestige of philosophy by contrast, say, with psychology or sociology. There is no doubt that theoretical knowledge often has to be tested in practice, but the 'pure' knower is the loftier knower.

Now professional expertise occupies a position midway between theory and practice: an expert *applies* established knowledge, but he does not (necessarily) create it. Hence the judges would have no difficulty establishing a doctor's credibility with claims that he is highly experienced, yet his experience may be in applying what he has learned theoretically, not in working with patients to generate knowledge. In fact, on the malestream medical model, doctors are textbook (= theory) trained. Their practice consists in recognizing what they 'already know' by producing a diagnosis, a prescription, a prediction—a problem solved. They work from knowledge that is imposed on experience (the patient's) rather than from knowledge that is informed by firsthand experience (theirs). In Chapter 5 I discuss the difficulty of contesting their knowledge with evidence presented from a patient's experience.

The public/private dichotomy helps to explain and reinforce these hierarchical distinctions. The assumptions that reason is alike in all men and that inquiry that follows the dictates of reason is most likely to produce truth do not alone warrant aligning reason with the 'public' side of the dichotomy. But the alignment is more readily explained in terms of the *opposition* of emotion to reason. In the individualist tradition, emotions are private matters, associated with particular, whimsical (= unruly) aspects of subjectivity.[39] Rational agents are passively subject to emotions, which should be suppressed in de-

[39]Shared, public emotions such as patriotism and loyalty pose something of a problem here, and even with 'private' love or hate it is arguable that there are public checks for reasonableness. But the generally accepted model contrasts private passion with public reason.

244 What Can She Know?

liberation and ratiocination. Only the products of these latter processes are deemed appropriate to place before the public eye, to become the bases of the policies and actions of authoritative public figures. People may *care* about the everyday affairs of practical life and about their personal associations. But these are private concerns that theoretical reason has to leave behind to attain universally valid, public knowledge.[40]

These dichotomies sustain and are sustained by the gender ideology that positions 'public' man and 'private' woman. The association of women with nature—with material, bodily seductiveness that distracts (male) minds from their highest pursuits—runs through the history of philosophy, in different guises, from Aristotle through Descartes, Rousseau, Kant and Hegel, to Sartre and even de Beauvoir. The historical, class, and racial specificities of these essentializing characterizations are smoothed out in a homogenizing process that keeps the gendered implications of the public/private alignment intact even as the boundaries and meanings of both public and private are differently drawn in varying historical, cultural, and economic circumstances. Women are represented (pejoratively) as emotional beings, whereas men, according to the received wisdom, are attracted to and excel in the life of reason. Thus is born the Man of Reason. Maleness pervades western constructions of reason as an intellectual character ideal. Conceptions of reason have, throughout a long history, been articulated through more or less conscious "exclusions of the feminine,"[41] as Lloyd demonstrates, and 'the feminine' has been constituted in terms of its exclusion. Because of their essentially emotional and more physical nature, women—at least the privileged women who are the complements and companions of the Man of Reason—are charged with the care of practical matters, leaving the theoretical realm a male preserve, often jealously guarded. Highly developed reasoning capabilities and a firm grasp of universal theoretical principles are the prerequisites for entry into the public domain. Hence women, who are more preoccupied with particularity and the practical, should naturally occupy themselves with private matters.

In the hierarchical confrontation between women and men which Baumgart describes, the men know and the women only have experi-

[40]Genevieve Lloyd observes: "From their earliest origins in Greek thought, our ideals of Reason have been associated . . . with the idea of a public space removed from the domestic domain. Reason is the prerequisite for, and point of access to, not just the public domain of political life but also a public realm of thought—a realm of universal principles and necessary orderings of ideas." Lloyd, "Reason, Gender, and Morality in the History of Philosophy," *Social Research* 50 (Autumn 1983): 490.

[41]Lloyd, *Man of Reason*, p. 109.

ence. The nurses are 'privatized' even with respect to their 'public' work; their 'experience' is evaluated differently from the universal, generalizable, publicly accessible, and experimentally testable experience that supports empirical knowledge claims. The nurses are credited only with practical experience, individually lived, inchoate, and unsystematic. Nurses are not expected to acknowledge or articulate links between what they know (often on the basis of experience) and the specific experiential situation of the moment. Paradoxically, they can construct knowledge out of praxis, yet, dislocated from the prestige of theory, it can claim minimal acknowledgment. The knowledge they dispense professionally is rarely their knowledge: consider its presentational style in such terms as 'the doctor says that this will help, that you must rest, that this will make you feel better'. A nurse cannot say; she has to defer to the doctor. Her knowledge does not empower her, because it is subject to mediation; it requires the doctor's approval of its validity. Doctors, therefore, are the rightful knowers in virtue of their access to knowledge that enables them to exercise control and claim obedience: laboratory tests, universal categories and diagnoses, theoretical warrantability, and a public, powerful, monologic voice. The dialogue of 'second person' contact with patients is a pale substitute.[42]

These facts attest to certain truths about the politics that inform the theory/practice dichotomy in ordinary appeals to knowledge: experience, within the middle-class professions, gains credibility for its possessors according to a gender-linked double standard. With women, it is *just* experience: women do not qualify as experts on its basis, and it is discounted as merely subjective. But men's experience carries a tacit assumption that it is not just experience; it is *objective* experience, informed by theory. Women's experience is thus accorded a circumscribed relevance when it is not denigrated outright, whereas men's experience counts as a trustworthy basis for the development and acknowledgment of knowledge and expertise. Variations on this pattern of relative valuation pervade the hierarchical arrangements that govern the professions, political organizations, and other forms of public participation. Faced with this pattern, it is difficult to maintain that the sex of the knower could have no epistemological significance.

---

[42]In extrapolating from the sociopolitical arrangements in the Grange Inquiry, I have presented a stark, essentialized picture of medical practice. My point is not that all doctors are objectifiers, nor all nurses disempowered. It is rather that the power/knowledge arrangements of professional medicine legitimate an uneven distribution of speaking and knowing positions that usually works to contain the knowledgeable practice of a nurse within stereotypical female roles.

As I have shown, the autonomy-of-reason credo suppresses the constitutive role of subjectivity in shaping 'objective' confirmations of stereotypes, especially of women. In the Grange Inquiry the argument might be that women's lack of rational authority legitimates the knowledge/experience-doctor/nurse parallel. Experience that is as particularized, as concrete as theirs cannot qualify as theoretically or professionally respectable. Yet the structures of power and privilege that construct the nurses as the disorderly and hence unknowledgeable Other are unmistakable. Stereotypes that tacitly inform these structures protect the protagonists from recognizing the contribution of their subjective interests in sustaining these structures and institutions and perpetuating the exclusionary ideals of reason and objectivity.

This assumed moral-political innocence is at least as ancient as the Aristotelian ranking of rational powers, in which the slave has no deliberative faculty; the woman has, but it is without authority; and the child has, but it is immature. Aristotle takes scant notice of the asymmetries in the ranking. Rational man, qua member of that natural kind, has a deliberative faculty that can claim authority; a child has no such faculty, qua child, but this lack is of no political consequence. A (male) child has the potential to develop authoritative reason in his normal growth to political maturity. De Beauvoir observes: "Childhood . . . is a natural situation whose limits are not created by other men and which is thereby not comparable to a situation of oppression. . . . To treat him as a child is not to bar him from the future but to open it to him."[43] Women are markedly different from children, slaves, and men: their capacities are given once and for all, as their nature. Whereas training produces male rational authority, and lack of training explains a slave's lack of authority, women alone are determined by their nature, come what may.

Aristotle's contention appears to be that women qua women lack deliberative authority. Yet many slaves were men, whose lack of authority could not be explained by their membership in the natural kind, 'man'. It would be explicable only because of their lack of access to the benefits that Greek citizenship affords in fostering rational development. But citizenship is an accident of birth or history, not a naturally occurring kind—an accident that separated male slaves from the social roles of rational deliberation and action. So the slave has no deliberative faculty not because he is a man (i.e., not because

---

[43]Simone de Beauvoir, *The Ethics of Ambiguity*, trans. Bernard Frechtman (New York: Citadel, 1948), p. 141.

of his nature), but because of the circumstances of his birth, upbringing, and captivity (i.e., because of nurture). Male children in the Aristotelian scheme are like the slave boy in Plato's *Meno*,[44] who can be taught a sophisticated geometrical proof in a pedagogical process that is possible precisely because of his hitherto unschooled mental powers.

It should follow from Aristotle's account of slavery and childhood that women lack rational authority *only* because they have no access to the activities in which such authority is acquired. Aristotle advances no argument to the effect that women are of a natural kind different from men, children, or slaves. Hence their differences require an explanation in terms of their place in the social order.[45] If all of the women Aristotle knew were intellectually unaccomplished—however implausible that may be—it would not be surprising for him to conclude that woman *qua* woman is intellectually inferior. One determines the nature of natural kinds from particular instances: people know whiteness from the experience of this or that particular whiteness.[46]

Now Aristotle clearly believes that development—training—is necessary for the realization of the best human potential. A young man learns what virtue is by observing the conduct of virtuous men and becomes virtuous by emulating it.[47] That a child's deliberative faculty is simply immature is consistent with a belief in the effectiveness of nurture in fostering its development. Hence consistency might have led him to find the source of women's lack of deliberative authority in their circumscribed position in the polis, their exclusion from its political life. But like subsequent biological determinists, Aristotle finds in women's political invisibility evidence for their lack of rational capacity, while he supports claims about their lack of rational capacity with evidence of their political invisibility. As in the Grange Inquiry, a privileged position in the political order informs conclusions about the nature and scope of rational authority, while claims about rational authority are used to justify positions within the political order. Hence Aristotle concludes that women are *more* biologically determined than men.

---

[44]Plato, *Meno*, trans. W. K. C. Guthrie, in *The Collected Dialogues of Plato*, ed. Edith Hamilton and Huntington Cairns (Princeton: Princeton University Press, 1961), 82b–85b.

[45]Spelman raises some related questions about the asymmetries and omissions in Aristotle's account of the social positions of men, women, and slaves. See chapter 2 of her *Inessential Woman*.

[46]See Aristotle, *The Categories*, trans. E. M. Edghill, in *Basic Works of Aristotle*, 2a34.

[47]See the *Nichomachean Ethics*.

Received conceptions of cognitive agency privilege modes of knowing that systematically suppress subjectivity in the name of objectivity. Because those conceptions are interwoven with stereotypes that affirm women's association with subjectivity *and* the essential femininity of women's stereotypical virtues and values, they suppress both subjectivity and femininity with the same stroke. In so doing, they conflate subjectivity with subjectivism, and femininity with both.

Such a conflation is peculiarly apparent in the construction of the stereotypically 'proper' virtues of a nurse. The maintenance of authoritarian expertise is associated with practices of keeping a judicious distance from the people who are subject to expert authority. By contrast, the responsive practices that derive from compassion, or from the sympathy that is continuous with friendship, assume second-person connections between people. The standard division of medical labor allows a doctor to treat 'a gall-bladder' or a 'coronary' with professional effectiveness, yet without reference to the *person* whose gallbladder or heart it is. That division of labor makes compassion the preserve of the nurse—compassion responsive to a particular person which, at its best, flouts the rules of authoritarian behavior, together with the maintenance of distance they enjoin. Yet compassion and the expertise *it* requires are accorded no more epistemic value than other aspects of a nurse's professional expertise. Compassion is relegated to the space 'down among the women' which nurses are expected to occupy. Because it is held to be a natural female trait, its effectiveness as a professional skill gains minimal esteem. And because it defies the rules of authority whose observance demands distance between people, Kathleen Jones observes, the dominant discourse constructs compassion as "nonauthoritative, marginal pleadings for mercy— gestures of the subordinate."[48] Professionals who would claim authority must eschew compassion and its analogues.

In the language of the Grange Inquiry, the nurses' experiences count merely as 'gestures of the subordinate'. The medical hierarchy reserves for them the role of responsive, compassionate beings, relegated to particularity and hence denied the authority that their expertise might prompt them to claim. Their efforts to achieve authoritative status are routinely read as disorderly and presumptuous, dismissed as out of order. Feminist critiques of the suppression of subjectivity

---

[48]See Kathleen B. Jones, "On Authority," in Irene Diamond and Lee Quinby, eds., *Feminism and Foucault: Reflections on Resistance* (Boston: Northeastern University Press, 1988), p. 121.

demand a reevaluation of objectivism and the constructions of cognitive agency it presupposes. This has been a central theme of this book so far. It has focused—in Hubbard's words—on why "certain ways of systematically interacting with nature and of using the knowledge so gained are acknowledged as science whereas others are not."[49] Late-twentieth-century capitalist societies downgrade manual labor just as they downgrade knowledge produced in noninstitutional settings—such as the household—however systematic, empirically warranted, and practically effective it may be. That they likewise downgrade knowledge produced in the lower, hands-on ranks of professions and institutions is clear from the proceedings of the Grange Inquiry.

The mask of neutrality behind which this downgrading takes place conceals connections between social distributions of power and privilege, and the conferral of knowledge status on an agent's cognitive products. Yet feminist *and* Foucauldian analyses reveal that facts found and/or constructed by people in positions of power have a greater presumption of validity than knowledge claims advanced by occupants of 'underclass' positions. Power is distributed in societies as much according to gender as in accordance with class, race, and other lines of difference. Commonly, in nontotalitarian regimes of truth, knowledge constructed from positions of power would not pass tests of validity if it were not constrained by 'reality', hence if it were not objective in some sense. But many well-established *facts* produced in creditable practices and processes of discovery do not earn the label 'knowledge' by simple empirical methods. The 'facts' about the alleviation of suffering which constitute the nurses' 'experience' are just one example. The alleged neutrality of judgments that confer epistemic warrant sounds increasingly like a confirmation of the *subjectivity*—that is, the values and practices—of the possessors of professional power, who are usually white, middle class, and male.

Now one avowed aim of feminist inquiry is the valorization of subjective experience, so it might seem that I am criticizing the apparent hegemony of *masculine* subjectivity only because it is masculine, not feminine. The problem is subtler than that, however. In its self-presentation, institutionalized objectivism disavows its subjective dimension: it is as ignorant of the forces that shape its constitutive assumptions as Aristotle was of the forces that shaped his conceptions of female rationality. Passive assertions—"It is observed that . . .", "It is concluded that . . ."—imply that the observation was not made by anyone in particular. It occurred out there in the

---

[49]Hubbard, "Science, Facts, and Feminism," p. 14.

world where no one need take responsibility for it. Making the data active, the knower passive ("the data suggest that . . .") presents cognitive agents as neutral receivers of truth. If the makers of hegemonic knowledge—both scientific and otherwise—were self-scrutinizing, presenting themselves as fact makers rather than fact finders—acknowledging that "every fact has a factor"[50]—then inquirers would be obliged to evaluate the locatedness of every discovery and to acknowledge the contingency of the privilege that positions certain 'knowers' as *fact makers*. The result might not be a radically different science or epistemology, but it would be a reconstructed politics of knowledge, free of some of the double standards that sustain hierarchy and oppression. If *his* knowledge is demonstrably shaped by his subjective position and masculine socialization, then it loses its prima facie claim to superiority over *hers*.

Implications

It is instructive to examine the implications, for a cognitive agent, of a systematic denigration of her experience, whereby the expertise it might be expected to produce is denied the status of knowledge. Established credibility determines a person's status in an epistemic community; status (authority) within the community determines public recognition of her contributions to knowledge; and capacities to contribute knowledgeably remain invisible when her achievements are structurally blocked from acknowledgment. Where presumptions against female credibility prevail, feminists are still learning to see how social expectations structure realizations of viable cognitive agency. Women can rarely *be* accredited members of an epistemic community; their knowledge rarely counts as part of a community's store of knowledge. In the final analysis, as I observe in Chapter 5, knowledge depends upon acknowledgment. Among the most immobilizing manifestations of epistemic oppression is the systematic withholding of such acknowledgment. On the strength of stereotype-informed readings of her biology, a woman's perceptions, feelings, subjective certainties, and professional experience are discounted, silenced, or denigrated.

It may be logically possible for every human mind, female or male, to know exactly the same things in exactly the same ways. Standard

[50]Ibid., p. 5. Many of the points I make in this paragraph are indebted to Hubbard's insights.

epistemology is written from the assumption that there is just such a standard mind capable, in principle, of attaining knowledge defined as the ideal product of closely specified reasoning processes. But appeals to logical possibilities are of little relevance when practical-political possibilities so clearly structure the situations under analysis.[51]

The problem for feminist epistemologists, then, in Haraway's words, is to discover how to have "*simultaneously* an account of radical historical contingency for all knowledge claims and knowing subjects, a critical practice for recognizing our own 'semiotic technologies' for making meanings, *and* a no-nonsense commitment to faithful accounts of a 'real' world."[52]

Maintaining that critical analyses of the construction of subjectivity and cognitive agency are central to any 'successor epistemology' project, I have been advocating a thorough re-examination of the position—or absence—of female subjectivity and agency in mainstream epistemological theories and the practices they inform. Mainstream epistemology denies validity and epistemological significance to women's experiences, leaving to feminists the task of reclaiming those experiences. Epistemologies that cannot account for women's experiences, that silence women in the name of authoritarian expertise, and/or that denigrate their experiential knowledge have to be displaced. Hence I have argued for a mitigated relativism, constrained by objectivity and a commitment to realism, but capable of taking subjectivity, accountability, and a range of perspectives seriously into account by refusing the tyranny of ideal objectivity, universality, and gender-neutrality. The primary theme running through these variations is that malestream epistemology has been instrumental in creating and maintaining women's oppression.

One recent study appears at first sight to offer a solution that takes specific locatedness into account in an analysis of women's successes in establishing effective cognitive agency. The work is *Women's Ways of Knowing*.[53] Because of the explicitly epistemological claims the authors make for the study, it is worth examining the text in some detail to

[51]The separation of theory from practice is a principal source of feminist disenchantment with traditional epistemology. Lloyd observes, "In the perception of many contemporary women, Philosophy is identified with theoretical thought in its most aberrant form—distanced from concern with human goods, distanced from the realities of life." Lloyd, "History of Philosophy and the Critique of Reason," p. 22.

[52]Haraway, "Situated Knowledges," p. 579.

[53]Mary Field Belenky, Blythe McVicker Clinchy, Nancy Rule Goldberger, and Jill Mattuck Tarule, *Women's Ways of Knowing: The Development of Self, Voice, and Mind* (New York: Basic, 1986).

evaluate the possibilities it creates for developing a 'successor epistemology'.[54] Feminists have received this work enthusiastically. It
speaks at a fundamental, experiential level to the structural drowning
of women's voices in the established authoritative spaces of late
capitalist societies and to the muted discourse that is often a woman's
only option in a traditional nuclear family. The authors' interviewing
techniques are plainly empowering in their (quasi-therapeutic) commitment to an unconditional acceptance of the weltanschauung of
each woman they interview.[55] Only when women can assimilate the
possibility of such an acceptance can they begin to recover from the
damage consequent on patriarchal oppression. The book shows its
readers how these possibilities can become real options, within the
grasp of women 'like themselves'.

Drawing on autobiographical stories, *Women's Ways of Knowing* analyzes the discursive shifts that enable women to find their epistemic
voices and learn to speak with authority. They work to establish relationships with authorities and experts, in which they can trust their
perceptions and speak for themselves even when their experiences
conflict with received, 'expert' knowledge. They become circumspect
in their respect for abstract canons of rationality and objectivity, and
resistant to impersonal, detached methods and practices. Taking examples from personal and interpersonal situations, the authors present listening, hearing, and speaking as primary routes to knowledge.
Hence they accord primacy to 'second person' interactions and to
senses other than sight. They note: "Unlike the eye, the ear requires
closeness between subject and object. Unlike seeing, speaking and
listening suggest dialogue and interaction."[56] These features make it
tempting to see in *Women's Ways of Knowing* the basis for a feminist
reconstruction of epistemology.

I shall argue that this temptation has to be resisted. In the conceptions of knowledge and of subjectivity it presupposes, *Women's Ways*

[54]The authors trace a pattern of progressive liberation from the oppressive effects of
silencing through to a declared recognition that "*all knowledge is constructed, and the
knower is an intimate part of the known*" (p. 137). En route from silence to this constructivist position, the women interviewed pass through three stages: 'received knowledge',
where they believe that truth comes from experts; 'subjective knowledge', where they
learn to trust their inner sense, to believe that the truth is "personal, private and
subjectively known" (p. 54); and 'procedural knowledge', which attends to the voice of
reason. The last-named is more objective than subjective knowledge because it adheres
to a methodological orthodoxy, yet it does not accord reason absolute respect. In the
final stage, 'constructed knowledge', knowledge acquired from personal experiences is
integrated with a newfound capacity to evaluate and discriminate.
[55]I am grateful to Diana Relke for this interpretation of the interviewing techniques.
[56]Belenky et al., *Women's Ways of Knowing*, p. 18.

of Knowing is epistemologically and politically more problematic than promising. Hence—perhaps paradoxically—it forces a recognition of the *political* importance of a residual commitment to certain—also problematic—tenets of mainstream epistemology. It reaffirms the need for a "doctrine and practice of *objectivity*,"[57] albeit one that accords pride of place to contestation, conversation, and fully acknowledged positionality. It calls for a reconstructed *realism*, engaged in dialogue with the 'objects' of knowledge, granting them the status of agent/actor, while acknowledging their recalcitrance to random, unrealistic structuring.

There can be no doubt about the stark poverty of 'S knows that p' epistemology, where 'S' is merely the vehicle that carries the project through. 'Knowing that' captures but a small part of what people know. I have argued that the inadequacies of the rubric are peculiarly evident in knowledge of other people. With its all-or-nothing connotation, it cannot accommodate knowledge that is incomplete, and it is inadequate for analyses of understanding. 'S knows that p' epistemology is a severely limited resource for feminists who expect epistemology to contribute to an emancipatory understanding of how real, historically and culturally situated knowers learn to cope in the 'real' world.

Ironically, *Women's Ways of Knowing* exhibits the reverse of these problems. As opposed to the near-exclusive concentration on 'knowing that p' of the mainstream, the authors concentrate so narrowly on S, upon the knowers, that it is not easy to determine *what* their subjects know. Questions about the truth and falsity and the justification of their knowledge claims rarely arise. What matters is the *manner* of S's knowing. Yet in the opening pages the authors approvingly cite William Perry's claim that cognitive maturity is marked by a complete comprehension that 'truth is relative'.[58] In consequence, the possibility is left open of maintaining that 'S knows that p, but p is false'. It is more than mere nostalgia for the safety of abstract malestream epistemology that prompts unease at such a consequence.

The possibility is most visible in the authors' discussion of 'subjective knowing', its frequent conflation with 'subjectivism', and the

---

[57]Haraway, "Situated Knowledges," p. 585, my emphasis.

[58]The authors observe: "It is only with the shift into full *relativism* that [Perry's] student completely comprehends that truth is relative, that the meaning of an event depends on the context in which that event occurs and on the framework that the knower uses to understand [it], and that relativism pervades all aspects of life . . . . *Only then is the student able to understand that knowledge is constructed, not given; contextual not absolute; mutable not fixed.*" Belenky et al., *Women's Ways of Knowing*, p. 10; first emphasis original, second emphasis mine.

authors' apparent conviction that subjectivism is not just a stage to be superseded, but a permanent epistemological possibility. Subjective knowers work from a "conception of truth as personal, private, and subjectively known or intuited." They move from silence, from the passivity of 'received' knowledge, to affirm an autonomy and independence that manifests a growing disdain for the public truth of remote and inaccessible experts, and a conviction that "the right-wrong criterion is irrelevant." The women's affirmation of their right to their own opinions is marked as a shift in the location of expertise, from outer to inner, and an alienation "from things scientific."[59]

Now this alienation marks a departure from silence and received knowing; yet it is neither epistemologically viable nor politically empowering tout court. Nor is it unequivocally an advance. 'Received' knowledge could be wisely received, and silence is sometimes powerful. Women frequently need to *know* that S is p in order to resist oppression or just to survive. A gut conviction is not good enough if what they 'know' is false, and a subjective knower's 'gut' often lets her down, prompting her to adopt a "cafeteria approach to knowledge," an approach scarcely conducive to empowerment.[60]

Even the women—primarily middle-class, affluent, and white—who advance to 'procedural knowledge' are epistemologically problematic. The authors characterize understanding as 'connected' procedural knowing that "precludes evaluation," equating evaluation with quantification and eschewing both together; they claim that "each of us construes the world differently."[61] But the question is not addressed as to whether any way of construing it is right or wrong, better or worse—or how one would decide.

'Separate knowers' reject subjectivism, yet the rejection is less apparent in their relation to the 'real' world than in their attitudes to other knowers. Hence even for procedural knowers, considerations of truth and falsity often give way to an emphasis on successful challenges to someone else's claims to know, on a successful defense against authorities.[62] Even procedural knowers argue that no one's experience can be called 'wrong'. It is not easy to see where *knowing* comes in, when even an appeal to objectivity amounts to standing back so other people can do "whatever feels right to them."[63] Al-

[59]Ibid., pp. 54–75.
[60]Ibid., p. 70.
[61]Ibid., pp. 101, 97.
[62]See ibid., pp. 106–107.
[63]Ibid., p. 120.

though I have, throughout this book, been critical of malestream, ideal objectivity, *Women's Ways of Knowing* provides a salutory corrective to this critique, with its demonstration of the slide into *unknowing* that subjectivism and unmitigated relativism prompts.

The irony is that these problems derive from features of the study that accord well with the feminist critique of epistemology I have been developing. Politically, women need to be less acquiescent to the dictates of expertise, more in control of their lives. To this end, they need to be knowledgeable and appropriately skeptical in the face of authoritarian, dislocated expertise. They need to know that experts can be wrong, and subjective knowers seem to have just these capacities. Yet the authors' conflation of subjectivity with subjectivism is no small matter. The point seems to be that where subjective knowledge clashes with 'expert' knowledge, the former will win without contest.

Now I have maintained throughout this book that knowledge is at once subjective and objective: subjective because it is marked, as product, by the processes of its construction by specifically located subjects; objective in that the constructive process is constrained by a reality that is recalcitrant to inattentive or whimsical structurings. Subjectivity requires theoretical analysis if epistemologists would maintain contact with the experiences of the subjects whose knowing they intend to explain. Yet if subjectivity is equated with a *subjectivism* unconstrained by a regulative realism, then the slide into radical, 'anything goes' relativism, into the conflation of fiction and fact, is inescapable. The dichotomous construal of knowledge as 'constructed not given . . . mutable not fixed' leaves the authors no space to argue that the construction might be *of* a given, the mutability *in* a stable, reality. Hence their claim that the truth is 'personal and private and subjectively known' undercuts the epistemological potential of the study.[64]

The subjectivists' expressed aim to learn through "direct sensory experience or personal involvement with objects of study"[65] also accords well with feminist wariness about the mystification of expertise. Yet it substitutes a naive realism and an innocent empiricism, both

---

[64]The authors do sometimes characterize subjectivists as anti-rationalist, thus withholding full approval (p. 72). But they present the alternatives as though 'rationalism' and 'antirationalism' (both undefined) are indifferently up for grabs. The possibility that the 'facts of the matter' might be more readily accessible in one of these modes— indeed, that the 'rationalist' (= scientific) mode has some successes to its credit—is not addressed.

[65]Ibid., p. 70.

unaware of the social location of knowledge seeking within a body of public knowledge that it would be simply foolish to retest personally.[66]

Moreover, in its commendable project of creating an approach to knowledge based in women's experiences, *Women's Ways of Knowing* risks making of experience a tyranny equivalent to the tyranny of the universal, theoretical, and impersonal expertise it seeks to displace. Where the mainstream cannot account for experiences that are not reducible to theoretical formulations, *Women's Ways of Knowing* makes experiences critically unassailable. From its beginnings in consciousness raising to its present-day scrutiny of knowledge and epistemology, however, feminism in its many articulations can attribute its greatest successes to critical engagement among feminists and with the sociopolitical and cultural world. The subjectivism that pervades this book obscures the need for critical interpretation and reinterpretation, both of women's experiences and of the 'real' world. In that respect its implications for women's empowerment are equivocal.

Paying little heed to feminist critiques of abstract individualism and the humanistic 'unified self', the authors of *Women's Ways of Knowing* take for granted that their subjects' autobiographical evidence can be read 'straight', unequivocally, without subtexts, hidden agendas, or gaps in the narrative line. The women's stories are detached from the psychological, sociological, material, and political structures that are constitutive of selfhood and subjectivity. The authors do not doubt that these woman are recounting authentic experiences that they *know* with all the certainty of an empiricist's privileged access. Hence they sustain the fiction of an unencumbered, self-making subject learning to speak authentically in her own voice—*and* to speak 'as a woman'— a member of a homogeneous category. These literal readings, from the surface, attest to a conviction that women's voices, their accounts of their experiences, need to be taken seriously and at face value. The history of experts' telling women what they really are experiencing is too long and too painful to be perpetuated. But an acritical acceptance is not the only—or the best—alternative. An equal and unconditional acceptance of all weltanschauungen does not translate well into critical political analysis.

---

[66]In his "How Do You Know?" (*American Philosophical Quarterly* 11, 2 [1974]: 113–122), Ernest Sosa counts a familiarity with state-of-the-art knowledge among conditions for being in a position to know.

In short, an unquestioned endorsement of what Bella Brodzki and Celeste Schenck call "the Western ideal of an essential and inviolable self, which, like its fictional equivalent, character, unifies and propels the narrative,"[67] informs *Women's Ways of Knowing*. Whereas the realization of that ideal has been promoted as the most natural—and best—outcome of the personal development of privileged white men, it has been less accessible to women, whom it has commonly constituted as 'Other'. Many feminists have argued that the hegemonic posturings of these privileged, unified selves have been a primary source of female and other 'underclass' oppressions in late capitalist societies. Yet *Women's Ways of Knowing* charts and applauds women's progress toward the production of just such a stable, unified self, whose "unique and authentic voice" will articulate its perspective confidently, to claim a place among malestream knowers. Neither the supremacy of such positions nor the possibility of bringing "the whole self into view"[68] is disputed.

The 'selves' that these women aim to realize are not easy to distinguish from the "male representative self"[69] of canonical autobiographies, and a presumption of individualism informs the discussions of connectedness.[70] Even the high tolerance of ambiguity that many of these women exhibit is described as a move toward unification.[71] The principal difference is that these women, including the constructivists, value a connectedness that is rarely part of masculine self-made subjectivity. Yet the claims made on behalf of reason and objective thought, in the characterization of constructivism, are the standard, mainstream ones, as is the individualized authority they confer.[72] Because it leaves the ideals and power structures of mainstream epistemology in place and unchallenged, *Women's Ways of Knowing* lacks political bite. Its principal contention is that women can learn—can be helped—to move *within* those structures to claim a more powerful, less marginalized, place. Yet their progress is charted within the limits of the system's terms, leaving the hierarchy of sexual, racial, ethnic, and economic differences intact in the politics of knowledge. The women who achieve the final, constructivist stage are, primarily, middle-class white students at an elite college, who have every (stra-

---

[67]Brodzki and Schenck, eds., *Life/Lines*; p. 5.
[68]Belenky et al., *Women's Ways of Knowing*, pp. 137, 32.
[69]Brodzki and Schenck, *Life/Lines*, p. 4.
[70]Belenky et al., *Women's Ways of Knowing*, p. 119.
[71]Ibid., p. 137.
[72]See ibid., pp. 134–135.

tegic) reason to emulate the masculine model. The achievement of this stage sounds like the discovery of a place for some women in a privileged segment of the male world.

Feminists do not have to demonstrate their political correctness by endorsing postmodern conceptions of subjectivity as multiple, conflicted, and contested, shaped by unconscious and partially conscious desires, encoded in language, and constituted by a complex of shifting sociopolitical, class, race, and gender relations—of subjectivity constantly positioning and repositioning itself in its meaning-creative activities. But it is not easy, in this post-Freudian and post-Marxist era, to justify assuming that a self-realization free from historical-material structurings is a real possibility. Autobiographical evidence needs to be read interpretively, read for the gaps as much as for the explicit presentation. An interpreter is implicated in the process and has to be accountable for her implication. Hence critical dialogue and self-criticism are integral to interpretation and critique and need to be visible in its explication.

Conceptions of selves as atomistic creatures whose experiences are unmediated by structural influences, as neutral inquirers in pursuit of the Truth, have legitimated epistemologies that wear the mask of political and perspectival neutrality, while perpetuating the Enlightenment illusion that it is possible to produce a single, authoritative representation of the objective nature of the 'real' world. Transparent, 'natural' selves claim to speak the truths that comprise that single account and to speak them 'from nowhere', in voices cleansed of ambiguity. In practice, however, such 'totalizing' and reductive discourses obliterate the facts of diversity; they marginalize people whose experiences do not conform, and smooth over the specificities that must be visible in any "faithful account of the real world."[73]

The authors of *Women's Ways of Knowing* are aware of the neutralizing and marginalizing effects of the Enlightenment legacy, but their representation of subjectivity impedes their endeavors to undo those effects. They assume that the women they study can indeed achieve an immediate apprehension, an unmediated grasp, of their situations and circumstances; can develop a sense of self that will enable them to be more assertive in encounters with 'authorities'. The experiences they report in this increasingly affirmative voice are theirs: without distortion and with the authoritative support of their unchallengeable direct access.[74] Their reports are the counterpart of the revelations

[73]See the Haraway quotation, p. 251, above.
[74]Mary Hawkesworth aptly suggests: "Operating at a level of assertion that admits of no further elaboration or explication, those who abandon themselves to intuition

claimed as the sensory deliverances of Universal Man, as he walks unencumbered through the pages of mainstream epistemology texts. Yet the strategic advantage remains on his side, for many of *his* utterances are falsifiable, in that they accord authority to how things are in the 'real' world. By contrast, these women's knowledge claims are incontestable. No space is left for the critical practice that could ravel the "semiotic technologies" through which meanings are made and remade, for no sense of the radical historical contingency of subjectivity and epistemic positions is conveyed.

It is not quite true that these autobiographies are utterly dislocated, for they are specifically presented as *women's* ways of knowing. Hence the women's location within the category *woman* shapes the analysis. Again, this location is at once promising and problematic. Where mainstream epistemology, in its putative gender-neutrality, homogenizes 'human' experience within analyses of the experiences of Universal Man, *Women's Ways of Knowing* explicitly aims to discover, in Mary Hawkesworth's words, "women's assumptions about the nature of truth, knowledge, and authority."[75] The promise inherent in these aims is problematic because of the authors' conviction that these 'ways of knowing' are essentially women's. Just as the representative male self speaks for all men, in virtue of a belief "that by discovering the meaning of his own life, he could offer a model of order to the world,"[76] so this project, in its attempt to produce a unified account, reclaims the mainstream's power to obliterate diversity.

I have described as a central tension in present-day feminist thought the problem of how to take women's differences and specificities adequately into account while retaining and extending the power to speak with political cohesiveness *about* and *for* women.[77] In *Women's Ways of Knowing* there is scant recognition of this tension. By their own account, the authors draw on a diverse sample from "different ethnic backgrounds and a broad range of social classes." Yet their endeavors to elicit a 'common voice' homogenize the sample and

conceive and give birth to dreams, not to truth." Hawkesworth, "Knowers, Knowing, Known: Feminist Theory and Claims of Truth," *Signs: Journal of Women in Culture and Society*, 14 (Spring 1989): 545.

[75]Ibid., p. 14.

[76]Brodzki and Schenck, *Life/Lines*, p. 4.

[77]Seyla Benhabib and Drucilla Cornell pose "the dilemma of feminine/feminist identity" as follows: "How can feminist theory base itself upon the uniqueness of the female experience without reifying thereby one single definition of femaleness as the paradigmatic one—without succumbing, that is, to an essentialist discourse on gender?" Benhabib and Cornell, "Introduction: Beyond the Politics of Gender," in Benhabib and Cornell, eds., *Feminism as Critique*, p. 13.

smooth over differences. Hence their claim that they studied and learned from "the ordinary voice"[78] reduces diversity to a harmonized, composite 'voice' in which specificities are effaced.

Apart from their source in the experiential reports of female subjects, it is unclear how these 'ways of knowing' count as 'women's ways'. The research legitimates the unsurprising conclusion that the women interviewed had a wide range of cognitive experiences. It does not legitimate the conclusion that these are *women's* 'ways'. Yet the authors' assertion that they listened to "the woman's voice"[79] points to the conclusion that women have these experiences *because* they are women. They do not ask whether such 'ways of knowing' are the products of women's oppressed social positions, nor do they consider whether a celebration of these 'ways' would be empowering and politically liberating. They cite no comparative studies to show whether (some) men manifest these same cognitive styles and attitudes; nor do they address the political question as to whether privileged men's occupation of positions of strength correlates with masculine 'ways of knowing'. The presentation in terms of ordered emancipatory stages, from silencing to constructed knowledge—of necessary stages en route to achieving an audible female voice—reinforces the essentialist tone. The fact that it is primarily affluent white women who pass beyond the early stages is granted minimal critical significance, nor is the developmental process contextualized to analyze its constitution within power structures and by forces other than the maturation potential inherent in a 'given' human nature.

Essentialist assumptions about 'women' are mirrored, in *Women's Ways of Knowing*, in essentialist assumptions about knowledge, expertise, and authority. Scientific knowledge and the experts who create and deploy it are represented as remote, authoritarian, on the alert to disable women and discredit their claims to know. There is no doubt that the power of science in western societies is commonly manifested thus: I make just this point in Chapter 5. But 'science'—whose reification is as infelicitous as the reification of 'woman'—has also produced many of the freedoms and advantages now available to women, albeit unequally. Labor-saving devices, reasonably safe birth control, quite good medical care, efficient and effective provision of an un-dreamed of variety of foodstuffs and consumer goods: all of these are creations of 'science'. Many women have demonstrated their abilities to make good use of these 'advantages'.

These material gains have their negative side: they are misused

---

[78]Belenky et al., *Women's Ways of Knowing*, pp. 13–14, 20.
[79]Ibid., p. 7.

and abused, often to the disadvantage of women and of underclass minorities. The same is true of the academic and political power structures that can render women mute but can also provide them with a place to learn—and to interrogate the structures themselves. The representation of women as victims, existing in an adversarial relationship with expertise and authority, has a greater capacity to act as a self-fulfilling prophecy than to empower women. Why, for example, would separate knowers "use [their] new skills to defend themselves against the authorities in their lives"[80] rather than to find solutions to their problems? It is as important to acknowledge the places where women's contributions and interventions have been effective as it is to demonstrate the oppressive powers of monolithic disciplines and bodies of knowledge. Otherwise there will be no doubt that women are natural victims after all.

Reviewing *Women's Ways of Knowing*, Monica Holland aptly observes that "discussion of epistemic justification risks deteriorating into an empty exercise if it is not grounded in the broader discussion of the nature of knowledge and the nature of *knowers*."[81] *Women's Ways of Knowing* might escape such deterioration if its conclusions were presented as cognitive styles and strategies, rather than 'ways of knowing'. Thus recast, silencing might still block strategic intervention. But it would be apparent that in some contexts an agent acts most effectively and responsibly as a 'received knower', others where she is best placed to know connectedly or procedurally. The appropriateness of these positionings would be determined by a critical examination of the 'real' world and her relation to it: different 'ways of knowing' would belong to different domains of inquiry, because of a knower's sociopolitical-experiential location. Her position would be determined as much by the politics of knowledge, as by her knowledge and experiences, as by the nature of the subject matter. Her approaches—and successes and failures—would be mapped accordingly. So an accomplished procedural knower could be silenced by the structures (both personal and substantive) of one research environment yet enabled by the structures of another. A constructivist who is empowered by a laboratory setting might be incapacitated in the kitchen; a scientist whose professional practice benefits from her skills as a subjective knower might be inept, and therefore more in need of expert advice, in personal relations. It is more plausible to expect these 'ways' to be operative variously throughout a cognitive history

[80]Ibid., p. 107.

[81]Monica Holland, review of *Women's Ways of Knowing: The Development of Self, Voice, and Mind*, ed. Belenky et al., in *Hypatia: A Journal of Feminist Philosophy* (Summer 1988): 179.

than to see them as a path toward increasingly valued, monolithic positions.

Reading these 'ways' as epistemological positions would make possible analyses of different positions either as loci for the active construction of meaning or as habits, practices, and discourses amenable to social critique. Such a reconstruction could make of the styles manifested in different positions a dynamic network of possibilities and constraints that can be enlisted for the political purposes of identifying appropriate places for supportive intervention in women's lives and for the validation of devalued strategies and techniques as marks of cognitive strength.

Once the contention is taken seriously that middle-class white masculinity is the hegemonic force in shaping dominant forms of knowledge, it becomes clear that women must reevaluate their position within and in relation to that knowledge. The claim that ideal objectivity is a masculine construct is not an accusation that philosophers, scientists, and 'experts' intentionally adopt a masculinist position from which they can distort theories, experiments, and results to sustain a male bias. Nor is it that, just because men have been the philosophers, scientists, and authoritative knowers, prevalent methodologies and criteria of truth and rationality are essentially 'masculine'. That scientists design and carry out research projects 'objectively' is not in dispute. What is at issue is more subtle. It is that, in the privileged classes of western societies, the construction of adult subjectivity takes place within a culturally transmitted and subsequently internalized 'sex/gender system'. Masculine agency tends to be shaped by this social construction, so that the orientation toward maximum autonomy and objectivity, and the adherence to universal principles of Gilligan's male subjects, mirrors the esteem accorded to objectivity, abstraction, generality, and theory-neutrality in malestream epistemology and scientific methodology. But the feminist solution is not to celebrate 'women's ways of knowing', pasting them on to received conceptions of good scientific practice to produce an androgynous amalgam. Such a solution would endorse an essentialism that is at best conservative and at worst obstructive of feminist efforts to break the binary opposition of masculine and feminine. It would be both simplistic and question-begging to argue that women qua gendered beings speak in a 'different' epistemic voice. Yet women as political beings, aware of the articulation of the politics of knowledge with the politics of gender, can transform 'the epistemological project'.[82]

---

[82]I owe this point to Hubbard, who suggests that although women as gendered beings may not have anything new or different to contribute to science, women as political beings do. Hubbard, "Science, Facts, and Feminism," p. 14.

To this end, the divisiveness at the core of traditional epistemology, produced by bipolar, dichotomous oppositions, has to be subjected to critical appraisal, not in order to create a new homogeneity, but to construct emancipatory theories of *difference*. Critiques of difference cannot be confined to sexual differences, whose emphasis on the differences of Woman *from* Man makes it difficult to articulate differences among women—or, as de Lauretis puts it, "the differences *within women*."[83] The point is, rather, to engage critically in pluralist analyses of differences, at once committed to revealing their interconnections and to refusing the quietism of liberal tolerance.[84]

Feminists need to develop politically informed, case-by-case distinctions between what scientific (and other) knowledge enables people to *understand* and what it enables 'man' to *do*. It is not enough for women simply to enter medicine, science, and other masculine preserves governed by gender stereotypes. The admission of a few women to carefully controlled places, so that they can serve as 'role models'—those cardboard and ephemeral constructs—offers minimal revolutionary promise. The problem exists at a deeper level, not in a role that can be put on and taken off at whim. It is about subjectivity and cognitive agency, about displacing entrenched thought structures. Ursula Franklin wisely cautions that it is "as important to know what cannot be done any more because a certain technology is put in place as what the technology actually achieves." The depersonalized techniques of modern medicine illustrate her point. The impressive achievements of medical technology often suppress the knowledge that caregivers acquire in hands-on, 'second person' experiences of healing. Technology, Franklin says, has "little use for experience":[85] she could be referring to the Grange Inquirers and the double standard that informs their proceedings.

Engagement in critiques of received knowledge generates anxiety as well as promise, however, for it seems to demand relinquishing the props that have kept epistemic endeavors manageable. So it is tempting to cling to the conviction that the development of pure theory, following the dictates of reason, adhering to strict canons of objectivity, according to publicly agreed-on procedures is the only route to

[83]De Lauretis, *Technologies of Gender*, p. 2.
[84]De Lauretis writes of "the possibility, already emergent in feminist writings of the 1980s, to conceive of the social subject and of the relations of subjectivity to sociality in another way: a subject constituted in gender, to be sure, though not by sexual difference alone, but rather across languages and cultural representations; a subject engendered in the experiencing of race and class, as well as sexual, relations; a subject, therefore, not unified but rather multiple, and not so much divided as contradicted." Ibid., p. 2.
[85]Ursula Franklin, "Will Women Change Technology or Will Technology Change Women?" *CRIAW Papers* 9 (Canadian Research Institute for the Advancement of Women, Ottawa), March 1985, pp. 5, 7.

clarity and certainty in knowledge, unassailed by the dark forces of passion and prejudice. Abandoning that route admits ambiguity and tentativeness into both process and product—a reckless, dizzying prospect.

It can be made steadier just at the point where the mitigated relativism I have been advocating articulates with a mitigated objectivism of partial perspective, limited location, situated knowledge: positions from which subjects can be answerable, accountable for what they learn how to see, for the knowledge they construct—not out of whole cloth, but out of the specific pieces they can claim to understand, carefully, responsibly.[86] Appeals to responsibility can be elaborated collectively, dialogically, and they can regulate epistemic activity just as care, justice, loyalty, and trust can regulate other forms of moral-political activity—not absolutely, but often well. A politically informed engagement in responsible epistemic practice can preserve the openness crucial to developing reconstructed feminist positions that can guard against the reductivism hitherto characteristic of malestream knowledge. Such reductivism is manifested in stereotype-based knowledge claims; in the assimiliation of human behavior to primate behavior; in what Ruth Benston calls "reducing the complexity of the real world by the construction of a model that represents an isolated, small part of that reality";[87] and, to end where this chapter began, in discounting subjective experiences in favor of granting authority only to knowledge produced by a specific, often quantitative, and plainly androcentric methodology.

[86]Here I am paraphrasing Haraway, who writes: "Only partial perspective promises objective vision. . . . Feminist objectivity is about limited location and situated knowledge, not about transcendence and splitting of subject and object. It allows us to become answerable for what we learn how to see." Haraway, "Situated Knowledges," p. 583.

[87]Ruth Benston, "Feminism and the Critique of Scientific Method," in Geraldine Finn and Angela Miles, eds., *Feminism in Canada* (Montreal: Black Rose, 1982), p. 62.

CHAPTER SEVEN

Remapping the
Epistemic Terrain

Epistemic Privilege

R ecently, I played the Poverty Game. Devised by six women from
British Columbia, who were on welfare, the game enables its
players to experience just a little of what it is like to live below subsistence level. Each player assumes the identity, and imagines herself
into the position, of one of the six women. Recordings of autobiographical stories, played as the game progresses, contribute to this
imaginative exercise. Facilitators act as welfare workers and other
public officials to simulate the pressures and obstacles the women
encounter. Months of living with not enough to live on and no pros-
pects of improvement are condensed into the day it takes to play the
game. Women on welfare are isolated, their checks arrive by mail,
they can rarely afford even the transportation costs of going out, and
they have limited, bureaucratically controlled access to their welfare
workers. That controlled access is strikingly apparent in their struggles to secure even the smallest bits of information. It is hard for them
to *know* about how to better their situation, cope with unexpected
crises, or claim their rights and privileges. To reproduce their isolation, players of the game are forbidden to converse, to consult one
another about how to cope with abusive expartners or disturbed children, about whether to spend a few dollars for a plant, or how to
afford coats for their children.

The game is designed to shock its players into awareness, and it
does. Playing it while my working life was devoted to writing this
book, I was reminded forcefully of the extent to which the knowledge

I write about is a commodity of privilege. Most white middle-class feminists are at least tacitly aware of this privilege—the class-specificity of higher education is evidence enough, as are the taken-for-granted correlations between level of education and quality of employment. But epistemologists tend to lose sight of these everyday facts or to deny them philosophical significance. Epistemology is about discerning the nature and conditions of knowledge, about justifying knowledge claims and refuting skepticism. As I have argued throughout this book, such inquiries assume that people *have knowledge* and that analyses of paradigmatic examples can reveal how knowledge as such acquires its status. In fact, the epistemic terrain is mapped out so that the welfare women can pose no problem. I am raising questions about their access to *information*, and that is not the stuff of which the knowledge that epistemologists study is made. These women's difficulties are merely practical; logically, it is as possible for them to *know* as it is for any rational man. Once they have knowledge, it will be indistinguishable from his, for epistemological purposes. To establish this point, simple, observationally based knowledge claims are usually cited.

These unsatisfactory dismissals of the problem the welfare women present for theorists of knowledge—with the gulf they reveal between theory and practice—show why feminists engaged in critiques of mainstream epistemology need to work toward remapping the epistemic terrain. As the map is currently drawn, there is no place for analyses of the availability of knowledge, of knowledge-acquisition processes, or—above all—of the political considerations that are implicated in knowing anything more interesting than the fact that the cup is on the table, now. In the received view, availability is a purely contingent matter, knowledge-acquisition is a subject for cognitive psychology, and politics should be expunged from analyses of knowledge per se. Practical possibilities and the experiences that reveal them occupy a no-man's land of the not-properly-epistemological. Their particularity, hence their assumed idiosyncrasy, makes them unsuitable candidates for the smoothed-over, unifying analyses that claim territorial supremacy in mainstream epistemology. Hence, according to the malestream view, the gulf between practice and theory should be admired rather than deplored: pure theory alone can yield the clear and controlled picture of knowledge that epistemologists require.

Now this sardonic description of mainstream epistemology may read like a caricature to feminists aware of the impact of recent critiques of epistemology, not just from feminist quarters but from "free-spirited" philosophers elsewhere.[1] But it is important regularly to rehearse the mainstream position and ritualistically to re-cognize the standards it upholds. Those standards still prevail.[2]

There may appear to be few points of contact between the welfare women's restricted access to information and a feminist critical project of reconstructing epistemological inquiry. Yet their epistemic situation, as I read it, is a stark revelation of the mechanisms of power and politics implicated in all processes of knowing. These mechanisms are visible as much in the kinds of knowledge that an epistemological position legitimates or finds worthy of analysis, contrasted with those it excludes, as in assumptions about the people who qualify as knowers. I have examined some of these mechanisms and assumptions in this book to demonstrate their alignment both with the androcentricity of epistemology and with the effectiveness of established epistemologies in serving white, privileged, masculine interests. Feminists who expect a theory of knowledge to address people's everyday cognitive experiences and to examine the place of knowledge in people's lives, who expect it to produce analyses and strategies that will contribute to the construction of a world fit for human habitation, can find little enlightenment in mainstream epistemology. Anne Seller aptly cautions that "one epistemology for the elite, another for the masses is embarrassing."[3] Yet this is just what mainstream epistemology offers, if indeed it offers anything for 'the masses' at all. It is for such reasons that remapping is required and that it is as much a political as a practical-theoretical issue.

Now philosophy has rarely claimed to be a theoretical pursuit of the people, by the people, and for the people, not even in Plato's time. Contrasts have always been drawn between thinking as a philosopher and thinking with 'the vulgar'. So women who claim a place for themselves within the discipline—even a reshaped place within a restructured discipline—do claim a certain continuity with the separateness that has been a philosopher's lot. But the political task, as I see it, is neither to require the welfare women to become philosophers and theorists nor for feminist philosophers to eschew

[1] I allude here to Sosa's characterization in "Serious Philosophy and Freedom of Spirit."

[2] Two typical examples of state-of-the-art epistemology, in which these standards are upheld, are Foley, *Theory of Epistemic Rationality*, and Alvin I. Goldman, *Epistemology and Cognition* (Cambridge: Harvard University Press, 1986). See my review of the former in *Review of Metaphysics* 42 (June 1989), and of the latter in *Canadian Philosophical Reviews* 8 (October 1988).

[3] Anne Seller, "Realism versus Relativism: Toward a Politically Adequate Epistemology," in Morwenna Griffiths and Margaret Whitford, eds., *Feminist Perspectives*, p. 171.

their philosophical training, even though they will need to repudiate parts of it. The task is, rather, to use the resources of that training to initiate a rapprochement between these equally unfeasible possibilities.

My thesis is that such a rapprochement can be effected through an elaboration of connections between theory of knowledge and ecological, community-oriented positions, and through a reexamination of the politics embedded in epistemological assumptions about subjectivity and cognitive agency. As I argue in Chapter 4, an obsession with the autonomy of reason that manifests itself in a conception of knowers as isolated and essentially self-sufficient beings, who are self-reliant in knowledge seeking, has characterized mainstream epistemology throughout a long and fairly consistent history. Standard representations of knowers are studiously neutral in their obliteration of specificity in the name of objectivity. Yet the class-, race- and gender-blindness of this assumed neutrality is by no means benign. In suppressing specificity per se, this neutral stance necessarily suppresses the effects of gender, race, class, and innumerable other specificities in shaping its own fundamental presuppositions.

The welfare women are not self-sufficient, and their isolation—paradoxically, perhaps—prevents their being self-reliant as knowers. Ironically, their experiential situation, which could, on a neutral description, approximate that of the autonomous moral and/or epistemic agent so closely as to seem identical to it, blocks their access to the knowledge that could empower them. In their stripped-down circumstances they can, indeed, know most of the things that the autonomous reasoner can know, and their knowledge would be exactly like his if the selection of examples were carefully controlled. Those stripped-down circumstances are startlingly like the ideal observational conditions in which, for an empiricist, objective knowledge is best acquired. Like the autonomous reasoner, they could know that the cat is on the mat (though they might not be able to afford a cat or a mat). Presumably, they could know that the door is open and the cup is on the table. They could probably arrive at those knowledge claims through their own resources, and their claims would be indistinguishable from the autonomous reasoner's propositionally identical claims. But this last point demonstrates nothing about the general neutrality, the paradigmatic nature, or the usefulness of simple, observationally based propositional knowledge claims. Indeed, it attests to their irrelevance in promoting efforts to see how knowledge fits into people's lives and to understand its contribution to the mapping out of livable relationships between knowing subjects and their environments—physical, material, and social/personal.

It is true that people have to know quite a bit about the nature and behavior of *things* in the world just to survive, whether on welfare or otherwise. But in arguing for a remapping of the epistemic terrain, I am taking issue with the implicit belief that epistemologists need only to understand propositional, observationally derived knowledge, and all the rest will follow. I am taking issue also with the concomitant claim that epistemologists need only to understand how such knowledge claims would be made and justified by autonomous, self-reliant reasoners, and they will understand all the rest. Beliefs of this sort are, in the end, politically oppressive in that they rest on exclusionary assumptions about the nature of cognitive agency and mask the experiences one might expect a theory of knowledge to explain.

Ecology and Community

My proposal is that an ecological model can shift epistemological inquiry away from autonomy-obsession toward an analysis explicitly cognizant of the fact that every cognitive act takes place at a point of intersection of innumerable relations, events, circumstances, and histories that make the knower and the known what they are, at that time. It is neither possible nor necessary to take all of these factors into account in every judgment, but sometimes a knower will need to take some of them very seriously into account—and they are all always there in the background. Nor is my point that knowers are at the mercy of these factors, determined to know only in certain ways, willy-nilly—hence that epistemology is meaningless. A recognition that knowledge construction is *dependent on* its 'location' is not tantamount to a claim that knowledge is *determined by* it. Rather, these factors constitute the stuff out of which knowers, as creators of meaning and as agents, must construct their meanings, purposes, and actions. They limit the constructive process, but they also give it shape. They do not obliterate it. Ecologically rather than individualistically positioned, human beings are interdependent creatures, 'second persons' who rely on one another as much in knowledge as they do for other means of survival.

An ecological model builds on the mutual relations of organisms with one another and the relations between organisms and their environment. The 'environment' is not just the physical environment, nor only the present one, but the complex network of relations within which an organism realizes, or fails to realize, its potential, be they historical, material, geographical, social, cultural, racial, institutional, or other. Any organism, at any moment in its history, exhibits its current state of accommodation both of and to such relations. But this is by no means a passive reflection: ecological analysis emphasizes the participation of organisms, whose choices (where the organism is such as to *have* choices) are relationally structured and who themselves have a shaping effect on relational choices.

Ecological thinking analyzes the implications, for organisms, of living in certain kinds of environments, and the possibilities, for those organisms, of developing strategies to create and sustain environments conducive to a mutual empowerment that is exploitative neither of the habitat nor of other inhabitants. Restating this point epistemologically, it is clearly of paramount importance for community standards of responsible cognitive practice to prevail if members of epistemic communities are to be able to know well and to construct environments where they can live in enabling rather than oppressive circumstances. Integral to ecological analysis is a recognition that any account of what it is to be a certain kind of organism, living in certain kinds of circumstances, will be tinged with provisionality, because it is made from a particular stance, at a specific time, and always subject to revision.

In many of its manifestations, feminist inquiry is continuous with ecological theory: ecofeminism, which elaborates connections between masculine domination, exploitation, and oppression both of women and of nature, has an increasingly audible voice in the construction of feminist theory.[4] Baier's interest in the interconnectedness of human lives, captured in the notion of 'second personhood' (which I discuss in Chapter 3) is continuous with this line of thought. Her arguments point to the centrality of relationships in constructing environments that contribute to the well-being of their participants. As Held aptly observes: "To sustain a society threatened with dissolution, we will have to pay attention before everything else to the relations between persons."[5] Threats of dissolution come not just from the dangers of nuclear annihilation and environmental pollution and

---

[4]A now-classic text is Merchant, *Death of Nature*. See also Susan Griffin, *Woman and Nature: The Roaring inside Her* (New York: Harper & Row, 1978); Vandana Shiva, *Staying Alive: Women, Ecology, and Development* (London: Zed, 1988); Carolyn Merchant, *Ecological Revolutions: Nature, Gender, and Science in New England* (Chapel Hill: University of North Carolina Press, 1989).

[5]Held, *Rights and Goods*, p. 84.

depletion, but from social structures and practices that are systematically unjust, discriminatory, remotely authoritarian, and based on principles of competitiveness, domination, and self-interest which serve a privileged minority at the expense of less-advantaged minorities. In such societies there is a general lack of concern with the living conditions of members who cannot or will not participate in competitive modes of living.

Ecology emphasizes the interdependence of human lives and the life of the biosphere, together with the value of healthy, balanced ecosystems to the maintainance of diversity. Elaborated in the context of an "integrative and transformative feminism,"[6] ecological theory and ecology-informed practices create space for developing responsible perspectives that make explicit the interconnections among forms and systems of domination, exploitation, and oppression, across their different manifestations. Hence an active, preservative respect for difference and diversity is central to them—diversity within the human and the nonhuman world. Ecologists are justifiably dismayed at technological excesses. In its more responsible forms, their dismay does not derive, naively, from a view that the existence of technology per se is deplorable: it is cognizant of the improvements in (some) human lives that technology makes possible. But it forces a sustained assessment of the ecological impact of every technological development, an awareness of the ecological price that such achievements exact. Such assessments are possible only in concert with relinquishing entrenched views about 'man's' natural right to control and exploit nature and with a critique of the mechanistic assumptions that, especially since Bacon and Descartes, inform western attitudes to nature. Values centered on preservation, on living harmoniously with one another and with the biosphere—not passively but creatively and commonally—are accorded high esteem in ecological thinking, creating a continuity between ecology movements and peace movements throughout the world.

An ecological model is both promising and problematic for feminists. I want to discuss some of its problems, in its ecofeminist form, before reaffirming its promise. I am concerned about essentialism and about suppression.

The essentialist problem derives from the same continuity of purpose between the feminist movement and the ecology movement from which its promise derives. An ecofeminist position, as Ynestra

---

[6]I owe this phrase to Karen J. Warren, "Feminism and Ecology: Making the Connections," *Environmental Ethics* 9 (Spring 1987): 17.

King describes it, is committed to "reconstructing human society in harmony with the natural environment,"[7] while respecting the integrity of nature and repudiating *man*'s right to dominate it. In a later piece, King restates the position: "An analysis of the interrelated dominations of nature—psyche and sexuality, human oppression, and non-human nature—and the historic position of women in relation to those forms of domination is the starting point of ecofeminist theory."[8] These are laudable purposes. The troubling aspect, especially in the earlier article, is that King accepts—indeed, endorses—the identification of woman with 'nature'. She wants to celebrate that identification by affirming women's responsibility and unique capacity to save the world from destruction. Thus romanticized, ecofeminism holds minimal promise as a transformative, liberating position. Its reliance on versions of an 'earth mother' stereotype that has constructed the space 'down among the women' where concern for taking care of people and things, providing nurture and support, is women's natural role, suggests a disempowering acceptance of biological determinism.

Now it would, admittedly, be unfair to hold King to her earlier, more frankly essentialist claims when she has modified them in this more recent piece. Her continued linking of women and nature is more subtly done, evidencing an awareness of recent feminist critiques of female essentialism and bipolar oppositions. Nonetheless, the ecofeminist dilemma to which I want to draw attention persists even as King endeavors to qualify it. Thus it is instructive, heuristically, to state the problem in its starker form to reveal its critical implications.

Ecofeminists, perhaps even more urgently than other feminists, have constantly to negotiate within the tension that I have been discussing throughout this book—the tension between celebrating the values and projects stereotypically constitutive of femininity and recognizing that women, especially privileged women, have been encouraged to cultivate those values and attributes in positions of powerlessness. The tension is, if anything, more acute in an ecofeminist context, because the identification of 'woman' with the sensuous, unruly chaos of nature has been as persistent as her identification with nurturant values and has been cited as justification for her con-

[7]Ynestra King, "Toward an Ecological Feminism and a Feminist Ecology," in Joan Rothschild, ed., *Machina Ex Dea: Feminist Perspectives on Technology* (New York: Pergamon, 1983), p. 119.

[8]Ynestra King, "Healing the Wounds: Feminism, Ecology, and Nature/Culture Dualism," in Jaggar and Bordo, eds., *Gender/Body/Knowledge*, p. 132.

tinued domestication and control. Hence a feminist politics that aims to derive its program from an alignment of woman and nature has to advance its claims very cautiously.

By definition, ecofeminism's preservative platform places it at the conservative end of the political spectrum, thus creating another area where careful articulation is necessary to affirm a transformative potential that avoids political stasis, quietism. To realize the promise of this preservative dimension, it has to be demonstrated that conservation can be productively—and even disruptively—conceived, as an active, radical reclamation, not a static maintenance of a status quo. Epistemologically, the route is opened, in King's later piece, for addressing this problem—in her plea for an epistemology based in "a noninstrumental way of knowing."[9] I argue in Chapter 4 that an epistemology that models itself on 'second person' relations would be just such an epistemology. The promise I see in an ecological model comes from the fact that it starts from a presumption of relationship in whose terms the analogical possibilities of reciprocity, respect—and friendship—between knowing other people and knowing inanimate objects are clearly visible.[10]

Just as essentializing and stereotyping block the development of knowledgeable friendship, blinding one to the unexpected, the unsettling humorous twist, so ecofeminism can realize its epistemological promise only if it resists fixed essentialist constructions not just of 'woman' but of 'man' and 'nature' as well. Lynne Segal criticizes early ecofeminists for their tendency to draw selectively on women's capacity for motherhood and on only a narrow range of possible ways of conceptualizing masculinity, femininity, and nature. She writes:

> In some of the symbols which we use to contrast nature and culture it is 'the male' which is seen as closer to nature: forceful, violent, animal-like and instinctive: 'the female' is the product of culture, tamed, domestic, civilised. In other symbolisations the dichotomy is reversed: 'the male' becomes the creator of culture, 'the female' becomes instinct and biology. Neither 'woman' nor 'man', then, is consistently connected with nature.[11]

---

[9]Ibid., p. 118.

[10]Haraway observes: "Ecofeminists have perhaps been most insistent on some version of the world as active subject, not as resource to be mapped and appropriated in bourgeois, Marxist, or masculinist projects. Acknowledging the agency of the world in knowledge makes room for some unsettling possibilities, including a sense of the world's independent sense of humor." Haraway, "Situated Knowledges," p. 593.

[11]Segal, *Is the Future Female?* p. 7.

Ecological projects that attempt to forge such connections universally or deterministically cannot claim epistemological or political adequacy. In fact, this deterministic position reinstates many of the dichotomies feminists have sought to eradicate. Recalling the metaphysical pervasiveness of the mind/body, culture/nature, reason/emotion, and public/private dichotomies, and their parallel with the male/female dichotomy, it is important to take note, in ecofeminist debates, of the fact that these pairs are not only hierarchically ranked and polarly opposed one to another, they are in fact governed by an instrumental assumption with oppressive political implications.[12] In these polarizations, the righthand, lesser terms play an instrumental role, with the consequence that these lower-ranking items *serve* the higher, in a relation of dominance, mastery, or control. If women are *naturally*, essentially aligned with nature, then women and nature alike can naturally—and uncontroversially—be enlisted in the service of men and of culture.[13] If women are naturally suited to be the preservers and protectors of nature, then it is just as plausible to maintain that men's historically demonstrated capacity for aggression and warfare is biologically determined—and hence that there is no reason to deplore it and no hope of transforming it.[14] Karen Warren notes: "The idea that one group of persons is, or is not, closer to nature than another group assumes the very nature-culture split that eco-feminism denies."[15]

Women may indeed have the capacity to save the world, in consequence, perhaps, of their cultural-historical relegation to a domain 'closer to nature' than men, whatever that means. Yet claims that such a capacity is uniquely, essentially theirs have consistently served as premises of arguments designed show that women should be the moral guardians both of 'humanity' and of nature. Such injunctions assign women responsibilities that are fundamentally oppressive, while excluding them from recognition as cognitive agents and creators of social meaning, precisely *because of* their alleged closeness to nature. An ecofeminism developed in this direction would be morally-politically unacceptable.

[12]I owe these points to Val Plumwood, in her "Ecofeminism: An Overview and Discussion of Positions and Arguments," *Australasian Journal of Philosophy* 64 (suppl.) (June 1986), esp. p. 132.

[13]See in this context Sherry Ortner, "Is Female to Male as Nature Is to Culture?" in Michele Rosaldo and Louise Lamphere, eds., *Women, Culture, and Society* (Stanford: Stanford University Press, 1974).

[14]This is Birke's point in *Women, Feminism, and Biology*, pp. 122–124.

[15]Warren, "Feminism and Ecology," p. 15.

A rather different problem derives from the fact that ecosystems notoriously survive at the expense of those of their members who, for one reason or another, endanger the balance of the system. Ecosystems sacrifice their old, their feeble, and their 'monsters' to promote the survival of the whole, which is able better to flourish when it is unencumbered by these burdens. Women have long been the chosen candidates for suppression as the 'dangerous' elements in a putatively rational society, as those who threaten to disrupt the social order, who must be controlled so that the whole can better, more efficiently survive.

It has been a central tenet of my argument that the autonomy-obsession of androcentric thinking endorses a stark conception of individualism that overemphasizes self-realization and self-reliance. I have argued against the supremacy of these values in favor of 'second personhood' and mutuality. But the ecological point is that it would be a mistake to conflate individual*ism* with individual*ity* and to repudiate the latter with the former. In the history of women's lives in patriarchal, capitalist societies, their struggles to claim individuality— a differentiated, empowered sense of self—have been bitter and often futile. Women's empowerment has been sacrificed to the smooth functioning of the whole: women have had to make do with an amorphous identity, as Woman, as Other, as submerged in the species.[16] Constructing an ecologically oriented feminist position and remapping the epistemic terrain require mindfulness of this history of suppression.

Now one of the most acute sources of the dismay occasioned by the Poverty Game is in what it reveals about a community where this situation can occur. The dismay demonstrates the value of linking the ecological model/metaphor with analyses of community in *its* political-epistemic dimension. The existence of welfare is not in itself deplorable, but the relegation of welfare recipients to a position of abjection is not a process born of a community in which ecologically informed feminists could want to live. It bespeaks an individualism according to which a person, alone, is responsible for her circumstances and must pay the price of penurious gratitude if she has not made of them what an individualistically based, autonomy-obsessed liberal society permits, at least in theory. An ecological model emphasizes mutual responsibility and the interconnectedness of people, environments, and events. In its morally and politically commendable

---

[16]Mackenzie analyzes women's immersion in the species in "Simone de Beauvoir."

forms it does not absolve members of a community (conceived as an ecosystem) from responsibility for the shape of their lives, but neither does it make that responsibility wholly theirs.

Thinking ecologically about communities where feminists could live requires a repudiation of contractarian constructions of community, where individual decision makers come together for mutual advantage and protection. In such communities, Hartsock observes, particularly when they are constructed on a market-economy model, it is taken for granted that individual rational agents "may dispose of their own persons and capacities freely, since they owe nothing to the community as a whole, either for who they are, or for the resources they possess."[17] Still more destructive of possibilities of commonality, in Hartsock's view, are communities structured around the relations of conquest and domination embedded in masculine eros as it is traditionally, heroically construed.[18] Neither conception of community is based on common interest and concern. In their existence around a core of self-interest, competitiveness, and mutual opposition, such communities are fragile in their dependence on shifting interests and allegiances and false in their lack of mutuality.

Ecological projects are committed to the creation of communities that depend on and foster the flourishing of their members. For this reason, they are more promising, heuristically, than communitarian thinking tout court, I am suggesting, despite the apparent feminist appeal of the latter as a repudiation of individualism. The conception of 'community' that informs the leading communitarian positions requires significant refinement if such positions are to be adaptable to feminist purposes.[19]

With its valorization of such 'found' or 'de facto' communities as families, neighborhoods, and nations, which provide identities for their members, standard communitarianism ignores the extent to which such communities have been systemically oppressive places for women to live[20] and have provided justifications for the exclusion and/or marginalization of other 'Others': sexual and racial minorities and other eccentric cultural groups. Communities to which people are 'naturally' bound, by the circumstances of their birth, impose attachments that are not chosen and values with which their eccentric

---

[17]Hartsock, *Money, Sex, and Power*, p. 39.

[18]See ibid., pp. 176–179.

[19]Influential recent versions of communitarianism are presented in Alasdair MacIntyre, *After Virtue* (London: Duckworth, 1981); and Michael Sandel, *Liberalism and the Limits of Justice* (Cambridge: Cambridge University Press, 1982).

[20]I am indebted in my thinking here to Marilyn Friedman's article "Feminism and Modern Friendship: Dislocating the Community," *Ethics* 99 (January 1989): 275–290.

members often disagree. Yet resistance to conforming, or active disagreement within such structures, calls forth judgments of deviance and occasions punitive action, both blatant and subtle. Communities have notorious histories not only of exploiting certain of their members, but also of discriminating against outsiders, either through arbitrary rules of exclusion or with hostility and outright aggression. Standard communitarian theory has little to say about the quality of relationships across community lines. It is silent about relationships between de facto, 'found' communities and such adult *chosen* communities as public interest groups, trade unions, and other self-identifying communities whose boundaries and practices are not always congruent with those of the larger, self-justifying, and normative community to which some kind of primary allegiance is presumed to be due. Moreover, a communitarian society could continue to endorse the exploitative, antiecological values of modern industrial societies in the name of the common good, nor is there any reason to believe that nationalistic chauvinism would be excluded from its political values.

For all its apparent repudiation of individualism, communitarianism, in most of its articulations, retains a presumption that community members are self-reliant, autonomous, liberal (male) individuals. Although they differ from orthodox liberal individuals in their collective orientation, there is no convincing indication that the community they comprise is anything *more* than the sum of its parts. Hence communitarian critiques of individualism rarely encompass the critiques feminists require. There is no doubt that, with its contention that selves are socially constituted, communitarianism improves on liberal assumptions of *abstract* individualism. But with its contention that all selves are *equally* socially constituted, communitarian thinking glosses over the unequal social pressures brought to bear on women and on other marginalized groups to develop a subservient, self-effacing subjectivity that facilitates the enforcement of norms not of their own choosing. In this aspect, communitarian thinking is as insensitive to gender, race, and class as most traditional political theories have been.

Nonetheless, it is my contention that a refined, "normative," ecologically constructed communitarianism has something to offer to feminists.[21] Normative ecological communitarianism would engage in evaluative, dialogical, self-critical debates—in open-ended conver-

[21]I owe the "normative" label to Julius Moravscik, "Communal Ties," in the *Proceedings and Addresses of the American Philosophical Association* 62 (suppl.) (September 1988): 211–225.

sations—about how the community can be made habitable and worthy of moral-political allegiance. Hence it would escape the normative complacency often consequent on the status granted to de facto communities in communitarian thinking. In its assessments of communities of choice, it would be especially critical of the varieties of complacency to which they, too, are prone. Solidarity is not intrinsically valuable, nor are choices as pure and unmediated as the conception of a *chosen* community suggests. The ethos and fundamental principles of chosen groups, communities, and societies are always open to critique. They can be assessed for their success in fostering open, nonrestrictive social structures that facilitate the well-being of their members and repudiate oppression and arbitrary privilege. Criteria of evaluation will encompass analyses of the *place* of a community in relation to other communities and of its global awareness and accountability. Does it use more than its share of resources? fail to replenish those it uses? distribute inequitably among its members? Ecology provides an evaluative framework sensitive to the interconnectedness of lives and processes, both local and global.

How, then, might these goals be achieved? In Chapter 3 I argue in favor of a model of personal relationships derived from friendship. Here I want to propose that certain features of friendship can be extended, by analogy, to construct a regulative ideal for communal living. My proposal will work on a larger sociopolitical scale only if the ideal is pursued in concert with the development of *ecological* strategies for creating social environments where a politics of difference is explicitly promoted. The trust, respect, and caring involvement that are essential to good friendship are the pertinent features here.[22] A community-oriented, ecologically responsible society would make participation and mutual concern central values and would restructure debates among community members as conversations, not confrontations. Its aim would be to promote mutual support and a nonoppressive ambiance.

It is instructive to think of the relationships that would constitute lives and histories in such communities as patterns of concentric circles, many of which intersect with the relationships that constitute other lives. In a strong, 'true' community (contrasted with the fragile, false communities Hartsock discusses) there would be a presumption in favor of commonality in forms of life and projects. But that pre-

[22]Moravscik argues that, in flourishing communities characterized by mutuality, trust will replace "constant surveillance or endless litigations" and that the presence of trust can change both "the quality of cooperation and the psychological background against which communal life develops." "Communal Ties," p. 220.

sumption could only viably be sustained against the background of a politics of difference in which claims to mutuality were not permitted to overwhelm affirmations of different, eccentric projects and positions. At the same time, there would have to be a systematic deconstruction of the adversarial assumption in whose terms human contacts are taken, initially at least, to be based on opposing and mutually exclusive interests. In the concentric picture, the 'outer' circles, representing more formal, less affectively central relationships, would work on an analogy with the more central ones. Hence a presumption in favor of the mutuality that governs initial encounters with potential friends would be allowed (perhaps cautiously) to structure less personal encounters. Such a reorientation might undermine the long-standing contention that there are two distinct kinds of relationships: public, formal, impersonal ones, and private, emotional, personal ones, dichotomously construed and mutually exclusive. For individualists, such relationships belong to distinct regions: they have relatively few features in common with respect to one's position and mode of participation within them. Hence there is an assumed split between a person's private and public 'self', with the projects of the latter commonly accorded greater value and requiring repudiation of the open, dialogic techniques of the former.[23]

In complex urban societies, it is unavoidable, and even desirable, for some relationships to be kept impersonal. My claim, however, is about starting points and points of emphasis. It makes a perceptible difference to the quality of relationships whether their principal focus is on commonality or on competitiveness and separateness. An assumed continuity rather than discontinuity between kinds of relationships would amount to an honest openness to the possibility of being one's 'private' self in 'public' encounters. Mastering the arts of personhood would involve learning how to interpret this assumed continuity with care, to avoid presumptuous, excessively familiar behavior, and to retain an appropriate sense of boundaries. There is always the option to retreat to a more formal, objective position, should the situation require it.

For autonomy-centered thinkers, this proposed dissolution of the public/private dichotomy would require a radical reconstruction of

---

[23]Of the autonomous self of the individualistic tradition, Benhabib observes: "He himself is divided into the public person and the private individual. Within his chest clash the law of reason and the inclination of nature, the brilliance of cognition and the obscurity of emotion. . . . In the discourse of modern moral and political theory, these dichotomies are reified as being essential to the constitution of the self." Benhabib, "Generalized and Concrete Other," p. 86.

subjectivity and agency. Its primary manifestation, as I suggest in my discussion of Baier, would be in relinquishing defensiveness. The fact that objective forms of social intercourse are commonly considered most suitable in 'public' arenas is well known, as is the fact that such domains are typically male, defined by men, occupied (often jealously) by them, and sustained by the exclusion of women and of 'feminine' values. I am suggesting that this is a pernicious exclusion and that an ecological acknowledgment of the extent to which persons *are* second persons could effect a rapprochement between domains whose distinctness is, at best, highly contrived. The idea that such reconstructions are possible is not based in a naive voluntarism, according to which people can effect total personal conversions at whim. Rather, it looks to the effectiveness of pedagogical, therapeutic, or business-professional practices that have, with conscious intent, slowly been reshaped by feminists and others committed to a gradual, systematic reorientation. Those reshapings tend to spread to the other practices such people are engaged in and to infect their associates and colleagues, often positively.

A project of working to construct a normative ecological community, I am arguing, holds considerable promise for social transformation consonant with feminist emancipatory goals and sensitive to the politics of difference. Yet feminists are by no means unanimous in endorsing such a project. Hence I want, at this point, to engage with one of the more persuasive voices of dissent to demonstrate more clearly the promise I claim for this project.

Against such advocates of community-oriented positions as Carol Gould, Seyla Benhabib, Michael Sandel, and Isaac Balbus, Iris Young argues that "the vision of small, face-to-face, decentralized units that this ideal [of community] promotes . . . is an unrealistic vision for transformative politics in mass urban society." In Young's view, an ideal of community that bases itself on a model of face-to-face relations is undesirably utopian. In its presumption that "subjects can understand one another as they understand themselves" and hence can achieve "wholeness and identification,"[24] it denies differences between them. In concentrating on the nurturant values of face-to-face relationships, it ignores the harsher realities of urban societies consequent on alienation and violence and temporal-spatial distancing—realities that are often also a part of face-to-face relations. Moreover, in claiming an authenticity for face-to-face relations which

---

[24]Iris Marion Young, "The Ideal of Community and the Politics of Difference," in Linda Nicholson, ed., *Feminism/Postmodernism* (New York: Routledge, 1990), pp. 300, 302.

contrasts with impersonal inauthenticity, constructing existing, impersonal society as a seamless whole impenetrable by transformative strategies, the ideal "totalizes and detemporalizes its conception of social life."[25] Hence it can neither accommodate a politics of difference nor make space for strategies of intervention. It is constructed as a closed, unified system.

Now Young's criticisms are well taken. Many of them, indeed, are consonant with the criticisms of maternal thinking I formulate in Chapter 3 and with the criticisms of communitarianism I have just put forward. Yet I think the oppositions in whose terms she structures her critique are, in turn, dichotomous and exclusionary to an extent that prevents her drawing on the promise of community-oriented politics without assuming that she would thereby endorse its (admittedly) troubling consequences. Her construction of a stark independence/intimacy dichotomy is particularly salient.

It would indeed be naive—and potentially coercive—to base a platform for political transformation on an empathetic 'second person' model that took for granted the possibility of perfect mutuality. Both in advocating friendship as an exemplary relationship and in proposing that knowledge construction should be patterned on processes of knowing other people, I have argued that it is the very tentativeness and instability, the necessary incompleteness of this knowledge, that recommends the model. It offers a salutory corrective to the arrogant expectations of perfect, complete knowledge that the 'S knows that p' model promises. Friendship requires separateness, distance, and a valuing of differences if it is to be a thoughtful, mutually sustaining relationship. It is often maintained across spatial-temporal distances. When it aims at perfect identification, total merging, it risks self-destruction. Young writes as though intimacy could be achieved only by sacrificing independence; and there is no doubt that face-to-face encounters have the potential to become exclusive, homogeneous places where differences are obliterated. But the likelihood of their taking that turn is clearly not so great as the likelihood that impersonal, bureaucratic structures will efface differences.

In fact, it is a problem for many communitarians that they expect to generate communal sentiments and loyalties out of a theoretical apparatus that makes little space for explicitly 'second person' relationships. True, such relationships can become sites for the obliteration of differences, but they also offer the potential for constructing places where differences can be clearly—narratively—articulated and un-

[25]Ibid., p. 302.

derstood. The Poverty Game is one such place; the politics of *glasnost*, in a global context, is another. In the latter, face-to-face encounters have succeeded in bringing irreconcilable differences within a range of comprehension and interpretation that might, in the early 1980s, have been thought merely utopian.

Young seems to assume that 'second person' relations are themselves seamless, so that they cannot be self-critical, cannot negotiate their commonalities and differences. Hence she does not believe that they can be starting points for the dialogic alliances out of which urban groups can work, both internally and with one another, to transform environments into the heterogeneous spaces she envisages. Yet the successes of pollution-control groups, legal advocacy groups, women's shelters and housing collectives, and other ecologically sensitive coalitions should not be permitted to disappear into a concentration on their ongoing internal and external political struggles to find ways of living together, independently *and* intimately. Young argues in terms of absolute identification or utter exclusion; she writes as though one kind of 'belonging' would use up all of a person's possibilities—as though people had only enough care, love, or commitment for one close relationship. This dualistic assumption truncates the argument, constrains it within too-narrow options.

For Young, the privileging of face-to-face relations "presumes an illusory ideal of unmediated social relations and wrongly identifies mediation with alienation."[26] Hence it is a dislocated ideal, out of touch with the material surroundings and structures of modern urban life. Again, there is no doubt that it can work out this way. My resistance to this part of the analysis derives from the fact that Young totalizes face-to-face relations even as she criticizes them for a totalized construction of social life to which they posit an alternative. Yet self-critical 'second person'-based relations and alliances eschew the monologic mold in which Young casts them, and many resist claiming unmediated authenticity. While claims for common goals and values are part of the glue that holds the relations together, they can avoid coming unstuck precisely in their efforts to negotiate, debate, discuss differences, maintain them in tension, work within them. There need not be the stasis, the smooth homogenizing unity that Young anticipates. In open, dialogic alliances, there will not be.

On a microlevel, Julius Moravscik urges professional philosophers to constitute themselves as just such a cooperative community, pursuing common aims. A reconstruction of the profession effected by a

26Ibid., p. 313.

construction of communal ties would foster mutual respect among people whose welfare is of mutual concern. The reconstruction would demand a trusting agreement to honor common aims with appropriate attitudes. Describing how a community orientation could manifest itself when philosophers are required to evaluate one another for positions or honors, Moravscik writes: "The best way to increase the probability that our performances will be shaped by such attitudes is to have these processes take place in public. . . . [It] takes trust to expect of the members of the community that such openness will not drive some people back into their shells or create personal enmity."[27] His proposal assumes just the continuity between so-called 'public' and 'private' selves which I advocate. One of its major advantages would be in its subversion of the adversarial paradigm that governs professional philosophy,[28] constructing fellow practitioners, primarily, as targets for criticism who must demonstrate their capacity to survive adversarial cross fire as an initiation rite into the ranks of the profession. The paradigm extends, in urban professional societies, across a much wider range of social encounters. Women, statistically, fare badly in such 'parry and thrust' situations and are often marginalized accordingly.

Moravscik does not address the place of this philosophical community in the society, nor does he analyze the exclusionary, hegemonic structures that determine and preclude membership in it. Its place would have to be established in cognizance of its expectations of and responsibilities to the society or culture where it thrives and to whose thriving it contributes, and the proposal is open to amplification in these terms. More pertinently, he does not address the issue of women's place in the philosophical community. Were he to do so, he would have to propose measures designed to ensure that the silencing of women in philosophy can never recur. The gender-neutrality of his proposals cannot guarantee that his 'trusting' community will care about women's interests or other 'marginal' interests as a matter of course. A place where 'Other' (than malestream) philosophical projects and interests can flourish can be created only with the introduction of special corrective measures designed to reveal and eradicate the androcentricity and ethnocentricity of professional philosophy, whose current self-presentation is that of the very homogeneous whole that Young wisely cautions against. Corrective measures would have to remain in place at least until there could be unequivocal

[27]Moravscik, "Communal Ties," p. 222.
[28]See my discussion of this paradigm in Chapters 1 and 4.

agreement that women—and other 'Others'—were explicit and equal participants in the aims and the principles of trust and concern that unite the community.

Knowledge and Empowerment

How, then, does this analysis bear on the *epistemic* circumstances of the welfare women? Against the background of Seller's astute observation, "As an isolated individual, I often do not know what my experiences are,"[29] consider what made it possible for the women who invented the Poverty Game to change the course of their lives. They receive an announcement of an innovative community program that provides free transportation and child care, and their new welfare worker is accessible and forthcoming. Out of these two developments—knowledge and solidarity—the six women are empowered to the extent that they can embark on the project of devising the game. Its success allows them, slowly, to overcome their inertia and—as they say in their recorded narratives—to draw on the strengths of commonality in taking charge of their lives. Knowledge made openly available, and new possibilities for friendship and cooperation radically alter their positions on the political-epistemic map.

There is no question that power is at work in this situation— power, I think, best understood in Foucault's terms. His analysis of power-knowledge circulating in myriad 'capillary' structures throughout a society to suppress loci of knowledge considered undesirable, and hence rendered invisible, helps to illuminate the women's situation.[30] For them, possibilities of acquiring the knowledge they need for reasonable survival are suppressed by impersonal bureaucratic structures, by a system that is everyone's and no one's responsibility. There is no explicit policy administered by a sovereign body, from above, specifying that welfare women are to be kept in ignorance lest they 'get uppity' and try to become active in dealing with their lives. Yet Foucault's power-knowledge analyses make clear what these women come also to realize: that knowledge and alliances put one in a position to claim the power to act, at least locally. The

[29]Seller, "Realism versus Relativism," p. 180.

[30]Foucault refers to "the capillary functioning of power" in *Discipline and Punish: The Birth of the Prison*, trans. Alan Sheridan (New York: Vintage, 1979), p. 198. In "Prison Talk," he comments, "In thinking of the mechanisms of power, I am thinking rather of its capillary form of existence, the point where power reaches into the very grain of individuals, touches their bodies and inserts itself into their actions and attitudes, their discourses, learning processes and everyday lives." Foucault, *Power/Knowledge*, p. 39.

bureaucratic structure is implicitly informed by this same conception in blocking the women's access to information. The official view evidently is that if welfare recipients are in a position to participate actively in shaping their circumstances, they will fail to pay the price of humiliation that the liberal society exacts from its members who do not pay their way.

The liberal society exacts its price according to a gender-related double standard. Although there are numerous male welfare recipients in North America, the majority are women. Nancy Fraser maintains that most U.S. social welfare programs are "officially gender neutral . . . [but] the system . . . has an unmistakable gender subtext."[31] The subtext is most plainly legible in the ideological and monetary structures that determine the availability and administration of unemployment insurance benefits, contrasted with those manifested in the distribution of welfare payments.

In effect, as Fraser sets it out, the gender subtext is polarized into an unemployment insurance/welfare dichotomy that parallels the traditional male/female dichotomy, and with it—both descriptively and evaluatively—the other dichotomies I have discussed throughout this book. The point is not that only men collect unemployment insurance, while women alone receive welfare. Rather, the processes of need interpretation, administration, and positioning of recipients as subjects take for granted a social division into a *masculine* realm of rights-bearers and a *feminine* realm of clients, or suppliants. When women enter 'male' territory, or men enter 'female' territory, they are expected to conform to the dominant structural norms: female unemployment insurance recipients to a 'masculine' model of individualistic labor-market participation, male welfare recipients to a passive 'feminine' model of a charity case.

As rights-bearers, recipients of unemployment insurance claim what they *deserve* as citizens of a society whose ideology conceptualizes them as proprietors of their own persons. They have paid with their labor power for benefits to which they are now entitled. Welfare recipients are represented as different in kind, not just degree, from unemployment insurance recipients. Unlike citizens claiming their due, they are passive beneficiaries of a system that routinely humili-

---

[31]Nancy Fraser, *Unruly Practices: Power, Discourse, and Gender in Contemporary Social Theory* (Minneapolis: University of Minnesota Press, 1989), p. 149. Although Fraser's account is based in U.S. practices, the parts I draw on here are consistent with the Canadian context in which the Poverty Game was invented. Fraser observes that some version of the fiscal crisis of the welfare state is taking place "in every late capitalist welfare state in Western Europe and North America" (p. 144).

ates and harasses them, while granting them 'benefits' that leave them well below subsistence level. With female recipients, the governing (if unsubstantiated) assumption is that welfare mothers do not work and have never worked: they are constituted as essentially dependent on an (absent) *male* breadwinner, and their needs are interpreted according to the heterosexual norm of the traditional (failed) nuclear family. Where male recipients are concerned, they are 'feminized' by the welfare process. As Fraser puts it: "In the 'masculine' subsystem . . . claimants must prove their 'cases' meet administratively defined criteria of entitlement; in the 'feminine' subsystem . . . [they] must prove conformity to administratively defined criteria of need."[32] A woman's needs are determined by the absence of a man, not by the claims she has, as a member of a community, to social support. Neither the unemployment nor the welfare system empowers its members; nor does the collection of unemployment insurance escape stigma and degradation in a liberal, capitalist society. But the utter lack of personal power and autonomy that characterizes the 'feminine' system is a reminder that although autonomy-obsession cannot claim feminist approval, a significant measure of female autonomy is indispensable for the realization of feminist aims. Without it, women cannot take control of their lives; their capacities for effective agency are systematically obliterated.

Now Fraser's point is neither that the gender subtext is the *only* subtext to be read out of the administrative and ideological structures of social welfare in the U.S., nor that it takes precedence, as a producer of injustice, over class, racial, or other subtexts. By focusing on gender for analytical purposes, she eschews abstract and gender-neutral conceptions of needs and values to examine specific patterns of 'needs interpretation' that are demonstrably detrimental to women's interests, if differently across lines of class, race, and sexual preference. That she claims to offer no comprehensive theoretical account of 'human' interests and needs is a strength, not a weakness, of her account. No politically acceptable general, abstract account of what those interests are or should be has yet been articulated; nor, a fortiori, is there an adequate *theory* of women's (aggregated) needs and interests, or of 'the good life' for women. The 'separate spheres' norms Fraser designates are not the only norms that shape a structure so complex as a welfare system. But an examination of their functioning reveals injustices that the discourse of conformity to "require-

[32]Ibid., p. 154.

ments of consistency and formal justice"[33] would serve simply to conceal. The women Fraser discusses are powerless to articulate their needs: no theory that ignores their powerlessness can pretend to adequacy. Nor can theorists presume, from a position of external privilege, to define the women's needs and interests for them. Fraser's analysis opens up a space where productive, dialogues between feminist theorists and activists, and the people whose well-being is at issue, could yield creative proposals for reshaping social structures and reinterpreting interests and needs.

There is no doubt that the welfare situations both Fraser and I discuss are situations of power and oppression. Yet this is not the top-down, monolithic power structure that standard political theories are designed to analyze. Hence the scope of political analysis has to shift, under feminist scrutiny, to address such issues. Foucault's focus on micropolitical structures provides some clues as to how this shift might be effected. The transformative political potential of micro-revolutions is more obviously within the grasp of small groups, or even of individuals reinforced by group-derived and -supported convictions, than the possibility of effecting global change. Foucault notes that the disruptive effects of microrefusals to fit smoothly into totalizing social structures are felt well beyond their points of origin. Hence he describes his "sense of the increasing vulnerability to criticism of things, institutions, practices . . . [and the] amazing efficacy of discontinuous, particular and local criticism" to which I refer in Chapter 5.[34] For the oppressed, too, connections between knowledge and power can be made to hold, and knowledge—experientially derived knowledge—can be empowering.[35] The creation of the Poverty Game is efficacious in just this sense, both for the women involved and for the possibilities it reveals to other women.

It would be a mistake, though, to move from a recognition of the empowering effects of the Poverty Game to a position that claimed it

[33]Bruce M. Landesman invokes these requirements in his critical comment "On Nancy Fraser's 'Women, Welfare, and the Politics of Need Interpretation,'" in *Hypatia: A Journal of Feminist Philosophy* 3 (Summer 1988): 158. My comments in this paragraph are prompted by Landesman's reading of Fraser's article. He brings abstract principles of autonomous reason to bear on a piece of work that explicitly demonstrates the oppressive practical consequences of such theoretical abstraction.

[34]Foucault, *Power/Knowledge*, p. 80.

[35]I argue this point at greater length in my "Tokenism," *Resources for Feminist Research* 16, 3 (1987); reprinted in Peta Tancred-Sheriff, ed., *Feminist Research: Prospect and Retrospect* (Montreal: McGill-Queen's University Press, 1988). There I claim that Foucault *equates* knowledge and power. I now see that the connections are more intricate.

as a hortatory model that all disadvantaged women should emulate to show that the liberal dream is realizable after all. Adopting such a position would be unjust and oppressive in a different way. In her early ecofeminist article, King claims: "Politically, ecofeminism opposes the ways that differences can separate women from each other through the oppressions of class, privilege, sexuality, race, and nationality."[36] Such an opposition is central to the dismay produced by living in a community that permits the welfare women's situation to exist; hence there are reasons to endorse King's point, cautiously. The caution is occasioned by a problem that her claim poses.

In recognition of their epistemic privilege, feminist philosophers and theorists might think that the way to promote a more ecologically viable community is for them to bring knowledge to women, or other oppressed groups, who do not know. It is tempting to believe that epistemically 'disadvantaged' women should be given the opportunity to benefit from the cognitive training and resources of the privileged. The point would be to obliterate their differences from *us* (where 'us' means 'those of us who do theory', represented as a unity for the sake of the argument). Based on the assumption that 'our' way would be best for them—a truth they would see if we helped them to know better—the project would aim at helping them to be just like us.[37] Such a mission is more problematic than promising. In interpreting as ignorance their lack of the training and resources that middle-class theorists have, it denigrates the knowledge and skills that economically oppressed women have had to acquire just to survive. A presumption that "those who do the theory know more about those who are theorized than vice versa"[38] would legitimate a blatant and unconscionable imperialism. In assuming that academic women, from their privileged place, can speak for other women and show them how they ought to live, the project would be as pernicious as any of the paternalistic practices feminists deplore. Re-dressing them in maternalistic garb neither disguises the oppressive effects of those practices nor dismantles the hierarchical assumptions that inform them.

[36]King, "Toward an Ecological Feminism," p. 124.

[37]The politics of 'we-saying' and of using the possessives 'our' and 'ours' is complex in feminist theory. I discuss it in greater detail below. Here I use 'our' and 'us' to refer, very loosely, to privileged white feminist philosophers, a group in which I claim membership.

[38]The phrase is from Maria C. Lugones and Elizabeth V. Spelman, "Have We Got a Theory for You! Feminist Theory, Cultural Imperialism, and the Demand for 'The Woman's Voice,'" in Marilyn Pearsall, ed., *Women and Values* (Belmont, Calif.: Wadsworth, 1986), p. 22.

It is important to frame the alternatives carefully. It would be politically irresponsible to argue that the oppressed just need to get on as best they can, for they are no concern of ours. But neither is it legitimate for the privileged simply to renounce their privilege in a guilt-ridden repudiation of hierarchy per se. There is no doubt that a community that immobilizes some of its members, by making access selectively difficult to everyday information/knowledge, is not a community where everyone has a fair chance. But unilateral renunciations and accusations would serve only to produce a stand-off in which each actor in the piece could present her position as fixed and argue abjectly or aggressively from it.[39] Women who have the insight and power that epistemic privilege confers need to acknowledge its value, so that they can draw on it to devise strategies for subverting oppressive structures. Analogously, women who do not have that (interim) power need to devise strategies of empowerment and resistance that do not "merely reflect the situation and values of the theorizer."[40] By finding ways of engaging in dialogue across the boundaries of their illusorily coherent positions, women can produce a collectively informed empowerment that neither group would realize alone. Foucault's conception of local strategies is useful here for articulating the functioning of the micropractices that were set in motion by some enlightened member(s) of the welfare organization in British Columbia and taken up, on their own terms, by the creators of the Poverty Game. Such microrevolutions could be more widely effected—with similar rippling spheres of influence. Philosophers and feminist theorists have skills they can devote to community activism. They can donate their critical and analytic skills to clarify problems and solutions from a differently informed perspective,[41] just as my Toronto doctor gives time and expertise to a sexual assault clinic;

[39]Biddy Martin and Chandra Talpade Mohanty note that "the assignment of fixed positions—the educator/critic (woman of color) and the guilty and silent listener (white woman)" in the Lugones and Spelman article "seem to exempt both parties from the responsibilities of working through the complex historical relations between and among structures of domination and oppression." Martin and Mohanty, "Feminist Politics: What's Home Got to Do with It?" in Teresa de Lauretis, ed., *Feminist Studies/Critical Studies* (Bloomington: Indiana University Press, 1986), p. 199.

[40]Lugones and Spelman, "Have We Got a Theory for You!" p. 27.

[41]Nye observes that even in the midst of struggles with "property law, prostitution, wife beating, homophobia, and racism," women seek ways of making sense of their experiences and of projecting effective programs of action (Nye, *Feminist Theory and the Philosophies of Man*, p. 2). It is not that theorists can do this *for* other women or can always do it better. But theorists often have insights that are not so readily available from the sites of specific struggles, and they are trained to put those insights to good use.

and a psychiatrist I know spends time counseling torture victims under the auspices of Amnesty International.[42]

It would be disingenuous to renounce all hierarchical differences between and among people or even to repudiate such differences between and among women. King's claim is therefore problematic: she apparently wants to obliterate differences as such. Yet the problem about hierarchy is that feminists are still in thrall to the influence of a dogmatic, rigid, and unidirectional malestream model. Reconceptualized in ecologically sensitive feminist terms, an acknowledgment of specific hierarchical differences can become a resource for political activism. There are people in every group—women in every group— who know better than others do, are wiser, more intelligent, more skilled, more capable in any number of ways, just as others manifest these or other capacities in greater measure than they do. It is difficult to see how women can get or give the knowledge, support, friendship, care, and power they need if they declare the political illegitimacy of such differences. But contrary to malestream conceptions of hierarchy, there is no single privileged place. Hence it is possible to eschew those aspects of the older conceptions that are damaging not just to women, but to any occupant of a 'lower' rung of the ladder. Feminist praxis, with its emphasis on the quality of 'second person' engagement, is amply able to effect reconstructions of epistemic hierarchy and authority.

The kinds of practice feminists can respect and work for are manifested in a doctor's willingness to explain to her patient whatever the patient wants to know, to indicate other directions she might investigate, to respect the patient's decisions about how to act on her advice, while refraining from claiming expertise where she has none. That same approach is apparent in a teacher's readiness to engage with students in cooperative, mutual investigations, and in a therapist's rejection of therapeutic power games. In none of these positions need the differences produced by knowledge and skill differential be denied. But neither is personal superiority affirmed, nor are the

---

[42]Paul Patton counts among the "non-discursive conditions of [the] production" of *Discipline and Punish* Foucault's 1971 involvement in the Groupe d'Information sur les Prisons (G.I.P.): "a movement of intellectuals, who were using their prestige . . . not to denounce the prison system in the name of any universal values, not, therefore, to claim to speak for the prisoners on their behalf, but rather to create conditions such that the prisoners could speak for themselves, and be heard." According to Patton, G.I.P. "demonstrated the possibility of direct engagement by intellectuals in local struggles, in a way that respected and made use of the specificity of the intellectuals concerned." Patton, "Of Power and Prisons," in Meaghan Morris and P. Patton, eds., *Michel Foucault: Power, Truth, Strategy* (Sydney: Feral Publications, 1979), pp. 109–110.

strengths and capacities of the occupant of the 'lesser' position minimized. Most feminists have experiences of such associations that they can use as resources for the development of innovative strategies. An ecological reading of this agenda would map the ways in which different members or aspects of an ecosystem draw on one another, in appropriate circumstances, for sustenance and support.

A noteworthy feature of such practices is the manner of listening they enjoin: a delicate process of taking the experiences of a female client/student seriously, while attempting to construct plausible reinterpretations of them. The process involves negotiation, seeking her confirmation of the resonance of alternative interpretations, attending to her denial of their pertinence. The person in the 'consulted' position must be aware of her fallibility in working with the other woman toward an interim, open-ended solution that is mutually plausible.

In this process, both parties have to resist the temptation to replace the old tyranny of an expertise deaf to experience with a new tyranny of experience hermetically sealed against criticism and reinterpretation. Some feminists maintain that I cannot be *wrong* about my experiences, that a person who challenges me violates my integrity. It is scarcely surprising that women who have lived with a centuries-old belief that they could not be *right* about what they were experiencing should insist on the validity of their experiences. Feminist inquirers need to realize that women can have credible access to what happens in their lives; theorists need to resist arrogating to themselves the power to define. Yet they need also to recognize that 'subjects' and clients frequently want 'expert' practitioners to produce interpretations. A theorist cannot always take experience at face value if she wants to construct an emancipatory analysis of its sources and structural location. Hence feminist inquirers have at once to resist treating experience as an inviolable, unconditioned datum and to resist claiming a position of theoretical expertise that exempts them from the need to understand.[43] A well-intentioned, self-abnegating liberal acceptance of feelings, experiences, and points of view at face value can inhibit an inquirer from engaging in critical analyses of their structure as social constructs, artifacts of politics and material/cultural circumstances.

[43]See Judith Grant, "I Feel Therefore I Am: A Critique of Female Experience as the Basis for a Feminist Epistemology," *Women and Politics* 7, 3 (1987): esp. pp. 108–111, for a discussion of some problems inherent in making women's experiences—either aggregated or reified—into a primary datum for the construction of a new epistemology. (Alison Wylie brought this article to my attention.)

Feminists have every reason to reject destructive, authoritarian critical tactics. But it would be a mistake to reject criticism per se. People with different histories, differently sensitive and astute, and differently trained can help one another to become conscious of aspects of their experiences that might have escaped their notice. Consciousness raising is still one of the most valuable tools of feminist inquiry. Hence the pertinence of Seller's observation: in isolation, I often do not know what my experiences are; privileged access is often unable to perform the role empiricists claim for it. If people who consult 'experts' could interpret their experiences with assurance and accuracy, they would not seek 'expert' advice. But a hierarchically deserved position of authority and expertise has to be assumed with an openness responsive to the establishment of trust, neither making it impossible for trust to be given nor requiring it. The process is ambiguous, but in that aspect it is free from the constraints of traditional hierarchy, hegemonic analysis, and the denial of differences. It is a matter, then, of developing communal strategies for mutual empowerment which grant intervention a place in open, nonpaternalistic, nonimperialistic conversations. At the same time, it is important to ensure that boundaries are respected, that making resources available is not designed to humiliate, that drawing on resources is never a degrading, compromising action. Globally stated, such a goal may sound utopian, but on a microlevel, such strategies have had considerable success. They do not require disadvantaged women to emulate the advantaged, but they make available new beginnings, from where the women *are*.

Alcoff's 'positionality' proposal, which I introduce in Chapter 5, suggests a productive way of converting specific positions into sites of emancipatory dialogue, while drawing on some of Foucault's best insights. The proposal is articulated partly out of Alcoff's enthusiasm for de Lauretis's 'identity politics', a position that explicitly takes its starting point from existing embodied, materially, culturally, and historically located selfhood. By contrast with essentialist conceptions of female subjectivity, for which a woman's 'own nature' is a given, a constant that she carries with her, so to speak, into every situation, a positionally defined identity is

> relative to a constantly shifting context, to a situation that includes a network of elements involving others, the objective economic conditions, cultural and political institutions and ideologies, and so on. . . . The position of women is relative and not innate, *and yet neither is it* "*undecidable.*" . . . [Moreover, it] can be actively utilized . . . as a loca-

tion for the construction of meaning. . . . [It is not] simply the place
where a meaning can be *discovered*.[44]

The promise of this proposal derives from its emphasis on recognizing, affirming, and interpreting a woman's position *as this woman*,
actively choosing what to make of her position, to the extent that the
situation and her resources allow. It explicitly affirms that, in plan-
ning political agendas, one cannot begin from an 'original position'.
Theories and actions are constructed in media res; they cannot abstract or extract themselves from their location without reconstituting
the theory/practice gulf that has left women's projects on the margins. There is nothing utopian or naive about the proposal, but neither is it defeatist. In repudiating essentialism, it resists acquiescing in
the view that circumstances and natures are given, once and for all,
hence that the only hope is in a—probably impossible and in any case
undesirable—transcendence of the sort de Beauvoir advocates.[45] In
its refusal of liberal individualist solutions, it is realistic in recognizing
the extent to which subjectivity is produced by environments, both
personal and natural, and the extent to which people can and cannot
take control of those environments. This is its ecological dimension.
    The proposal refuses the liberal assumption of human inter-
changeability, engaging at the outset with the myriad differences out
of which subjects must somehow construct meaning. Hence feminist
identity politics is continuous with other forms of identity politics
resistant to marginalization. Black, Aboriginal, Irish, and Hispanic
identity politics are obvious examples, with their projects of reclaiming knowledge, languages, cultures, and values threatened with ex-
tinction as 'subjugated knowledges'. These reclamations draw on resources that the homogenizing climates of liberal societies threaten to
efface. With other such political movements, feminist identity politics
can recognize the historical-cultural constitution of subjectivity and
assume responsibility for constructing the meaning of that identity
toward emancipatory ends.
    The proposal is that women identify themselves by their position
within a material, structural network of relations out of which meaning can be constructed and acted on. In their darkest moments, the
welfare women could be described as existing in negative space, in
direct consequence of their near-total isolation. Their relationships

---

[44]Alcoff, "Cultural Feminism," pp. 433–434, emphasis added.
[45]See Lloyd's discussion of conceptual barriers to female transcendence in *Man of
Reason*, pp. 93–102.

with their children, in the main, drain their identity, rather than en-hancing their sense of self. They are in no position to offer much to those children, either materially or emotionally, and their constant need to deny subtracts increasingly from their sense of self-worth. Nonetheless, the women who were able, even from that negative space, to respond to the possibilities that materialized with the wom-en's group managed to reconstruct their situations according to a new set of meanings that they used, ultimately, to transform their practical circumstances and their sense of self. Those possibilities spoke di-rectly to the women *as they were*: no impossible tasks were set or goals implied; no denial was required of their identity as welfare women, whose situation made it feasible for them to respond only to certain options. They find an opportunity to engage in a form of identity politics that requires them to deny nothing of who and what they are, but enables them to make that identity mean something new and positive—to move out of its most austere restrictions. The point is not that their new situation is immediately or entirely positive, but that unexpected openings make affirmative action possible, not in the macropolitical sense but in a micropolitical sense of notable significance.

Although Alcoff draws productively on Foucault in her articulation of identity politics as a locus of resistance, she finds in his work a set of problems that poses questions about whether his power-knowl-edge analyses can be useful for feminist political purposes. The prob-lems derive from her reading of the construction of subjectivity on which his genealogies center—from Foucault's claim, for example, that "one has to dispense with the constituent subject, to get rid of the subject itself."[46] Many feminists commend Foucault's rejection of *humanistic* subjectivity, which is demonstrably androcentric.[47] His stated aim to develop "an analysis which can account for the constitu-tion of the subject within a historical framework . . . a form of history [that does not have to] make reference to a subject which is either transcendental in relation to the field of events or runs in its empty sameness throughout the course of history"[48] has considerable femi-nist appeal. An analysis that explicitly refuses ahistorical, disengaged accounts of subjectivity cannot endorse essentialism in any of its vari-

---

[46]Foucault, *Power/Knowledge*, p. 117.

[47]My point is not that Foucault rejects it for its androcentricity, but that his rejection opens a space where feminist reconstructions can take place. (De Lauretis remarks that "Foucault's theory . . . excludes, though it does not preclude, the consideration of gender." De Lauretis *Technologies of Gender*, p. 3.)

[48]Foucault, *Power/Knowledge*, p. 117.

ants. The problem is that, in Foucault's analyses, the subject-as-*agent*—who is accorded implausibly dislocated, self-making capacities in autonomy-centered theories—is often difficult to locate. Foucault sometimes appears, in Alcoff's view, "totally to erase any room for maneuver by the individual within a social discourse or set of institutions." She is troubled by the possibility that, "following Foucault and Derrida, an effective feminism could only be a wholly negative feminism, deconstructing everything and refusing to construct anything."[49] And it is true that Foucault's analyses of the disciplinary, normalizing power of discursive practices often convey a sense that 'individuals' are so powerlessly swept along by the forces of hegemonic discourse that no space could be found for strategies of resistance.[50] Hence he sometimes appears to substitute for the old biological determinism of essentialism an equally constraining discursive determinism that is just as impervious to intervention.

There would be every reason to resist such a consequence of Foucault's position. Not only is the implication of powerlessness *theoretically* undesirable, but feminists have discovered, in practice, that creative resistance is possible and effective—perhaps not as effective as liberal ideology promises, yet much more effective than the more deterministic Foucauldian passages suggest. Foucault himself grants this point in his observation about local struggles. Hence a feminist elaboration of his genealogies needs to draw upon those features that can promote the creation of transformative strategies. The resistance of the inventors of the Poverty Game could not be explained on a stark reading of his position.

The question, then, is whether Foucault has to be read negatively on issues of agency and possibilities for occupying innovative, oppositional positions. I side, in what follows, with those who argue that he does not. Foucault's 1982 claims that his project is "to show people that they are much freer than they feel," that all of his analyses "are against the idea of universal necessities in human existence . . . [that they] show the arbitrariness of institutions and show which space of freedom we can still enjoy and how many changes can

---

[49]Alcoff, "Cultural Feminism," pp. 417, 418.

[50]See esp. *Discipline and Punish*, pt. 3, chaps. 1 ("Docile Bodies") and 2 ("The Means of Correct Training"). For example, Foucault writes: "Discipline 'makes' individuals; it is the specific technique of a power that regards individuals both as objects and as instruments of its exercise" (p. 170). "The individual is no doubt the fictitious atom of an 'ideological' representation of society; but he is also a reality fabricated by this specific technology of power that I have called 'discipline'. . . . power produces; it produces reality; it produces domains of objects and rituals of truth. The individual and the knowledge that may be gained of him belong to this production" (p. 194).

still be made" are evidence of his commitment to developing an emancipatory politics.[51] He concludes Volume 1 of *The History of Sexuality* with a set of ironic injunctions to ponder "the stratagems," "the ruses" by which sex has been transformed into discourse; to work imaginatively with the possibility that there can one day be "a different economy of bodies and pleasures" that, presumably, will render those ruses incomprehensible—and hence contestable.[52] Foucault's characterization of his project as a "critical ontology of ourselves, . . . a historico-practical test of the limits that we may go beyond,"[53] speaks frankly against implications of stasis and hard determinism. The plainly Socratic flavor of his pride in the fact that people see him as a "danger for the intellectual health of students"[54] attests to his persistent defiance of institutional hegemony and stability. Yet Foucault's demonstrations that people are 'freer than they feel' could not be read as straightforward reclamations of a humanistic, 'natural', and authentic self who is there to be discovered beneath the surface of discursive productions. So the problematic of subjectivity and agency remains contested among Foucault readers.[55]

This critical contestability is, I think, a response to Foucault's ambivalence about matters of subjectivity, which comes through in the ambiguities of many of the texts. Ambivalence and ambiguity are productive, not aporetic, postures in this instance, for they leave open places for developing interpretations that at once build on and depart from textual starting points.

One source of the ambiguity is that Foucault simultaneously re-

---

[51]Luther H. Martin, Huck Gutman, and Patrick H. Hutton, eds., *Technologies of the Self: A Seminar with Michel Foucault* (Amherst: University of Massachusetts Press, 1988), pp. 10, 11. True, the evidence is equivocal. Peter Dews, for example, notes the difficulty, for Foucault, of claiming normative superiority for any power-knowledge complex. Yet he argues that Foucault is "clearly unable entirely to abandon an emancipatory perspective." Dews, "The Return of the Subject in Late Foucault," *Radical Philosophy* 51 (Spring 1989): 38.

[52]Foucault, *History of Sexuality*, 1:159.

[53]Michel Foucault, "What Is Enlightenment?" in Paul Rabinow, ed., *A Foucault Reader* (New York: Pantheon, 1984), p. 47.

[54]Martin et al., eds., *Technologies of the Self*, p. 13.

[55]Joan Cocks claims that "Foucault *goes so far in denying the capacity for agency in everyone* that if one were to go all the way with him, any talk, not of dominative power but of dominating social groups, would be extremely hard to sustain." Cocks, *The Oppositional Imagination: Feminism, Critique, and Political Theory* (New York: Routledge, 1989), p. 48, emphasis added. By contrast, John Rajchman claims: "Foucault invents a philosophy which would 'free' our experience of ourselves or our subjectivity. . . . We are 'really' free because we can identify and change those procedures or forms through which our stories become true, because we can question and modify those systems which make (only) particular kinds of action possible, and because there is no 'authentic' self-relation we must conform to." Rajchman, *Michel Foucault: The Freedom of Philosophy* (New York: Columbia University Press, 1985), p. 122.

nounces the normative apparatus of the liberal humanist tradition and needs something very like it to show why certain power regimes invite opposition.[56] Hence he frequently appears to retain some of the fundamental assumptions of humanism while repudiating not just its (Cartesian) vocabulary,[57] but its belief in the possibility of access to an unconstructed, dislocated, transparent self. These gaps—these harkings back to the normativity of a reconstructed humanism—are places where affirmations of agency and accountability can enter. The tension created for the genealogical enterprise by this residual humanism that does not quite 'fit' is productive in that it permits feminists to draw on Foucault's analyses of power and situated subjectivity while escaping some of the constraints that the lack of an explicitly articulated normative apparatus entails. Crucial to elaborating the emancipatory potential of his work is a recognition that there is no incompatibility in arguing for a more opaque subjectivity than the humanistic tradition posits, and arguing, at the same time, in favor of reflexivity, of self-understanding as politically empowering. It is a *positional* self-understanding that he advocates: hence the aptness of his analyses for Alcoff's purposes. Constructing answers to the normative questions that Foucault leaves unanswered has to proceed from an acknowledgment that all positions are implicated in power relations; that it is nonetheless necessary to take up positions and to be "aware of the possibilities for new pleasures and new forms of resistance created in every confrontation."[58]

The very assertion that such awareness can be politically effective requires a Foucault reader to draw on the reciprocal dimension of constructive processes. It is clear, for example, that the panoptic regime of a disciplinary society works best—is most successful in producing 'docile bodies'—when members of the society are complicit, self-surveillant. Social/institutional discipline produces subjective self-discipline; subjective conformity confirms and consolidates social regimes. On this reciprocity the continuous, smooth, capillary circulation of power depends. Yet it is this very reciprocity that, to quote de Lauretis,"leaves open a possibility of agency and self-determination at the subjective and even individual level of micropolitical and everyday practices."[59] Subjects can refuse to reciprocate, to speak from within hegemonic discourse—a point that is crucial to

---

[56]I am indebted here to Fraser, *Unruly Practices*, chap. 1–3, and esp. pp. 29–33.
[57]Ibid., p. 38.
[58]The phrase is Biddy Martin's, in "Feminism, Criticism, and Foucault," in Diamond and Quinby, eds., *Feminism and Foucault*, p. 13. It is clear to Martin that "Foucault's work does not negate the possibility of concrete political struggle and resistance" (p. 12).
[59]De Lauretis, *Technologies of Gender*, p. 9.

the development of feminist resistance. Feminism produces a subject located at once inside and outside ideologies of gender, conscious of this 'doubled' location, empowered by the doubled vision this ambiguous position affords. The empowerment derives from an ability at once to see and criticize the ideology of gender, and to perceive imaginatively, creatively in its ambiguities and gaps, the possibilities of detachment, resistance, and transformation they allow. Having achieved a resistant detachment, feminists can develop strategies for engaging in those local struggles whose effectiveness Foucault himself acknowledges. Detachment, paradoxically, is always located, positioned, and *precisely* if not permanently so—hence Alcoff's crucial insistence that the position of women is not *undecided*. Her positionality proposal could allow Alcoff a route around the (intermittent) Foucauldian erasure of subjectivity: positioned subjects can be self-conscious and creative in reconstructing their situations. The successes of local struggles—and their capacity, as in the 1989 events in eastern Europe, to generate global transformations—attest to the promise of a subjectivity that works, collectively, from an emancipatory awareness of its positionality.

The articulation of the proposal as an identity politics at once sharpens its political edge and poses another set of problems. Without doubt it is necessary to name and occupy a specifically identifiable position in order to engage in identity politics. Yet the articulation of an identity politics is a complex task that has also to be performed ambiguously, framed as it is by the terms of another paradox that it would be premature to dissolve. As Denise Riley states the paradox, "both a concentration on and a refusal of the identity of 'woman' are essential to feminism. This its history makes plain."[60] The problem extends beyond the identity 'woman' to affirmations and attributions of identity more widely conceived.

'The identity crisis in feminist theory'[61] is, I think, a crisis on two levels. On one level, it is a crisis about how a woman can identify herself as a feminist within one of the options that 'second wave' feminism makes available, about the implications of labeling oneself, of identifying with feminist theoretical positions.[62] But the crisis is

[60]Denise Riley, *"Am I That Name?" Feminism and the Category of Women in History* (Minneapolis: University of Minnesota Press, 1988), p. 1.

[61]Readers will recall that the title of the Alcoff article I have been discussing is "Cultural Feminism versus Post-Structuralism: The Identity Crisis in Feminist Theory."

[62]Alcoff convincingly reduces the categories to two, classifying 'liberal', 'radical', and 'socialist' feminists as 'cultural feminists', constituted as a group by their varied belief in a distinctive 'femaleness'—that is to be celebrated, for socialist and radical feminists, or assimilated into male-defined structures, for liberals. As a group (and

also located at a subterranean level, below (hence before) the moment of political self-identification: namely, as a crisis in the very possibility of claiming an identity as a woman, as a feminist simpliciter. This is the crisis Riley points to. The question is no longer simply about *which* feminism can command allegiance, but how, in an intellectual climate in which the instability of labels and selves is constantly declared, one can claim an identity at all. Insufficiently nuanced affirmations and assignments of identity, with the essentialist, stereotyped implications they carry, have been instrumental in marginalizing women in the name of their differences from men, and in marginalizing 'minority' or 'Other' women in the name of their differences from a newly installed feminist norm. The 'second wave's' early cooptation of the experiences of black, working-class, and lesbian women in the hegemonic theoretical discourses of white middle-class heterosexual feminism is just one example of the problems inherent in identity claims. Even particularized, carefully specified identities tend to solidify, to acquire a nostalgic appeal in their capacity to offer a "home," a resting place, an illusory coherence and stability.[63] Yet the emancipatory necessity of claiming identities, of infusing them with political content, and of constructing sites for action that is not merely passive resistance, but active reconstruction, cannot be overestimated.

Every reader of this text will know that feminist theory was born and has developed out of a political urgency to address issues of women's oppression. Its initial emphasis was on a commonality in women's experiences: whatever their social, political, or economic circumstances, women were alike both in their femaleness and in their oppression. These were the universals—femaleness and oppression—on which early 'second wave' feminism turned: the rhetoric of sisterhood captures its pivotal conviction. Like everyday linguistic universals such as 'chair', 'rock', and 'tree', these universals derive from particulars; and like physical-object universals, they

---

Alcoff apologizes for the simplified taxonomy) these 'female essentialists' contrast with poststructuralists (posthumanists, antiuniversalists, postessentialists), who repudiate essential femaleness and deconstruct subjectivity—not destructively, but to uncover and name the processes of its structurings in social, racial, class, political, and other contexts.

[63]I allude here to the title of Martin and Mohanty's article "Feminist Politics: What's Home Got to Do with It?" Alert to the problematic of false unities, Martin and Mohanty argue: "When one conceives of power differently, in terms of its local, institutional, discursive formations, of its positivity, and in terms of the production rather than suppression of forces, then unity is exposed to be a potentially repressive fiction" (p. 204).

efface the particularities of the particulars in the derivation process. Noting the intractability of a language of pure particulars reveals these effects as an inevitable by-product of the construction of universals.[64] Perhaps with physical objects these effects are insignificant: at least they are differently so. But for feminists, the old universals have outlived their usefulness. Neither as epistemological nor as political tools can they serve the unifying purposes of constructing a platform for political action that feminists once envisaged for them. Hence affirmations of women's commonality yielded, in the 1980s, to calls for increasingly nuanced analyses of differences among women— indeed, of differences *within woman*.[65]

Engagement in identity politics requires care, then, but it need not invite gloom and despair.[66] De Lauretis, who is one of its most articulate articulators, writes of its "radical epistemological *potential*," which she elaborates as

> the possibility . . . to conceive of the social subject and of the relations of subjectivity to sociality in another way: a subject constituted in gender, to be sure, though not by sex differences alone, but rather across language and cultural representations; a subject en-gendered in the experiencing of race and class, as well as sexual, relations; a subject, therefore, not unified but rather multiple, and not so much divided as contradicted.[67]

This multiplicity, this contradiction, generates a problematic of identity with which the humanist tradition did not have to contend, because all of its master narratives are written with interchangeable, whole, unified selves in the main speaking parts.

I have noted the feminist appeal of postessentialist structurings of subjectivity. There is not the slightest doubt about who the main characters are who populate the pages of humanism. Nor is there any doubt about the parts women play in relation to them.[68] The essen-

---

[64]I note the intractability of a language of pure particulars in my discussion of stereotypes in Chapter 5.

[65]De Lauretis, *Technologies of Gender*, p. 2.

[66]I am thinking of the despair Hartsock evinces when she asks: "Why is it that just at the moment when so many of us who have been silenced begin to demand the right to name ourselves, to act as subjects rather than objects of history, that just then the concept of subjecthood becomes problematic?" Hartsock, "Foucault on Power," *Feminism/Postmodernism*, p. 163.

[67]De Lauretis, *Technologies of Gender*, p. 3.

[68]There is a telling asymmetry here: talk of women's relation to them flows easily and imperceptibly, but talk of their relation to women would be awkward, uneasy.

tialist, universal pretensions of Enlightenment humanism created easily specifiable, 'natural' spaces for women to occupy, and generated complex power structures for keeping them there, while ensuring that they would not notice their disempowerment. Postessentialist subjectivity refuses the coherence of humanistic labeling to affirm a multiple subjectivity liberated from the constraints of the old dogmas and the political processes they inform. It may seem, therefore, to offer just the emancipatory route that feminists require.

Even as they reveal their promise, however, postessentialist theories force feminists to recognize the import of Riley's question. The name 'woman' is a sociopolitical construct, not a mere label. It is encrusted with all of the meanings that have provided the rationale for women's disadvantaged sociopolitical positions, yet it also designates the attributes that feminists seek to reclaim as women's strengths. Hence Spelman cautions that "though all women are women, no woman is only a woman. Those of us who have engaged in it must give up the hunt for the generic woman—the one who is all and only woman, who by some miracle of abstraction has no particular identity in terms of race, class, ethnicity, sexual orientation, language, religion, nationality."[69] Whatever identity a woman claims, there will always be a part of her history and location that does not fit and may provide the occasion for her marginalization. Nor is it possible just to ask her, for post-Freudian postessentialist analyses reject the surety of privileged access, of a translucent self-consciousness that would allow a person always to be a reliable witness on her own behalf. Yet if women cannot claim reasonably coherent (if not static) identities that incorporate an acknowledgment that "one is always *somewhere*, and limited,"[70] it is not easy to see how feminists can continue to develop responses that challenge the persistent hegemony of white male societies and institutions. The tension in feminist theory, to which I have been referring throughout this book, exerts its pull strongly here. Politically effective action, on however 'micro' a level, requires its agents to assume specific positions, identities, allegiances, for which they can claim responsibility and to which they are answerable. Feminists need, often, to be able—clearly and self-critically—to answer Riley's question in the affirmative.

Speaking in the first-person plural, as 'we', claiming a collective identity, poses a different kind of problem. The contestedness of the

---

[69]Spelman, *Inessential Woman*, p. 187.
[70]The phrase is from Bordo's "Feminism, Postmodernism, and Gender-Skepticism," in Nicholson, ed., *Feminism/Postmodernism*, p. 145.

category 'woman' destabilizes the site from which early feminists were able, quite confidently, to speak collectively as women, as 'we'. Yet any possibility of sustaining an allegiance to an ongoing, if changing, women's movement makes it imperative to find ways of negotiating the politics of 'we-saying'. The politics is delicate for feminists, yet it is a simple matter for mainstream epistemologists, to an extent that the contrast is instructive.

Richard Foley's *Theory of Epistemic Rationality* illustrates my point. In this undisputed, state-of-the-art work of epistemology,[71] Foley bases his theory on a criterion of first-person persuasiveness, calling it a "subjective foundationalism." He does not worry that its 'subjective' aspect will force him into subjectivism or solipsism, precisely, it would seem, because of the blithe confidence with which he can say 'we'. Exemplary knowledge claims are presented in the standard 'S knows that p' rubric; and Foley's appeals to S's normality—to his being 'one of us', 'just like the rest of us'—to his not having "crazy, bizarre [or] outlandish beliefs," or "weird goals," "weird perceptions,"[72] evidently warrant his assumption that in speaking for S he is speaking for everyone—or at least for 'all of us'. There are no problems, no politics of 'we-saying': this is an epistemology that masks its political investedness, even to its own gaze. In so doing, it consigns to epistemic oblivion anyone who would profess a 'crazy, bizarre, or outlandish belief'. The book is instructive for its revelation of the presumption of uttering an inclusive, unself-conscious 'we'.

For feminists, such utterances are not so easy. Recently, I participated in a collaborative ethics project with four other feminist philosophers.[73] We produced an interwoven (interleaved) text out of a sporadic correspondence, interspersed with a series of cooperative working sessions. The processes were positive; initially, it seemed that we could have spoken in unison, have said 'we' almost as blithely as Foley does. But the aspects of our positions that did not fit insisted increasingly on being heard, until it was clear that we could not always use the first-person plural; sometimes we had to say 'I', differentiating ourselves explicitly from the others in so doing. It was at once a necessary move and one that produced unease about lack of cohesiveness, even about political disloyalty. The problem of how to

---

[71]I refer to Foley's book in Chapter 1, n. 7, and again in Chapter 5.

[72]Foley, *Theory of Epistemic Rationality*, pp. 114, 140.

[73]Part of this project is published as Lorraine Code, Maureen Ford, Kathleen Martindale, Susan Sherwin, and Deborah Shogan, "Some Issues in the Ethics of Collaborative Work," in *Explorations in Feminist Ethics: Theory and Practice*, ed. Eve Browning Cole and Susan Coultrap-McQuinn (Bloomington: Indiana University Press, 1991).

speak together in 'a feminist voice' faced us on the levels both of how to identify the feminism with which we were aligning ourselves and how to identify ourselves as women and as feminists. Only by articulating and rearticulating our positions in an ongoing dialogue are we learning to talk across these differences. In the process we have learned that identities can be interrogated and renegotiated, as the ongoing consciousness raising of feminist practice dislocates us and requires us to relocate ourselves more self-consciously. But not every relocation is equally possible for everyone—or equally desirable. A noncoercive politics of difference has to come to terms with this fact.

Finally, engagement in identity politics raises a set of moral-political problems of a rather different order, problems inherent also in Foucault's work. The central issue, which I have already signaled, is the lack of a conceptual apparatus in whose terms one can distinguish, evaluatively, between the identity politics espoused and practiced by feminists, blacks, and native people, and the practices of REAL women, white supremacists, the IRA—or even sexists—all of whom make strong claims for their identities and values which, superficially, resemble claims made for feminist identity politics.[74] A similar problem attached to the celebration of *engagement* in the early Sartrean philosophy: just as it became clear that Sartrean engagement *tout simple* could not merit full approval, for it had morally reprehensible forms—fascism was commonly cited—so it is, too, with identity politics. Because it is potentially problematic, morally, its practice always demands moral evaluation; because of its affinities with the exclusionary features of communitarian politics—where identities always create Others, produce we/they distinctions—it cannot be practiced monologically. Foucault imports a loose 'falsifiability' test into his work, on the subject of oppression: it emerges, implicitly, that many sorts of oppression are deplorable; hence, perhaps by default, that freedom is desirable.[75] But the unstated criteria seem to be variants on the old humanist celebrations of freedom, even though the

[74]Citing Minnie Bruce Pratt, Martin and Mohanty ask: "When we justify the homogeneity of the women's community in which we move on the basis of the need for community, the need for home, what . . . distinguishes our community from the justifications advanced by women who have joined the Klan for 'family, community, and protection?'" Martin and Mohanty, "Feminist Politics," p. 209.

[75]Gary Gutting concludes, for example, that Foucault's "techniques of critical history provide a model for how we can maintain our awareness of the dangers implicit in all bodies of knowledge and effectively oppose those that, at a given time, have become sources of evil" (*Michel Foucault's Archaeology of Scientific Reason* [Cambridge: Cambridge University Press, 1989], p. 288). Whether or not Foucault can make the further move of providing criteria for discerning 'evil' remains an unanswered question.

constructed, localized, specified freedoms he gestures toward are not quite the same old humanist freedoms. Alcoff's failure to offer the normative guidelines that contestable identities call for does not vitiate her proposal, but it leaves gaps that need to be filled. The task of filling them adequately is too large for the present context, but ecological analyses provide an entry into the problematic. The projects of white supremacists and sexists thwart the realization of the mutually sustaining societies that ecological commitments promote. Feminist projects align well with those commitments and can enlist them in affirmations of political identities. That alignment reveals that feminist struggles, like ecological ones, are by no means confined within the local boundaries of their strategic articulation. Though they may begin there, their impact can be global.

Philosophers, Theorists, and Others

It would be difficult to underestimate the role that knowledge plays in the welfare women's capacities to take up new positions from which they can embark on new initiatives. For this reason, I return to the problematic of epistemic privilege to see how its structures can be enlisted for feminist political ends. It does not follow, naively, from Alcoff's proposal, that women have wide open choices, unconstrained by circumstance; but she argues for the possibility of gaining control over "internalized oppressive mechanisms" whose capacity to "hold us in check" is powerful.[76] Epistemologically, one of the most intransigent of such mechanisms, I would suggest, is rooted in the belief, embedded in western society at least since the time of the ancient Greeks, that women cannot think. Such a conviction is bound to be especially strong in a woman down on her luck, who lives in a society that makes it entirely her fault. She is faced with the assumption that, like every other self-realizing individual, she should have been able to 'make it' entirely by her own efforts. As the invention of the Poverty Game has shown, extrication from the tenacity of this sort of mechanism is fundamental to developing transformative strategies for restructuring one's social and political position.

Engagement in positionality and identity politics works somewhat differently for women of epistemic privilege, and particularly for women philosophers. One of the most significant aspects of identity politics, contrasted with the homogenizing, macropolitical theories

---

[76]Alcoff, "Cultural Feminism," p. 432 n. 67.

commonly taught in the academy, is that it requires people to work from their specificity in creating an emancipatory position. Rather than following the traditional philosophical path of suppressing that specificity for the sake of constructing universal, global theories untainted by the untidiness and impurity of taking particularity into account, identity politics derives explicitly from "one's personal, subjective engagement in the practices, discourses, and institutions that lend significance (value, meaning, and affect) to the events of the world."[77] It is political not in the sense that it requires people to take a stand dogmatically committed to demonstrating the truths of what they already know, but in its commitment to analyzing, trying to understand the specific, material conditions that constrain marginalized groups of women. Critical reexaminations of 'our' philosophical identity, such as many feminist philosophers are currently engaged in, can create space for the construction of positions from which a rapprochement of mutual understanding can be effected between situations of epistemic disadvantage and privilege and across other divisive differences.

Women who identify themselves as philosophers have evidently repudiated the assumption that women cannot think. It has been an uneasy rejection. Historically, some women have succeeded in performing it only through the mediation of a male mentor (as with Abelard's Eloise or Descartes's Elizabeth), in a process Michele Le Doeuff calls an "erotico-theoretical transference."[78] Others have absorbed the tradition of their teachers and mentors so well that their philosophical discourse is indistinguishable from that of the male philosophical establishment both in style and in the problems they address. Hence women who can think like men have, in the last half century, become increasingly visible, and more or less acceptable, in mainstream philosophy. Many of them have succeeded to the extent that they have acquiesced in the exclusions and suppressions in 'received' philosophical discourse. Yet given that their choice may have been either to reason according to the established model or to be refused acknowledgment as practitioners of professional philosophy, the point is not to blame them. Rather, it is to understand the exclusionary and assimilationist powers of hegemonic discourse in order to subvert them, to reconstruct the philosophical 'community'.

The main assumption to be countered is that there can be a single, monolithic philosophy that yields access to the Truth, and that all

---

[77]Ibid., p. 423.
[78]Michele Le Doeuff, "Women and Philosophy," p. 2.

rival discourses should be dismissed or suppressed as diversions from the true path. As Le Doeuff observes: "Up to now, logocentrism has left its mark on the entire history of philosophy, separating this history from what could be a 'history of ideas' and turning it into a 'fundamental' thesis, that of the power of true discourse. A discourse is philosophical if it expresses the power of philosophy (confused with the possession of true *knowledge*)." That discourse smooths over communality and differences in the name of the autonomy of reason. It takes as its model the reasoning of self-actualizing individuals who are committed to developing, monologically, a complete, error-free, theoretical position that betrays no insecurities, reveals no gaps in understanding, and is perfectly clear about its self-determined rightness and consistency. By contrast, feminist philosophy in Le Doeuff's conception is informed by a recognition that " 'I do not do everything on my own', that I am a tributary to a collective discourse and knowledge, which have done more toward producing me than I shall contribute in continuing to produce them."[79] The ecological flavor of this observation is unmistakable. The river imagery captures the sense that this discourse is fluid, moving, and that as it flows it gathers from, and is a resource for, its environment.

In Chapter 3 I affirmed the creative possibilities of a style of moral analysis and practice which would be committed to doing without a moral theory.[80] Starting from the contention that moral *theories* close off possibilities of understanding and of nuanced judgment, I argued that a suspension of claims on behalf of theory creates space for critical practice, committed to experimenting with the implications and effectiveness of different ways of being moral philosophers. Systematic epistemological theories have an analogous exclusionary history. Doing without an *epistemological* theory creates space for the critical practice necessary to the development of analyses of knowledge that can take into account the positions people occupy on the epistemic terrain, who need to be variously resourceful in their occupancy.

Maintaining a creative tension within this diversity of meanings and epistemic 'products' enables feminists to resist the closure of theory building, to refuse techniques designed to make the strange familiar by slotting it into preconstructed categories or spaces, where

---

[79]Ibid., pp. 8, 11.

[80]In the discussion there I draw on Baier's article "Doing without a Moral Theory," in her *Postures of the Mind*.

its uniqueness is obliterated. McClintock's respect for difference, which I discuss in Chapter 4, illustrates the point, as does the positioning and repositioning in the moral domain in which Gilligan's subjects engage. At once committed and self-critical, such practices interrogate monolithic ideologies, methodologies, and categories, while guarding against collapse into a supremely tolerant relativism that amounts merely to epistemic and political quietism. Feminist epistemological projects, informed by ecological principles, have to be mapped out of a commitment to creating "institutions and communities that will not permit *some* groups of people to make determinations about reality for *all* as Bordo puts it."[81] They will aim to engage with differences that strengthen community and to develop political strategies sufficiently contextualized to address diverse experiences of dominance and subjugation. In inveighing against oppression, these practices point to the necessity of constructing revisionist normative stances; yet they remain open to questioning, to being accountable, and to renegotiating any position they may adopt. The project demands an ongoing consciousness of the fact that an inquirer is implicated in every inquiry and is as culturally and historically constituted as any of her allies, collaborators, or subjects of study. That feminists have been so successful in generating such creative and self-aware projects should dispel any idea that women cannot think.

The next step in the political process of rethinking women's capacities to think is a move into the conversational mode that I discuss in Chapter 5. There I maintain that thinking, both with other people and by oneself, is conversational: with others, because inhabitants of this postessentialist age are in a position to think of themselves as constituted in relationships; by oneself, because inhabitants of this post-Freudian age are aware of the dynamic interaction of the 'voices' within their psyches. According to Young-Bruehl, thinking becomes "a constant interconnecting of all sorts of representations of our experiences as we hear ourselves and others and reflexively interpret ourselves in and through novel conjunctions or conversational moments . . . if we take this idea seriously, *live* this idea richly, we cannot become . . . mental monists. And . . . we cannot become prescriptivists of the mental realm."[82] Extending these ideas across situations of unequal privilege has the potential to set in motion a conver-

---

[81]Bordo, "Feminism, Postmodernism, and Gender-Scepticism," p. 142.
[82]Young-Bruehl, "Education of Women as Philosophers," p. 216.

sational format in which there are no absolutely privileged places or participants, yet no participant need deny the unique contribution that her interim privilege or lack thereof enables her to make.

Productive conversations have to be open, moving, and resistant to arbitrary closure; sensitive to revisions of judgement; prepared to leave gaps where no obvious consensus is possible. They will be characterized by what Moira Gatens calls "productive ambiguity"[83]— an idea rich in possibilities, and anathema to the philosophical tradition. The emphasis on ambiguity signals the thoroughly interpretive tenor of such conversations: a hermeneutic dimension committed not to seeking a single, privileged *Urtext* beneath conversational variants, nor aiming primarily at a fusion of horizons in which differences would be dissolved, but to working dialogically to preserve the best features of the consciousness raising that participated at the birth of the women's movement. No assumptions can be made, from the outset, about the commensurability of the languages spoken or the experiences spoken about, even when the participants ostensibly speak 'the same' language. Yet such a process is peculiarly effective in countering the isolation to which Seller refers, in which one does not know what her experiences are. It goes beyond the tyranny of 'experientialism' to draw on the strengths of women's devalued conversational arts—beyond the trivialization of gossip, the denigration of 'second person' relationships, to acknowledge their mutually sustaining, ecological function—and their truth-producing capacities. In productive, reciprocally interpretive conversations, rapprochements could be effected among women of disparate epistemic and political circumstances.

My claim is not that philosophers have to be the initiators, seeking out epistemically 'less privileged' women to engage them in conversation. In fact, the Poverty Game is an effective emancipatory tool partly because it subverts an established pattern. There the privileged (charitably) seek out the less privileged to find out how it is where they are, a pattern that replicates the old social-scientific observer/observed hierarchy and attests to a belief that the 'privileged' themselves are nowhere—at least nowhere that makes *their* position contestable. The game, by contrast, is the first move in a conversation that the welfare women initiate, inviting economically and epistemically advantaged people—women and men—to enter a conversational format patterned on their rules. The level of engagement, of

[83]Moira Gatens, "Feminism, Philosophy, and Riddles without Answers," in Carole Pateman and Elizabeth Gross, eds., *Feminist Challenges*, p. 28.

struggle, that participation in this conversation requires leaves no position absolutely privileged or uncontested. Yet, when it works, it fosters an understanding from which ongoing, dialogic negotiations can develop across hitherto resistant structural boundaries. It would be foolish for the participants to become careless about the politics of 'we-saying'—to claim to understand everything after playing the game. But it would be equally trivializing of the efforts of the participants of both 'sides' of the conversation to minimize its effectiveness in revealing commonalities as well as differences.

The larger project, which draws at once on Foucault's analyses of local struggles and micro-political intrications of power and knowledge, and on positionality and identity politics, is to remap the epistemic terrain into numerous, fluid conversations. Some of them will merge into one another and reshape one another, some of them will reveal gaps in others, will take place in the interstices; others will be engaged in specific and specialized research whose results are analyzed, interpreted, reinterpreted, still others will mount explicitly political campaigns whose effects, again, are caught up in many other conversations. Living one's life as a feminist is something like this, and there is no reason why the process could not be more widely generalized. In a sense I have been engaged in conversation about the welfare women with myself ever since I played the Poverty Game. It has revealed gaps and ambiguities in my feminist politics— ambiguities that produce different ways of engaging with these issues and that enter my other conversations at many levels. Moving this conversation from its present internal location to a position of actual engagement with other women demands an approach simultaneously responsive to differences and productive of mutually supportive dialogue.

It is no coincidence, as questions about how to articulate identities across experiential differences are acquiring such urgency for feminist theorists, that at the same time 'a biographical/autobiographical turn' is occurring, whose relevance to problems of identity, difference, and positionality cannot be overestimated.[84] Autobiography, Brodsky and Schenck observe, "localizes the very program of much feminist theory—the reclaiming of the female subject—even as it foregrounds the central issue of contemporary critical thought—the problematic

[84]The appearance within just a few months in 1988 of Carolyn Heilbrun, *Writing a Woman's Life*; Shari Benstock, ed., *The Private Self: Theory and Practice of Women's Autobiography* (Chapel Hill: University of North Carolina Press, 1988); Brodzki and Schenck, *Life/Lines* as additions to a growing corpus of biographical/autobiographical analysis must be more than just a coincidence.

status of the self."[85] It would be a mistake to characterize this 'turn' as a unified project, since it works to fracture illusory unities. Nor is it an attempt to reclaim a place for privileged access after all, this time through appeals to first-person utterances that are more elaborated, yet differ only quantitatively, not qualitatively, from the old empiricist, foundational, privileged access claims. Rather, autobiography becomes an exercise at once of critical tellings and critical readings. There is no final, definitive, or incontestable autobiography, but neither are autobiographies undecided, pure text. They speak a subjectivity that is specifically located, yet open to interpretation, dialogue, and analysis, on the basis of the positions it occupies and those it refuses.

Nor would it be legitimate to read women's autobiographies as efforts to construct a representative self who could stand for all women of a certain 'kind' or 'group', rather as Foley's knower stands for those of us—or them—who are 'normal'. In fact, female autobiography is distinct from the traditional masculine genre on precisely this point. A female autobiography is no mirror of a woman who is a spokeswoman for her sex or her era. Female autobiography cannot speak in "the Western, transcendent, and masculine norm of autobiographical selfhood,"[86] not just because it is not masculine, but because that script is not available for women. Because many women's biographies/autobiographies reveal the bits of a woman's life that do not fit the society's master narratives, they interrogate those narratives, break through their smooth surfaces, expose their presuppositions to doubt. Feminist readings of autobiographies in their insistent specificity challenge "the dream of a common language," calling attention, to what Biddy Martin calls "the impossibility of neutral or unmediated speech."[87] At the same time, it would be incorrect to cast this 'turn' as a withdrawal into auto/biography, occasioned by despair over lost community. In its critical dimension, for reader, writer, and critic, auto/biography works as a form of address, an engagement that speaks from a specified position and makes itself available for uptake, critique, and multiple interpretive readings.

[85]Brodzki and Schenck, *Life/Lines*, pp. 1–2. Joan Scott likewise sees in biographies "the best efforts . . . so far . . . to examine the ways in which gendered identities are substantively constructed and [to] relate that to a range of activities, social organizations, historically specific cultural representations." Scott, "Is Gender a Useful Category of Historical Analysis?" in Joan Wallach Scott, *Gender and the Politics of History* (New York: Columbia University Press, 1989), p. 44.

[86]Brodzki and Schenck, *Life/Lines*, p. 4.

[87]Martin, "Lesbian Identity," p. 96. *The Dream of a Common Language* refers to Adrienne Rich's collection (1978).

Hence Carolyn Steedman's *Landscape for a Good Woman*[88] is at once an autobiography and a biography of her mother, and an exercise in sociopolitical analysis. Steedman demonstrates that neither her mother's life nor her own childhood fits into the rhetorical scripts that designate woman's place and venerate motherhood. In consequence, she casts doubt on the viability of the scripts, rather than constructing the lives she tells as aberrations. They are neither bizarre nor weird, yet they disrupt the categories to reveal their instability. Keller's biography of Barbara McClintock achieves something similar in detailing McClintock's approaches to the construction of a knowledge that achieves the highest intellectual accolade—the Nobel prize—yet is produced out of nonstandard methods and attitudes.[89] These studies point to the arbitrariness of the norms against which they speak, revealing their *partiality* in two senses: (a) they are neither whole nor all-encompassing; (b) they are politically partial (= partisan) despite their self-proclaimed neutrality. The point is not to find in any single autobiographical narratives 'an answer', 'a solution' to the identity crisis. It is to find ways of understanding "how individual self-reflection and critical practice might translate into the building of political collectivity."[90]

For reasons I have discussed throughout this book, engagement in critical practices and conversations that are committed to the construction of collectivities needs to start from a readiness to model political, working relationships and alliances on the principles of friendship. Here it is especially clear that a maternal thinking model will not do, and its inappropriateness attests further to its inadequacy as a paradigm for feminist practice. The power and dependency differentials that characterize stereotypical mother-child relations during the immaturity of the child, and often throughout the relationship, have to be overcome if the relationships are to mature into a mutual respect and reciprocity conducive to good friendship. Rarely does that differential disappear without leaving inhibiting marks. Inequalities of status, power, and privilege across diverse histories and positions—for example, between middle-class professional women and women on welfare—would condemn relationships modeled on maternal thinking to replicate, in female form, the paternalistic and patronizing postures that members of 'higher' social orders have consistently assumed toward their 'lesser' brothers and sisters. To struc-

[88]Carolyn Steedman, *Landscape for a Good Woman* (London: Virago, 1986).
[89]Keller, *Feeling for the Organism*.
[90]Martin and Mohanty, "Feminist Politics," p. 210.

ture *chosen* personal encounters on that model would be disempowering for all participants and hence politically ineffective. It would be equally outrageous for middle-class professional white women to assume that they can bestow their friendship on less privileged women and that the bestowal will be gratefully received. The rhetoric of such thinking perpetuates the initial power differential under the guise of a friendship that is no friendship at all, but an act of demeaning charity.

Lugones and Spelman's project of writing together "without presupposing any unity of expression or of experience" approaches the question of how such friendships and conversations could productively be structured. Writing "in a Hispana voice," Lugones contends that the only motive out of which Anglo women could legitimately join with Hispanic women to interpret the relations between women's experiential stories and theorizers' interpretations of them is a motive of friendship.[91] Self-interested, conscience-appeasing motives and the common theorizer's motives of remaking the other in her own image are barred.[92] Only by taking the trouble to know other people well, in *their* circumstances, sensitive to what their circumstances mean *to them*, can people participate responsibly in each other's lives. It is not that the disadvantaged—or the privileged—are always right, but rather that understanding has to precede criticism and take it seriously. Friendship and its analogues can provide a valid context for such conversational engagement.

Shifting conversational locations on an epistemic map can be evaluated qualitatively, according to the extent that they demonstrate a commitment to mutual understanding at once ready to acknowledge its power and to assent to its incompleteness. Such conversations will be characterized by conscious efforts on the part of each participant to find out how her interlocutors understand their positions on a complex epistemic-political map and to be responsible about her self-presentation. As I note in Chapter 5, discussions of responsibility often have a bad odor in feminist circles, for women have been assigned oppressive responsibilities for so long, in patriarchal societies, that the very word signals one more female burden. Yet quite a different responsibility consideration is at issue here, a responsibility the creators of the Poverty Game *want* to be able to take. They need to

---

[91]Lugones and Spelman, "Have We Got a Theory for You!" pp. 20, 22–24.

[92]Hence, for example, Gail Stenstad notes that middle-class American feminists who support birth control in the Third World because they perceive continuous pregnancies as oppressive, have been surprised to note that the Third World women see this intervention as genocidal. Stenstad, "Anarchic Thinking," *Hypatia: A Journal of Feminist Philosophy* 3 (Summer 1988): 98.

know well enough that they can take responsibility for their lives, according to the best understanding of their abilities and circumstances.

Like everyone else, they will have to accept some of the requisite knowledge on authority, for not even the epistemically super-privileged have the expertise, time, and resources to do the primary research independently that must inform their most important decisions. People have to be able to judge which 'expert' conversations merit confidence and trust: they have to situate themselves within many of the ongoing conversations before they can become clear about what they need to reject. But such dependence need not be abject. Seller draws a valuable contrast between the practice of an expert who *tells people* what is true and an exchange in which views are tried out, considered, and reconsidered. In the best forms of teaching, for example, people are introduced "to ideas they can play with and use (or ignore) to create and correct their own views"[93]— and to which they contribute their ideas, from which the 'experts' are prepared also to learn. Conversations like this must have prompted the creation of the Poverty Game: the welfare workers were prepared to challenge existing practices, to make ideas, possibilities, and knowledge available, to listen responsively and responsibly to proposals in which the proposers had much of themselves at stake; the welfare recipients were able to imagine how their proposals could transform their lives and had the courage to articulate them and pursue ways of bringing them into effect. People need to be in positions to know and to live in societies that ensure that everyone can occupy such positions. The creation of the Poverty Game shows that such a dream is not merely utopian.[94]

[93]Seller, "Toward a Politically Adequate Epistemology," p. 174.

[94]Susan J. Hekman's *Gender and Knowledge: Elements of a Postmodern Feminism* (Boston: Northeastern University Press, 1990), which I read after completing this book, is an important contribution to discussions of the significance of Foucault's work for feminist epistemological inquiry.

CHAPTER EIGHT

A Feminist Epistemology?

The product of my investigations in this book cannot unequivocally be called 'a feminist epistemology'. Indeed, my principal conclusion is that the question whether a feminist epistemology is possible or desirable must be left unanswered. So seemingly outrageous a claim, at this stage, demands an explanation.

As long as 'epistemology' bears the stamp of the postpositivist, empiricist project of determining necessary and sufficient conditions for knowledge and devising strategies to refute skepticism, there can be no feminist epistemology. I have shown that the conceptions of knowledge and subjective agency that inform this project are inimical to feminist concerns on many levels: ontological, epistemological, moral, political. Ideals central to the project—ideals of objectivity, impartiality, and universality—are androcentrically derived. Their articulation maps onto typical middle-class white male experiences to suppress the very possibility that the sex of the knower could be epistemologically significant. But my project has been to take that possibility very seriously and to argue that once its implications are examined, 'the epistemological project' will demand reconstruction. It would not be possible to develop a feminist epistemology that retained allegiance to the pivotal ideas around which epistemology—for all its variations—has defined itself. Hence there can be no feminist epistemology in any of the traditional senses of the term.

Feminists can be epistemologists, however, and epistemologists can be feminists. Feminists have to understand 'the epistemological project' to be in a position to see its androcentrism and to comprehend the political consequences of its hegemony. They need to engage in dialogues with the tradition to analyze its strengths and limitations; they need to develop politically informed critiques and to create space for productive relocations of knowledge in human lives. My contention that feminists have to engage in epistemological analysis without articulating their project as the creation of 'a feminist epistemology' is not merely a semantic quibble. Epistemological analyses that are compatible with feminist political commitments—however varied—sit uneasily with amalgamating the labels while attempting to decenter androcentricity so that it can include women. Feminists cannot participate in the construction of a monolithic, comprehensive epistemological *theory* removed from the practical-political issues a theory of knowledge has to address. My discussions of women and madness, of the nurses in the Grange Inquiry, and of the creation of the Poverty Game have shown why theories that transcend the specificities of gendered and otherwise situated subjectivities are impotent to come to terms with the politics of knowledge. So there can be no feminist epistemology in the received sense—yet epistemological questions are fundamental to feminist inquiry.

Even if androcentricity could be decentered to make space for gynocentric concerns, it is not obvious that 'a feminist epistemology' would be the most desirable result. A feminist epistemology would seem to require a basis in assumptions about the essence of women and of knowledge. Hence it would risk replicating the exclusionary, hegemonic structures of the masculinist epistemology, in its various manifestations, that has claimed absolute sovereignty over the epistemic terrain. A politically adequate 'successor epistemology' would have to give pride of place to questions such as, Whose knowledge are we talking about? Is it the knowledge that interchangeable observers have of cups, pens, and books on tables, or is it knowledge that committed Marxists have about capitalism? that committed supporters of apartheid have about blacks? Is it the knowledge of privileged intellectuals with the leisure to analyze the nature of freedom and oppression, or is it the knowledge that women who desperately need work must have so that they can weigh the dangers of radiation in a factory job against the humiliation of unemployment and welfare? The diversity of situations and circumstances in which people need to be in a position to know makes it difficult to see how *a* theory of knowledge, *an* epistemology, could respond to their questions.

Some of these reservations bear on the difficulty of seeing in feminist empiricism the best alternative to androcentric epistemology.[1] Feminist empiricism advocates a new empiricist project informed by the privileged vision of feminist consciousness and hence peculiarly equipped to eradicate sexism and androcentrism, represented as social biases. In its feminist dimension, it disrupts the smooth impartiality of the standard empiricist credo by introducing a specificity—a declaration of specific interests—to contest the very possibility of a disinterested epistemology. Hence it can claim subversive potential. But its scope is constricted by the fact that it makes these claims from within a structure that is itself indelibly tainted.

In arguing that social biases permeate 'the context of discovery' in any inquiry so thoroughly that it would be naive to hope for their eradication in the 'context of justification', feminist empiricism demonstrates its radical potential. In requiring—especially in the social sciences—that researchers locate themselves on the same critical plane as their 'objects of study', feminist empiricism takes issue with the very idea that there could be valid, detached observation. And in urging more rigor in scientific and other inquiry, to detect the influence of gender bias in shaping research, feminist empiricism refuses to accept any claims for value-free inquiry.[2] Paradoxically, by acknowledging its engaged, interested position and taking the socio-political identity of inquirers into account *epistemologically*, feminist empiricism promises enhanced objectivity and diminished bias.

Yet that very emphasis on screening for bias restricts the promise of feminist empiricism. The idea that a 'truer' account of reality, a more rigorously empirical and hence objective account, can be achieved through self-conscious stripping away of bias threatens to reproduce the old liberal split between 'the individual' and the discourses and power structures constitutive of her or his place on the epistemic terrain. It evinces a belief in a detached position from which biases will indeed be visible and can be washed away. The thought that the—possibly unconscious—androcentrism of mainstream epis-

---

[1]In examining feminist empiricism and a version of feminist standpoint theory as possible 'successor epistemologies', I am drawing on Harding's classifications in *The Science Question in Feminism*. In her "Conclusion: Epistemological Questions" in *Feminism and Methodology*, Harding characterizes them aptly as *transitional epistemologies* (p. 186). It will be apparent that the 'standpoint' I sketch here is somewhat different from Harding's.

[2]In her book *Toward a Feminist Epistemology* (Totowa, N.J.: Rowman & Littlefield, 1990), which I read after this book had gone to press, Jane Duran develops a version of empiricism that draws on 'naturalized epistemologies'. Her analysis aims to make it possible for empiricists to take human specificities more plausibly into account while retaining their central empiricist commitments.

temology is imposed and maintained from outside on an otherwise neutral subject matter fails to take into account the constitutive role of ideologies, stereotypes, and structures of epistemic privilege in creating the only institutionally legitimate possibilities for the construction and growth of knowledge. It does not grant sufficient credence to the claim that facts are often made, not found. Feminist empiricism—like the master discourse from which it takes its name—opts for a position outside the material and historical conditions that most urgently require analysis. Hence, despite its subversive potential, it cannot, alone, provide the theoretical position that feminist epistemologists require.[3]

How, then, can the terrain be remapped so that the space required for feminist epistemological analyses can be created? A productive imagery is that of creating a clearing, an open middle ground where an inquirer can take up a position, a standpoint, within a forest of absolutes: the exigencies of objectivism, the fervor of ideology, the quietism of extreme relativism, and the hegemony of universal Truth—to mention only a few. This idea of 'taking up a position' resumes the positionality analyses of previous chapters. Positionality, I think, is a sophisticated elaboration of earlier feminist standpoint theories that argued for the possibility of developing a unified, authoritative construction of reality anchored in the experiences and socioeconomic positions of women, deriving their inspiration from Marxist analyses of the standpoint of the proletariat.[4] Recent feminist concentration on differences and specificities makes the possibility of *a* feminist standpoint both remote and suspect, for it would presuppose an artificial unity in diversity. Intricated as it is with a complex configuration of specificities, *positionality* responds more adequately to the historical/political exigencies of the 1990s.

On this middle ground, responsible critical inquiry could take place, and effective forms of cognitive agency could thrive. Yet middle grounds have a bad name in professional philosophy. Too often, occupying such a position is condemned as a refusal to take a stand, a plea for undecidability and indifferent tolerance, a desire to have

---

[3]Wylie notes that "feminist empiricists are caught in the awkward position of exploiting the epistemic advantages of their standpoint as women while endorsing the ideal that scientific inquiry is objective in that an inquirer's social, political standpoint is irrelevant." Wylie, "The Philosophy of Ambivalence: Sandra Harding on *The Science Question in Feminism*," in Hanen and Nielson, eds., *Science, Morality, and Feminist Theory*, p. 64.

[4]A landmark feminist standpoint position is elaborated in Nancy Hartsock, "The Feminist Standpoint: Developing the Ground for a Specifically Feminist Historical Materialism," in Harding and Hintikka, eds., *Discovering Reality*.

things both—or all—ways, hence a feeble form of fence sitting. More-over, as I have shown in Chapter 2, the dichotomous thinking of most mainstream philosophy obliterates the very possibility of 'middle grounds'. My claim, however, is that a well-mapped middle ground offers a place to take up positions of strength and maximum produc-tivity from which exclusionary theories can be tapped critically and creatively for criticism and reconstruction. Occupancy of these posi-tions is compatible with a strong commitment to engagement in prac-tices designed to eradicate women's oppression and to the creation of environments ecologically committed to the promotion of so-cial/political well-being. It draws on the theoretical and practical re-sources that surround it to incorporate what is best in them and to reject what is damaging and oppressive. From these positions it is clear that analyses of damage, constraint, well-being, and empower-ment are all themselves situated and revisable, based on the best understanding available at the time, open to renegotiation. The provi-sionality—the revisability—of the resources no more leaves them 'un-decided', unstable sites for theory building and activism than a 'falli-bilist' standpoint in scientific inquiry would make it impossible to proceed with research. Like scientific research, politically informed activism and theory building have to go on, from where they are, for the gaps in their knowledge will not become visible except in practice, in further research that shows where revision is demanded. 'Second wave' feminists made remarkable progress working from the hypoth-esis that women could be analyzed as a class; that same progress destabilized the hypothesis, yet while it was in place it made quantities of high-quality, emancipatory research and action possible.

Feminists committed to breaking with the monolithic, hegemonic tradition, to working as philosophers and feminists at once, have revealed gaps in the malestream totalizing discourse which leave them no choice but to refuse obedience to it. These refusals are *anar-chic* in breaking away from the rules of established methodologies, challenging the most taken-for-granted philosophical assumptions, theories and goals.[5] Challenges and refusals are marks not of trucu-lence and aimless rebellion, but of strategies for uncovering the struc-tures of an order that is imposed to check an imagined threat of 'chaos', the exaggeration of whose dangers conceals its emancipatory potential. This is a 'chaos' of plurality, ambiguity, and differences: plurality of methods and methodologies; ambiguity in theoretical conclusions; differences that refuse the reductivism of universality

---

[5] I borrow the 'anarchic' characterization from Stenstad, "Anarchic Thinking."

and univocity. Only by thinkers wedded to a rigid conception of order and orthodoxy could this multiplicity be interpreted as chaotic in a derogatory sense. Yet such thinkers prevail, and such interpretations are the stuff of which their theories are made. For Stenstad, an anarchist persists in "questioning, working and playing with ambiguities, being alert for the presence of the strange within the familiar, and allowing for concealment or unclarity in the midst of disclosure."[6] The questioning takes place *from somewhere* and is committed to finding answers that make action possible.

One of the traditionally problematic features of a middle ground is that a refusal to occupy a position of pure objectivism is equated with an assertion of value in relativism. I have made such a claim at many places in this book. I have done so cognizant of the fact that there are cogent and persuasive arguments against relativism available in the philosophical tradition: that relativism can take an 'anything goes' form that would make criticism and responsible epistemic choice into meaningless ephemera—hence that absolute relativism forces perfect tolerance, which would have to include tolerance of sexism, racism, homophobia, and other oppressive practices. But the middle ground has no place for absolutes, relativist or otherwise. Participants in standard objectivist/relativist debates work with a false dichotomy according to which any move toward relativism amounts to a flat rejection of realism. My claim is that epistemological relativism does not entail antirealism.

Politically, feminists could not opt for an absolute relativism that recognized no facts of the matter—no objective, external reality—but only my, your, or our negotiated reality. Consider feminist concern with what "science has proved" about women's natural inferiority to men, about the safety of drugs to safeguard or prevent pregnancy, about the harmlessness of pesticides and nuclear power. That concern will not be put to rest by an assurance that there are many ways of looking at these things, all equally valid. No politically informed woman will be convinced by an argument that it is all relative—that for some people these things are wrong or harmful and for others they are valid and harmless. Nor could feminists agree that 'the realities' of sexism, the wage gap, violence against women, inadequate day care, class and racial injustices are all in their minds. It would fly in the face of the well-documented experiences of countless women to deny that these are realities, if perhaps not in the idealized physical science sense. If there are no objective social realities—in a sense that

---

[6]Ibid., p. 89.

allows for perspectival differences—there are no tools for the realization of feminist political projects.

However various their political allegiances, feminists are united in their commitments to ending women's oppression in patriarchal societies. Their ideological differences may produce different causal analyses of oppression and prompt diverse solutions. Yet differences in knowledge about oppression do not preclude possibilities of transformative dialogue. Were the oppression not demonstrably there *at all*, no debate would be possible; were it known identically by everyone, no debate would be necessary. Hence the impact of feminism on epistemology recommends a mitigated relativism. Mitigated relativism takes different perspectives into account. The claim that it must be mitigated affirms that there is something there, in the world, to know and act on—hence to constrain possibilities of knowledge and analysis. Were this not so, the findings of feminist research could simply be dismissed as one set of opinions, no better than any others. Indeed, they could be read as manifestations of ideological paranoia, and a relativist would have no way of countering the charge. Feminists need to demonstrate the reality of social injustices and practices and to work as hard for change in larger social structures and institutions as for change in the 'personal' areas of women's lives. Because of the dominance of received 'objectivist' knowledge in producing the social institutions in which they live, women cannot opt for a *radical* relativism that is unable to name those institutions and productions. They can, and I think must, opt for the mitigated, critical relativism implicit in asking, *Whose* knowledge are we talking about? Such a relativism would recognize the perspectival, locatedness of knowledge *and* its associations with subjective purposes. Yet it would develop strategies for evaluating perspectives and purposes.

This claim for evaluative possibilities might appear to recommend a mitigated *objectivism* instead of a mitigated relativism, and the suggestion would be plausible.[7] On a continuum between extreme objectivism and radical relativism, the mitigated versions of each would approach one another quite closely. I prefer to characterize the position I advocate as a *mitigated relativism*, however, for the freedom it offers from the homogenizing effects of traditional objectivism, in which differences, discrepancies, and deviations are smoothed out for the sake of achieving a unified theory. With its commitment to difference, critical relativism is able to resist reductivism and to accommodate divergent perspectives. Mitigated in its constraints by

[7]Marilyn Friedman made this suggestion to me.

'the facts' of material objects and social/political artifacts, yet ready to account for the mechanisms of power (in a Foucauldian sense) and prejudice (in a Gadamerian sense) that produce knowledge of these facts, and committed to the self-critical stance that its mitigation requires, such relativism is a resourceful epistemological position.

Wariness of relativism may be prompted by a suspicion that only knowers of supreme privilege, able to step outside the harsher constraints of inadequate material and epistemic resources, could claim the possibility—and right—to construct 'their world' from their own vantage point. The suspicion is not unfounded. But it cannot, I think, justifiably be countered with a move to objectivism with its history of laying claim to 'a view from nowhere'. That view will never be available to everyone; only God and his would-be successors can pretend to a God's-eye view. Those who are not sufficiently privileged to occupy such a position will always find that their position is constructed relative to it, and the old illusions and oppressions will remain firmly in place.

No single, monolithic scheme has been able to claim adequate explanatory power; and projects to devise such a scheme have been impressive for their failure to acknowledge their gaps, exclusions, and suppressions. Yet the fact that the scheme that has claimed absolute authority has proved wanting does not count as a reason to conclude that no scheme is better than any other. Perspectival explanations are constrained by reality: relativism is stopped in its feared slide into nihilism, solipsism, or subjectivism by the 'brute facts' of the world and by the discursive limits of speaking positions. Sexism, racism, and environmental harm are as demonstrably part of the world as tables and chairs, though they are open to more varying interpretations. So an endorsement of relativism in no way amounts to a denial of realism.

The adversarial method gains strong endorsement from the anti-relativism of objectivist theories. On the adversarial paradigm, any philosopher worthy of the name—hence any philosopher worth engaging with in adversarial combat—will have located himself in an entrenched position to which his allegiance is complete and perfect. One could not *be* a bit of a utilitarian, with Kantian and existentialist sympathies, and claim respect as a disputant under the adversarial paradigm. So a philosopher who finds truth in Kantian ethics but believes that it would offer better guidance to real people if it were tempered with consequentialist, situational, and care-oriented considerations will have difficulty claiming the credentials of a bona fide moral philosopher. To occupy a utilitarian position for some situations, a Kantian one in others, is to occupy a middle ground where the malestream assumes that no debate can take place and that only inferior philosophy, therefore, can be done. Analogous charges are advanced against self-proclaimed epistemologists who argue the advantages of reliabilism, coherentism, foundationalism, and perspectivism, or claim that knowledge is both objective and subjective.

The occupancy of a middle ground is a political act that refuses confinement within the narrow, cramped space that the adversarial paradigm allows for philosophical conversation. This refusal is not simply a negative act. It amounts to an explicit requirement for openness to debate; it resists closure and is committed to developing a politics of difference. Nor is it merely a reactive gesture. It is true that it creates clearings in the middle of the absolutes out of a radical disillusionment with the pretensions and political implications of unified theory building. So it would be preposterous for the refusal to amount simply to constructing an alternative theory of just the same kind, with 'masculine' modes simply displaced by 'feminine' ones. But only within the adversarial paradigm is the lack of a whole, universal theory equated with impotence. The middle ground is located within experiences, histories, social structures, material circumstances. Its occupants are committed to examining the resources and contradictions these experiences and circumstances yield. Its openness is a source of power in which the productiveness of an ambiguity that refuses closure can be realized. De Beauvoir argues that "the notion of ambiguity must not be confused with that of absurdity." Nor, in this context, must it be confused with anti-realism or irrationalism. She continues: "To say that [existence] is ambiguous is to assert that its meaning is never fixed, that it must constantly be won . . . it is because man's [sic] condition is ambiguous that he seeks, through failure and outrageousness, to save his existence."[8]

An ecological analysis of how, from a middle-ground position, feminists could engage in viable epistemological critique and reconstruction would emphasize the power of feminist philosophy as a collective, not an adversarial, project. Its nature is apparent in the practice of citing and drawing on one another's work as sources for theoretical-practical growth, bases for constructive critique, contributions to ongoing conversations committed to understanding the environments and structural locations where people are positioned and position themselves. Feminist philosophy in general, and epistemological inquiry in particular, engages with traditional philosophical

---

[8]De Beauvoir, *Ethics of Ambiguity,* p. 129.

discourse and takes a stand in relation to it. From its middle-ground position it can perceive interconnections among various traditionally separate 'branches' of philosophy, and of philosophy with other disciplines and projects. It is committed to developing "an *explanatory-diagnostic analysis* of women's [epistemic] oppression across history, culture and societies, and [to] articulating an *anticipatory-utopian critique*" of current epistemololgical norms and values—to developing new modes of cooperative existence and "of relating to ourselves and to nature in the future."[9] Ecologically mapped, the epistemic terrain can accommodate many locations on a middle ground, whose influence spreads to promote other transfomations and emancipatory strategies, which go on to inspire still others, and so on.

In Chapter 4 I note that, despite its problems of autonomy and austerity, Kantian philosophy affords a resource for the process of taking subjectivity into account while resisting the slide into subjectivism. Kant's revolutionary contribution to the history of philosophy is in his demonstration that knowledge is a *construct*—not a construct ex nihilo, or out of whole cloth, but one in which cognitive agents have considerable freedom. Feminist unmaskings of the political implications of constructive processes demonstrate that it matters how responsibly the project is undertaken. Feminist demonstrations of the interweaving of epistemological issues with moral, political, and ontological questions reveal the intricacy and ubiquity of accountability requirements.

Committed at once to emancipatory and ecologically sensitive goals, feminists have to devise strategies for remapping the epistemic terrain which acknowledge the demands of social-political-moral accountability while addressing specific, located, structurally produced needs. The point is not that scientific inquiry, or knowledge production more generally, should eschew its commitment to objectivity and accurate prediction. But such commitments have to be balanced against ecological and emancipatory projects—balanced responsibly so that investigators *consciously* control for sexism, for insensitivity to other specificities, and for human and environmental exploitation. Hence there must be an explicit acknowledgment that methods and methodologies always raise ethical-political questions, and inquirers must ensure that they can address these questions. In science, ecological commitments demand the development of cooperative, noninvasive ways of understanding nature and using its resources. Scientists cannot continue to present themselves as free, autonomous, asocial

[9]The phrases are from Benhabib, "Generalized and Concrete Other," pp. 80–81.

agents who can follow "the lure of the technically sweet"[10] without regard for its social-political impact. Feminist involvement in the ecology and peace movements requires a reconstruction of all projects of inquiry, from the microcosmic to the macrocosmic, toward a productive, critical elaboration of strategies for promoting and fostering cooperation—among people and with the environment.

Writing of her vision for women, in the concluding paragraphs of *The Second Sex*, de Beauvoir remarks: "It remains only for women to continue their ascent, and the successes they are obtaining are an encouragement for them to do so. It seems almost certain that sooner or later they will arrive at complete economic and social equality, which will bring about an inner metamorphosis."[11] That ascent has been slower and more arduous than de Beauvoir anticipated, yet the transformations in women's lives have been more wide-ranging and radical than she envisaged. Each success has revealed another step to be taken. Women have far to go to end economic, political, and social oppression, and they will not achieve it until they succeed in obliterating epistemic oppression. But the impact of the women's movement has been nothing short of astonishing. The metamorphosis de Beauvoir envisages is not confined to 'inner', private transformations; it is visible in transformations in social structures; in women's refusals to remain Other.

Posing the question Whose knowledge are we talking about? is a revolutionary step in this refusal. The next steps cannot merely be the addition of some notes about women's subjugated knowledge to the existing corpus of received knowledge, or the integration of women on equal terms into received epistemological theories. They must transform the terms of the discourse, challenge the structures of the epistemological project. Such transformations will reveal that the discourses feminists are developing are themselves empowering, informing innovative practices, and producing a resistance against domination that signals profound inner metamorphoses.

[10]The phrase is attributed to Robert Oppenheimer, by James Eayrs, in *Science and Conscience* (Toronto: C.B.C. Publications, 1968), the transcript of a Canadian Broadcasting Corporation television symposium (p. 5).
[11]De Beauvoir, *The Second Sex*, p. 811.

Bibliography

Addelson, Kathryn Pyne. "The Man of Professional Wisdom," in Harding and Hintikka, eds., *Discovering Reality*.

Alcoff, Linda. "Justifying Feminist Social Science." *Feminism and Science*. Edited by Nancy Tuana. Bloomington: Indiana University Press, 1989.

——. "Cultural Feminism versus Post-Structuralism: The Identity Crisis in Feminist Theory." *Signs: Journal of Women in Culture and Society* 13 (Spring 1988): 405–436.

Arendt, Hannah. *Thinking*. Vol. 1 of *The Life of the Mind*. New York: Harcourt, Brace, Jovanovich, 1978.

Aristotle. *The Categories*. Trans. E. M. Edghill. In *The Basic Works of Aristotle*. Edited by Richard McKeon. 1941. New York: Random House, 1971.

——. *Nichomachean Ethics*. Trans. W. D. Ross. In *The Basic Works of Aristotle*.

——. *Politics*. Trans. Benjamin Jowett. In *The Basic Works of Aristotle*.

Arnault, Lynne S. "The Radical Future of a Classic Moral Theory." In Jaggar and Bordo, eds., *Gender/Body/Knowledge*.

Ayer, A. J., ed. *Logical Positivism*. New York: Free Press, 1959.

Baier, Annette. "Trust and Antitrust." *Ethics* 96 (January 1986): 231–260.

——. *Postures of the Mind: Essays on Mind and Morals*. Minneapolis: University of Minnesota Press, 1985.

Balbus, Isaac. *Marxism and Domination*. Princeton: Princeton University Press, 1982.

Barnes, Barry, and David Bloor. "Relativism, Rationalism, and the Sociology of Knowledge." In Hollis and Lukes, eds., *Rationality and Relativism*.

Barrett, Michele. *Women's Oppression Today: Problems in Marxist Feminist Analysis*. London: Verso, 1980.

Baumgart, Alice. "Women, Nursing, and Feminism." *Canadian Nurse*, January 1985, 20–22. An interview with Alice J. Baumgart by Margaret Allen.

Belenky, Mary Field, Blythe McVicker Clinchy, Nancy Rule Goldberger, and Jill Mattuck Tarule. *Women's Ways of Knowing: The Development of Self, Voice, and Mind*. New York: Basic, 1986.

Benhabib, Seyla. "The Generalized and the Concrete Other." In Benhabib and Cornell, eds., *Feminism as Critique.*

Benhabib, Seyla, and Drucilla Cornell, eds. *Feminism as Critique: Essays on the Politics of Gender in Late-Capitalist Societies.* Minneapolis: University of Minnesota Press, 1987.

Benjamin, Jessica. "The Bonds of Love: Rational Violence and Erotic Domination." In *The Future of Difference.* Edited by Hester Eisenstein and Alice Jardine. New Brunswick, N.J.: Rutgers University Press, 1985.

Benson, John. "Who Is the Autonomous Man?" *Philosophy* 58 (1983): 5–17.

Benstock, Shari, ed. *The Private Self: Theory and Practice of Women's Autobiography.* Chapel Hill: University of North Carolina Press, 1988.

Benston, Ruth. "Feminism and the Critique of Scientific Method." In *Feminism in Canada.* Edited by Geraldine Finn and Angela Miles. Montreal: Black Rose, 1982.

Berkeley, George. *Principles of Human Knowledge.* New York: Scribners, 1929.

Bernstein, Richard. *Beyond Objectivism and Relativism.* Philadelphia: University of Pennsylvania Press, 1983.

Biology and Gender Study Group. "The Importance of Feminist Critique for Contemporary Cell Biology." *Hypatia: A Journal of Feminist Philosophy* 3 (Spring 1988): 61–76.

Birke, Lynda. *Women, Feminism, and Biology.* Brighton: Harvester, 1986.

Bleier, Ruth. "Science and Belief: A Polemic on Sex Differences Research." In *The Impact of Feminist Research in the Academy.* Edited by Christie Farnham. Bloomington: Indiana University Press, 1987.

———. "Lab Coat: Robe of Innocence or Klansman's Sheet?" In de Laurentis, ed. *Feminist Studies/Critical Studies.*

———, ed. *Feminist Approaches to Science.* New York: Pergamon, 1988.

Bloor, David. "A Sociological Theory of Objectivity." In *Objectivity and Cultural Divergence.* Edited by S. C. Brown. Cambridge: Cambridge University Press, 1984.

———. *Knowledge and Social Imagery.* London: Routledge & Kegan Paul, 1977.

Bordo, Susan. "Feminism, Postmodernism, and Gender-Scepticism." In Nicholson, ed., *Feminism/Postmodernism.*

———. *The Flight to Objectivity: Essays in Cartesianism and Culture.* Albany: State University of New York Press, 1987.

———. "The Cartesian Masculinization of Thought." *Signs: Journal of Women in Culture and Society* 11 (Spring 1986): 439–456.

Braidotti, Rosi. "Ethics Revisited: Women and/in Philosophy." In Pateman and Gross, eds. *Feminist Challenges..*

Brittain, Vera. *Testament of Friendship: The Story of Winifred Holtby.* London: Macmillan, 1947.

Brodzki, Bella, and Celeste Schenck, eds. *Life/Lines: Theorizing Women's Autobiography.* Ithaca: Cornell University Press, 1988.

Calhoun, Cheshire. "Responsibility and Reproach." *Ethics* 99 (January 1989): 389–406.

Callahan, Daniel. "Autonomy: A Moral Good, Not a Moral Obsession." *Hastings Center Report* 14 (October 1984): 38–42.

Campbell, Beatrix. *Unofficial Secrets.* London: Virago, 1988.

Carnap, Rudolf. "Psychology in Physical Language." In Ayer, ed., *Logical Positivism.*

Carson, Rachel. *Silent Spring*. New York: Fawcett, 1962.

Chodorow, Nancy. "Toward a Relational Individualism: The Mediation of Self through Psychoanalysis." In Heller et al., eds., *Reconstructing Individualism*.

———. *The Reproduction of Mothering: Psychoanalysis and the Sociology of Gender*. Berkeley: University of California Press, 1978.

Clark, Kenneth. *Landscape into Art*. Harmondsworth: Penguin, 1956.

Cocks, Joan. *The Oppositional Imagination: Feminism, Critique, and Political Theory*. New York: Routledge, 1989.

Code, Lorraine. "Will the 'Good Enough' Feminists Please Stand Up?" *Social Theory and Practice*, Spring 1991.

———. "Collingwood's Epistemological Individualism." *The Monist* 72 (October 1989): 542–567.

———. *Epistemic Responsibility*. Hanover, N.H.: University Press of New England, 1987.

———. "Tokenism." *Resources for Feminist Research* 16, 3 (1987). Reprinted in *Feminist Research: Prospect and Retrospect*. Edited by Peta Tancred-Sheriff. Montreal: McGill-Queen's University Press, 1988.

———. "Second Persons." In Hanen and Neilson, eds., *Science, Morality, and Feminist Theory*.

———. "Persons, and Others." In *Power, Gender, Values*. Edited by Judith Genova. Edmonton: Academic Printing and Publishing, 1987.

———. Review of *Postures of the Mind: Essays on Mind and Morals*, by Annette Baier. *Dialogue* 26 (Spring 1987): 201–207.

———. Review of *Sexual Divisions in Law*, by Katherine O'Donovan. *Canadian Journal of Women and the Law* 2, 1 (1987): 190–198.

——— "Simple Equality Is Not Enough." *Australasian Journal of Philosophy* 64(suppl.) (June 1986): 48–65.

———. "Stories People Tell." *New Mexico Law Review* 16 (Fall 1986): 599–606.

———. "The Importance of Historicism for a Theory of Knowledge." *International Philosophical Quarterly* 22 (June 1982): 157–174.

———. "Is the Sex of the Knower Epistemologically Significant?" *Metaphilosophy* 12 (July/October 1981): 267–276.

———. "Language and Knowledge." *Word: Journal of the International Linguistics Association* 31 (December 1980): 245–258.

Code, Lorraine, Maureen Ford, Kathleen Martindale, Susan Sherwin, and Deborah Shogan. "Some Issues in the Ethics of Collaborative Work." In *Explorations in Feminist Ethics: Theory and Practice*. Edited by Eve Browning Cole and Susan Coultrap-McQuinn. Bloomington: Indiana University Press, 1991.

Collingwood, Robin George. *The Principles of Art*. Oxford: Clarendon, 1938.

Covina, Gina. "Rosy Rightbrain's Exorcism/Invocation." In *The Lesbian Reader*. Edited by Gina Covina and Laurel Galana. Oakland, Calif.: Amazon, 1975.

Daly, Mary. *Gyn/Ecology: The Metaethics of Radical Feminism*. Boston: Beacon, 1978.

Davidson, Donald. "On the Very Idea of a Conceptual Scheme," *Proceedings and Addresses of the American Philosophical Association* 47 (1974): 5–20.

Day, Elaine Buckley. "A Twentieth-Century Witch Hunt: A Feminist Critique of the Grange Royal Commission into Deaths at the Hospital for Sick Children." *Studies in Political Economy* 24 (Autumn 1987): 13–39.

de Beauvoir, Simone. *The Second Sex*. Translated by H. M. Parshley. New York: Vintage, 1972.

———. *The Ethics of Ambiguity*. translated by Bernard Frechtman. New York: Citadel, 1948.

de Lauretis, Teresa. *Technologies of Gender*. Bloomington: Indiana University Press, 1987.

———, ed. *Feminist Studies/Critical Studies*. Bloomington: Indiana University Press, 1986.

Descartes, René. *Discourse on the Method of Rightly Conducting the Reason and Seeking for Truth in the Sciences*. In *The Philosophical Works of Descartes*, vol. 1. Translated by Elizabeth S. Haldane and G. R. T. Ross. Cambridge: Cambridge University Press, 1969.

———. *Meditations*. In *The Philosophical Works of Descartes*, vol. 1.

———. *Rules for the Direction of the Mind*. In *The Philosophical Works of Descartes*, vol. 1.

Dews, Peter. "The Return of the Subject in Late Foucault." *Radical Philosophy* 51 (Spring 1989): 37–41.

Diamond, Irene and Lee Quinby, eds. *Feminism and Foucault: Reflections on Resistance*. Boston: Northeastern University Press, 1988.

Dietz, Mary. "Citizenship with a Feminist Face: The Problems with Maternal Thinking." *Political Theory* 13 (February 1985): 19–37.

Dinnerstein, Dorothy. *The Mermaid and the Minotaur: Sexual Arrangements and Human Malaise*. New York: Harper Colophon, 1976.

Duran, Jane. *Toward a Feminist Epistemology*. Totowa, N.J.: Rowman & Littlefield, 1990.

Ehrenreich, Barbara, and Deirdre English. *For Her Own Good: 150 Years of the Experts' Advice to Women*. New York: Doubleday, 1978.

Eisenstein, Zillah. *The Radical Future of Liberal Feminism*. New York: Longmans, 1981.

Elster, Jon. "Belief, Bias, and Ideology." In Hollis and Lukes, eds., *Rationality and Relativism*.

Faderman, Lillian. *Surpassing the Love of Men: Romantic Friendship and Love between Women from the Renaissance to the Present*. New York: Morrow, 1981.

Fee, Elizabeth. "Women's Nature and Scientific Objectivity." In *Woman's Nature: Rationalizations of Inequality*. Edited by Marian Lowe and Ruth Hubbard. New York: Pergamon, Athene Series, 1983.

Firestone, Shulamith. *The Dialectic of Sex: The Case for Feminine Revolution*. New York: Bantam, 1971.

Flanagan, O. J., Jr., and J. E. Adler. "Impartiality and Particularity," *Social Research* 50 (October 1983): 576–596.

Flax, Jane. "Political Philosophy and the Patriarchal Unconscious: A Psychoanalytic Perspective on Epistemology and Metaphysics." In Harding and Hintikka, eds., *Discovering Reality*.

Foley, Richard. *The Theory of Epistemic Rationality*. Cambridge: Harvard University Press, 1987.

Foucault, Michel. "What Is Enlightenment?" In *A Foucault Reader*. Edited by Paul Rabinow. New York: Pantheon, 1984.

———. *The History of Sexuality*. Vol. 1. *An Introduction*. Translated by Robert Hurley. New York: Vintage, 1980.

———. *Power/Knowledge: Selected Interviews and Other Writings, 1972–1977*. Edited by Colin Gordon. Translated by C. Gordon, Leo Marshall, John Mepham, and Kate Soper. New York: Pantheon, 1980.

——. *Discipline and Punish: The Birth of the Prison*. Translated by Alan Sheridan. New York: Vintage, 1979.

——. "The Discourse on Language." In *The Archaeology of Knowledge*. Translated by Alan Sheridan. New York: Pantheon, 1972.

——. *Madness and Civilisation*. Translated by Richard Howard. London: Tavistock, 1967.

Franklin, Ursula. "Will Women Change Technology or Will Technology Change Women?" *CRIAW Papers* 9 (Canadian Research Institute for the Advancement of Women, Ottawa), March 1985.

Fraser, Nancy. *Unruly Practices: Power, Discourse, and Gender in Contemporary Social Theory*. Minneapolis: University of Minnesota Press, 1989.

Friedman, Marilyn. "Feminism and Modern Friendship: Dislocating the Community." *Ethics* 99 (January 1989): 275–290.

Frye, Marilyn. *The Politics of Reality: Essays in Feminist Theory*. Trumansburg, N.Y.: Crossing Press, 1983.

Fuller, Margaret. *Woman in the Nineteenth Century*. 1845. New York: Norton, 1971.

Gadamer, Hans Georg. "The Universality of the Hermeneutical Problem." In *Philosophical Hermeneutics*. Translated by David E. Linge. Berkeley: University of California Press, 1976.

——. *Truth and Method*. Translated by Sheed & Ward, Ltd. New York: Seabury, 1975.

Gage, Matilda Jocelyn. *Women, Church, and State*. 1893. Watertown, Mass.: Persephone, 1980.

Gatens, Moira. "Feminism, Philosophy, and Riddles without Answers". In Patemen and Gross, eds. *Feminist Challenges*.

Genova, Judith. "Women and the Mismeasure of Thought." *Hypatia: A Journal of Feminist Philosophy* 3 (Spring 1988): 101–117..

Gergen, Kenneth. "Feminist Critique of Science and the Challenge of Social Epistemology." In M. Gergen, ed., *Feminist Thought and the Structure of Knowledge*.

Gergen, Mary M., ed. *Feminist Thought and the Structure of Knowledge*. New York: New York University Press, 1988.

Gilligan, Carol. "Remapping the Moral Domain: New Images of the Self in Relationship." In Heller et al., eds., *Reconstructing Individualism*.

——. *In a Different Voice: Psychological Theory and Women's Development*. Cambridge: Harvard University Press, 1982.

Ginzberg, Ruth. "Uncovering Gynocentric Science." *Hypatia: A Journal of Feminist Philosophy* 2 (Fall 1987): 89–105.

Goldman, Alvin I. *Epistemology and Cognition*. Cambridge: Harvard University Press, 1986.

Goodfield, June. *An Imagined World*. Harmondsworth: Penguin, 1982.

Gornick, Vivian. *Women in Science*. New York: Simon & Schuster, 1983.

Gornick, Vivian, and Barbara K. Moran, eds. *Woman in Sexist Society*. New York: Basic, 1971.

Gould, Stephen Jay. Review of *A Feeling for the Organism*, by Evelyn Fox Keller. *New York Review of Books*, March 1984. 3–6.

Gramsci, Antonio. *Selections from the Prison Notebooks*. Translated and edited by Quintin Hoare and Geoffrey Nowell Smith. New York: International, 1971.

Grant, Judith. "I Feel Therefore I Am: A Critique of Female Experience as the Basis for a Feminist Epistemology". *Women and Politics* 7, 3 (1987): 99–127.

Griffin, Susan. "The Way of All Ideology." In *Feminist Theory: A Critique of Ideology.* Edited by Nannerl O. Keohane, Michele Rosaldo, and Barbara Gelpi. Chicago: University of Chicago Press, 1982.

———. *Woman and Nature: The Roaring inside Her.* New York: Harper & Row, 1978.

Griffiths, Morwenna, and Margaret Whitford, eds., *Feminist Perspectives in Philosophy.* Bloomington: Indiana University Press, 1988.

Grimshaw, Jean. *Philosophy and Feminist Thinking.* Minneapolis: University of Minnesota Press, 1986.

Gutting, Gary. *Michel Foucault's Archaeology of Scientific Reason.* Cambridge: Cambridge University Press, 1989.

Habermas, Jurgen. *Knowledge and Human Interests.* Translated by Jeremy J. Shapiro. Boston: Beacon, 1971.

Hacking, Ian. "Language, Truth, and Reason." In Hollis and Lukes, eds., *Rationality and Relativism.*

Hanen, Marsha, and Kai Nielson, eds., *Science, Morality, and Feminist Theory.* Calgary, Alberta: University of Calgary Press, 1987.

Haraway, Donna. "Primatology Is Politics by Other Means." In Bleier, ed., *Feminist Approaches to Science.*

———. "Situated Knowledges: The Science Question in Feminism and the Privilege of Partial Perspective." *Feminist Studies* 14 (Fall 1988): 575–599.

———. "A Manifesto for Cyborgs: Science, Technology, and Socialist Feminism in the 1980s." *Socialist Review* 15, 80 (1985): 65–107.

Harding, Sandra. *The Science Question in Feminism.* Ithaca: Cornell University Press, 1986.

———. "Why Has the Sex/Gender System Become Visible Only Now?" In Harding and Hintikka, eds., *Discovering Reality.*

———. "The Social Function of the Empiricist Conception of Mind." *Metaphilosophy* 10 (January 1979): 38–47.

———, ed. *Feminism and Methodology.* Bloomington: Indiana University Press, 1987.

Harding, Sandra, and Merrill Hintikka, eds. *Discovering Reality: Feminist Perspectives on Epistemology, Methodology, and the Philosophy of Science.* Dordrecht: Reidel, 1983.

Hardwig, John. "Epistemic Dependence." *Journal of Philosophy* 82 (July 1985): 335–349.

Harris, Roy. *The Language Makers.* Ithaca: Cornell University Press, 1980.

Hartsock, Nancy. "Foucault on Power: A Theory for Women?" In Nicholson, ed. *Feminism/Postmodernism.*

———. *Money, Sex, and Power.* Boston: Northeastern University Press, 1986.

———. "The Feminist Standpoint: Developing the Ground for a Specifically Feminist Historical Materialism." In Harding and Hintikka, eds., *Discovering Reality.*

Hawkesworth, Mary. "Knowers, Knowing, Known: Feminist Theory and Claims of Truth." *Signs: Journal of Women in Culture and Society* 14 (Spring 1989): 535–557.

Heidegger, Martin. "Being Dwelling Thinking." In *Martin Heiddeger: Basic Writings*. Edited by David Farrell Krell. New York: Harper & Row, 1977.
——. "The Origin of the Work of Art." In *Martin Heidegger: Basic Writings*.
——. *Being and Time*. Translated by John Macquarrie and Edward Robinson. New York: Harper & Row, 1962.
Heilbrun, Carolyn. *Writing a Woman's Life*. New York: Norton, 1988.
Held, Virginia. *Rights and Goods*. New York: Macmillan, Free Press, 1984.
Heller, Thomas C., Martin Sosna, and David Wellbery, eds. *Reconstructing Individualism: Autonomy, Individuality, and the Self in Western Thought*. Stanford: Stanford University Press, 1986.
Higonnet, Anne. "A Woman Turned to Stone." *Women's Review of Books* 5 (September 1988): 6–7.
Hintikka, Merrill B. and Jaakko Hintikka. "How Can Language Be Sexist?" In Harding and Hintikka, eds., *Discovering Reality*.
Holland, Monica. Review of *Women's Ways of Knowing: The Development of Self, Voice, and Mind*, by Mary Field Belenky et al. *Hypatia: A Journal of Feminist Philosophy* 3 (Spring 1988): 177–179.
Hollis, Martin. "The Social Destruction of Reality." In Hollis and Lukes, eds., *Rationality and Relativism*.
Hollis, Martin, and Steven Lukes, eds. *Rationality and Relativism*. Cambridge: MIT Press, 1982.
Hollway, Wendy. *Subjectivity and Method in Psychology: Gender, Meaning, and Science*. London: Sage, 1989.
Houston, Barbara, and Ann Diller. "Trusting Ourselves to Care." *Resources for Feminist Research* 16 (September 1987): 35–38.
Hubbard, Ruth. "Science, Facts, and Feminism." *Hypatia: A Journal of Feminist Philosophy* 3 (Spring 1988): 5–17.
——. "Some Thoughts about the Masculinity of the Natural Sciences." In M. Gergen, ed., *Feminist Thought and the Structure of Knowledge*.
——. "Have Only Men Evolved?" In *Biological Woman: The Convenient Myth*. Edited by Ruth Hubbard, Mary Sue Henifin, and Barbara Fried. Cambridge, Mass.: Schenkman, 1982.
Humboldt, Wilhelm von. *Humanist without Portfolio: An Anthology of the Writings of Wilhelm von Humboldt*. Translated with an Introduction by Marianne Cowan. Detroit: Wayne State University Press, 1963.
Hume, David. *An Inquiry concerning Human Understanding*. Indianapolis: Bobbs-Merrill, 1955.
——. *A Treatise of Human Nature*. Edited by L. A. Selby-Bigge. Oxford: Oxford University Press, 1969.
Hurtado, Aida. "Relating to Privilege: Seduction and Rejection in the Subordination of White Women and Women of Color." *Signs: Journal of Women in Culture and Society* 14 (Summer 1989): 833–855.
Jaggar, Alison M. "Love and Knowledge: Emotion in Feminist Epistemology." In Jaggar and Bordo, eds., *Gender/Body/ Knowledge*.
Jaggar, Alison M., and Susan R. Bordo, eds. *Gender/Body/ Knowledge: Feminist Reconstructions of Being and Knowing*. New Brunswick, N.J.: Rutgers University Press, 1989.
Jay, Nancy. "Gender and Dichotomy." *Feminist Studies* 1 (1981): 35–56.
Jones, Kathleen B. "On Authority." In Diamond and Quinby, eds., *Feminism and Foucault*.

Kant, Immanuel. *Critique of Judgement*. Translated by J. H. Bernard. New York: Hafner, 1972.

———. *Groundwork of the Metaphysic of Morals*. Translated and analysed by H. J. Paton. New York: Harper Torchbooks, 1964.

———. *The Critique of Pure Reason*. Translated by Norman Kemp Smith. London: St. Martin's, 1929.

Keller, Evelyn Fox. "The Gender/Science System: Or, Is Sex to Gender as Nature Is to Science?" *Hypatia* 2 (Fall 1987): 37–49.

———. *A Feeling for the Organism: The Life and Work of Barbara McClintock*. New York: Freeman, 1985.

———. *Reflections on Gender and Science*. New Haven: Yale University Press, 1985.

———. "The Anomaly of a Woman in Physics." In Ruddick and Daniels, eds., *Working It Out*.

Keller, Evelyn Fox, and Christine Grontkowski. "The Mind's Eye." In Harding and Hintikka, eds. *Discovering Reality*.

Keller, Evelyn Fox, and Helen Moglin. "Competition and Feminism: Conflicts for Academic Women." *Signs: Journal of Women in Culture and Society* 12 (Spring 1987): 493–511.

King, Ynestra. "Healing the Wounds: Feminism, Ecology, and Nature/Culture Dualism." In Jaggar and Bordo, eds., *Gender/Body/Knowledge*.

———. "Toward an Ecological Feminism and a Feminist Ecology." In *Machina Ex Dea: Feminist Perspectives on Technology*. Edited by Joan Rothschild. New York: Pergamon, 1983.

Kittay, Eva, and Diana Meyers, eds. *Women and Moral Theory*. Totowa, N.J.: Rowman & Littlefield, 1987.

Koblitz, Ann H. *A Convergence of Lives. Sofia Kovalevskaia: Scientist, Writer, Revolutionary*. Boston: Birkhauser, 1983.

Kramarae, Cheris, and Paula Treichler. *A Feminist Dictionary*. London: Pandora, 1985.

Kramer, Cheris, Barrie Thorne, and Nancy Henley. "Perspectives on Language and Communication." *Signs: Journal of Women in Culture and Society* 3 (Spring 1978): 638–651.

Kuhn, Annette. *Women's Pictures: Feminism and Cinema*. London: Routledge & Kegan Paul, 1982.

Kuhn, Thomas. *The Structure of Scientific Revolutions*. 2d ed. Chicago: University of Chicago Press, 1970.

Kuper, Hilda. "Colour, Categories, and Colonialism: The Swazi Case." In *Colonialism in Africa 1870–1960*. Vol. 3. *Profiles of Change: African Society and Colonial Rule*. Edited by Peter Duignan and L. H. Gann. Cambridge: Cambridge University Press, 1971.

Lakoff, Robin. *Language and Woman's Place*. New York: Harper & Row, 1975.

Landesman, Bruce M. "On Nancy Fraser's 'Women, Welfare, and the Politics of Need Interpretation.'" *Hypatia: A Journal of Feminist Philosophy* 3 (Summer 1988): 157–161.

Le Doeuff, Michele. "Women and Philosophy." *Radical Philosophy* 17 (Summer 1977): 2–11.

Lippmann, Walter. *Public Opinion*. 1922. New York: Free Press, 1965.

Lloyd, Genevieve. "Feminist Philosophy and the Idea of the Feminine." Unpublished manuscript, 1986.

——. "History of Philosophy and the Critique of Reason." *Critical Philosophy* 1, 1 (1984): 5–23.

——. *The Man of Reason*. London: Methuen, 1984.

——. "Reason, Gender, and Morality in the History of Philosophy." *Social Research* 50 (Autumn 1983): 490–513.

Locke, John. *An Essay concerning Human Understanding*. Book II. New York: Dent, 1961.

Longino, Helen. *Science as Social Knowledge: Values and Objectivity in Scientific Inquiry*. Princeton: Princeton University Press, 1990.

Lugones, Maria C., and Elizabeth V. Spelman. "Have We Got a Theory for You! Feminist Theory, Cultural Imperialism, and the Demand for 'The Woman's Voice.'" In *Women and Values*. Edited by Marilyn Pearsall. Belmont, Calif.: Wadsworth, 1986.

MacIntyre, Alasdair. *After Virtue*. London: Duckworth, 1981.

——. "Epistemological Crises, Dramatic Narrative, and the Philosophy of Science." *The Monist* 60, 4 (1977): 453–472.

Mackenzie, Catriona. "Simone de Beauvoir: Philosophy and/or the Female Body." In Pateman and Gross, eds., *Feminist Challenges*.

MacKinnon, Catharine A. "Feminism, Marxism, Method, and the State." In Harding, ed., *Feminism and Methodology*.

Martin, Biddy. "Feminism, Criticism, and Foucault." In Diamond and Quinby, eds., *Feminism and Foucault*.

——. "Lesbian Identity and Autobiographical Difference[s]." In Brodzki and Schenck, eds., *Life/Lines*.

Martin, Biddy, and Chandra Talpade Mohanty. "Feminist Politics: What's Home Got to Do with It?" In de Lauretis, ed., *Feminist Studies/Critical Studies*.

Martin, Jane Roland. "Science in a Different Style." *American Philosophical Quarterly* 25 (April 1988): 129–140.

——. *Reclaiming a Conversation: The Ideal of the Educated Woman*. New Haven: Yale University Press, 1985.

Martin, Luther H., Huck Gutman, and Patrick H. Hutton, eds. *Technologies of the Self: A Seminar with Michel Foucault*. Amherst: University of Massachusetts Press, 1988.

Matthews, Jill Julius. *Good and Mad Women: The Historical Construction of Femininity in Twentieth-Century Australia*. Sydney: Allen & Unwin, 1984.

Merchant, Carolyn. *Ecological Revolutions: Nature, Gender, and Science in New England*. Chapel Hill: University of North Carolina Press, 1989.

——. *The Death of Nature: Women, Ecology, and the Scientific Revolution*. New York: Harper & Row, 1980.

Merleau-Ponty, Maurice. *The Phenomenology of Perception*. Translated by Colin Smith. London: Routledge & Kegan Paul, 1962.

Miller, Jean Baker. *Toward a New Psychology of Women*. Boston: Beacon, 1976.

Mitchell, Juliet. "Femininity, Narrative, and Psychoanalysis." In Juliet Mitchell, *Women: The Longest Revolution*. London: Virago, 1984.

Montaigne, Michel de. "Of Friendship." In *The Complete Essays of Montaigne*. Translated by Donald M. Frame. Stanford: Stanford University Press, 1965.

Mooney, Edward F. "Gender, Philosophy, and the Novel." *Metaphilosophy* 18 (July/October 1987): 241–252.

Moravscik, Julius. "Communal Ties." *Proceedings and Addresses of the American Philosophical Association* 62 (suppl.) (September 1988): 211–225.

Moulton, Janice. "A Paradigm of Philosophy: The Adversary Method." In Harding and Hintikka, eds., *Discovering Reality*.

Nead, Lynda. *Myths of Sexuality: Representations of Women in Victorian Britain*. Oxford: Blackwell, 1988.

Nelson, Lynn Hankinson. *Who Knows: From Quine to a Feminist Empiricism*. Philadelphia: Temple University Press, 1990.

Neurath, Otto. "Sociology and Physicalism." In Ayer, ed., *Logical Positivism*.

Nicholson, Linda, ed. *Feminism/Postmodernism*. New York: Routledge, 1990.

Norwood, Vera. "The Nature of Knowing: Rachel Carson and the American Environment." *Signs: Journal of Women in Culture and Society* 12 (Summer 1987): 740–760.

Nussbaum, Martha. *The Fragility of Goodness*. Cambridge: Cambridge University Press, 1986.

Nye, Andrea. *Feminist Theory and the Philosophies of Man*. London: Croom Helm, 1988.

——. "The Unity of Language." *Hypatia: A Journal of Feminist Philosophy* 2 (Summer 1987): 95–111.

O'Brien, Mary. "Resolute Anticipation: Heidegger and Beckett." In Mary O'Brien, *Reproducing the World: Essays in Feminist Theory*. Boulder, Colo.: Westview Press, 1989.

——. *The Politics of Reproduction*. London: Routledge & Kegan Paul, 1980.

O'Donovan, Katherine. *Sexual Divisions in Law*. London: Weidenfeld & Nicholson, 1985.

Ortner, Sherry. "Is Female to Male as Nature Is to Culture?" In *Women, Culture, and Society*. Edited by Michele Rosaldo and Louise Lamphere. Stanford: Stanford University Press, 1974.

Pateman, Carole. *The Sexual Contract*. Stanford: Stanford University Press, 1988.

Pateman, Carole, and Elizabeth Gross, eds. *Feminist Challenges: Social and Political Theory*. Sydney: Allen & Unwin, 1986.

Patton, Paul. "Of Power and Prisons." In Meaghan Morris and Paul Patton, eds., *Michel Foucault: Power, Truth, Strategy*. Sydney: Feral, 1979.

Peirce, Christine. "Philosophy." *Signs: Journal of Women in Culture and Society* 1 (Winter 1975): 487–503.

Penfold, P. Susan, and Gillian Walker. *Women and the Psychiatric Paradox*. Montreal: Eden, 1983.

Plato. *Meno*. Translated by W. K. C. Guthrie. In *The Collected Dialogues of Plato*. Edited by Edith Hamilton and Huntington Cairns. Princeton: Princeton University Press, 1961.

——. *Republic*. Translated by Benjamin Jowett. In *The Collected Dialogues of Plato*.

Plumwood, Val. "Ecofeminism: An Overview and Discussion of Positions and Arguments." *Australasian Journal of Philosophy* 64 (suppl.) (June 1986): 120–138.

Polkinghorne, David. *Narrative Knowing in the Human Sciences*. Albany: State University of New York Press, 1988.

Potter, Elizabeth. "Modeling the Gender Politics in Science." *Hypatia: A Journal of Feminist Philosophy* 3 (Spring 1988): 19–33.

Rajchman, John. *Michel Foucault: The Freedom of Philosophy.* New York: Columbia University Press, 1985.

Raymond, Janice. *A Passion for Friends.* Boston: Beacon, 1986.

Reiter, Rayna, ed. *Toward an Anthropology of Women.* New York: Monthly Review, 1975.

Rich, Adrienne. *On Lies, Secrets, and Silence. Selected Prose 1966–1978.* New York: Norton, 1979.

———. *The Dream of a Common Language: Poems 1974–1977.* New York: Norton, 1978.

———. *Of Woman Born: Motherhood as Experience and Institution.* New York: Harper & Row, 1976.

Riley, Denise. *"Am I That Name?" Feminism and the Category of Women in History.* Minneapolis: University of Minnesota Press, 1988.

Rorty, Amélie. "Akratic Believers." *American Philosophical Quarterly* 20 (April 1983): 175–183.

Rorty, Richard. *Consequences of Pragmatism.* Minneapolis: University of Minnesota Press, 1982.

———. *Philosophy and the Mirror of Nature.* Princeton: Princeton University Press, 1979.

Rose, Hilary. "Dreaming the Future." *Hypatia: A Journal of Feminist Philosophy* 3 (Spring 1988): 119–137.

Ross, W. D. *Aristotle: A Complete Exposition of His Works and Thought.* 1923. New York: Meridian, 1959.

Rossiter, Margaret. *Women Scientists in America: Struggles and Strategies to 1940.* Baltimore: Johns Hopkins University Press, 1981.

Rubin, Gayle. "The Traffic in Women: Notes on the Political Economy of Sex." In Reiter, ed., *Toward an Anthropology of Women.*

Ruddick, Sara. *Maternal Thinking: Toward a Politics of Peace.* Boston: Beacon, 1989.

———. "Maternal Thinking." *Feminist Studies* 6 (1980): 342–367.

Ruddick, Sara, and Pamela Daniels, eds. *Working It Out: 23 Women Writers, Scientists, and Scholars Talk about Their Lives.* New York: Pantheon, 1977.

Russell, Bertrand. *Mysticism and Logic.* London: Allen & Unwin, 1917.

———. *The Problems of Philosophy.* Oxford: Oxford University Press, 1912.

Russett, Cynthia Eagle. *Sexual Science: The Victorian Construction of Womanhood.* Cambridge: Harvard University Press, 1989.

Ruth, Sheila. "Methodocracy, Misogyny, and Bad Faith: Sexism in the Philosophic Establishment." *Metaphilosophy* 10, 1 (1979): 46–61.

Rycroft, Charles. Review of *The Man Who Mistook His Wife for a Hat and Other Clinical Tales,* by Oliver Sacks. *New York Review of Books,* March 13, 1986. 11–12.

Sacks, Oliver. *The Man Who Mistook His Wife for a Hat and Other Clinical Tales.* New York: Summit, 1985.

Sandel, Michael. *Liberalism and the Limits of Justice.* Cambridge: Cambridge University Press, 1982.

Sarton, May. *As We Are Now.* New York: Norton, 1973.

Sayers, Janet. *Biological Politics.* London: Tavistock, 1982.

Sayre, Anne. *Rosalind Franklin and D.N.A.: A Vivid View of What It Is Like to Be a Gifted Woman in an Especially Male Profession.* New York: Norton, 1975.

Scheman, Naomi. "Othello's Doubt/Desdemona's Death: On the Engendering of Scepticism." In Judith Genova, ed., *Power, Gender, Value*. Edmonton: Academic Printing and Publishing, 1987.

Schiebinger, Londa. *The Mind Has No Sex? Women in the Origins of Modern Science*. Cambridge: Harvard University Press, 1989.

——. "Women and Science." *Signs: Journal of Women in Culture and Society* 12 (Winter 1987): 305–332.

Scott, Joan. "Is Gender a Useful Category of Historical Analysis?" In Joan Wallach Scott, *Gender and the Politics of History*. New York: Columbia University Press, 1989.

Segal, Lynne. *Is the Future Female? Troubled Thoughts on Contemporary Feminism*. London: Virago, 1987.

Seller, Anne. "Realism versus Relativism: Towards a Politically Adequate Epistemology." In Griffiths and Whitford, eds., *Feminist Perspectives in Philosophy*.

Sherwin, Susan. "Ethics: Towards a Feminist Approach." *Canadian Woman Studies/Les cahiers de la femme* 6 (Spring 1985): 21–23.

Shiner, Roger. "From Epistemology to Romance via Wisdom." In *Philosophy and Life: Essays on John Wisdom*. Edited by Ilham Dilman. The Hague: Martinus Nijhoff, 1984.

Shiva, Vandana. *Staying Alive: Women, Ecology, and Development*. London: Zed, 1988.

Shorter, Edward. *Bedside Manners: The Troubled History of Doctors and Patients*. New York: Simon & Schuster, 1985.

Showalter, Elaine. *The Female Malady: Women, Madness, and English Culture, 1830–1980*. New York: Penguin, 1987.

Smith, Dorothy. *The Everyday World as Problematic*. Toronto: University of Toronto Press, 1988.

Soble, Alan. "Feminist Epistemology and Women Scientists." *Metaphilosophy* 14 (1983): 291–307.

Sosa, Ernest. "Serious Philosophy and Freedom of Spirit." *Journal of Philosophy* 84 (December 1987): 707–726.

——. "How Do You Know?" *American Philosophical Quarterly* 11, 2 (1974): 113–122.

Spacks, Patricia Meyer. *Gossip*. New York: Knopf, 1985.

Spelman, Elizabeth V. *Inessential Woman: Problems of Exclusion in Feminist Thought*. Boston: Beacon, 1988.

——. "On Treating Persons as Persons." *Ethics* 88 (1978): 150–161.

Spender, Dale. *Man Made Language*. London: Routledge & Kegan Paul, 1980.

Stanley, Liz, and Sue Wise. *Breaking Out: Feminist Consciousness and Feminist Research*. London: Routledge & Kegan Paul, 1983.

Steedman, Carolyn. *Landscape for a Good Woman*. London: Virago, 1986.

Stenstad, Gail. "Anarchic Thinking." *Hypatia: A Journal of Feminist Philosophy* 3 (Summer 1988): 87–100.

Taylor, Gordon Rattray. *The Natural History of the Mind*. London: Granada, 1979.

——. "A New View of the Brain." *Encounter* 36, 2 (1971): 25–37.

Thorne, Barrie, and Nancy Henley, eds. *Language and Sex: Difference and Dominance*. Rowley, Mass.: Newbury House, 1975.

Thurber, James. "The Unicorn in the Garden." In *Further Fables for Our Time.* New York: Harper & Row, 1939.
Treblicot, Joyce, ed. *Mothering: Essays in Feminist Theory.* Totowa, N.J.: Rowman & Allenheld, 1984.
Trollope, Anthony. *The Warden.* 1855. New York: Washington Square, 1962.
Tronto, Joan. "Beyond Gender Difference to a Theory of Care." *Signs: Journal of Women in Culture and Society* 12 (Summer 1987): 644–663.
Tuana, Nancy. "The Weaker Seed: The Sexist Bias of Reproductive Theory." *Hypatia: A Journal of Feminist Philosophy* 3 (Spring 1988): 34–59.
Unger, Rhoda. "Psychological, Feminist, and Personal Epistemology: Transcending Contradictions." In M. Gergen, ed., *Feminist Thought and the Structure of Knowledge.*
Walsh, Mary Roth. "The Quirls of a Woman's Brain." In *Biological Woman: The Convenient Myth.* Edited by Ruth Hubbard, Mary Sue Henifin, and Barbara Fried. Cambridge, Mass.: Schenkman, 1982.
Warren, Karen J. "Feminism and Ecology: Making the Connections." *Environmental Ethics* 9 (Spring 1987): 3–20.
Weisstein, Naomi. "Adventures of a Woman in Science." In Ruddick and Daniels, eds., *Working It Out.*
———. "Psychology Constructs the Female." In *Woman in Sexist Society.* Edited by Vivian Gornick and Barbara K. Moran. New York: Basic, 1971.
Wells, H. G. *Ann Veronica.* 1909. London: Virago, 1981.
Wenzel, Helene Vivienne, eds. *Simone de Beauvoir: Witness to a Century.* Yale French Studies 72 (1986).
Whitbeck, Caroline. "Feminist Ontology: A Different Reality." In *Beyond Domination.* Edited by Carol Gould. Totowa, N.J.: Rowman & Allenheld, 1983.
Williams, Bernard. *Descartes: The Project of Pure Enquiry.* Harmondsworth: Penguin, 1978.
Winch, Peter. "Understanding a Primitive Society." *American Philosophical Quarterly* (1964): 307–324. Reprinted in *Rationality.* Edited by Bryan R. Wilson. Oxford: Blackwell, 1971.
———. *The Idea of a Social Science and Its Relation to Philosophy.* London: Routledge & Kegan Paul, 1958.
Wisdom, John. *Paradox and Discovery.* Oxford: Blackwell, 1965.
Wittgenstein, Ludwig. *On Certainty.* Edited by G. E. M. Anscombe and G. H. von Wright. Translated by Denis Paul and G. E. M. Anscombe. New York: Harper Torchbooks, 1971.
———. *Tractatus Logico-Philosophicus.* Translated by David Pears and B. F. McGuinness. London: Routledge & Kegan Paul, 1961.
———. *Philosophical Investigations.* Translated by G. E. M. Anscombe. Oxford: Blackwell, 1951.
Wolff, Robert Paul. *The Autonomy of Reason.* New York: Harper & Row, 1973.
Woolf, Virginia. *Night and Day.* 1919. New York: Harcourt Brace Jovanovich, 1973.
Wylie, Alison. "The Philosophy of Ambivalence: Sandra Harding on *The Science Question in Feminism.*" In Hanen and Nielson, eds., *Science, Morality, and Feminist Theory.*
———. "Gender Theory and the Archeological Record." In *Women and Prehistory.* Edited by Margaret Conkey and Joan Gero. Oxford: Blackwell, in press.

Wylie, Alison, Kathleen Okruhlik, Leslie Thielen-Wilson, and Sandra Morton. "Philosophical Feminism: A Bibliographic Guide to Critiques of Science," *Resources for Feminist Research* 19 (June 1990), 2–36.

Young, Iris Marion. "The Ideal of Community and the Politics of Difference." In Nicholson, ed., *Feminism/Postmodernism*.

Young-Bruehl, Elisabeth. "The Education of Women as Philosophers." *Signs: Journal of Women in Culture and Society* 12 (Winter 1987): 207–221.

Young-Eisendrath, Polly. "The Female Person and How We Talk about Her." In M. Gergen, ed., *Feminist Thought and the Structure of Knowledge*.

Index

Abortion, 162
Accountability, 3, 151, 160, 323
Active/passive dichotomy, 22
"Adequate seeing," 151, 170
Adversarial method, 23–24, 120, 132–133, 279, 283, 321
Aesthetic judgments, 8
Aesthetics, 8; vs. technology, 14
Affectivity, 120–121. *See also* Emotion
Age, 58, 73
Agency: autonomous moral, 71–79; cognitive (*see* Cognitive agency)
Agreement, voluntary, 185
Akrasia, 72, 189
Alcoff, Linda, 81–82, 179, 180–181, 237–238n, 292–299 passim
Alliances, 95; political, and trust, 183
Ambiguity, 257, 296–297
Ambivalence, in Descartes and *Othello*, 52–53
Analysis: case-by-case, 167–168; hermeneutic, in social sciences, 164; vs. interpretation, 122
Animal behavior, 228–231
Animality, 195; passion as, 212–213
Anonymity, in science, 158. *See also* Autonomous knower/reasoner
Anorexia nervosa, 226
Anthropology, 40, 44; feminist critiques of, 191n
Anxiety: Cartesian, 50–51, 134–139; of separation, 52
Arendt, Hannah, 103, 122

Aristotle: contraries in, 29; on friendship, 97–105 passim; on slaves, 246–247; on vision, 140; on women's lack of rational authority, 9, 21, 181, 186, 195, 223
Arnault, Lynne, 78n, 126n
Art, 69: and artistic vision, 145; perspective in, 135, 136; post-Reformation, 135, 136; sciences as, 233–234
Atomistic self, 76–78, 258
Authority: of academic learning, 57; authoritative vs. authoritarian, 185; cognitive, 224; and credibility, 224 (*see also* Credibility); defense against, 254; deference to, as rational act, 132; dictionary as, 63; and expertise, 181–188; illegitimate, stereotypes' appeal to, 189; of inner conviction, 135; of knowledge claims, 119; lexical inventory as reflection of, 59–60; medical, over women, 206–214 passim; as status, 250; withheld from women's traditional knowledge, 68; of women in science, 9n; women's lack of, in Aristotle, 9, 21, 181, 186, 195, 223
Autobiography, 252, 258, 309–310; canonical (male), 257, 310; scientific, 165–166
Autonomous knower/reasoner, x, xi, xii, 4–6, 73, 170, 179, 279n; childhood of (*see* Child: separation from mother); as "economic man," 79; masculine rationality, 117–130 passim; scientific breakthroughs attributed to, 10–11

339

Collingwood, R. G., 145
"Common sense" as ideological structure, 196
Communication, acts of, and translation, 58
Communitarianism, 276–277; normative ecological, 277–284
Community, 79, 123, 275–284; epistemic, 132n, 224, 233, 234
Compassion, 248
Competition, 79
Conflict of interest, 75, 76
Connectedness, 106. *See also* Holism; Wholeness, maternal
Consciousness: false, 22; of self, 38
Consciousness-raising, 197, 221; groups, 220
Consent, informed, 184
Consequentialism, 321
Constructed knowledge, 252n
Constructivism, 257
Consumer movements, 188
Contexts, moral, abnormal, 240
Context stripping, 160, 161, 238
Continuity vs. contraries, 29–30. *See also* Dichotomous thinking
Contractarianism, 78
Control: autonomy and, 179; over emotions, through detached-observer posture, 50–51; of nature, through mechanistic approach, 48–49; of own body experiences, 50; science without, 150–151; of self, 89; vision as, 143–144
Conversational engagement, 312, 313
Conversational mode, 307–308. *See also* Second persons
Cookery, 68, 233
Cooperation, 55, 57, 324
Corpuscular paradigm: and the atomistic self, 76–78, 258; Boyle's, 235–236, 238
Corroboration, 216
Covina, Gina, 15, 17
Craft labor, 165
Creativity: and cultural location, 56–57; in knowledge construction, 46, 114
Credibility, 7; of cluster-concepts, 192; of sense perceptions, 213; from status, 250. *See also* Authority; Experts
Credulity, 219
"Cultural feminism," 80–81
Culture: individual, as construct, 11; lore of, stereotypes as, 189–190; transition from oral to literate, 150

Dalkon Shield, 47
Daly, Mary, 14–15, 17, 58n, 221
Darwinism, 230

Dasein, 146–148
Davidson, Donald, 59n
Day, Elaine Buckley, 224n
Day care, 319
De Beauvoir, Simone, ix, 178, 193n, 232, 246, 293, 322, 324
Defensiveness, 130, 131–133, 280
De Lauretis, Teresa, 197, 263, 292, 294n, 297
Dependence, excessive, 217. *See also* Interdependence
Derrida, Jacques, 295
Descartes, René, 69, 242, 244; anxiety in, 50–51; on autonomy of the knower, 5–6; on childhood, 116; denies male monopoly on reason, 118; distrustful of testimony, 131; and Elizabeth, 305; intellectual vs. physical perception in, 141; posits universals from self-concept, 128; rational autonomy in, 112; second person in, 115–116; skepticism of, 129, 134–139, 164; on vision, 140
Determinism: biological, 228, 231–232, 247, 272; discursive, 179, 180, 295
Deviance, 195, 202, 277; madness as, 210
Dichotomies: abstract/concrete, 29; active/passive, 22; art/science, 233–234; culture/nature, 212, 274; fact/value, 31, 46; fixed/mutable (knowledge), 255; form/formlessness, 118; given/constructed (knowledge), 255; good/bad, 118; hard/soft (sciences), 243; independence/intimacy, 281; intellectual vs. physical perception, 141; knowledge/experience, 222–224, 241–250; light/dark, 118; limit/limitless, 118; mind/body, 29, 141, 212, 242, 274; public/private, 59, 194n, 206, 242–244 passim, 274, 279–280; pure/applied (science), 243; Pythagorean, 118; reason/emotion, 29, 47, 212, 242, 243–244, 274; right/wrong, 254; square/oblong, 118; theory/practice, 29, 242/243, 251n, 266; universal/particular, 29
Dichotomous thinking, 28–31, 47, 118, 119, 255, 263, 318, 319
Dictionaries, 63–65
Dietz, Mary, 99n, 100–101
Difference: construction of, 58; and cooperation with second persons, 55; vs. dichotomy, 263; politics of, 303 (*see also* Identity politics); science respectful of, 151; within women, 300
Diffidence, 185
Dinnerstein, Dorothy, 54

Library of Congress Cataloging-in-Publication Data

Code, Lorraine.
What can she know? : feminist theory and the construction of knowl-
edge / Lorraine Code.
    p.   cm.
Includes bibliographical references and index.
ISBN 0-8014-2476-3 (cloth : alk. paper).—ISBN 0-8014-9720-5 (paper : alk. paper)
1. Feminist theory.   2. Knowledge. Theory of.   I. Title.
HQ1190.C64   1991
305.42'01—dc20

90-55755